The
South
Atlantic
Quarterly
Spring/Summer 2003
Volume 102
Number 2/3

Visit Duke University Press's Web site at www.dukeupress.edu.

Subscriptions. Direct all orders to Duke University Press, Journals Fulfillment, 905 W. Main St., Suite 18B, Durham, NC 27701. Annual subscription rates: institutions, $120; e-only institutions, $108; individuals, $35; students, $21. Add $16 for foreign subscriptions. Back volumes (institutions): $120. Single issues: institutions, $30; individuals, $12. For more information, contact Duke University Press Journals at 888-387-5687 (toll-free in the U.S. and Canada) or 919-687-3602; subscriptions@dukeupress.edu.

Permissions. Photocopies for course or research use that are supplied to the end user at no cost may be made without explicit permission or fee. Photocopies that are provided to the end user for a fee may not be made without payment of permission fees to Duke University Press. Address requests for permission to republish copyrighted material to Permissions Coordinator, Duke University Press, 905 W. Main St., Suite 18B, Durham, NC 27701; permissions@dukeupress.edu.

Advertisements. Direct inquiries about advertising to Journals Advertising Specialist, Duke University Press, 905 W. Main St., Suite 18B, Durham, NC 27701; journals_advertising@dukeupress.edu.

Distribution. The journal is distributed by Ubiquity Distributors, 607 DeGraw St., Brooklyn, NY 11217; phone: 718-875-5491; fax: 718-875-8047.

The *South Atlantic Quarterly* is indexed in *Abstracts of English Studies, Academic Abstracts, Academic Index, America: History and Life, American Bibliography of Slavic and East European Studies, American Humanities Index, Arts and Humanities Citation Index, Book Review Index, CERDIC, Children's Book Review Index (1965), Current Contents, Historical Abstracts, Humanities Index, Index to Book Reviews in the Humanities, LCR, Middle East: Abstract and Index, MLA Bibliography, PAIS,* and *Social Science Source.*

The *South Atlantic Quarterly* is published, at $120 for institutions and $35 for individuals, by Duke University Press, 905 W. Main St., Suite 18B, Durham, NC 27701. Periodicals postage paid at Durham, NC, and additional mailing offices. Postmaster: Send address changes to *South Atlantic Quarterly,* Box 90660, Duke University Press, Durham, NC 27708-0660.

Copyright © 2003 by Duke University Press

ISSN 0038-2876

Relocating the Fault Lines: Turkey beyond the East-West Divide

SPECIAL ISSUE EDITORS: SIBEL IRZIK AND
GÜVEN GÜZELDERE

The
South
Atlantic
Quarterly
Spring/Summer 2003
Volume 102
Number 2/3

Sibel Irzık and Güven Güzeldere

Introduction

During the last couple of decades, Turkish economy, society, and culture have undergone intense hybridizations under influences no longer easily characterized as importations of a Western modernity. In February 2001, the liberalized market economy instituted within, if not by means of, the repressive political environment following the 1980 military coup produced a major crisis bearing all the marks of a full-scale integration with global capitalism. The consequences of this economic crisis are currently being experienced in the form of sharply escalated rates of unemployment and poverty. The increasingly more visible manifestations of poverty in urban settings coexist with material and symbolic displays of what Tanıl Bora calls a "neoliberal chauvinism of prosperity" personified in "Euro-Turks."

Ayşe Buğra's description of the changes in the place of the economy in contemporary Turkish society shows that the current dissolution of "society-specific arrangements, which, until recently, were able to prevent the worst forms of social exclusion and poverty" cannot be interpreted as a sign of modernization in the sense

The *South Atlantic Quarterly* 102:2/3, Spring/Summer 2003.
Copyright © 2003 by Duke University Press.

of the replacement of such arrangements with the rules of the competitive market, formalized labor relations, and formal mechanisms of redistribution. While the new orientation toward a globalized market renders informal relations of reciprocity such as family support incapable of continuing to function as systems of social protection, the same types of informal relations are mobilized to deregulate the labor market, to facilitate flexible production, and to accelerate the use of public resources to support private sector development. The emergence of "Euro-Turks" is largely due to the fact that "liberalization and deregulation have provided ample opportunities for the mobilization of networks for private gain, and what was critically labeled as populism has given way to downright corruption." The currently experienced shocks of Turkey's insertion into the global market are thus not accompanied by a promise of evolving toward what used to be a Western model of justly and rationally regulated configurations of economic and social life.

While the Westernized prosperous elite was busy distinguishing itself from the impoverished lower classes it viewed as a hindrance to membership in the EU, a predominantly right-wing coalition government including the radical nationalist MHP (Nationalist Movement Party) recently surprised both the Turkish public and the European authorities with a speedy enactment of a number of significant legal reforms required by the EU. Soon after, in October 2002, the EU released its latest report on Turkey's progress toward accession to membership. It praised the new reforms but also cited several antidemocratic practices and human rights violations as serious obstacles in the way of starting membership talks. Although Turkey's possible membership in the EU continues to be a contested issue, and although several representatives of the state challenged the accuracy of the claims in the report, the standard objection to the EU's demands as interferences with Turkey's internal affairs was not voiced as loudly as it would have been even a few years ago. It seems to have lost much of its appeal in a widely shared knowledge and acceptance of the permeability of national borders.

Tanıl Bora's taxonomy of nationalist discourses in Turkey becomes especially interesting in this context. It registers the rising appeal of a liberal "neonationalism" largely shaped by an ideology of economics. This brand of nationalism sees the self-interest of the nation in merging with the globalization process, defining Turkishness as an "intrinsic" capacity to harmonize with universal standards. This "sterile, narcissistic, and hedonistic" nationalism coexists with official, racist, and Islamic varieties, each involving "articulations, osmoses, and 'syntheses' alongside its 'Eastern' and 'Western,' ethno-essentialist and civil aspects."

Against this background, the sense of belatedness and the fear of inauthenticity that accompanied the traumatic late-nineteenth-century encounter with the Western model have become complicated by a bewildering sense of simultaneity with the rest of the world. Analyses in terms of Turkey's geographical and cultural situation "between two worlds" are becoming increasingly untenable in a world that seems all too "single." The immediately perceivable dependence of people's lives upon the uncertainties of a global economic system is not the only reason for this untenability. More important, the timeless spatial model in which Turkey is purportedly situated between two roughly symmetrical worlds, the "East" and the "West," does not accord with the ways in which economic, political, and cultural alternatives are imagined and articulated in the Turkish public sphere.

The "West" is a permanent, if shifting, signifier in the language of this public sphere, and it exerts a powerful pressure on the imagining of modern Turkish identity, both positively as a developmental ideal and negatively as the figure of alienation. But there is no corresponding presence of something called the "East" as an alternative paradigm of identity. Although Islam is the one phenomenon automatically associated with an "Eastern" identity by "clash of civilizations" discourses, such an association is far from being necessary and meaningful in conceptualizing the role Islam continues to play in the definition of different identities in the Turkish public sphere, or in the volatile oppositions and alignments among different lifestyles, different economic and political interests.

Turkey is neither caught between nor a successful synthesis of an "East" and a "West." It is, rather, a country in which many of the fundamental social divisions have been experienced, articulated, concealed, or displaced in a cultural/ideological vocabulary mobilizing the "West" in different power and justification strategies. An imagined state of "non-Westernness" or "not-yet-Westernness" has served to found national identity upon a sense of lack and has not yet been remedied under the custody of elites and institutions cast as guardians of a narrow range of features of Western modernity. Today, as this authoritative paradigm of Westernization has largely exhausted its capacity to generate social cohesion and legitimation, it becomes possible and necessary to confront the fault lines running through what Meltem Ahıska calls "the historical fantasy of the modern" that is identified with the "West" in Turkey.

This collection of articles aims to do this through a number of different but related strategies. The first is to ask what mechanisms of repression supported the construction of the fantasy; that is, the exclusions and displacements involved in the modernizing elite's highly selective appropriation of a limited set of ideals associated with European modernity.

Viewed in this way, the "secular" character of the Turkish state does not support the cliché about Turkey's exceptional role as a bridge between the Islamic world and the secular West. It appears, rather, as a specific appropriation of one ideal of Western modernity, only partially realized through the exclusion or adulteration of such other ideals as democracy and individual autonomy. The shape this specific appropriation takes is largely determined by the fault line separating the state from the society and the pressures exerted upon this divide by the dialectics of domination and autonomy structured along it. The continuing importance of this fault line in contemporary Turkey is addressed most directly in Ahmet Insel's interpretation of the results of the general elections that took place as this issue went into production, and in Ümit Cizre and Menderes Çınar's analysis of the role of the military in shaping the country's political landscape. Insel sees the AKP's (Justice and Development Party) victory as having created the possibility of lifting at least some of the inhibitions imposed on the political development of Turkish society by the statist, authoritarian regime established after the 1980 military coup. Along sılımar lines, Cizre and Çınar discuss how the Turkish state's "visible distaste for politics as a societal activity" is operative in the military's ability to close public debate about religion and secularism, "pitting the rhetoric of 'contemporariness' against 'Islamic anachronism'" and proclaiming itself the primary agent of the Westernizing/civilizing Kemalist project.

Andrew Davison's reconsideration of Turkey's identity as a secular state addresses the question of what mechanisms of repression support the construction of the fantasy. Davison points out the ways in which the new Turkish Republic's secularizing reforms "actually created a new structure of control and oversight between the state and Islam in which the republic's founders sought to use the powers of state to interpret, oversee, and administer religious doctrine and practice." He describes how the Kemalist state promoted the principle of secularization as an essential requirement of "catching up" with the modern West while interpreting and practicing it in such a way as to support its own version of "true" Islam and to maintain what it considered the right relations between religion, state, and society.

The displacements produced by the collisions and transformations of Islam, Turkishness, and the "West" both in Turkey and in an international context support Meltem Ahıska's assertion that "a new theoretical conceptualization is necessary in order to comprehend the historical interdependence between Turkey and the West." Ahıska attempts to lay the groundwork for such a conceptualization by exploring the figurations of the West as a phantasmic element in the imagining of modern Turkish national identity. She stresses the temporal paradoxes that arise from the Occidentalist conceptions that locate Turkey in both a temporal statis and a permanent crisis, making the experiential reality of its present impossible by defining that present only through its relation to an immutable past that must be annihilated and a future that must be caught by a radical leap.

The echoes that the notions of Islam and secularization find in Haldun Gülalp's and Katherine Ewing's articles illustrate further displacements of these notions along other fault lines in widely disparate contexts. Gülalp provides an interesting example of religion's capacity to take on multiple meanings in everyday life and political behavior in Turkey. Rejecting the assumption that Islam represents an intrinsically non-Western essence that needs to be rigidly circumscribed or outgrown on the way to modernization, Gülalp suggests that both the people's and the dominant ideology's conceptions of Islam are shaped along the widening fractures separating social and communal identities, especially those determined by class. A lower-class woman can associate practices such as wearing the headscarf with lifestyle and identity rather than religion, while categorizing an Islamist political leader as not a good Muslim because he can afford to have his children educated abroad. Similarly, Islam often stands in for class identity in Kamalist state ideology, since, "according to official dogma, the nation's trajectory from Islamic traditionalism to Western modernity is to be replicated in the lives of individual Turks who come from rural backgrounds to the big city and aspire to upward mobility. As they move up the class ladder, they are supposed to shed their Islamic cultural traditions and become Westernized."

According to Katherine Ewing, a similar transformation is expected of Turkish Muslims in Germany. They are supposed to shed their Islamic identities, seen as incompatible with Germanness, as they become integrated into German society. German nationalist discourses transport the political and social tensions around Islam and secularism within Turkey to the German public sphere and map them onto the previously existing tensions surrounding German national identity. In this way, "the precariousness of the notion of 'German,' its ambivalent links to a disavowed Nazi past," are covered over, and the visible, practicing Muslim becomes the "phantasmic, abjected other" of Germanness while the "hybrid" culture of secularist Turkish-Germans is celebrated as a demonstration of the new multicultural identity of Germany.

In a collection of cartoons by Behiç Ak, whose daily cartoon strip is published in *Cumhuriyet*, the paradoxes and absurdities—fantasies, as it were—are confronted and dismantled by AK's distinctly personal wit and understatement.

Bruce Kuniholm's consideration of Turkey's future in the world while "the fault lines that help to frame the tectonic shifts in Turkey's evolving identity are unquestionably being redrawn" is clearly distinguished from these phantasmic constructions of temporality. Kuniholm's careful delineation of the regional and global dynamics determining Turkey's concrete alternatives for the future is enhanced by the insights the other articles in this first section of the issue provide into the past and the present of its economy, politics, and culture. After all, as Kuniholm points out, the best way to evaluate projections about the future is to judge them "not on *how* they turn out but on *the quality of our thinking about how they might turn out.*"

Levent Soysal's more general interrogation of the "culturalist" paradigm for constructing immigration and integration stories about Turkish-Germans complements this perspective. He suggests that this paradigm is blind to the transnational dimensions of contemporary migrants' existence as well as to the "rapid incorporation of migrants into legal and societal institutions, regimes of rights and membership, and economies of ownership and inequity in Europe." This blindness turns Turkishness and Islam into reified parameters of difference and identity and uses the Turk as the ultimate signifier of the migrant who "is tied to an unyielding past, the past of his home and culture, and a persistent present, the present of his host place, his bureaucratic shackles, and his otherness."

Ahıska's elaborations of Occidentalism and its paradoxes, both temporal and representational, inspire the second strategy that this collection uses to confront the fault lines running through the Turkish configurations of the modern: the turn to literature. The second part of this double issue is devoted to articles on Turkish novels and poetry not simply because they provide thematic illustrations of the denial of an Ottoman past and the development of ideals about Turkishness as a result of an ambivalent encounter with the Western model. Although they certainly do provide such illustrations, these articles attempt to do more. They approach literature as a special register of the conundrums and the aporias involved in the construction and representation of the subjectivities of a peripheral modernity. They trace the oppositions between the original and the imitation, the indigenous and the foreign, the public and the private, the traditional and the innovative along the fractures *within* the subjectivities constituted through the literary and epistemological crises generated by belatedness.

Hülya Adak's remarkable treatment of *Nutuk* [The speech], the "sacred" text of Kemalist ideology and nationalist historiography, as a literary narrative resonates with the notion of national allegory. Adak characterizes *Nutuk* as the self-narrative of the "new individual" representing his life as complete, unified, and exemplary by inscribing it in the narrative of the nation. *Nutuk*'s fantasy of "a unified nation and unified self, interchangeable and intertwined," an "'I-nation' above the problematics of narrative representation," forms the reverse image of the deeply fissured selves depicted in modern Turkish novels. Adak sees the explorations of *bildung*, interpersonal dimensions of identity, the agency of the people, and the permeability of ego boundaries in the autobiographical narratives of Halide Edib as critical responses to the hegemonic narcissism of *Nutuk*.

Necmi Zeka's critique of modern Turkish poetry's "imprisonment in language" through the literary establishment's narcissistic elevation of Turkish to the status of a uniquely poetic language producing superior but untranslatable poetry could be considered an interesting variation on the theme of the illusory nature of self-enclosed native traditions.

Both the figure of the carriage and the problem of genre find modified echoes in Jale Parla's delineation of the car narratives in Turkish novels as constituting a subgenre dominated by the thematics of "the machine in the psyche." These narratives of "possession and dispossession, maturation and infantilism, narcissism and fetishism, fragmentation and self-destruction" unfold the ironies of Turkish modernization through the use of machines "as metonyms of incompletion and lack, on the personal-psychological level as well as the cultural-aesthetic." According to Parla, the significance of the carriage or the car as a cultural object in these narratives and in the lives of Turkish people during the entire period of modernization results from the fact that it offers a semiprivate space in which to negotiate, usually without success, the newly emerging and volatile boundaries between the public and the private.

Sibel Irzık considers the possibilities and limitations of "national allegory," the defining form of Third World literature according to Fredric Jameson. She follows the implications of regarding allegory as the expression of a healthy lack of a split between the public and the private in Third World cultures. Irzık points out the authoritarian thrust in the demand for an identification between private and national destinies and reads a number of modern Turkish novels as both fulfilling and nullifying this demand, "acknowledging but also attempting to overcome the contortions that language, narrative, and individual lives have to go through under social conditions that provide neither a protected private sphere within which individuals can have at least the illusion of sovereignty and freedom, nor a public sphere in which their demands for sovereignty can be freely negotiated."

Orhan Koçak's chronicle of "the catastrophic births of modern Turkish poetry," which uses Harold Bloom's theory of the anxiety of influence to conduct a "geoculturally" informed study of how poetic influence works in the context of Westernization, is a complicated example of articulating the problems of modern literature through the notion of belatedness. Koçak points out the at least initially "outlandish" nature of "attempting to transfer the ideas of the author of The Western Canon to quite alien terrain, where they would seem to lose much of their relevance, and by way of a type of concern which has been branded as 'the culture of envy' by the author of those ideas." But in showing how the poetic movement called "the Second New" turned "the positional weaknesses of modern Turkish literature, its off-centeredness and its belated novitiate, into the formal law of great poetry," Koçak deconstructs the notion of belatedness even as he places it at the center of his argument. This is a double move most of the articles in this issue make in various ways.

Nurdan Gürbilek probes "the desire to be the other and the fear of losing one's self in the other" through the late-nineteenth-century novelistic figure of the snob and then asks, "What if the place called *inside* consists of an outside? . . . What if what is called *Turkishness* itself involves at the very origin the currently irremovable rift between a snobbish self and an authentic one?" Gürbilek suggests that the breaking down of the carriage in Recaizade Ekrem's *The Carriage Affair* is paralleled by the breaking down of the Western representational form that is the novel precisely because of this rift, this necessity to represent the self only through the impasses of a form that is foreign to the self, to signal at an interiority only through its impossibility.

A much more radical undermining of identity narratives is at work in Oğuz Atay's *Tutunamayanlar* [The disconnected], the 1972 novel many of the literary critical articles in this issue reference. Suna Ertuğrul reads this novel as marking the impossibility of subjectivity as the ground of meaning in the face of a confrontation with modernity experienced as a loss of world. She then goes on to assert that *Tutunamayanlar*'s articulation of cultural difference as that which refuses to be appropriated by the modern project does not reveal something only about Turkey, but also something about modernity itself: "The experience of 'belatedness' is not being late to a historically determined essence; it is the recurrence of the essential lack of ground that defines the modern project." As an experience of the loss of origin, the loss of transcendental structures that guarantee meaning, "modernity is always belated vis-à-vis itself." If this is the case, what is called "belated modernity" may be, from the perspective of Western modernity, the "inside" consisting of an "outside."

Ertuğrul also sees Oğuz Atay's taking the modern crisis to its limits as a demonstration that "there is no outside to modernity in the sense of native and aboriginal traditions or non-Western narratives that can open up the possibilities of an alternative to Eurocentric modernity." At a more general level, Meltem Ahıska's critique of theories of alternative modernities reiterates Ertuğrul's point. One could claim, however, that there *is* a possibility opened up by the attempt to go beyond the East-West divide. The fault lines that run so visibly through the self-constructions of a belated modernity may be cracks through which the epistemological, cultural, and political contradictions of the West also become visible, revealing modernity as a still incomplete project.

The problematic relationship between the public and the private is taken up in Erdağ Göknar's discussion of ambivalence toward social responsibility in Ahmet Hamdi Tanpınar's *Those outside the Scene*. Göknar sees the indecision of Tanpınar's characters between "East" and "West," modernity and tradition, Ottoman past and Turkish national future as these characters' "form of bourgeois protest," their form of forging private selves out of a "debilitating state of ambivalence."

Davison's, Gülalp's, and Ewing's references to the incomplete conceptualizations and practices of secularism in the West "reveal modernity as a still incomplete project." So, too, do Soysal's and Ewing's criticisms of migration stories that are geared toward maintaining national order and containing anxieties about national identity. Ahıska makes this revelation more explicit when she states that her aim "is not simply to go beyond the East-West divide; instead, it is to re-member the historical divide as constitutive of both the 'Western' and 'Eastern' modernities." In a similar move, Gürbilek brings Recaizade Ekrem's Bihruz together with Flaubert's Emma, making use of René Girard's theory to reveal in the figure of the snob the imitated nature of all desire. She also sees Oğuz Atay as "working through the literary problems of belatedness and affectation, problems not only of belatedly modernized literature, but all literature, itself always belated to what we call individual experience."

Ahmet Insel

The AKP and Normalizing Democracy in Turkey

The parliament that emerged from the general elections on November 3, 2002, in Turkey has created an unexpected possibility of exit from the authoritarian regime established after the military coup of September 12, 1980.[1] The 1982 Constitution, to which I will refer as the September 12 regime, aimed to impose on the society an authoritarian and conservative statist conception of politics. The September 12 regime made the concept of the state sacred. It placed a radical statism at the center of the principle of republicanism, and it took care to have this principle hang over politics like Demokles's sword. It systematized the authoritarianism that was one of the innate characteristics of the Turkish Republic, and institutionalized the transfer of the administrative center of this authoritarianism from the civil to the military bureaucracy,[2] to achieve a politically and socially stable but economically dynamic new regime.

Thanks to the intensification of the internal contradictions of the September 12 regime, the results of the November 3 elections created the possibility of leaving this conservative statist-authoritarian regime behind under the

The *South Atlantic Quarterly* 102:2/3, Spring/Summer 2003.
Copyright © 2003 by Duke University Press.

leadership of a conservative-democratic political/social movement. This development signals a possibility of political transformation that is important in the context of Turkey's recent history. To assess the potential significance of this event, it will be useful to consider the 1982 Constitution, which inhibited the political development of Turkish society for twenty years, and the structure determining the qualities of the institutions and traditions deriving from that Constitution.

The Characteristics of the September 12 Regime

The architects of the September 12 regime desired to construct a political sphere with the state at its center. This project reflected a political conception that perceived the state as the center and the society as the periphery. The different wings of politics, its left and its right, were to be determined according to this center. With this aim in view, it was stipulated that political parties would conform to a single type in their establishment and operation, that organic ties between political parties and other social organizations would be prevented by means of a series of prohibitions, and that the clustering of votes around a few central parties would be made obligatory by means of the 10 percent threshold for representation in the parliament. To this was added the opportunity for military tutelage institutionalized through the strengthening of the political powers of the National Security Council (MGK, or Milli Güvenlik Kurulu). Because the 1982 Constitution was legitimized under the shadow of military intervention and by means of a referendum during which oppositional propaganda was prohibited, it was not difficult to put in place this new regime of military tutelage that went beyond the traditional military-politics relationship in the Turkish Republic.

The architects of the regime hoped that political actors adapted to the new conditions would emerge in the sphere vacated through political prohibitions. They therefore banned the prominent political figures of the "old regime" from politics. In this way, the tradition of "ban from politics" due to political activities was established—a tradition whose effects continue to this day. After a brief period of liberalization between 1983 and 1985, the state-centered structure was consolidated by the conservatives by the institution of a state-of-emergency environment, in response to the rapidly escalating confrontations with the PKK (the illegal Kurdish Labor Party and its armed forces). In this way, the authoritarian conception of politics that constituted the heart of the third republican regime was prevented from weakening. The political parties that were obliged to conduct their activities in an extremely limited sphere stiffened even further the authoritarian reflexes that already existed in the Turkish political tradition because they had to adopt these authoritarian conceptions in order to remain legitimate.

The September 12 regime initiated a political period during which the greatest number of parties were closed down in Turkish history. Not only were the small and marginal parties outside the parliament closed down, but parties represented in the parliament as well.[3] A category of *political activity crime* was created, the political immunity of some "illegitimate" members of parliament was lifted, their membership in parliament was cancelled, and they were imprisoned. At the same time these threats were directed at other political actors.

The September 12 regime had trapped itself: it had the state at its center, saw the society as the threat besieging this center, and considered authoritarian methods legitimate in defending itself against that threat. It mainly relied on the reproduction of political and social stagnation to maintain its control. The concept of stability, which was obsessively reiterated, referred to a state of immobility in which the institutions of the September 12 regime and the hierarchy among them would not be upset. The aim was to compensate for this immobility by means of economic dynamism and to direct the social energy that could not flow into political and cultural channels to the area of economic growth. In the 1980s, the liberty that was not permitted in the areas of politics and culture was permitted in the economic sphere. It was not possible, however, for a social energy that had been repressed and restricted in the spheres of politics, culture, and identity to create a long-lived and constructive force of attraction in the economic sphere. It was doomed to remain limited to occasional bursts of dynamism that quickly died out.

From 1980 to today, the only breach in the authoritarian state-centered view occurred through the economic liberalization attempt under Özal's masterly leadership. Özal belonged to the same modernizationist conservative world as today's AKP. In 1978, he ran for parliament as a candidate for the National Salvation Party (MSP, or Milli Selamet Partisi), but failed to be elected. As prime minister after 1983, he enacted a program for economic liberalization, which the architects of the September 12 regime could not quite stomach but unwillingly accepted as being dictated by modern times. This liberalism of enterprise remained weak in terms of ramifications in the political sphere and gave precedence to opportunism and a "fixer" mentality in pursuit of easy profits. This urge was not balanced by social institutions, and the autonomous activity in the political sphere was reduced to the distribution of economic spoils, which promoted a certain kind of primitive accumulation of capital; that is, the attempt to appropriate already-produced value and to use political power to procure a larger share in distribution, rather than accumulating value by means of production. In addition to causing wage earners' share in the national income to become smaller and the inequalities among wage earners to increase, this struggle over distribution intensified the rivalry between the rising enterprise groups in the provinces and the traditional republican bourgeoisie.

The conservative-liberal synthesis that found fertile ground for self-expression in Özal's pragmatism hoped that social and political stability/immobility could be secured through economic dynamism alone. As a result, the economy, which was the only space for action, drew politics into itself and instrumentalized it. The political parties, whose capacities for action in the political sphere had been restricted, had no choice but to shape their political activities according to this mechanism of distribution and to become brokers for it. Politics became much more subjected to the periodic fluctuations of economic activity. The rapid erosion of the public's confidence in the future further strengthened the instability of economic life. The crisis of February 2001, in fact not only an economic crisis but also a sign of the institutional collapse and paralysis of the September 12 regime, was the beginning of the end: the complete and almost irreparable breakdown of the economy, which had until then been the only sphere of free social activity. Soon after, the regime collapsed as well.

At the end of a process in which the inner contradictions of the September 12 regime intensified, the system became clogged, and the circuits of economic and political crisis became accelerated by mutually reinforcing each other, an electoral system that had been the invention of the authoritarian regime suddenly precipitated the conditions for leaving itself behind. A purging wave swept the political stage, leaving almost all of the parties shaped according to the political philosophy of September 12 and their traditional leaders outside the parliament. Like every rigid structure, the narrow and hardened political structure imposed by the September 12 regime was incapable of adaptation, and the party located at the greatest distance from the state obtained a sweeping majority in the parliament.

This was not the first time the mechanisms of this electoral system backfired. Earlier, thanks to the simple majority system instituted by the September 12 regime, Tayyip Erdoğan had become the mayor of Istanbul in 1994, even though only a quarter of the voters voted for him. Everybody in Turkey, especially the conservative statists, knew that this electoral system had to change. But no mobilizing force that could realize this change emerged. The political energy of the September 12 regime had been exhausted. It was able to defend itself only by pushing the limits of jurisprudence, availing itself of far-fetched interpretations that perverted the intent behind the laws and seeking shelter under the shadow of the covert military intervention that occurred on February 28, 1997. Rather than introducing a just electoral system and thus preventing Erdoğan from getting reelected as mayor with only, say, one third of the total votes, the political authority chose to imprison Erdoğan and permanently ban him from politics because he had recited a poem of mediocre literary quality with a nationalist content including Islamic motifs. Even this was sufficient proof that the regime had been deprived of the capacity to reproduce itself within its own parameters. The September 12 regime had entered its glacial period.

The New Middle Class

The economic policies implemented in the politically repressive environment of the September 12 regime dealt a serious blow against the traditional middle classes favored by protectionist policies. This middle class, comprised of urban artisans and midsize traders and farmers in Western Anatolia, wage earners, most of whom worked in the public sector, and large private-firm employees who had been able to raise their purchasing power thanks to the right of collective bargaining, lost its economic standing because of the new policies. The traditional middle class began to be replaced by a new one. The conservative cultural affinity between the traditional class of provincial artisans and traders on the one hand, and, on the other hand, the small- and midrange enterprisers who live mostly in midsize cities and some of whom are employer and employee simultaneously, and the young executives who have received university education, especially in technical fields, caused these groups to become united and to constitute the nucleus of a new middle class. The great distance separating the traditional republican bourgeoisie from this new middle class, which is culturally conservative, politically nationalist and moderately authoritarian, economically liberal, or rather, on the side of free enterprise, became considerably more marked during the last period. This rising class of conservative enterprisers chose to be represented in the new Association of Independent Industrialists and Businessmen (MÜSIAD, or Müstakil Sanayici ve İşadamları Derneği) rather than in the previously established Association of Turkish Industrialists and Businessmen (TÜSIAD).[4] The natural political representatives of this new middle class were the Motherland Party (ANAP, or Anavatan Partisi) and the True Path Party (DYP, or Doğru Yol Partisi), both having evolved from the tradition of the Justice Party (AP, or Adalet Partisi), rather than the Islamist parties of the National Order Party/National Salvation Party line. However, ANAP and DYP, both of which came into power several times in various coalitions in the 1990s, rapidly lost the capacities for political representation and mobilization.[5] The vacuum that the traditional rightist parties were unable to fill became one of the principal causes of instability dominating the parliament from 1995 up to the November 3 elections in 2002.

The results of the November 3 elections show that, for now, the AKP is the clear winner in the struggle to become the political representative of the new middle class. Whether this representation is permanent depends mostly on the ability of the AKP government to fulfill its promises of economic stability and growth in the middle term. Viewed in this perspective, it is evident that the main axis of the AKP government program is constituted by the aim of increasing production through the reestablishment of stability and trust. The AKP sees the small- and midsize firms as the main force in the realization of the aims of creating jobs and economic vitality. When one considers the approach of this capitalist group, and especially of MÜSIAD, to labor relations, one sees that it defines wage labor "not as a social stratum possessing rights pertaining to trade unions and social security at the level of class or the individual, but as a 'member providing services' for the organic unity of the economy."[6] In this sense, the AKP's defense of social justice is based on the strengthening of traditional relationships of charity and cooperation rather than the strengthening of individual and social rights. The AKP brings its conservatism to the foreground by emphasizing such traditions, especially those related to the family.

The political and economic careers of a significant number of the AKP elites were determined by their exclusion by the republican elites. A real class struggle continues to be waged between the traditional upper-middle class and the new middle class—a struggle whose external appearance is characterized by the symbols of identity politics but, at the same time, related to economic positions. The instinctive reactions and fears of the laicist elite in the face of the AKP and the political stance it represents have their source mainly in the anxiety of losing a hegemonic position; they reflect a certain kind of class position. The clash between the radical laicists and the Islamists in Turkey is not only a clash between modernizationists and traditionalists, but also a clash between the high (*havas*) and the low (*avam*) dating from the final period of the Ottoman Empire. The AKP's coming to power with a parliamentary majority, enabling a single-party government, constitutes an important threshold in this nearly century-old conflict.

In addition to receiving the votes of the new middle class the AKP received votes from a good portion of the working class. A sense of belonging that blended political and cultural values resulted in many from the working classes, which did not occupy the position of a middle class but which aspired to such a position, to turn to the AKP. The new middle-class sense of belonging that finds expression in the person of Tayyip Erdoğan has determinations that go beyond his being a "child of the people" who has risen from the bottom. Erdoğan consolidated this sense of belonging by virtue of being someone who has for the most part avoided the paths followed by the traditional republican elites. The new, growing middle class was able to identify easily with Erdoğan, who did not fit the traditional republican elite image. The other leaders could at best be "on the side of the people." Among the political leaders prominent in the history of the Turkish Republic, Erdoğan was the person most clearly and authentically "one of the people." He represented a new middle-class elite that deserved to displace the republican elites formed and thus "domesticated" by the state, even if they had originally come from among the people.

The AKP's assumption of a more *authentic* and more *humble* posture compared to the executive staff of the other parties, or at least, their behavior facilitating such a perception, impressed the mass of voters. This authenticity and humility evident in the majority of the people constituting the AKP administration produces an important power of attraction in the eyes of the new conservative modernizationist middle class. Viewed in this way, the AKP's "unstoppable march to power" could be understood as a more authentic and humble continuation of the process that started with Özal.

It would be more correct to say that the new middle class rather than the AKP now occupies the center of politics since the November 3 elections. Consequently, the other rightist parties trying to attract voters away from the AKP will have to conduct a politics oriented toward this conservative modernizationist world. The reactions and expectations of this new middle class, whose conflict with the state is historically conditioned rather than being a matter of principle, will force the rightist parties to abandon the sphere of state-centered politics. If the AKP government achieves relative success in relation to EU membership, the solution of the Cyprus problem, and economic growth, there will be a flow of political elites from such central rightist parties as ANAP and DYP, and even from the Nationalist Movement Party (MHP, or Milliyetçi Hareket Partisi), toward the AKP. As a result, the number of proponents of the Islamist "National Outlook" (Millî Görüş) within the party will decrease, and the other rightist parties will for the most part disappear into history, which could lead to the isolation of such radical nationalist-conservative-authoritarian movements as MHP and BBP (the Great Unity Party, or Büyük Birlik Partisi). Provided that the leftist–social democratic movements do not aspire to the status of state parties, the mission of being the "party of the state" could become limited to a narrow archaic nationalist group.[7] Such a development would mean the achievement of a democratic transformation from the bottom. At the end of that development, a quiet, mild transition that would nevertheless be radical in terms of its consequences would be possible toward a normal democratic regime in Turkey—a regime in which the center of gravity of politics would be distanced from the military-civil bureaucracy, and the political movements nourished by large sections of the society would establish themselves at the center of politics.

If the state-society relations in Turkey had been realized on a normal democratic basis, the AKP would have had to take its place as a rightist "establishment" party in the political arena, in view of the values it represents and its economic-social program. But the distortions of political representation in the traditional republican order, its structure based on the hegemony of statist-laicist forces, the deep suspicion these forces harbor against the majority of the society, and, in more general terms, the transformation of the authoritarian project of modernization from above that is almost cotemporaneous with the republic into a more rigid conservatism, gave the AKP an opportunity to act as a democratic movement and to constitute a social force of attraction without abandoning its conservative posture and values. The AKP was able to claim with sufficient credibility that it had achieved a developmentalist, moderately solidaristic synthesis between free enterprise and conservative values.

AKP Conservatism

The AKP has undertaken the mission of ending the September 12 regime whether it likes it or not, but its capacity to fulfill this undertaking should be assessed by considering the characteristics of the social groups it represents. The AKP is a culturally conservative movement that harbors strong authoritarian tendencies and a vigorous nationalistic vein. The authoritarian patriarchal reflexes of the family tradition rooted in the Turkish soil are reflected in the values and the behavior of the AKP cadres in the form of traditionalism.[8] The tendency to transform these authoritarian patriarchal reflexes into a nationalist-statist conservatism is represented within the AKP by the cadres coming from the tradition of the Turk-Islam synthesis. But aspirations to become a pragmatic middle-class party also have an important place in this structure. This pragmatism corresponds to such values of economic liberalism as entrepreneurship and efficiency. The confidence produced by the belief that the party reflects the cultural values of a sweeping majority in Turkish society can also lead this pragmatism to manifest itself in the form of tolerance.

The dominant profile that emerges from a blend of all these tendencies is reminiscent of popular American conservatism. Indeed, it is not a coincidence that the American conservative circles forming the heart of the Republican Party constitute the one social formation outside Turkey with which an important section of the AKP elites feels the closest affinity, both in terms of background and aspirations.

Among all the Western societies, America is the most religious, and this is not a recent phenomenon,[9] originating in the eighteenth century and continuing today. The religiosity of Americans constitutes an anomaly against the law, articulated by such sociologists as Comte and Weber, that modernity is accompanied by "the disenchantment of the world." In this sense, the American exception continues to pose a question that is not completely answered for sociologists. Americans, who create the most advanced applications of modern science, who have adapted to the requirements of science and technology, who have in many respects been the most modern society of the last century, who live in a society in which materialist values dominate daily life, and who should thus be the least likely people, according to Weber, to turn to religion for the interpretation of the world and human existence, continue to be the most religious people among economically advanced Western societies. Raymond Boudon is of the opinion that the solutions Adam Smith, Alexis Tocqueville, and Max Weber provided for this mystery are still valid and not transcended.[10]

Outside the radical but marginalized circles that represent the extremes of conservatism in the United States, religion is experienced as a body of moral precepts, and not as the concrete manifestation of dogma. For this reason, American laicism is extremely tolerant in allowing people to practice their religious beliefs fully and freely, but it is uncompromising about the principle that the requirements of religious dogma cannot be imposed on people despite their wishes. American popular conservatism attributes an absolutely superior value to the freedom of enterprise. It holds the belief that the organization of social solidarity through the mediation of the state encourages laziness and dependence. It believes, not in the social state, but in the institution of the family, individual generosity, and voluntary acts of charity conducted through foundations. It sees the home as the natural place and child-rearing as the natural duty of women. It is "prolife" in this context, too, not only in its opposition to abortion. On the other hand, in contrast to elitist conservatism, popular conservatism does not hold itself superior to society by virtue of lineage. In terms of tastes, lifestyles, and family relationships, it represents, not an upper-class attitude, but a much more common cultural world.

This approach, which interprets religious values as moral values guiding social behavior, which is very sensitive about the freedom of conscience, and which understands and values nationalism, not as love of the state, but as love of country, is much closer to the AKP than the Christian-democratic traditions of continental Europe. It would of course be meaningless to look for all the characteristics of American conservatism in such a political formation as the AKP, which originated in a different history and geography. But the cultural codes of the AKP do exhibit similarities with moderate and popular American conservatism. It is not a coincidence that the views of the AKP's young executive cadres resonate closely with the American Republican conservative movement. The AKP enterprise represents a modernizationist conservative stage of the Turkish Muslim tradition, which is in the process of secularization. It presents a mature, more consistent, and more authentic version of the American-style liberal-conservative development that had partially started with Özal.

Conservative-Liberal versus Conservative-Democrat?

The November 3 election results show that the field of action for the left has become even narrower in Turkish society.[11] Such a movement as the AKP, which comes from within the conservative world and claims to be democratizing that world through modernization, has an opportunity to become the initiating force for a normalized regime of democracy. In recent years, statist-laicist elites have narrowed the limits of the political legitimacy of democracy and have defended a concept of republic with strong overtones of authoritarianism. They have been inflexible and harsh in their reaction to the demands for the recognition of a Kurdish identity and in their reaction to the demands for the acknowledgment of the existence of authentic Muslim identities in the public sphere. In some cases, for instance in the matter of female students' demand to attend universities wearing head scarves, the reaction of the traditional republican elites smacked of class clash: the upper class disturbed by "the people" invading the public sphere. The AKP was also able to channel the reactions against the unjust distribution of wealth that had become even more severe as a result of the economic crisis of the late 1990s, and the reactions against corruption revealed in the wake of the November 3 election: the fraudulent bankruptcies of banks, the ties of mutual interest that politicians established with business circles, and a sort of "jet set" lifestyle widely displayed in the media. It assumed the role of the patron of "the victimized, the excluded, and the oppressed," filling a space that should normally have been occupied by leftist-social democratic parties.

The AKP takes pains to avoid defining itself as a religious party, and from a political point of view its program has the characteristics of a democratic party program.[12] It takes as its basis the principle that "nobody is free unless everybody is free," and proposes that "democratization be achieved

by placing the individual at the center of all policies." It declares its acceptance of Turkish society "with all its colors, its points of commonality and
difference," emphasizing the potential for enrichment and strength offered
by this fact. The program's emphasis on the consolidation of a "state based
on the rule of law" instead of "law based on the rule of the state," its reitera-
tion of the necessity that "decisions concerning public life must be made
by elected representatives," its statement that democracy is distinguished
from all other regimes by the fundamental principle of the sovereignty of
the people, and its definition of democracy as a system based on tolerance
are all signs that the AKP could be a consistent defender of a pluralist parliamentary regime.

On the subject of laicism as well, the AKP program expresses a democratic approach in a consistent way. It characterizes laicism as an indispensable condition of democracy and the guarantee of the freedom of religion
and conscience. Laicism is presented in this framework as a "principle of
freedom and social peace." As for the conservative dimension, it comes to
the foreground in the conception of "religion as one of the most important
institutions of humanity," and the emphasis that is placed on "preventing
behavior that offends religious people."

The AKP states that it considers "the historical experience and cultural
wealth of our nation a solid ground for our future" and defines itself as conservative. It compares society to a "living organism that survives by replen-
ishing itself in the cultural environment constituted by such entrenched
institutions as the family, education, property, religion, and morality." It
describes the development of this organism by means of an anticonstructiv-
ist argument in the style of Hayek, thus clearly marking its distance from
the Kemalist project of modernization: "The local culture and institutions
that are produced and unified within their own natural processes without
external intervention do not conflict with universal values."

The AKP expresses its conservatism most clearly and strongly with regard
to the subject of the family and women. The program emphasizes the priority that "family centered policies" have for the party and chooses to discuss the participation of women in economic life from the perspective of
"its connection to peace in the family." Instead of acknowledging the existence of a distinct problem regarding women, it prefers to treat this issue
in the context of the institution of the family defined as "a strong institution of social security" and as the institution that has enabled "the society

to remain intact despite the economic problems it experienced." In certain cases, the women's organizations of the AKP have also expressed the view that it is more natural and appropriate for women to remain in the home. For instance, some of the AKP's women members of parliament have asserted that working in "home-offices" is more suitable for women.[13] The same popular conservative approach is reflected in Tayyip Erdoğan's declaration, in the summer of 2002, of "a Muslim-Turkish Turkey with a population of one hundred million as a target," and his claim, in this context, that "population-planning for development is a betrayal of country."

The program, which defends a classical liberalism in the economic sphere, does not go beyond a very moderate principle of social solidarity in terms of social policies. It claims, in popular conservative fashion, that corruption lies at the root of social injustice. This claim reflects the belief that the state can never be effective in the economic and social sphere. Along the same lines, the program does not neglect to promise a massive reduction in general and social security taxes. To sum up, the program constitutes a synthesis of conservatism and liberalism.

In terms of its government program, the properties that distinguish the AKP from other political parties are not found in the areas of the economy and social policy. Almost everybody in Turkey acknowledges that a very narrow margin for choice exists regarding these issues, considering the dimensions of the economic crisis and the international commitments that have been made. Naturally, the AKP's voters will look for the criteria of its success or failure in its achievements in the areas of economic growth and employment. But this is not a short-term expectation. The AKP represents a new stage in the Westernization movement in Turkey—the stage at which the society becomes involved. In this sense, it represents a threshold for a process through which Turkish Westernization can be turned upside down. The new middle class supporting the AKP will measure its success with reference not only to its economic performance, but also the political and social consequences of this conservative democratic transformation from below. For this reason the AKP feels the need to become much more engaged with such issues as solving the Cypress problem, finalizing Turkey's membership in the EU, and putting the democratization package into practice. It is also highly probable that its economic and social liberalism will have precedence over its democratic sensibilities while realizing these goals.

The fact that the program of the AKP government places the greatest emphasis on the economy does not mean that this party has no claims regarding transformation in other areas. An important reason for the prominence of the economy in the program is the fact that the identity of the middle class it represents is shaped primarily through economic activity. The AKP can expand its space of action in its relations with the state by relying on a legitimacy articulated in economic terms. Its leaders expect to be empowered by the legitimacy that their economic achievements will provide for them and to use this power to eliminate the premodern residues located in the state, or to force them to subjection. When such a stage is reached, it will become possible to tell whether the AKP will be content to defend democracy only for itself or whether it will try to build the new social order on democratic foundations.

The Exit from the September 12 Regime

The results of the November 3 elections had the effect of an earthquake on Turkey's political order. The unexpected new composition of the parliament, the fact that the party positioned at the most distant point from the state has formed a majority government, and the aspirations and expectations of the new middle classes supporting this party provide reasons to think that an opportunity for a mild but radical exit from the September 12 regime has arisen. The realization of such an exit, not by the traditional Westernizers, but by a movement like the AKP, which Westernizing-statist elites regard with suspicion, will finally make the normalization of Turkey's century-old Westernization adventure possible. Turkey is now going through a paradoxical period in which statist-Westernizing elites are forced to swerve into anti-Western positions, and the West is defended by Islamic, Kurdish, and other movements of identity politics, which shows that the exit from the authoritarian regime will be realized when the polarization that traverses the entire republican history, the polarization that appears to be between modernizationists and traditionalists but is actually between the republican elites and the people, loses effect and leaves its place to more normal dynamics of social polarization and conflict. Such a development, if it indeed occurs, will be one of the most important transformations determining the future of Turkey.

Notes

1   In the elections, in which the rate of participation was 79 percent, the Justice and Development Party (AKP, or Adalet ve Kalkınma Partisi) won 34.3 percent (10,779,489 votes), and the Republican People's Party (CHP, or Cumhuriyet Halk Partisi) won 19.4 percent of all valid votes. Because a party needs to receive at least 10 percent of the votes on a national basis in order to be represented in the parliament, the other parties that entered the elections and received 46 percent of the valid votes collectively could not send any representatives to the parliament. The new parliament opened with 366 members from the AKP, 191 members from the CHP, and eight independent members.

2   Ahmet Insel, "Otoriterizmin Sürekliliği" [The continuity of authoritarianism], *Birikim*, no. 125/126 (1999): 143–67.

3   In 1994 the Democracy Party, which conducted political activities targeting the Kurdish problem, was closed down, the immunity of its thirteen members in the parliament was lifted, and these members of parliament were arrested. Four of them are still in prison. The Welfare Party (RP, or Refah Partisi) was closed down in 1998, and the party established in its place, the Virtue Party (FP, or Fazilet Partisi), met the same fate in 2001. Between 1983 and 2002, a total of twenty-one political parties were closed down by the decision of the Constitutional Court.

4   For a discussion of how MÜSIAD was founded to organize the entrepreneurs who had been historically excluded from state favors in order to bind them into a coherent community through ample use of Islamic references, and a consideration of the close relationships between MÜSIAD and the leaders of Islamic politics, see Ayşe Buğra, "Class, Culture, and State: An Analysis of Two Turkish Business Associations," *International Journal of Middle East Studies*, no. 30 (1998): 521–39.

5   The most significant sign of the crisis of representation experienced in the world of business during the 1990s was the rapid increase in the number of political/religious organizations of businessmen. In addition to TÜSIAD, representing the owners of big firms, and MÜSIAD, representing Muslim businessmen, the Association of Nationalist Industrialists and Businessmen (USIAD, or Ulusalcı Sanayiciler ve İşadamları Derneği) formed by leftist Kemalist businessmen opposed to Turkey's membership in the EU, the Association of Republican Industrialists and Businessmen (CUSIAD, or Cumhuriyetçi Sanayiciler ve İşadamları Derneği) formed by Alawi businessmen, and the regional businessmen associations constitute a telling manifestation of the crisis of representation experienced by this social group.

6   Fuat Keyman, "Demokratikleşme ve AKP" [Democratization and the AKP], *Radikal2*, December 1, 2002.

7   In the short time since the new parliament started to operate, it has been possible to observe that the "social democratic" CHP bases its parliamentary opposition on not straying too far from the axis of a state party.

8   In the opinion poll conducted by Yılmaz Esmer, voters who have voted for different political parties agree that raising a child "to be respectful toward elders" has greater priority than raising a child "to be industrious and tolerant toward others, and to know how to protect his or her own interests." This shows how widespread patriarchal conservatism

is. Two-thirds of AKP voters and 41 percent of CHP voters are of this opinion. *Milliyet*, November 16, 2002.

9   For a comparison of developed European societies and the United States in terms of religious values, see R. Inglehart, M. Basavez, and A. Moreno, *Human Values and Beliefs: A Cross-Cultural Sourcebook* (Michigan: University of Michigan Press, 1998).

10 Raymond Boudon, "Les croyances collectives," in *Qu'est-ce que la vie psychique*, ed. Y. Michaud (Paris: Odile Jacob, 2002).

11 The total percentage of votes for the left in the last election is 29 percent. If a complete system of proportionate representation had been used, the entire left would end up with fewer seats in the parliament than those CHP has today. If we divide the votes that are not represented in the current parliament roughly between right and left, it becomes evident that voters with rightist preferences have a lower representation than the total votes they have cast. Granted, in a system of proportionate representation without a minimum vote threshold, voting behavior would have been different. It is also true that one cannot compare the relative significance of a member in the current parliament with that of a member in a parliament composed of more than two parties. A single member in the latter has much greater weight than in the former. Despite all this, however, one could not claim that the left currently has a lower representation in the parliament than the total number of votes it received in the November 3 election.

12 "Adalet ve Kalkınma Partisi Programı" [The program of the Justice and Development Party] (Ankara: AKP, 2002).

13 "AKP'nin Cinsiyetçiliği" [The sexism of the AKP], *Postexpress*, November 2002.

Ümit Cizre and Menderes Çınar

Turkey 2002: Kemalism, Islamism, and Politics in the Light of the February 28 Process

In the 1990s, Turkish politics witnessed the fragmentation of the political center and the rise of the Islamist Welfare Party (Refah Partisi, or RP) from fringe party to a major partner in the coalition government, Refahyol, it formed with the center-right True Path Party (Doğru Yol Partisi, or DYP) in June 1996. With the benefit of hindsight, one might suggest that the Turkish military took the accession of the RP into government as confirmation of its belief that Islamist reactionism, *irtica* in Turkish, had become a substantial threat to the secular character of the republic. Consequently, on February 28, 1997, the military-dominated National Security Council (NSC) issued the Refahyol coalition government with a list of measures designed to nullify the supposed Islamization of Turkey and fortify the secular system. Subsequent pressure from the NSC, in tandem with the civilian component of the secular establishment, led to the collapse of the coalition government in June 1997.

The ousting of the Refahyol government signaled the start of the military's plan to refashion Turkey's political landscape along Kemalist lines

The *South Atlantic Quarterly* 102:2/3, Spring/Summer 2003.
Copyright © 2003 by Duke University Press.

without actually having to take over power directly. Hence, the phrase "February 28 process" was coined to indicate not only the far-reaching implications of the NSC decisions, but also the suspension of normal politics until the secular correction was completed. This process has profoundly altered the formulation of public policy and the relationship between state and society. No major element of Turkish politics at present can be understood without reference to the February 28 process.

This essay takes issue with three things. First, it seeks to unpack the rationale that underpins the February 28 process and critically assess its impact on Turkish politics and society. Next, it examines the way in which the February 28 process has afforded the Turkish Armed Forces (TAF) even greater scope to influence public policy and to do so with virtually no oversight by the civilian constitutional authority. Finally, it addresses the ways in which political Islam has responded to the process.

Reconfiguring Politics

Since the inception of the republic, Kemalism has comprised its guiding vision. It is in essence a Westernizing/civilizing ideology whose incontrovertible maxims are secularism, understood as the separation of religion from political rule; a modern/Western identity and lifestyle; and the cultural homogeneity and territorial unity of the nation. Because the Kemalist Westernization project has relied more on symbols than substance, it has associated publicly visible instances of Islamic identity with reactionism. The ideology is also marked by a visible distaste for politics as a societal activity, and an ambivalent attitude toward the notion of popular legitimacy. Over time, it has been adjusted, at times stalled, but never abandoned or discontinued. Even if the TAF has at times deployed the Kemalist doctrine to suit its own agenda, its basic tenets have not lost their power of appeal and legitimacy both across classes and across the civilian-military divide.

Kemalism Redefined or Entrenched? The architects behind the February 28 process grounded their actions in the need to ensure the "continuity" of the basic assumptions of the Kemalist model. The Turkish military, former President Süleyman Demirel (1993–2000), the civil societal network of the secular establishment, media, and large sectors of the populace believe that Islamic reactionism constitutes the chronic, if at times undetectable,

Demonstration by the Association for Atatürkist Thought. Photo by Arif Aşçı.

malaise of the Turkish polity. The former Chief of General Staff General Hüseyin Kıvrıkoğlu expresses this sentiment: "Radical Islam may appear gone one day to reemerge the next day . . . it is not possible to say that the danger has vanished."[1] As a result, the secular establishment's natural reflex is to remain in a permanent state of alert. They also hold that by sticking to a "purist interpretation of the Kemalist bases of the republic,"[2] civilian politics can be reconstructed so as to ensure continuity of the Kemalist regime and thereby accrue popular support for it.

Contrary to the "neorepublican" policies that prevailed after the post-1980 military rule when elements of Islam were incorporated into public discourse to provide a moral basis, ideological unity, and some certainty in the face of global capitalism,[3] the February 28 process seeks to usher back the republic's radical secularism. That represents a complete reversal from the republican pattern of state-Islam relations that, in the past, allowed for negotiation, compromise, and reconciliation between Turkey's political Islamists and the establishment.[4] This time, however, a string of drastic prosecular policy measures were introduced: All primary and secondary school curricula were altered so as to emphasize both the secularist history and character of the republic and the new security threats posed by political Islam and separatist movements. Teaching on Atatürkism was expanded to cover all courses taught at all levels and types of schools.[5] The secondary school system for prayer-leaders and preachers (*imam hatip*) was scrapped and an eight-year mandatory schooling system was introduced. Appointments of university chancellors since 1997 were pointedly made from among staunch Kemalists. Teaching programs on Kemalist principles, the struggle against reactionism, and national security issues were also extended to top bureaucrats and prayer leaders.[6] Finally, military institutions and personnel were actively involved in administering the programs.

If we add to these measures the closing of the Islamic parties and the banning of their key policy makers from active politics, it is clear that the architects of the process aim to ensure that the key political players toe the line—namely, comply with the need to both stabilize the rule of the original Kemalist project and revive the myth of a homogenous nation and society. The moralizing mentality that elevates a suprapolitical Kemalism and secularism to the level of a moral consensus of society is clearly exemplified by the deputy chief of general staff: "Countries that could not create a common value system are by definition in a state of conflict. Our common value is secular and democratic Turkey within the framework of unitarianism and Atatürkist thought. All movements that do not meet with us on this common value are the enemies of the nation and country, and must be fought against."[7]

The actual dynamics of the process, however, point at a compromise between a zero-sum understanding of Kemalism and the new realities on the ground. In its drive to reassert secularism, the establishment has run into two principal problems: the political resistance put up largely by the center-right Motherland Party (Anavatan Partisi, or ANAP), which has been part of all governments since June 1997, and the reforms required if Turkey's EU membership application is to be successful.

Because Tansu Çiller, the chairwoman of the DYP, had already been sidelined and the RP and its successors were clearly discredited and intimidated, Mesut Yılmaz, the chairman of the ANAP, emerged as the main opposition to the secular establishment's assessment and justification of the necessity and management of the struggle against *irtica*. The Center-Right's claim is that *irtica*, like the preceding communist and Kurdish questions, is a pretext to maintain the power, position, and large budget share of the TAF. In taking a critical stand against the TAF over who should fight against Islamic activism and how, Mesut Yılmaz as the prime minister (July 1997–January 1999) repeatedly expressed the view that *irtica* was not the number-one question for Turkey: "It is only if they (Islamists) rebel against the state authority that we would have to assign the task to the TAF."[8] This attitude implies that intervention is justified only if there is "clear and present danger," as opposed to the view that a preemptive strike is required against the *possibility* of Islamic dominance. Yılmaz, who ironically enough was favored by the secular establishment to unite the Center-Right as part of the combat against *irtica*, explicitly accused the high command of trying to reap political gains from the campaign against the Islamists.[9] Furthermore, he argued that he would act against assertions of Islamic identity publicly only on the basis of court verdicts rather than intelligence reports compiled by the military's working groups.[10] The underlying conundrum for the Center-Right has been the fear of hurting "genuinely devout Muslims," the conservative bedrock from which they draw their popular support. Their dilemma lies in the fact that the center-right tradition can neither embrace radical secular policies, nor reject or ignore the secular state ideology. In other words, as Islam-as-culture is the most important icon of its claim to be "modern," this tradition simultaneously opposes both politicized Islam and radicalized secularism.

The Center-Right's challenge against the post–February 28 interpretation of secularism has created some political space to engage the secular establishment in an extended process of protest, warning, defiance, and sometimes cooperation and negotiation. The subsequent story of Turkish political life after 1997 can be said to be a constant stretching of the limits imposed by the February 28 process.

The other issue that has at least partly diluted the force of the war mentality against Islamic activism has been the support for Turkey's firm commitment to Westernize proffered by the Helsinki European Council's meeting on December 10–11, 1999. To stave off criticism from prodemocracy circles and the European Union (EU), in the official declaration of the historic NSC meeting on February 28, 1997, the high command justified the intervention by arguing that it upheld Turkey's commitment to full EU membership and presented secularism as "a guarantee not only for the regime but at the same time of democracy, societal peace and the modern lifestyle."[11] Moreover, pitting the rhetoric of "contemporariness" (a piece of imagery in Turkey that centers around the idea of being Westernlike) against the opposite imagery of "Islamic anachronism" is one way for Ankara to show its endorsement of Western values. In the post-Helsinki era, at least until the Kurdish insurgency was firmly under control, there was also a shift of discourse on the part of the military establishment from a rhetorical language denying violations of democratic norms to an "argumentative rationality" when engaged with its domestic and international critics over specific accusations of democratic deficiencies and human rights violations.[12] The argumentative discourse affirmed the democratic deficiency in Turkey's political landscape in terms of civil-military relations, individual rights, and the securitization of public life, but tried to justify them on the grounds that, as part of the military's combat against internal enemies, these measures were "exceptional" and "corrective," expressing some awareness of the importance of the democracy-centered security architecture in post–Cold War Europe.

However, as the high command is clearly in favor of a controlled entry into the EU, it has simultaneously adopted another discourse claiming that

Street photographer with Atatürk portraits. Photo by Arif Aşçı.

democratic compromises required in order to join the EU would be too high a price to pay for a state committed to countering *irtica* and separatist terror. Thus, accession measures should be accepted only on condition that they do not inflame ethnic differences and provide a breeding ground for Islamic principles. The conservatizing impetus that has followed the September 11 attacks has introduced extra incentives for the Turkish general staff to move toward a more conservative-nationalist position with regard to Ankara's fulfillment of the EU's Copenhagen Criteria. Moreover, the high command is of the opinion that the EU is a bloc that displays a negative bias toward Turkey and will therefore not let her in. Tuncer Kilinc, secretary-general of the NSC, expressed his opinion in early March 2002 that "the EU will never accept Turkey. . . . Thus, Turkey needs new allies, and it would be useful if Turkey engages in a search that would include Russia and Iran."[13]

Implementation: Shaping Turkish Politics. The protagonists of the February 28 intervention saw the roots of political Islam in the "irresponsible" policies of Turkey's political class that uses Islam for partisan purposes and also in the division of the Center-Right into DYP and ANAP, which was regarded as obstructing the formation of strong, effective, and stable government. Therefore, foremost in their minds was a structural redesign to strengthen Turkey's political center so as to minimize the importance of what they considered the "noncentric" forces of political Islam and establish a center-party majority rule. This objective would be achieved by the bold use of state power to discipline representative institutions, forge the fragmented center around ANAP, and engage the judiciary in wresting control of political power from the RP and its successors by closing them down. In the end, there are two principal aspects of existing politics that can be attributed to the makings of the February 28 process. They are the crystallization of state-friendly features by almost all political persuasions and a pervasive sense of political inertia, both of which have exacerbated the weakness and instability of Turkey's civilian politics.

Gravitating toward the State. The principles that informed the February 28 process have exposed the state-dependent and state-defending characteristics of all representative platforms in Turkey. Turkey's Center-Left, as the founder of official republican politics, has always acted as a force fully complicit with the military-civil bureaucracy in subordinating politics and economics to the logic of secular state power. It has also been badly battered since the 1980s by being outflanked by the free-market rhetoric of the New Right. When it gradually embraced the same agenda rather than articulating welfare-state policies, it lent respectability to neoliberalism. Not surprisingly, since the 1997 intervention, the two center-left parties, the Democratic Left Party (Demokratik Sol Parti, or DSP) of Prime Minister Bülent Ecevit and the Republican People's Party (Cumhuriyet Halk Partisi, or CHP) have acted as the agents and defenders of the reconsolidation of nation-state behind the totalizing language of secularism.

Turkey's Center-Right, which also comes from a tradition articulating rural and urban interests that seemingly oppose puritan Kemalism, has gravitated toward a state-centered discourse. This is so because the political discourse of this tradition was built on an ambiguous and fuzzy set of principles encompassing political, economic, and religious liberalism.[14] Those principles allowed the Center-Right to satisfy its power base through the distribution of state largesse while paying lip service to liberal values. The DYP's problems with the February 28 process were over the party's loss

Peddler of Atatürk portraits. Photo by Arif Aşçı.

of power and relegation to the sidelines, rather than based on an ethically motivated opposition to the intervention. The ANAP, locus of power in the 1980s, upheld the free-market ideology without seeing any contradiction between supporting the state-imposed political design of the February 28 process and political and economic liberalism. It was only when the party's alignment with the process was observed to be causing a major electoral slide for the party that it became the major challenger to the new political design.

Since February 28, 1997, Turkish political parties have retreated from a constituency-serving position to a state-supporting one. Neither the rising star of Turkish politics in the 1990s, the nationalist camp represented by the Nationalist Movement Party (Milliyetçi Hareket Partisi, or MHP), nor the Islamists can claim to have articulated an alternative democratic political platform that can act as "the significant other." The nationalist MHP and the Islamist parties have failed to formulate a solid political bedrock from which to constructively oppose the moral consensus laid down by the February 28 process. Hence, EU accession has become the only instrumental issue with the power to compel progressive change in the country.

The Politics of Inertia. Despite the vast changes in political, social, economic, and geopolitical realities, the thrust of politics has stagnated since February 28, 1997. The current three-party coalition government comprising the center-right ANAP, the center-left DSP, and the nationalist MHP has been in office longer than any coalition in Turkish history. But the government does not owe its durability to imaginative politics, empathy with the fears and hopes of the masses, and its outward-looking, competitive drive for power. On the contrary, it owes its durability to a new version of the politics of inertia, or bloc-politics, which is promoted by domestic and international business circles to bring stability and inspire confidence in the markets. The core bloc of the government, comprised of ANAP and DSP, first emerged as an alternative to the Refahyol coalition government in 1997. With the inclusion of the conservative-nationalist MHP after it emerged as the second largest party in the April 1999 elections, it was thought that this bloc would bring some stability into politics. The formation and survival of this bloc have also been facilitated by the decline of the Turkish Left as well as by the tacit understanding that there is a de facto military veto against any prospective governments where DYP and RP and their successors can participate.

Given that the bloc politics is basically due to the failure of Turkey's political persuasions, be it on the left or right, to articulate any pattern of thought other than that of defending the status quo, the troika stays in power because it is a government by default. That it stays despite its policy failures—culminating in the most serious economic crash in the history of the republic on February 21, 2001, which effectively forced the government to seek a massive new standby emergency aid package from the International Monetary Fund (thus saddling the Turkish taxpayer with even further international debt)—is a sign of the absence of political synergy or a credible parliamentary alternative, and the officials' abject disregard for the concerns of those they represent.

Moreover, in the absence of a tradition of resigning from public office, Prime Minister Ecevit's refusal to step down, despite his deteriorating health and massive defections from his party in the summer of 2002, plunged the country into a state of political uncertainty.[15] The government could survive only by calling for early elections on November 3, 2002. The EU-required political reforms, necessary to start accession negotiations by the end of this year to qualify Turkey for full membership, could be passed only thanks to the last-minute initiative of the ANAP, itself desperate to institute the reforms for the elections and thereby avoid political extinction.

It would not be wrong to suggest that the pervasive sense of political inertia in the country and the absence of serious challenges to the extant hierarchy of power is largely a function of a trend in evidence since February 28, 1997, namely, the urge to secure the country against potential threats to the Kemalist doctrine. That outlook has led to the closure of public debate on key issues and caused the existing political class to subcontract the resolution of crucial problems to the civil-military bureaucracy.[16] One writer, in referring to the dominance of the security-first outlook, speaks of a "dual-track government," in which there is a certain division of labor between the TAF and the representative institutions: "It is not that the military has assumed the power of governing; rather, they have set much of the contentious political agenda and then put pressure on the government to enact it. The power of the military (exerted through the NSC) has, in the past two years, increasingly encroached on areas traditionally . . . the prerogative of the nation's elected civilian leaders."[17] Without formally governing, the military's behind-the-scenes maneuvering has successfully managed, perhaps unintentionally, to snuff out any meaningful space for democratic debate and carefully considered renewal.

All in all, the post–February 28 political design has been implemented only to a limited extent, mainly because the problems of political Islam and a fragmented center are seen from a rather mechanical prism and regarded as being alterable by manipulating the technical rules of the game that organize political life. The new model also aimed at promoting stability by enhancing discipline and authority in the public sphere rather than promoting regime capabilities through more effective governance, political legitimacy, and expanded democracy. Considerations of connections between the transformative effects of market policies specific to the countries of the near-periphery and their effect on the empowerment of political Islam are absent. Furthermore, as the "creeping Islamization of Turkey" is attributed to the strategies of irresponsible, weak, inefficient political agents, politics is understood as needing a dose of moral injection in terms of framing public interest as the triumph of the "good" forces against "evil," the victory of secularism against the creeping threat of the Islamization/feudalization of life. The question to address therefore is whether the February 28 process, in steering civilian politics in a particu-

Peddler with picture of the Islamic place of pilgrimage in Mecca. Photo by Arif Aşçı.

lar direction to strengthen center politics and keep Islamic parties out of power, has perilously enhanced the weakness of civilian politics in Turkey.

TAF As Guardians

The Turkish constitutions have not openly proclaimed any guardianship role for the military. However, the esteem with which the military has historically been held and the broad definition of what constitutes a security issue and who defines it[18] means that the realm of influence of TAF goes significantly beyond its counterparts in other democratic societies. It is "not only a professional military organization but a core element of Turkey's political system,"[19] enjoying a high degree of political and institutional autonomy.[20] Backed by that mantle of authority, it is well positioned to pursue its historically mandated guardianship role, a mandate that effectively provides the military with an "ideal for following a political agenda of its own."[21]

In the 1990s, the TAF has expanded its domain of jurisdiction by redefining the idea of national security.[22] By identifying Islamic and Kurdish groups as potential internal enemies, it is effectively able to control the public agenda. In doing this, it takes advantage of the privileged powers and position that it has by virtue of its role within the NSC.[23] Hence, the extent of the TAF's influence over public policy has increased, while at the same time the ability of civilians to correct the imbalance in civil-military relations has decreased. Given that the magnitude of the Islamic threat is perceived to be potentially present in all parts of the country and in all sectors of society, national security considerations are now enshrined in legislation on anti-terrorism, media, public order, political parties, education, civil rights, and liberties. The insertion of national security concerns into public policy has significantly altered the meaning of democracy in Turkey by subordinating individual and group rights and liberties to the demands of security. The endorsement of Turkey's candidate status in the Helsinki Summit in 1999, however, acts as the main driving force behind the parliamentary initiative to either modify or repeal the draconian features of national security laws and practices.

Perhaps the most disturbing concern is that what qualifies as an internal defense threat is defined by the military itself. The military sets the standards for measuring and judging the Islamic threat as a life or death question and has created new organizational devices to combat it.[24] Especially after the 1995 elections, the TAF has been involved in making and breaking governments, initiating crucial policy decisions, becoming directly involved in political intrigue, issuing public demands and warnings to civilians, structuring new bills through its own research units and departments, launching campaigns to inform the public about the possibility that political Islam might be acting as cover for reactionary intentions, having the final say on whether or not the 1999 elections would be held, shaping foreign policy, and continuously impinging on the daily operations of elected governments.

Consequently, the military is more exposed to charges of partisanship and is more vulnerable to criticisms. Given the fact that the military's traditional "most trusted institution" status was based on its image of being "above politics," one could argue that by remaining in the political arena it weakens the very foundations of its own strength. The increasing intolerance of the military for any criticism or alternative views, which we can observe in the frequency with which the institution responds to what it considers counterpositions taken by public figures, reflects its increasing sense of insecurity about its status. It is perhaps for this reason that the military aims to construct its own support base by acting like a political party directly addressing the public. However, this strategy feeds back into the weakening of the military's carefully nurtured "above politics" image.

A major element of rupture with the past is the way the military's priority has shifted from invoking societal indifference and fear to producing consent and support. In trying to undermine the RP's popular appeal and create an order characterized by social discipline, centralized authority, and hierarchical integration, the military has been very successful in establishing a new relationship with targeted groups in society. It has appealed directly to the organized groups of the modernized urban-secular sectors—the business world, media, academia, public prosecutors, judges, leaders of civil societal associations—and even held briefing meetings with them to warn of the extent and magnitude of the Islamic threat. The rising salience of civil society for the general staff, however, has not arisen from the search for a free public space, rule of law, limited state power, democratic consensus and compromise over power sharing. On the contrary, there is a widespread belief among the secular-urbanites that the intensity of the Islamic threat may require the suspension of democratic freedoms and limitation of representative principles and institutions. To this end, these sectors have given the TAF a strong hand in crushing what they see as a threat to the regime's existence.

Islamist Politics: Division, Adaptation, and Change

Thus far we have discussed the nature of the February 28 process, the way in which it modified the political landscape, and the way it signaled the military's appropriation of civilian policy making. However, we have yet to consider the way in which the process affected those who were its explicit target, as well as the ways in which they reacted to it. The main target of the process, the RP, was founded in July 1983 as the third political party of the Islamist National Outlook Movement (Milli Gorus Hareketi, or MGH), the expression of Islamism in the political arena since 1970. It was closed down by the Constitutional Court on January 16, 1998, on the grounds that it had become a focal point of antisecular activities. With this closure, a five-year ban on the political activities of its leader, Necmettin Erbakan, and five other top policy makers was imposed. The RP was succeeded by the Virtue Party (Fazilet Partisi, or FP, founded in December 1997), again closed down on June 22, 2001, for its antisecular activities and for violating the constitutional stipulation that a permanently closed party, the RP, cannot be opened again. Although the FP claimed to be a different party than the RP and tried to follow a different political style, until its closure it too was under the questioning eyes of the secularist establishment of Turkey, which charged it with being the new flag bearer of the RP and disguising its reactionary nature from the public.[25]

What has been the impact of this intimidation on political Islam? The question cannot be answered adequately without reference to the division of the movement into the reformist and traditionalist factions.[26] The ban imposed on Erbakan, the founder of the MGH and its authority figure, enabled the FP to break free from his direct influence and enabled the reformists to publicize their discontent with the policies of the traditionalists.[27] The movement was eventually divided into two parties after the closure of the FP: the traditionalists' Felicity Party (Saadet Partisi, or SP, founded on July 20, 2001) and the reformists' AKP, founded on August 14, 2001. In what follows we will delineate and discuss the different readings of the February 28 process as reflected by each faction's preferred policies and political styles.

The Traditionalist Wing: Paying Lip Service to Kemalism and Democracy? In terms of their politics, both the RP and the FP tried to adapt themselves to the February 28 process conditions by de-Islamizing their discourse, emphasizing a discourse that avoided any societal tensions, and taking a low-profile, nonconfrontational, and moderate stance. On the basis of what he called "unripe and transitory" conditions, Erbakan rejected the RP's provincial leaders' demands for a strong opposition against the crackdown of the February 28 process.[28] Its successor party, FP, also employed a consensus-seeking strategy, expressing no discontent over the undemocratic nature of the crackdown on Islamic identity. Its leader, Recai Kutan, for example, went as far as declaring that "they will not be a party to any conflict"[29] and that "they will not bring up the issue of the headscarf even though it is the right thing to do so."[30] He even lent some legitimacy to the February 28 process by indicating that they understand the TAF's sensitivity on secularism.[31] It must be pointed out that this obedient stance was motivated by the FP's massive sense of insecurity—so much so that on that particular point, the party even asked the opinion of the chief of staff about its political program.[32]

The FP's acquiescence was redressed by a discourse endorsing democ-

Demonstration against the headscarf ban at the university. Photo by Arif Aşçı.

racy and the idea of a "nonideological state" as the basic principles of the modern world. "We know," Kutan stated, "what it is like to be threatened, blackmailed, silenced," and "therefore no one could value democracy better than us."[33] Before the February 28 process, the Islamist movement saw the false consciousness of the Westernizing elite as Turkey's basic problem. This elite, it was argued, prevented people's moral development, which was the prerequisite of economic development and democracy. Erbakan and his team did not question the nonpluralist form of state-society relations, but singled out only the secularist substance of it as a focus of criticism. More-over, Erbakan's RP claimed that the MGH represented the true national will of the whole society and appealed to the majoritarian principle to sup-port that conclusion. The RP, therefore, seemed to be willing to utilize the Kemalist legal and political framework, which was instituted to enforce a Western lifestyle by the republican regime, to switch the secular bias of a nonpluralist state-society relationship to one that was Islamic.[34] Hence, for example, the idea of making Friday a holiday—as is the case in Islamic societies—was defended not in terms of the right of believers to practice Islam in a democratic context, but rather in terms of the fulfillment of the state's legal duty to provide religious services within the framework of secularism as drawn by Atatürk.[35] Consequently, it was not unthinkable for the secular Turkish public to conceive that the RP posed a threat to their lifestyle.

Although the FP endorsed the idea of a nonideological state, it still main-tained its predecessor's nonpluralist understanding of society. For example, in one of his visits to EU authorities in Brussels, the FP's pro-Erbakan leader, Kutan, denied that there is a Kurdish problem in Turkey.[36] When, on rare occasions, the existence of the Kurdish problem was acknowledged, the FP's alternative was little more than to uphold the solution once pro-posed by the RP: relying on the assumption that the real source of identity is Islam, the suggested solution was to strengthen the national and moral values by relaxing the pressures on religion so as to maintain the "com-munity," rather than a democratic-pluralist restructuring.[37] Consequently, the FP's understanding of democracy was self-servingly restricted to legal and constitutional amendments that would make the closure of the parties difficult and remove the ban on Erbakan's political activities. As a corol-lary, instead of pressing for institutional and noninstitutional changes that would make the state nonideological, which was the FP's declared priority, the FP used democracy as a window dressing to endear itself to the public in a democracy-dominated age.

According to a distinguished former deputy of the RP, Aydın Menderes, the traditionalists not only lack the ability to carry out radical reforms in the party, but also seem willing to return to the substance and style of politics they conducted in the RP whenever the grip of the February 28 process relaxes.[38] Indeed, both Erbakan and Kutan, after the closure of their parties, asserted that they will not change their political stance and ideals, which they believed were correct. The traditionalists' current political party, the SP, not unexpectedly adopts a course of return to the basic tenets of the RP's discourse in a somewhat modified manner.

Lessons the Reformists Drew from the Past. The reformist faction, which eventually formed the AKP under the leadership of the prominent ex-mayor of Istanbul, Recep Tayyip Erdoğan, reads the February 28 process and the RP's role in the making of it somewhat differently. Unlike the traditionalists, the reformists are (self-)critical of the political style and policies of the RP, which, they believe, contributed to the February 28 process with its political mistakes.[39] For them, the RP's policies reached an impasse because it let religious issues dominate its political agenda, it underplayed the importance of consensus-seeking and dialogue-building with the other sectors of the society, and it did not address itself to a broader public.[40] As such, the reformist group's moderate discourse seemed to spring from the recognition of the heterogeneous nature of the society. Another conclusion the reformists have drawn from the Refahyol experience is the need to acknowledge the guardianship role of the military in Turkey, which, they considered, should be taken into account as a historical reality. "If we are to be realistic," a leading reformist said, "we should not come up against and clash with the military."[41]

The reformists' stated goal was to establish a party that would refrain from employing a rhetorical discourse, would not restrict its political horizon to Islamic issues, would pay special attention to pluralism by building a dialogue with non-Islamist sectors of the society, and would be predictable, dynamic, and open to change, with no hidden agenda on critical issues.[42] In wanting to bring about the transformation of Islamism, they tried to eliminate what they saw as the root cause of the maladies of the RP, namely the lack of intraparty democracy, self-criticism, and transparency.[43]

Demonstration/prayer at Beyazıt Square. Photo by Arif Aşçı.

The reformist AKP persistently rejects being Islamist, defines itself as a conservative democratic party, and emphasizes the democratic character of the party organization, its spirit of teamwork, and the importance of consensus-seeking in politics. But since for Erdoğan, politics by definition should take up popular issues and demands related to religious life, the AKP's moderation does not mean that it will not bring religious issues to the political arena,[44] especially when the AKP's intention to broaden its support base without alienating the traditional constituency of the Islamist movement is taken into account. Hence, for example, it aims to raise the issue of the ban on the wearing of headscarves in educational institutions in the political arena as a matter of basic rights, but not as an issue of religion or religiosity. The AKP cites its attempt to address itself to a broader public while taking up the issues related to public visibility of Islamic identity as evidence of its will to reconcile secularism and Islam through a pluralist public sphere in Turkey. Turkey's secularist establishment, they believe, will respect moderate religiosity in a pro-Islamic party if it refrains from employing a rhetorical discourse and if it maintains a transparent political agenda.

Despite some doubts,[45] legal pressures, and ambiguities concerning Erdoğan's eligibility to be elected as a member of parliament,[46] according to almost all opinion polls, the AKP is the most popular party in Turkey. Admittedly, this is due to the AKP's capitalization on the political vacuum created by the immobility of Turkey's existing political contenders. In doing so, the AKP promises a government that will not sacrifice the system's stability and development merely for the sake of acquiring political benefits. In a context in which corruption is rampant and the economy is in severe crisis, such a discourse is appealing. Nevertheless, as it is a promise of "performance" and not a societal vision in which Islam and secularism can be reconciled, such a discourse is more technocratic than political in its outlook.

Conclusion

The political language of the February 28 process presents itself in the form of an ambiguous double discourse. This represents the crisis of epistemology in Kemalist thought. On the one hand, it is correct to say that the central element in the February 28 strategy is the subordination of the present to the past, politics to the market, individual to the wisdom and moral guardianship of the secular establishment, and sociopolitical differences to unity and uniformity. Yet both the establishment and the actors of political Islam, in the process, appropriate a language of holding themselves up as believers in "democracy." Given that the iron rule of Turkish politics is that the practice of democracy is not permitted to have a hallow content but must be rooted in a secular existence, this is hardly surprising. Nor can the logic of power based on the belief that "the confession of secularism is identical with democratic conviction"[47] be sustained in modern global circumstances in a country struggling to obtain EU membership. Likewise, political Islam provides the mirror image of Kemalism in terms of its conception of democracy not as a hallow notion, but as a totalizing and restrictive sense.

Notes

1   "Kıvrıkoğlu: Sinsi Irtica" [Kıvrıkoğlu: Sinister reactionism], *Radikal*, June 14, 2001.
2   Heinz Kramer, *A Changing Turkey, the Challenge to Europe and the United States* (Washington, DC: Brookings Institution Press, 2000), 71.

3 Faruk Birtek and Binnaz Toprak, "The Conflictual Agendas of Neo-Liberal Reconstruction and the Rise of Islamic Politics in Turkey," *Praxis International* 13.2 (1993): 192–212.

4 Ümit Cizre Sakalhoğlu, "Parameters and Strategies of Islam-State Interaction in Republican Turkey," *International Journal of Middle East Studies* 28 (1996): 231–51.

5 "Atatürkçülük Her Derste Okutulacak" [Atatürkism is going to be taught in all courses], *Hurriyet*, June 27, 1998.

6 "Yönetici Memura Inkilap Tarihi Dersi" [History of the republic course (given) to top bureaucrats], *Milliyet*, December 12, 1995.

7 "GATA Açılışında Laiklik Uyarısı" [Secularism warning in the opening ceremony of GATA (Gülhane Military Medicine Academy)], *Radikal*, October 2, 2001.

8 "Yılmaz'dan Askere Sınır" [Yılmaz constrains the officers], *Radikal*, July 11, 1998.

9 "Hükümetin Zor Günleri" [Hard days for the government], *Milliyet*, March 14, 1998.

10 "Yılmaz: Komutanların Hakkıdır" [Yılmaz: It is the right of the commanders], *Sabah*, March 21, 1998.

11 Muzaffer Şahin, *MGK, 28 Şubat Öncesi ve Sonrası* [NSC, before and after February 28] (Ankara: Ufuk Kitabevi, 1998), 77.

12 We borrow the idea that at one stage of internalization of human rights norms, there is a move from "rhetorical discourse" to an "argumentative rationality," from Thomas Risse and Kathryn Sikkink. The significant component in this move is that the logic of argumentation over human rights violations in public entraps the political class in its own rhetoric, enabling them to move toward a true dialogue. See Thomas Risse and Kathryn Sikkink, "The Socialization of International Human Rights Norms into Domestic Practices: Introduction," in *The Power of Human Rights, International Norms and Domestic Change*, ed. Thomas Risse, Stephen C. Ropp, and Kathryn Sikkink (Cambridge: Cambridge University Press, 1999), 2–3.

13 Jon Gorvett, "Turkish Military Fires Warning Shot over EU Membership," *Middle East*, no. 323 (2002): 33.

14 Ümit Cizre, "Liberalism, Democracy and the Turkish Center-Right: The Identity Crisis of the True Path Party," *Middle Eastern Studies* 32.2 (1996): 142–61; and Ümit Cizre, "From Ruler to Pariah: The Life and Times of True Path Party," in *Political Parties in Turkey*, ed. Barry Rubin and Metin Heper (London: Frank Cass, 2002), 82–101.

15 The political crisis deepened when Foreign Minister Ismail Cem, six other ministers, and about seventy defected deputies left Ecevit's party to launch a new party on July 12, 2002, in defiance of Ecevit's refusal to step aside and name a successor. Kemal Dervis, the former minister of state and the overseer of the ongoing IMF-designed stabilization program, was expected to join in the new movement, which later became the New Turkey Party. Until Dervis's declaration in mid-August 2002 that he would not join the New Turkey Party, the initiative was hailed by Turkey's secular establishment and business and international circles as potentially capable of stemming the tide of the Islamic Justice and Development Party (Adalet ve Kalkınma Partisi, or AKP) and speeding up the process of starting Turkey's accession talks with the EU.

16 Menderes Çınar, "Mission Impossible?" *Private View* 2–5 (1997): 72–78.

17 Heath W. Lowry, "Turkey's Political Structure on the Cusp of the Twenty-First Century,"

in *Turkey's Transformation and American Policy*, ed. Morton Abramowitz (New York: Century Foundation Press, 2000), 48.

18 The chief example is Act No. 2945 on the NSC and the National Security Council General Secretariat, which assigns significant and broad political powers to the NSC, placing it on par with the executive.

19 See Kramer, *A Changing Turkey*, 30.

20 Ümit Cizre Sakallıoğlu, "The Anatomy of the Turkish Military's Political Autonomy," *Comparative Politics* 29.2 (1997): 153.

21 Kramer, *A Changing Turkey*, 30.

22 On April 29, 1997, the Turkish General Staff announced a radical change in their basic doctrine (the National Military Defense Concept). Henceforth priority would be given to combating internal threats from, primarily, Islamic activism and, secondarily, the Kurdish separatism, rather than safeguarding against interstate wars and external threats. This new document replaced the one formulated on November 18, 1992, singling out Kurdish terrorist acts as the primary security threat to the state. Both documents were prepared by the secretariat of the NSC and became governmental policy. The parliament was not fully informed about this decision. The defeat inflicted on the PKK by the capture, arrest, trial, and conviction of its leader, Abdullah Öcalan, reinforced this shift.

23 Article 35 of the Military Internal Service Code assigns the military the task of safeguarding the territorial unity and the republic itself. Furthermore, Act No. 2945 assigns three important functions to the NSC secretariat, which enables it to act like the council of ministers. First, the secretary (a general) has the authority to prepare the agenda of the meetings. Next, he is authorized to follow up the implementations of the decisions reached in the NSC meetings and passed to the ministers to act upon with priority consideration. Finally, the secretary can present his suggestions on domestic and foreign policy to the council of ministers directly.

24 A new unit called the Western Study Group (Batı Çalışma Grubu, or BCG) was instituted within general staff headquarters to collect information about the political orientations of civil society groups, mayors, governors, government employees, political party cadres, and media personalities. Moreover, by a governmental decree published in the official gazette on January 9, 1997, a new organ called the Prime Ministerial Crisis Management Center (Başbakanlık Kriz Yönetim Merkezi) was formed within the NSC secretariat to observe and report on "crises," a vaguely defined term in the decree, and formulate responses to them. As the center was placed within the NSC but called "Prime Ministerial," it had an ambiguous structural and functional position. It bypassed parliamentary control of its activities and was seemingly responsible to the prime minister but was, in reality, answerable only to the NSC.

25 When the Constitutional Court was handling the closure case filed against the FP, the military issued a judgmental statement that the FP is a source of reactionism, indicating the direction that the case would follow. Before April 1999 general elections, the then-president of the republic, Süleyman Demirel, also equated the FP with the RP.

26 The reformist group constituted usually the younger generation of the MGH such as Abdullatif Sener, Salih Kapusuz, Abdullah Gül, and their leader Recep Tayyip Erdoğan.

Bulent Arınç, who has been in the movement ever since its inception, was with the reformists as well as the newcomers to FP such as Ali Coşkun, Abdulkadir Aksu, and Cemil Çiçek, all from the conservative wing of the ANAP. The traditionalists, on the other hand, included the leader of the FP, Recai Kutan, as well as the top administrative officials of the party such as Bahri Zengin, Veysel Candan, and Oğuzhan Asilturk.

27 Hence, the first convention of the FP, held on May 14, 2000, was also the first competitive convention in the whole history of the MGH. In this convention, despite Erbakan's disapproval, the reformist faction challenged the traditionalist leadership of the party and lost by only a small margin, which is usually taken as evidence that Erbakan's moral authority over the movement was no longer intact.

28 "Refah Örgütünde Çiller Tepkisi" [Çiller reaction in the rank-and-file of the Refah], *Milliyet*, October 27, 1997.

29 "Kutan'dan 'Kavga Yok' Sözü" [Kutan promises "no fight"], *Hürriyet*, February 11, 1999.

30 "Tansu Bize Gelecek 3: Türbanda Dikkatliyiz" [Tansu will join us 3: We are careful about headscarf], *Hurriyet*, February 8, 1999.

31 Bilal Çetin, "Kutan'dan FP'nin 'Sistem Partisi' Olduğuna Inandırma Çabası" [Kutan's attempt to convince that the FP is a 'systemic party'], *Radikal*, February 11, 1999. This acquiscent stance does not really represent a radical break from the past, when we bear in mind that the main actors of this tradition considered the military the biggest defender and guardian of democracy in Turkey, denied the obvious role of the military in the making of the February 28 process, and refrained from publicizing or precluding the operations of the BCG, which gathered the intelligence that made the process possible in the first place.

32 "Enine Boyuna Fazilet 2: 28 Subat Ayni Şiddetle Devam Etmiyor" [Comprehensive virtue 2: February 28 process is not continuing with the same momentum], *Sabah*, March 28, 1999.

33 Recai Kutan, "Birinci Olağan Kongre Açılış Konuşması" [First convention opening speech], May 14, 2000, ASKI Sports Hall (Ankara: [n.p.], 2000), 12.

34 For a detailed analysis of the RP's politics and vision of state-society relationship, see Menderes Çınar, "From Shadow-Boxing to Critical Understanding: Some Theoretical Notes on Islamism as a 'Political Question,'" *Totalitarian Movements and Political Religions* 3.1 (2002): 35–57.

35 See Süleyman Arif Emre, "Atatürk'ün Çizdiği Laiklik Çerçevesi" [The framework of secularism as drawn by Atatürk], *Milli Gazete*, February 8, 1997.

36 See Bilal Çetin, "Anlamlı Randevu" [A meaningful appointment], *Yeni Şafak*, September 29, 2000.

37 Abdullah Karakuş, "Kutan: Türk-Kürt Ayrımı Yapılmıyor" [Kutan: There is no differentiation between Kurds and Turks], *Milliyet*, March 20, 2000. For a detailed study of the Islamist movement's approach to the Kurdish question, see Burhanettin Duran, "Approaching the Kurdish Question via Adil Duzen: An Islamist Formula of the Welfare Party for Ethnic Coexistence," *Journal of Muslim Minority Affairs* 18.1 (1998): 111–28.

38 Aydın Menderes, interview by Mustafa Karaalioğlu, "Önce Refah Mezara Girdi" [First the RP was buried], *Yeni Şafak*, November 6, 2000; Aydın Menderes, interview by

Naki Özkan, "Erbakan'in Son Kullanma Tarihi Geçti" [Erbakan's expiration date is past], *Milliyet*, November 8, 2000.

39   "Erbakan'a Gül Dikeni" [Gül (rose) thorn to Erbakan], *Radikal*, January 22, 1998; "Abdullah Gül: Hatalarımız Oldu" [Abdullah Gül: We have made mistakes], *Zaman*, August 30, 1998.

40   Bulent Arinc, interview by Nilgun Cerrahoglu, "Libya Gezisi Bir Felaketti" [Visit to Libya was a disaster], *Milliyet*, February 22, 1998; Bulent Arinc, interview by Kemal Can, "Refah Partisini Ozlemiyoruz" [We do not miss the RP], *ArtiHaber*, June 20–26, 1998, 54–55.

41   Bülent Arınç, interview by Mehmet Gündem, "Askerle Polemik Hataydi" [Polemic with the military was a mistake], *Zaman*, February 6, 2000.

42   Bülent Arınç, interview by Yurdagül Erkoca, "FP"li Arınç Büyük Konuştu" [Arınç spoke rigorously], *Radikal*, May 25, 1998; Abdullah Gül, interview by Neşe Düzel, "Ben 28 Şubatı Imzalamazdım" [I would not have signed the February 28 decisions], *Radikal*, June 5, 2000.

43   Abdullah Gül, interview by Ruşen Çakır, "Şeriatçılar Marjinal" [Reactionists are marginal], *Milliyet*, February 9, 2000.

44   Recep Tayyip Erdoğan, interview by Eyüp Can, "Şeriat Devletini Ciddiye Almıyorum" [I do not take a Sharia state seriously], *Zaman*, February 6, 2000.

45   For example, the current president of the republic, Ahmet Necdet Sezer, drew Erdoğan's attention to the Constitutional Court's sensitivity on secularism and equated his demand for "a state that respects religion" with "a state based on religion." See "Sezer'den Erdoğan'a Rejim Uyarisi" [Sezer warns Erdoğan on regime], *Cumhuriyet*, December 5, 2001.

46   Although he benefited from a law that postponed the penalties of December 2000, Erdoğan's position as the chairman of the party as well as his eligibility to be elected and to be prime minister remain legally ambiguous. This is so because in January 2002, the Constitutional Court upheld the charge of the Chief Public Prosecutor of High Court of Appeals that Erdoğan could not be a founding member, and therefore not the chairman of the AKP, because of his previous conviction for inciting religious hatred. The court ordered the AKP to comply with its decision within six months. The implications of this decision have divided lawyers. Whether he can lead a party and stand as a candidate for the parliament in the elections is still not clear.

47   Kramer, *A Changing Turkey*, 87.

Andrew Davison

Turkey, a "Secular" State?
The Challenge of Description

The analytical reason for suggesting that what is known as secularism in Turkey be understood and consistently redescribed as laicism, indeed as a limited, inconsistent, and ambivalent form of laicism,[1] is that *secularism* and *laicism* are not two different words for the same institutional arrangement, but rather two distinct, complex, varied, contested, and dynamic possibilities in the range of nontheocratic politics. In this essay, I review the conceptual, empirical, and normative-theoretical bases for this suggestion and examine some of their consequences for the study of Turkey and the politics of secularization and laicization.

As concepts, secularism and laicism, while synonymous in some limited senses, have different etymologies, institutional histories, and normative theoretical implications. *Secularism* derives from the Latin *saeculum*, meaning generation or age, and originally meant "of the world" as opposed to "of the church." *Laicism*, by contrast, derives from the French word *lai* (or *laïque*, in contemporary usage), meaning "of the people" as distinguished from "the clergy." *Secular* thus originally conveys the early

The *South Atlantic Quarterly* 102:2/3, Spring/Summer 2003.
Copyright © 2003 by Duke University Press.

Christian "requirement of distance, of non-coincidence"[2] between matters of religiosity and matters of the world (seen as corrupted and to be resisted), while *laicism* underscores the distinction between lay members of a church, or *ecclesia*, and its religiously wise, clerical strata.

Lay certainly has some secularized meanings (e.g., "nonexpert"), but its English usage still seriously conveys its core original affiliation with the nonclerical, but still religious, members of a community of believers. By contrast, because of the core contradistinction it conveys between belonging to the world/worldly/temporal matters, on the one hand, and belonging to religion/religious/spiritual/heavenly matters, on the other, the concept *secular* today connotes a wide range of ideas, institutions, worldviews, ways of living, and other matters that extend well beyond the contours of any religious imagination. (Note that we call the "nonexpert" meaning of *lay* a "secularized," not a "laicized," meaning.) *Secular* is associated, for instance, with varieties of materialisms, humanisms, atheisms, and antitheisms that conceptualize worldliness and "the world" in ways that sharply differ and depart from the original Christian conception. Indeed, the term *secular* would not be what it is without connotations of jettisoning, divorcing, or dissociating religious doctrine, practice, and especially the premise and idea of God from all aspects and levels of human experience and social organization—from individual conscience and ordinary behavior to outlook on reality, symbolic experience, forms of art and inquiry, social norm, custom, education, administration, law, ideology, governance, and politics. *Secular* may thus convey a negative relation to religion and religiosity. George Holyoake, who coined the term *secularism*, described it as "a policy of life for those who do not accept theology."[3] Sociologists have defined the process of secularization as the "diminution of the social significance of religion," and "the growing tendency . . . to do without religion."[4]

The original Christian usage of *secular*, of course, complicates contemporary discourse regarding secular organizations of power between state and religion, but only to some extent. In one sense, "secular" political arrangements that delineate separate spheres for religion and politics by separating the two may do so precisely on Christian grounds of maintaining a distance between affairs of the world (state/politics) and affairs of the tradition. This was the case for the founders of the United States, who, in building a "wall of separation" between state and religion with the First Amendment to the Constitution believed, as James Madison noted, that religion is as much "hurt by establishment" as civic order is threatened. Garry Wills notes, "Neither Jefferson nor Madison thought that separation would lessen the impact of religion. . . . Quite the opposite, churches freed from the compromise of establishment would have greater moral force."[5] The religion-free, secular status of the federal government was designed largely to ensure the vitality of religion at all other levels of experience. Indeed, according to Michael Sandel, "at the time of its adoption, six of the thirteen states maintained religious establishments. Far from prohibiting these arrangements, the First Amendment was enacted in part to protect religious establishments from federal interference."[6] Hence, "highly differentiated" relations between religion and the state that are designed to secure a high measure of autonomy for both spheres,[7] insofar as they reiterate the early Christian distinction, can be seen correctly as one institutional manifestation of the Christian ideal, as Marx pointed out long ago in his reflections on the Abrahamic qualities of modern liberalism.[8]

In another sense, however, *secular* is quite often used as well to describe non- or antireligious, philosophically liberal-, social-, or socialist-democratic forms of separating religion and politics. These uses borrow on non- and/or antireligious connotations of the term stressing the availability of "secular moralities that are logically independent of religion."[9] Although the relationship between secularism and democracy has been subject to great contestation recently, secularism's rejection of religious imposition and citizenship criteria (for both religious and nonreligious citizens) along with its legitimation of non- and antireligious ways of thinking and living — the multiple and dynamic ways of being that one may find within a given political space — has made it a common centerpiece of democratic political theory. As an ideal, democratic secularism enables more inclusive, tolerant polities and more varied forms of social and public experience — ensuring "freedom from religion as well as freedom of religion."[10] Difficulties have emerged recently with the claim, heard around the world, that secularism is hostile to free religious expression in political life — either as a consequence of "neutrality" or "control" — and is thus highly antidemocratic. It's not clear whether or not the root cause of such critiques is "secularism." Still, philosophically, an important debate has emerged over whether or not secularism is an indispensable tool for creating political norms in contexts of radical difference "whatever else one may believe about human life and God's demands"[11] or a narrow, dogmatic, and colonizing metaphysic that

assimilates and does violence to difference and must therefore itself be jetti-
soned.[12] What is important in the context of the present essay is that the concept *secular* largely maintains a meaning of "nonreligious" in these debates.
Contemporary democratic secular arrangements certainly do not satisfy all
religionists or nonreligionists, but they satisfy many, and the reason they
do is that, by dissociating religion from politics or the state, such forms of
secularism secure the loyalty of nonreligious people (who see no imposition
of religion) for, inter alia, nonreligious reasons (e.g., "democracy") and religious people (who see no interference by the state) for, inter alia, religious
reasons (e.g., "worldly power corrupts"). A great deal of global evidence
suggests, moreover, that, in the context of modern political power relationships, these religionists include members of religious traditions other than
Christianity.[13] In terms of the meaning of *secular*, it should be noted that
even the friendly or nonantagonistic relationship toward religion and religious practices found in some such arrangements does not compromise the
nonreligious meaning ascribed to the character of the state. In such cases,
the meaning of *secularism* itself remains "nonreligious." By "secular state,"
one understands a "religion-free" state. Thus, secularism's association with
historical Christianity does not preclude its usage in non- and antireligious
senses.

   Just as *secularism* contains meanings related to the "nonreligious" connotations of *secular*, the political principle *laicism* contains within it meanings
related to the "religious" connotations of *lay*. The lay members of a community of believers may have quite varied orientations toward the components
of their tradition and many different understandings of the legitimate relationship between their tradition and power, politics, and the state (some
may even be clericalists). That is to say that, like secularism, laicism does
not imply a single ideology or ideal institutional arrangement. But the lay
are, by definition, "of the religious community." Laicization is the process
of rendering something (e.g., governance, education, etc.) lay or transfer-
ring it to lay control, and, while this process may entail a radical separating
of religious and state affairs (as in French laicism after 1905), this separation may certainly be less extensive than that found in secularist arrangements for the simple reason that lay are not expected to be non- or antireligious. It is indeed a fine distinction that may not always be evident in
practice, but it is a distinction that allows for more mixed relations—of various kinds—between affairs of the world and/or politics and those of religion

in laicist arrangements than in secular ones. While laicist political relations may separate affairs of the tradition from the state to some extent and in some ways, they may also retain the religion in a prominent, lay-defined, official role, something not anticipated in the meaning of secular practices or arrangements. Even in its original meaning, secularism connotes a possibility of standing outside of the moral realm of religiosity—"belonging to the world," not to the religiously spiritual zone. Thus, laicism is not equivalent to secularism; the latter is not the anglophone form of the French word for the former. Both, of course, have various, complex, and dynamic articulations in both theory and practice. But they are distinct as well, even if there are some overlapping dimensions.

The founders of the contemporary institutional relationship between the state and Islam in Turkey named that relationship *laiklik*, after the French term *laïcisme*, and it was, in terms of the conceptual possibilities for describing the new relation between the state and Islam, a relatively good choice. *Laiklik* emerged as a governing principle of the Republican People's Party (RPP) during the 1920s as it maneuvered and battled for control over the reins of the new state. In this context, the RPP abolished the Caliphate, the Sharia, and the *medrese* school system, demoted Islam from its previous place of constitutional and legal significance, banned the use of religion for political purposes, closed the institutions of folk Islam, created a new, nationalist education system, and promulgated nonreligious codes of governance (e.g., revised Swiss civil and Italian penal codes)—all secularizing moves of significance.[14] But it did not remove religion from the state. The founding and operative institutional matrix is best understood as a form of laicism, not secularism.

The abolition of the Caliphate and Sharia in 1924, for example, was accompanied by the founding of General Directorate of Religious Affairs (DIR) authorized to oversee "all cases concerning the Exalted Islamic Faith which relate to beliefs (*itikadat*) and rituals of worship (*ibadat*)." Its head was to be "appointed by President on the recommendation of the Prime Minister," to whose office it was "attached" (Article 4). Its responsibilities included the "administration of all mosques . . . as well as the appointment and dismissal of all *imams* [preachers], *hatibs* [orators], *vaizs* [preachers], *şeyhs* [leaders of dervish houses], *müezzins* [callers to prayer], *kayyims* [sextons], and all other employees of a religious character"—who, in Binnaz Toprak's felicitous phrase, all became "paid employees of the state."[15] The law further stipulated that the DIR is the "proper place of legal recourse" for the jurisconsults (*müftülük*) of Islamic law (Article 5). This institutional structure comprises what Şerif Mardin has termed "official Islam" in the modern Turkish Republic.[16] The dramatic abolition of the Caliphate and Sharia, seen as the definitive act of *laiklik* by its many interpreters, actually created a new structure of control and oversight between the state and Islam in which the republic's founders sought to use the powers of state to interpret, oversee, and administer (including financially) religious doctrine and practice (more on this later in this essay).

A similar structural arrangement was established in the republic's new educational system, created in the Law for the Unity of Education (1924). Often seen as a thoroughly secularizing reform due to its primary goal of creating a new system of national—as opposed to religious—education, the purposes of aspects of this law nonetheless dovetailed with those found in the law establishing the DIR. Article 4 empowers the Ministry of Education to establish a Faculty of Divinity at the Darülfünün (later Istanbul University) "with the duty of training officials"—those employed by the DIR—"such as preachers, for the performance of religious services." It also empowers the ministry to open "separate *mekteps*" (*ayrı mektepler*) to serve as lower-level religious schools for the same purpose. In this regard, the law created educational mechanisms for service in the state's mosques. The *mekteps* were closed in 1933, the same year the Faculty of Divinity was transformed into the Institute of Islamic Research, but the DIR opened Koran Study Courses in 1934 "and the number of teachers and students grew steadily."[17] Moreover, even in the larger national education system, the state never ended its interest in supporting opportunities for religious instruction, in specific schools, at specific times. While religious education in the national schools was phased out in urban areas in the 1930s and 1940s, it continued to be taught in village schools until the early 1940s, was reintroduced into all primary and intermediate schools by the late 1950s (first as an extracurricular elective and then as a requirement for which parents could request exemption), and then made compulsory after the 1980 coup (in courses on "Religion and Moral Culture").[18] The policy pattern through time suggests, especially with the growth of the Imam Hatip schools after 1950, that while the state has engaged in some restriction of religious education in the state school system (e.g., closure of religious classes in the early thirties, and recent restrictions) it has also enabled its growth (reopening and expansion through the mid-1990s) *and* its continuation, suggesting that the operative understanding of the founding principle of *laiklik* is that state-sponsored religious training and instruction and "national education" go together. It is not that *laiklik* "does not prevent" the mixing of religious instruction and state education. The relation is stronger than that: *laik* institutional arrangements make their mixing possible in "national education." Also noteworthy in this regard is the religious socialization given by the military to its general recruits.

It should not be overlooked that *laiklik* was not a constitutional principle until 1937. It makes its first appearance in the RPP principles in 1927. But between 1922 and 1928, the constitution declared Islam to be the official religion and the state to be the executor of the Islamic law (Articles 2, 26). Even after 1937, when those articles are gone, strictly speaking, Islam was not removed from the state. This is one reason *laiklik* in Turkey is an ambivalent, partial, and inconsistent form of laicism. The very existence of the DIR, for example, weakens even the officially declared laicism. To this day, it routinely convenes conferences on matters of doctrine and practice to the end of describing and defining belief and ritual (including, recently, on the ceremonial roles of women). In addition to shaping Friday sermons, it uses its publishing houses and programs on state television (or, better, "the state uses . . .") to fulfill its official charge of "enlightening the public on the subject of religion." In early summer 2002, for example, I watched a DIR program on television in which the meanings of the Islamic concept of jihad were described. A written text stating the official view as explained by the head of the DIR (emphasizing the concept's nonviolent elements as well as Islam's categorical rejection of the murder of innocent people) was shown against a video background of the terror attacks in New York City.[19] As one observer has noted, "Friday sermons are used to invite citizens to engage in acts supportive of government. The [DIR] sends out model sermons to imams which may encourage the citizens, for example, to pay their taxes, or to contribute to foundations established to assist the armed forces."[20] Regarding the "often heard" analogy between laicism in Turkey and the laicism of the French Third Republic, Alfred Stepan has commented that "France in 1905 never assumed this degree of management of religion."[21] But it is not only the state's influence over religion that weakens its declared laicism. It's also the *state's* religion's influence over individual and social morality; that is, its direct role in shaping the content of belief and norm. Article 136 of the 1982 constitution, which reiterates *laiklik* as a foundational principle, illustrates this well. It declares that the DIR "fulfills its duties . . . in compliance with the principles of *laiklik* [*laiklik ilkesi doğrultusunda*] remaining outside of all political views [*bütün siyasî görüş ve düşünüşlerin dışında*], and having national solidarity and integrity as its goal." If, however, the DIR is involved in ensuring national solidarity and integrity, then it is difficult to say that its duties can be fulfilled "outside of all political views and thinking." The DIR is the *state's* DIR— its institution of Islamic thought and practice usable for its ideological and legitimation objectives. Along with the structure of religious education, then, the state actively participates in ensuring belief—"religious" as such as well as "religious" in relation to "nationalist"—shaping the content of both individual and social morality, consistent, since the earliest days of the republic, with the regime's understanding of Turkish nationalism and the proper relationship between nationalism, national solidarity, and Islam. Religion from the perspective of the state is a constitutive element of the larger national bond.[22]

Members of the state *laik* elite have often exaggerated the extent of separation between the state and Islam (in both English and Turkish discourse), but they have rarely denied their goal of promoting their own version of "pure" and "true" Islam. Even the abolition of the Caliphate was not undertaken as a fully non- or antireligious act. In the words of Mustafa Kemal Atatürk—who had previously praised Islam as the most reasonable (*makul*) and natural (*tabii*) religion[23]—it was designed to "raise and purify Islam," by removing it "from its condition of being a political instrument which it had been for centuries through habit."[24] The RPP's 1927 statutes echoed this goal, describing "the complete separation of religion from the world in matters of state and nation" as part of "rescuing matters of belief and conscience from politics and various complications of politics."[25] Here, too, one sees a bit of classical *laik* obfuscation—overstating the degree of separation and neglecting to mention what Niyazi Berkes described as the regime's "new religious policy."[26] To be sure, the regime "considered religion and the world separate"[27] in some affairs: their operative interest in controlling Islam should not occlude the ways in which they separated, reduced, or eliminated the role of Islam in areas of symbolic legitimation and governance, especially in civil and judicial matters. But the new Kemalist state never made religion or Islam an entirely separate (and, thus, "private") matter. Rather, in its terms, it "rescued Islam" as a matter of "belief" and "conscience" by institutionally supporting, financing, and promulgating a different version of Islam and its view of its relation to power and social life. The separation of religion from its previous position of influence constituted a shift in Islam's institutional and legitimation position, not its formal, full elimination. How to explain, for example, the new state religious establishment, the state religious educational interest, the marking of religious identity on state identity cards, and the like? Islam was not disestablished; it was differently established. Religion became a separate concern among other state concerns, not separate from politics or the state. Thus it may be said that the RPP removed Islam from the condition of being used as a political instrument in the way it was previously used, but not from the condition of being an instrument of politics as such, since they understood well the role that the state would play in fostering a specific interpretation of Islam, support for which they have been quite explicit about over the years.[28]

It is true that the various reforms designed to integrate Turkey into the economic and social patterns of Europe (e.g., calendar, script, sartorial regulations) constituted assaults, in important respects, on specific Muslim cultural practices in Turkey. Much needs to be said about these policies, and, in the context of the concern of this essay, especially how they helped cultivate the view that Kemalism's *laiklik* was antireligious, anti-Islamic, and radically secularist. To some degrees and in some ways, these claims are compelling. But the overall interpretive and institutional landscape of both the reforms and the power relationship between the state and Islam created during the years of *laiklik*'s formation suggests that none of the reforms were undertaken with the view that "religion as such is bad or harmful" or "Islam must go into the dustbin of history." Rather the operative idea was that certain forms of Islamic control and expression—derogatorily labeled and rejected as superstitious, fanatical, reactionary, and obscurantist—are wrong according to Kemalism's version of Islam and its relation to politics. The constitutive discourse of this conflict does not bear a "secularist" or "atheist" versus "Muslim" exchange, rather, it is a heated contest between different accounts of politicized Islam.[29] The Kemalist understanding of Islam may be weak and/or at odds with the vast understandings found among the people at large, but it is still an understanding of Islam. The perception that *laiklik* was "antireligious secularism" ignores the regime's religious policy and fails to consider the existence of different accounts of politicized Islam in Turkey, one of them enshrined in power and the others outside it.

The new set of relations between the state and Islam in the contemporary Turkish republic are thus difficult to describe as "secular" or "secularist" for the very reason that neither the state, nor politics, nor indeed "matters of worldly policy" have become "nonreligious." The meanings conveyed by the concepts *secular* and *secularism* ("staunch," "rigid," "strict," "radical," "militant," etc.) are at odds with the concepts and practices comprising the relation between state and Islam in Turkey. Indeed, rather than constituting a radical break from the Ottoman tradition of integrating and subordinating Islam to the requirements of state,[30] the power relations of *laiklik* constituted an alteration in the basic pattern, a shift with ruptures in some regards (legitimation ideology, constitutional, legal, and educational status of Islam), but continuities in others (integrated, established apparatus of religious governance, education, and socialization). The shift was carried out by political agents who understood themselves as fostering a different account of Islam and its legitimate relation to political power (disestablished in some regards, established in others). Without entering the complex questions of Islam's conceptualization of "the world" or its orthodox rejection of a clergy,[31] it is rather clear that connotations of the word *secular* and the political principle of secularism do not relate fully to the dynamics of *laiklik*. The question, to be clear, is not, what is the essence of secularism and does *laiklik* exhibit that essence? The question is, given what is and what was meant to be the case in Turkey by the founders and participants in the conceptual core of the laicist power relations, are those relations adequately described by the term *secular* as it is commonly used to mean "nonreligious" or "structural separation and differentiation"? Secularism carries the meaning of divorcing religion and politics, and this divorce has not occurred in Turkey. Furthermore, since there is an English translation of *laiklik* available, it seems that, methodologically speaking, the only grounds for not choosing that term would be if the self-understanding of the Kemalists was so at odds with the empirical reality that we would need to "correct" their description.[32] In this case, this doesn't seem warranted. Rather, and especially since "laicism" is not the same as "secularism," the English form of laicism is quite well suited, with the caveat that laicism in Turkey—which evidences a substantial degree of integrated state-religious relations and matters—does not describe all manifestations of possible laicist political arrangements.

The complex laicist admixture of certain secularized elements of governance and certain established elements of governance raises important questions for research in the politics of laicization. Those areas in which religious practice has been divorced from the state suggest that *laiklik* evidences some *secularizing* dimensions, without becoming secular. This is not to suggest that *laiklik* tends toward greater secularization. That would depend on the policies adopted, and these have wavered in important ways in the nearly eighty years of *laiklik* practice in Turkey. Nor does comparative experience suggest any particular linear relationship between laicism and secularism. Anything seems possible. In Iran, laicist intellectuals were prominent in supporting Rule by the Grand Jurist (*marja'e taqlid*). Hamid Dabashi notes that the economist Abolhassan Bani-Sadr was among the first to describe Ayatollah Khomeini as "Imam," thus lending "a measure of legitimacy to the reinterpreted [clericalist] religious cause."[33]

Laicism does not, indeed, always tend toward secularism. The Turkish case suggests that laicism can assume a far less nonreligious set of relations between religion and state than those found in laicist arrangements in France, where anticlericalism, irreligiosity, and the active "refusal of the interpenetration of political values and religious values" constitute the norm.[34] Kemalist laicism was anticlerical to some extent, but the elevation, not elimination, of "lower level religious personnel"[35] to serve, within the state, in the new republic's DIR should not be overlooked. The practice of using the people's money to fund religion and religious education was ended in French laicism in 1795 and religious instruction in state schools in 1882. In the first years of the French Republic, "fluctuations of revolutionary religious policy" were "inspired in part by the conviction that the unity of the nation must be founded on a national religion, and in part by the opposite and growing idea that religion must be set aside as a purely personal matter."[36] Whereas fluctuations in Turkey, especially the growth of the administration of religious practice, suggest that Islam is a component of the national religion. While the official view may be "religion is a personal affair," the means of making it such—indeed, publicly and extensively insuring that religion *is* a "personal" affair—are quite formal. Thus, relative to theocratic arrangements, Turkish laicism is not "at the opposite end of the spectrum," where Esposito places the "secular Turkish repub-lic,"[37] but rather somewhere in between—ambivalent, partial, and even religiopolitical in some aspects. In those respects, *laiklik* may be seen as an obstacle to secularization, notwithstanding other laicized and even secular-ized elements.

Comparative analysis aside, the dynamics of power found in *laiklik* are, I think, important to understanding organizational power relations in repub-lican Turkey more generally. *Laiklik* created a structure of power in which Islam was separated from areas of governance in some respects within an overall and overarching integrated relationship of state control. The rela-tions of separation (e.g., in the civil code) are not unimportant, for they con-stitute the basis for the perception that the relationship between Islam and the state is more extensively "separated" than is empirically the case, and they underlie the habitual identification of the state as "secular." The com-bination of all of these elements—control, separation, perception of more of the latter than the former, "secularism"—constitutes a certain puzzle for observers of the dynamics of *laiklik* and deserves some attention.

In a related context, Şerif Mardin has written recently of the republic's combination of Ottoman patrimonial, statist modes of authority and more modern, populist "ideals"—ideals that, as I noted earlier in this essay, his-torically inform democratic versions of secularism:

> Whereas the Ottoman patrimonial-sultanic scheme had defined gov-ernment as underscored by the duties of the rulers to provide good gov-ernment *for* the people, the Turkish republic conceptualized its ideal of government—*even though it was an ideal* [this emphasis added]—as government *of* the people and *by* the people. This was a plus for the Republic. Although it did not spell it outright, the new principle inti-mated an even more radical conceptual change: people not only made their own personal history but also were prisoners of recurring cycles of history.[38]

This is a very important statement, to my mind, intimating a power dynamic that is perhaps as much a key to understanding power relations and political possibilities in Turkey as the "Center-Periphery" paradigm Mardin fruitfully injected into the study of Turkish politics over a quarter of a century ago.[39] For, among other things, what his comment suggests implicitly is that the complex power relations constituting *laiklik* exemplify a broader pattern of authority in the republican period: achievements of institutional "autonomy" take shape within recurring, but altered, patrimonial relations of domination and control, not independent of them. In this relationship, the latter modes of power—those of domination and control—are modified by the existence of the former—the improved spaces for autonomy—but the former are always affected by the influence of the latter. As in *laiklik* power relations, autonomy and domination are mutually constituted. Any reference, say, to the autonomy of religion within the power structure of *laiklik* invokes its lack of autonomy as well, its being bound up with the preferred designs of the republic's *laik* authorities. This may constitute a difference between laicist and secularist arrangements more generally.

To be clear, Mardin's point, I think, is not simply a reminder of Weber's important insight that "in a great number of cases the emergence of rational association from amorphous social actions has been due to domination and the way in which it is exercised."[40] It also suggests that, in contemporary Turkish politics, autonomous spaces are not fully autonomous, and spaces of domination are not fully permeating. In the experience of institutional power, the "autonomy" of the subordinate is palpably truncated by the reiterable remaining patrimonial power of the superior, whose expression of will must survive review according to the new, but truncated, ideals. Moreover, these dynamics are *known*, as Weber might describe the interpretive domain, by those who occupy the different positions of power. In *laiklik*, even as politics/the state and Islam are "separated" in some senses, they are also deeply interconnected. Their separation enables the interesting, but often overstated, public representation of the "ideal" of secularism (the people governing history), as well as its continual pursuit. The institutional arrangement and will to control religion by the state represents the demonstrable recurring cycles of history (the protection of "the state"). The two coexist and interpenetrate. Those aspects of *laiklik* that have affected a separation of realms are not independent of the overall inherited significance of the state tradition, and thus of the overall structure of control. Any autonomy religious expression and practice enjoy is fundamentally bound up with its lack of autonomy.

This is one reason why contemporary discussions about abolishing the DIR may be difficult to empower on a broad scale. The idea is that for the state to be more secular, the DIR should be abolished. But the status of the DIR cannot be conceptualized entirely apart from other elements of *laiklik*, including those that have made religion a separate matter *as a result of the authority of the state.* It must be recognized that the areas in which the "ideal" has apparently been achieved emanate from within the larger apparatus of domination. In discussing any reform aimed at greater secularization, the point should not be "to make the state more secular," but "to make the limited laicist state secular." Achieving greater secularization requires reexamining the entire apparatus of *laiklik*, its scope and limitations included. Mardin's point suggests that if the means of domination are to be further restricted; if, that is, the range of autonomous practice for the expression of conscience and culture (of all sorts) is to be extended in more democratic directions, then the larger complexities of state authority, of which *laiklik* is a part, must be addressed as well. This is one reason why it is crucial to think in detailed, nuanced terms about the character of different aspects of *laiklik*'s power relations. Possibilities for transforming their structural bases in more democratic directions depend upon more precise descriptions of *laiklik*'s achievements and limitations as they have taken shape in practice. Too often laicism is seen by its observers as representing one "ideal" or another—either the paradigmatic secularizing or the paradigmatic authoritarian move—rather than expressive of a more complex amalgam of power relations that one finds, I think more generally, in contemporary Turkey.

The so-called modernization of Turkey, therefore, evidenced a hybrid, alternative arrangement in the politics of secularization at its founding, and it has taken many of us in social science a long time to catch up. Regrettably, *laiklik* is routinely translated as, and thus equated with, "secularism" in current, highly influential literature, both scholarly and journalistic, on the topic. There are too many examples. One may be found in a "glossary" accompanying a recent special edition of a prominent journal of international affairs on contemporary Turkey. Its listing of *secularism* as "the separation of mosque and state, one of the founding tenets of the state"[41] reiterates the highly misleading identification that I have argued against here.

One may object that qualifying the usage of *secularism* along the lines that I have argued would imply that many arrangements that are regarded as "secular" should not be described as such either. But that is precisely the point. They may be "secular" in some ways but not in other ways, and both analytical and political theoretical discourses remain empirically limited as long as careful descriptions of the conceptual and practical varieties and variations are missing. Calling, for example, the structure of governance in the United States "secular" obscures important aspects of established and daily religiopolitical realities in the affairs of governance that neither the wobbling wall of separation nor the pocked principle of neutrality prevents or constrains. The organization of power between state, politics, religion, culture, matters of conscience, and tradition there (and elsewhere) may be better described in terms other than "secular."

Rather than attending rigorously to the specifics of the interpretive and empirical relations of specific cases, the dominant habit is to see "secular" outcomes wherever there is no "theocracy." The dichotomous template "either secular or religious" is implicitly and explicitly read onto more varied and interesting conceptual and practical formations. "Covering secularism" like this with vague generalities, to borrow from Edward Said, distorts more complex conceptual and practical realities, weakens the concept's analytical and political theoretical purchase, and deprives us of valuable insight on particular and various ways of organizing the relationship between power and tradition, or matters of culture and conscience more broadly, whereas careful empirical work can provide a better, comparative understanding of actual experiences in the politics of secularization and laicization as well as a better opportunity to conceptualize alternative projects. I am not proposing a strict schema, only a more analytically fruitful sense of practical and theoretical options, including those critical of secularism as such. Understandings and experiences of secularism have demonstrably been very different. "The meaning of the term secular," notes Timothy Mitchell, "is not something self-evident or universal."[42] Like other essentially contested concepts, it has "multiple faces."[43] As Rajeev Bhargava emphasizes, "The separation thesis means different things . . . and is interpreted differently at different times," and these meanings and interpretations, along with the practices generated by them, must be more precisely described.[44]

Perhaps this underscores the empirical and political theoretical significance of the study of *laiklik* in Turkey. It confirms the analytically progressive value of deconstructing false dichotomies, such as "secular or religious,"[45] and it opens us to occluded forms of political practice that are insufficiently described according to that dichotomy (using either prong). In terms of the widely felt need for evaluating and creating more democratic institutional arrangements in contexts of radical plurality and difference, a generalized critique of secularism, where historical experience is quite varied, may leave us without a basis for revision. The various, alternative efforts to relate matters of tradition, culture, and conscience to power and politics need understanding. The challenge, then, lies in the description.

Notes

I am grateful to Andrew Bush, Sibel Irzık, Gürol Irzık, Gün Kut, Şule Kut, Paul Soper, and Taha Parla for invaluable discussion and argumentation about these matters. Some of the conceptual and empirical considerations offered in this essay are more extensively discussed, with different emphases, in Taha Parla and Andrew Davison, "Secularism and Laicism in Turkey," in *World Secularisms at the Millennium*, ed. Janet R. Jakobsen and Ann Pellegrini (Durham: Duke University Press, forthcoming) and Andrew Davison, *Secularism and Revivalism in Turkey: A Hermeneutic Reconsideration* (New Haven: Yale University Press, 1998), esp. 153–54, 181–88.

1   See Parla and Davison, "Secularism and Laicism."
2   Charles Taylor, "Modes of Secularism," in *Secularism and Its Critics*, ed. Rajeev Bhargava (Delhi: Oxford University Press, 1998), 32.
3   George Jacob Holyoake, *The Principles of Secularism*, rev. 3d ed. (London: Austin and Company, 1870), 6.
4   Roy Wallis and Steve Bruce, "Secularization: The Orthodox Model," in *Religion and Modernization: Sociologists and Historians Debate the Secularization Thesis*, ed. Steve Bruce (Oxford: Oxford University Press, 1992), 8–9; Owen Chadwick, *The Secularization of the European Mind in the Nineteenth Century* (Cambridge: Cambridge University Press, 1975), 17.
5   Garry Wills, *Under God: Religion and American Politics* (New York: Simon and Schuster, 1990), 25.
6   Michael J. Sandel, "Religious Liberty: Freedom of Choice or Freedom of Conscience," in Bhargava, *Secularism and Its Critics*, 75.
7   See Gabriel Almond, "Comparative Political Systems," *Journal of Politics* 18 (1956): 398.
8   Karl Marx, "On the Jewish Question," in *Karl Marx: Selected Writings*, ed. Lawrence H. Simon (Indianapolis: Hackett, 1994), 6–7.
9   Kai Nielsen, "Morality and the Will of God," in *Critiques of God: Making the Case against Belief in God* (Amherst, NY: Prometheus, 1997), 249.
10 Ellen Willis, "Freedom from Religion: What's at Stake in Faith-Based Politics," *Nation*, February 19, 2001, 12.
11 Taylor, "Modes of Secularism," 33.
12 See, for example, essays in Bhargava, *Secularism and Its Critics*; John Keane, "The Limits of Secularism," in *Islam and Secularism in the Middle East*, ed. John L. Esposito and Azzam Tamimi (New York: New York University Press, 2000), 31–36; and William E. Connolly, *Why I Am Not a Secularist* (Minneapolis: University of Minnesota Press, 1999).
13 See, for example, Dale Eickelman and Joseph Piscatori, *Muslim Politics* (Princeton: Princeton University Press, 1996), 52.

14 Much of this discussion is based on evidence presented in Andrew Davison, *Secularism and Revivalism*, 134–88, and Parla and Davison, "Secularism and Laicism."

15 Binnaz Toprak, "Islam and the Secular State in Turkey," in *Turkey: Political, Social and Economic Challenges in the 1990s*, ed. Çiğdem Balım, et al. (Leiden: E. J. Brill, 1995), 35.

16 Şerif Mardin, "Religion in Modern Turkey," *International Social Journal* 29 (1977): 287, and "Turkey, Islam, and Westernization," in *Religion and Societies: Asia and the Middle East*, ed. C. Caldarola (Berlin: Mouton, 1982), 179.

17 Howard A. Reed, "Atatürk's Secularizing Legacy and the Continuing Vitality of Islam in Republican Turkey," in *Islam in the Contemporary World*, ed. C. K. Pullapilly (Indianapolis: Cross Roads, 1970), 330.

18 See Ismail Kaplan, "The National Education Ideology in Turkey and Its Implications for Political Socialization" (Ph.D. diss., Boğaziçi University, 1998) and David Shankland, *Islam and Society in Turkey* (Cambridgeshire: Eothen, 1999).

19 See www.diyanet.gov.tr/duyurular/istisariingl.htm. For further research, see www.diyanet.gov.tr — *Diyanet* is the first word of the Turkish title of the DIR, so that's the DIR-*dot-gov*, emphasis added.

20 İlter Turan, "Religion and Political Culture in Turkey: Islam in Modern Turkey," in *Islam in Modern Turkey*, ed. Richard Tapper (London: I. B. Tauris and Co., 1991), 42.

21 Alfred Stepan, *Arguing Comparative Politics* (New York: Oxford University Press, 2001), 245.

22 I borrow the phrasing from Jean Bauberot, "The Two Thresholds of Laïcization," in Bhargava, *Secularism and Its Critics*, 97.

23 For analysis, see especially Taha Parla, *Kemalist Tek-Parti İdeolojisi ve CHP'nin Altı Ok'u (Türkiye'de Siyasal Kültürün Resmi Kaynakları: Cilt 3)* [*The Ideology of the Kemalist Single-Party and the RPP's Six Arrows*, vol. 3 of *The Official Sources of Political Culture in Turkey*] (Istanbul: İletişim, 1992), 256–89.

24 Mustafa Kemal Atatürk, *A Speech Delivered by Ghazi Mustapha Kemal, President of the Turkish Republic* (Leipzig: K. F. Koehler, 1929), 684.

25 See analysis in Davison, *Secularism*, 160ff.

26 Niyazi Berkes, *The Development of Secularism in Turkey* (Montreal: McGill University Press, 1964), 484.

27 Mahmut Esat Bozkurt, "Preface to the Turkish Civil Code [1926]," translated and analyzed in Davison, *Secularism*, 167–73.

28 For evidence of continuity on this theme, see Davison, *Secularism*, 232.

29 For fuller elaboration, see Parla and Davison, "Secularism and Laicism."

30 Şerif Mardin, "Religion and Secularism in Turkey," in *Atatürk, the Founder of a Modern State*, ed. Ergun Özbudun and Ali Kazancıgil (London: C. Hurst and Co., 1981), 194; and "Religion and Politics in Modern Turkey," in *Islam in the Political Process*, ed. James Piscatori (Cambridge: Cambridge University Press, 1983), 139.

31 Important considerations that often conclude by suggesting that the Turkish case may be the case of "secularism in an Islamic context," a usage of the term *secular* that I don't find compelling for reasons stated above. See Davison, *Secularism*, 184–87.

32 See Davison, *Secularism*, 83.

33 See Hamid Dabashi, *Theology of Discontent: The Ideological Foundation of the Islamic Revolution in Iran* (New York: New York University Press, 1993), 407.

34 Alain Bergounioux, *La laïcité, valeur de la République,"* *Revue Français d'études constitutionnelles et politiques* 75 (1998): 17–26; quotation from 18, translated and quoted in Susanna Kalitowski, "A Reevaluation of French *Laïcité* (unpublished seminar paper, "Theorizing Secularity," Vassar College, May 8, 2001).

35 Şerif Mardin, "Islam in Mass Society: Harmony Versus Polarization," in *Politics in the Third Turkish Republic*, ed. Metin Heper and Ahmet Evin (Boulder, CO: Westview, 1994), 165.

36 Bauberot, "Two Thresholds," 100–1.

37 John L. Esposito, "Introduction: Islam and Secularism in the Twenty-First Century," in Esposito and Tamimi, *Islam and Secularism in the Middle East*, 3.

38 Şerif Mardin, "Projects As Methodology: Some Thoughts on Modern Turkish Social Science," in *Rethinking Modernity and National Identity in Turkey*, ed. Sibel Bozdoğan and Reşat Kasaba (Seattle: University of Washington Press, 1997), 70.

39 Şerif Mardin, "Center-Periphery Relations: A Key to Turkish Politics?" *Daedalus* 102 (December 1973): 169–96.

40 Max Weber, "Domination by Economic Power and by Authority," in *Power*, ed. Steven Lukes (New York: New York University Press, 1985), 28.

41 "Turkey: A Struggle between Nation and State," a special issue of *Journal of International Affairs* 54.1 (Fall 2000): 338.

42 Timothy Mitchell, introduction to *Questions of Modernity*, ed. Timothy Mitchell (Minneapolis: University of Minnesota Press, 2000), xiii.

43 Gerald F. Gaus, *Political Concepts and Political Theories* (Boulder, CO: Westview, 2000), 33.

44 Rajeev Bhargava, introduction to *Secularism and Its Critics*, 3. A good example is found in Rochana Bajpai, "The Conceptual Vocabularies of Secularism and Minority Rights in India," *Journal of Political Ideologies* 7.2 (2000): 179–97. Bajpai underscores the need to study "shifts in emphasis between the constellation of concepts that have defined secularism" (194).

45 I have in mind the understanding of deconstruction found in Nancy Fraser, *Justice Interruptus: Critical Reflections on the "Postsocialist" Condition* (New York: Routledge, 1997), 11–40.

Meltem Ahıska

Occidentalism: The Historical
Fantasy of the Modern

> A place on the map is also a place in history.
> —Adrienne Rich, "Notes toward a Politics of Location"

> One who goes too far East,
> Because of geography arrives in the West,
> The reverse is also true.
> —Ece Ayhan, *Yort Savul*

Europe has been an object of desire as well as
a source of frustration for Turkish national identity in a long and strained history. Turkey, who
has long been trying to be a member of Europe,[1]
regarded 2002 as an especially critical year in its
relations with the European Union (EU). Hoping
to be given a date for "negotiations" for full
membership at the end of the year, the Turkish
government concentrated its effort to initiate
legislative reforms concerning human rights.
Although the political target of full membership to Europe found support in most segments
of the society, the enthusiasm was nevertheless shadowed by a doubt whether Europe or
"the West" would at last accept Turkey's self-
consciously crafted Western identity. It turned
out that the anxiety was not without reason. In
December 2002, the EU leaders' meeting came

The *South Atlantic Quarterly* 102:2/3, Spring/Summer 2003.
Copyright © 2003 by Duke University Press.

to the conclusion that "if the European Council in December 2004, on the basis of a report and a recommendation from the Commission, decides that Turkey fulfills the Copenhagen political criteria, the European Union will open accession negotiations with Turkey without delay."[2] The ambiguity of the "if" condition is causing further debates in Turkey as to the possible reasons of this recurring "delay." The debates take new shades given that a pro-Islamic party has been in government since November 2002. However, instead of analyzing the trajectory of the debates, I would like to focus on the year 2002 when both the hopes and the anxieties concerning membership in the EU found significant social and cultural expressions, which I find relevant to my discussion of Occidentalism in this article.

One of the striking themes that emerged in the pro-European campaigns emphasizing the urgency of accomplishing the required legislative reforms in 2002 echoes the persisting anxiety over the possibility of finally "catching the train"[3] of modern civilization. I remember seeing a comic strip in one of the popular comic magazines in Turkey years ago that brilliantly captures and mocks the train metaphor. The comic strip shows a "typically" dressed Kurdish man lazily sitting in a forlorn train station looking at a "typically" Western-style dressed young woman waiting for the train with a big suitcase. He says, "The last train has long gone, Miss. So, marry me." The message is clear: The train metaphor is functional to deploy the desire for a Western future embodied in the figure of a Western-looking woman, yet the present is the problem-stricken Turkey unable to deal with its Kurdish or other ethnic-identity problems. Instead of concentrating on the present problems and their solutions, the hegemonic imaginary looks beyond the present with the aid of an already-late and always-postponed ideal.[4] Despite the apparent emphasis on movement and speed best exemplified in the metaphor of "catching the train" before it is too late, I argue that there is a certain temporal stasis, even timelessness involved in the way the EU was perceived in public discussions in 2002. As I discuss later, "speed" is symptomatic of a much earlier condition of modernity in Turkey, which urges one to think that the emphasis on speed has nothing to do with movement, but rather is static.

My aim in this article is neither to discuss the specific case of the EU membership of Turkey in its highly contested political and economic aspects, nor to dwell on its long and frustrating history. Instead, I point at the temporal constructions of modernity appropriated in discussing the EU as part of a larger historical framework in order to elaborate the conception and experiencing of modernity in Turkey in relation to "the West." The "present" cannot simply be reduced to a naturalized and privatized time embedded in everyday life or to a segment in the national-durational time of modern history that connects past and future in the moment. The present has its own politics of time and space that is overdetermined by what is called history, itself a geographical-temporal representation.

I offer the term *Occidentalism* to conceptualize how the West figures in the temporal/spatial imagining of modern Turkish national identity. From its initial conception in the process of defining the Turkish national identity in the late nineteenth century to this day, "the West" has been contrasted to "the East" in a continuous negotiation between the two constructs. "The West" has either been celebrated as a "model" to be followed or exorcised as a threat to "indigenous" national values. I argue that in theorizing the construction and representation of Turkish modernity, we can neither unproblematically herald the Western model nor dismiss the fantasy of "the West" that informs the hegemonic national imaginary.[5] Turkey, which has been labeled by both outsiders and insiders as a bridge between the East and the West,[6] has an ambivalent relation not only to the geographical sites of the East and the West, but also to their temporal signification: namely, backwardness and progress. Turkey has been trying to cross the bridge between the East and the West for more than a hundred years now, with a self-conscious anxiety that it is arrested in time and space by the bridge itself. In other words, the meaning of the present has a mythical core that has persisted over years and which remains as a source of frustration and threat, and as a symptom of internalized inferiority.[7]

A study of Occidentalism means being receptive to the problems on the very boundary of the East-West divide. Therefore, it is neither an emic analysis that tries to "see things from the actor's point of view,"[8] nor an etic analysis that looks at things from imposed frames of reference, such as those based on Western representations. I pursue, rather, a theoretical framework that claims to analyze the gaps and mismatches that emerge on the boundaries of interconnected projections of the Occident and the Orient. This framework attends to questions of modernity in a non-Western context and aims to evoke the historicity of the non-Western other rendered invisible in the hegemonic conceptions of Western modernity, and even in some existing social theories that attempt to analyze these conceptions. Therefore, the aim of the article is not simply to go beyond the East-West divide; instead it is to re-member the historical divide as constitutive of both the "Western" and "Eastern" modernities. This seems to be an even more necessary task at a time when intellectual maneuvers try to transcend the divide, yet the war positions continuously reproduce violent versions of it.

The "Time Lag" and the West

The wide gap between the present and the future, captured in the train metaphor, is not contingent to Turkish modernity. Nilüfer Göle argues that non-Westerners are "alienated from their own present which they want to overcome by projecting themselves either to the utopian future or to the golden age of the past"[9] due to the "time lag" stigmatized and internalized as "backwardness" in representations of non-Western modernity. Halil Nalçaoğlu makes a similar point: the self-identity of those countries where modernization is attempted in a non-Western context is significantly determined by "being late."[10] Catching the train is a metaphor that signifies the destination of history to which the "latecomers" are *always already* late.[11] Nalçaoğlu points at the "chronic anxiety" and the "universe of symbolic crises" thereby produced.[12]

The "time lag" is paradoxically immobile and stands apart from the constantly onward-moving chronological sequence of Western progress.[13] It is a timeless element of the self-definitions of the non-Western. Yet, as I argue later in the article, it does not originate from the culture of the specific sites labeled as non-Western and cannot be reduced to essential traits of a past heritage. Instead the past that figures in this state of stasis should be thought of in connection to the historical dynamics of modernity. The movement is arrested and bracketed in the formula that equates the present with stasis points to the dislocated time and space of the non-Western.

When seen in this larger framework, it is not surprising to find that the same anxiety of the "time lag" plays itself out in the way the EU is currently perceived and discussed in Turkey. Although it is not easy to portray the complexity of the long- and short-term political interests of each actor participating in the discussions, it is noteworthy that, positively or negatively, the EU was evoked as a symbolic marker for the future of Turkish society.[14] What all the parties in the ongoing discussions shared was the ambivalence[15] about the *transcendental* meaning of the reforms required by the EU for membership. The reforms were not discussed *as such*, as solutions to present social problems, but signified as a code for the desired or feared Westernization.[16] It is striking that the ambivalence persisted even after the reforms were finally and "miraculously" enacted in the national parliament at the last minute.[17]

More concerned with the question "How does Europe see us?" the public discussions defer the practical-political meaning of the reforms.[18] The gap between what the reforms imply—for example, the rights given to ethnic communities to speak and broadcast in their own language—and the continuing political pressures over the same groups becomes disturbing only if pointed out by the EU representatives. This makes it more apparent that the reforms were not meant for addressing the present problems in Turkish society,[19] but they were part of a performance geared for the gaze of the West.

The hegemonic imaginary concerning the EU displaces the present and focuses on the future. Nevertheless, the future is overshadowed by a fixed past. This is best illustrated in the campaign of "Europe Movement 2002." This is a "civil society"[20] movement supported by a large number of primarily business and trade organizations; the specific campaign consists of newspaper ads and billboards advocating the urgent need for Turkey to become a member of the EU.[21] The slogan of the campaign is "There is no other tomorrow." The campaign evokes an emphasized feeling of urgency by both the slogan and the text of the ads. The first ad uses the old Kemalist motto, "Turk, be proud, work and trust," and supplements it with the phrase "and be quick." It links the present anxiety about the future to the "centuries-long struggle" of Turkish nationalists to become part of "contemporary civilization." The stagnant past is revisited in the light of the urgency of choosing a future. The second one accentuates the anxiety with a threat. It portrays a crying baby and, using ironic language, claims that without the "European future," Turkey is doomed to stay in the unbearable present (past?) crisis. The infantalization of the national identity that desperately needs the West to survive is again a resurrection of a past theme that will be addressed later in this article as I develop the theoretical construct of Occidentalism. The third ad is especially significant in bringing in the past issues of national identity. Showing identical-twin images of an Oriental-looking man with a moustache, the ad invites us to look at the "difference." We learn that the difference, which doesn't show but has a major impact on the present, is the difference in the life quality between a Greek who is a member of the EU, and a Turk who is not. The past when the Greeks were part of the Ottoman Empire, and hence joined in sameness with them, is reclaimed yet cancelled by the national difference, in fact a product of the invisible mediation of the West.[22] The final ad gives the clues for the long-awaited solution. The headline "Golden Goal" makes a reference to Turkey's unexpected "victory" in the World Cup. It says that with a little "willpower" and "courage," Turkey will make a final "attack" to win the match. Once again, the meaning of the reforms as code words for the EU are severed from their present meanings (such as the ongoing painful struggles for human rights in the society)[23] and reduced to a clever tactic in a game conducted and viewed by the Western world.

As the ads' themes show, the campaign conveys a discourse deeply shaped and burdened by the past, yet never passing, symbolic crises of Turkish national identity. It tells much about the temporal constructions of modernity and national identity. The urgent call to the future reinscribes the past as the immutable and timeless origin of the present, which should be annihilated by a radical leap into a future that has no connections with the present. The present time is denied in its heterogeneous experiential terms and reduced to a permanent crisis that the Turkish national elite has "struggled" to evade from the very beginning.

The present is very much haunted by beginnings.[24] The timeless fantasy of "the West" in contrast to "the East" is not a construction in void. It has its dialogical references to the fantasy of "the East" produced in the historical encounter of the West and East, as accounted by Edward Said's *Orientalism*.[25] The fantasy still informs the present images of Turkey utilized by Western-ers. It is not at all a coincidence that Western journalists also made reference to the "beginnings" of Turkish national identity in their comments on Turkey's membership to the EU.[26] For example, their envisaging Turkey as the "sick man" of Europe implies a double meaning: While pointing to the present—to the poor condition of health of Bülent Ecevit (then prime minister of Turkey)—it invigorates the late-nineteenth-century phrase that the Europeans used to denigrate the Ottoman Empire. Another "classical" type of comment that came from the Western journalists and infiltrated the Turkish media raises doubt about the authenticity of Turkish modernity. It reads that Turkey, after the enactment of the reforms, is now *like* Europe.[27] Once again, this is not a new perspective. The Western "model" and Turkish "copy" have been recurring themes not only in journalistic representations but also in social theory for a long time. The distinction historically made between the model and the copy lies at the heart of the hegemonic imaginary concerning the constructs of the East and the West. The Turkish hegemonic imaginary has been structured within an encounter with the West, which imposed a "model" for modernity in its colonialist and imperialistic history, and which has always reproduced itself through insufficient "copies."

Let us now look briefly at how the concepts of *model* and *copy* figure visibly or invisibly in theories that address "Turkish modernity."

The Time Difference between the Model and the Copy

Modernization theorists regarded the process of Westernization and/or modernization as a movement of Western values and techniques from the center of modernity to its "developing" margins.[28] In this Eurocentric conception, the complexity and the crisis of modernity are neglected, being reduced to a "model" which is taken as an *"exclusively European* phenomenon."[29] However, as long as the so-called modernizing mission is integral to this view, the linear-time model of modernity that is expected to travel from the modern to the traditional is paradoxical. The homogenizing attempt of modernization is premised upon a differentiation that, according to Peter Osborne, "must first be recognized in order to be negated, so that "the results of synchronic comparisons are ordered diachronically to produce a scale of development which defines 'progress' in terms of the projection of certain people's presents as other people's futures, at the level of the development of history as a whole."[30] In this sense, the linear time model is also an invisibly spatial one.[31] The resulting paradox is that the movement of time is cancelled by the stasis of space. Modernization is bound to be distorted in the end because of the essential particularities of the specific space under consideration. This means that modernization theories, which preach that modernization is possible in non-Western contexts, at the same time posit an opposition of time and space, which is not resolvable within their paradigm.[32] The "essential space" of the non-West is stagnant and is defined in opposition to time and change.[33] For example, it is not surprising that Bernard Lewis, who celebrated "the emergence of modern Turkey" more than thirty years ago, recently evaluated the Turkish case as still facing "important choices" between the Middle East and the West.[34] Turkey is not "there" yet because "catching up with the modern world means more than borrowing or buying modern technology."[35] For Lewis, too, Turkey could not still cross the bridge. As can be clearly seen from this example, modernization theory is quite ambivalent about the inevitability of modernity in places such as Turkey. Modernity does not have its inherent dynamic in non-Western sites but is always dependent on an ever-appearing critical choice between the East and the West, which is paradoxically inscribed on its essential space.

Recent research on modernity and nationalism in Turkey is very critical of modernization theories. In opposition to classical modernization theories that celebrated the "asymptotic" adoption of Western modernity in Turkey, critiques of this approach "publicly debate and criticize the Kemalist doctrine as a patriarchal and antidemocratic imposition from above that has negated the historical and cultural experience of the people in Turkey."[36] Whereas modernization theories saw a more or less successful *example*[37] of universal modernity in the Turkish case, the critique treats this case as a failure to achieve a democratic and modern society.[38] However, both views share the reference point of the implicit model. Whether the history of Westernization is designated as a success or failure, both versions imply that Turkey, which "imitated" the West, is an exceptional case: an inept vehicle for Western modernization. It is bound to be a "copy."

Furthermore, in recent critical approaches there is a tendency to interpret the making of the Turkish nation in terms of "fabrication" from a model.[39] This seems to be a mirror image of the nationalist ideology that prioritizes the successful initiative of the political and cultural leadership in the interconnected processes of nationalization/modernization/Westernization. If the official nationalist representation emphasizes "good intentions," the critique points to the "dictatorial intentions" of the initiative. According to the latter view, the Turkish "modernizing elite" voluntarily adopted the model of Western civilization and forcefully imposed it on the masses, which, of course, falls short of the "democratic" Western model. Both views deal with Turkish identity within a problematic of imitation, hence maintaining the necessary temporal/spatial difference between the model and the copy. Even those scholars who are critical of Western dominance pursue the same logic to emphasize the evils of imitation. According to Kevin Robins, for example, Turkish culture "has been imitative and derivative in its emulation of the European model." "But, of course," he continues, "however good the simulation, it does not amount to *the real thing*."[40] The West is posited as the original stage for modernity to play out its concepts and institutions. This approach renders Turkish modernity a nonhistorical and nonsociological phenomenon.

So, one is confronted with several questions deriving from the above perspectives concerning Westernization/modernization in Turkey: the problem of how one might conceive of "impact" and "influences"; the problem of what "imitation" may mean; and, of course, the problem of what the "real thing" is. These questions pose a theoretical, practical, and political challenge. Obviously, the problem of model and copy is not unique to Turkey. This very challenge is addressed, for example, in postcolonial theories. Postcolonial theories attempt to deconstruct the historical representations of the model/copy or the self/other by attending to the colonial history of these dichotomous oppositions.[41] However, what can be considered unique to Turkey is its uneasy relation to colonialism and its consequent invisibility in postcolonial theories.

The Turkish case has not really attracted the attention of postcolonial critics.[42] Modernization theories have more to say on this case; they advance the idea that Turkey was Westernized without being colonized.[43] It then becomes worthwhile to ponder Turkey's invisibility in postcolonial criticism. It is even more striking that Edward Said omitted Turkey in his study of Orientalism, given that his critical investigation of the Western conceptions of the non-West made a big impact on studies of modernity, including postcolonial criticism. Not only does Said skip the long Ottoman history that has been the object of Orientalist visions of desire and derision in many areas such as philosophy, travel writing, and art;[44] he also does not address the complications of the "defeat of Turkey and the West's appropriation of its former imperial possessions"[45] after the First World War. Said's silence on this issue is significant, since he describes the same period as a time when the "Orient" increasingly "appeared to constitute a challenge . . . to the West's spirit, knowledge and imperium."[46] Said primarily locates the "Oriental" other in the Arabic world to which he partially belongs, and his neglect of the Turkish case implies that Turkey stands in a very problematic relationship to the Arab world, the Ottoman Empire being the former colonial power there. This may reflect Said's own ambivalence toward the history of the Ottoman colonization of Palestine: the Ottoman Empire disrupts the binary oppositions of East and West, colonizer and colonized that inform his analysis.

Hence, the status of Turkey in relation to the history of colonialism is further complicated by the fact that the Ottoman Empire was itself a colonizing force.[47] The major challenge to Ottoman rule came from the so-called West starting in the eighteenth century. The invasion of Western sciences, know-how, and artifacts, which contested Islamic and traditional ways of life and invoked the existence of a "lack," was accompanied by actual Western enterprises that established and monopolized certain trades and industries. Thereafter Ottoman rule underwent a period of decline, which can be described as the colonization of the colonizer.[48] The impact of this period, either the Western colonization of Ottoman life or the problem of the Ottoman colonies, was not openly addressed in the Kemalist discourse that reigned after the foundation of the Turkish Republic.[49] The Kemalist rupture that tried to set a zero point in time has contributed to the predominantly ambivalent attitude toward both the West and the Ottoman past in Turkey. In parallel to the maneuver of the Kemalist discourse that rendered the dynamics of the colonization of the colonizer Ottoman invisible, social theory has also not fully addressed the complexities involved. Consequently, the Turkish "replica" of modernity is either taken too literally or remains invisible in theories of modernization, Orientalism, and postcolonial criticism.

The Meaning of the "Present": Alternative or Multiple Modernities

If the postcolonial critique is mostly oblivious to the case of Turkey, a line of critique that stems from postcolonial criticism but frees itself from the dialogism of self and other celebrates the hybrid and multiple (or alternative) modernities in Turkey and other non-Western countries. This is, in a sense, a partial liberation from the burden of the history of modernity and colonialism. The oppressive framework of "model" and "copy" is refuted. Instead, "a site-based reading of modernity"[50] is privileged. According to Dilip Parameshwar Goankar, "modernity today is global and multiple and no longer has a governing center and master narratives to accompany it."[51] But of course, this does not mean for the authors who engage with the idea of alternative or multiple modernities that the Western discourse of modernity could or should be abandoned. A mere celebration of cultural difference would be too naive. In order to overcome the difficulty of defining the "universal" and the "local" meanings of modernity, a distinction between "societal modernization" and "cultural modernity" has to be made albeit in a dialectical way. In Taylor and Lee's words, "A viable theory of multiple modernities has to be able to relate both the pull to sameness and the forces making for difference."[52] Hence, it is posited that societal modernization provides the axis of convergence for the divergent "site-specific 'creative adaptations'" Goankar advances on this distinction to pursue the meaning(s) of modernity.[53] Inspired by Foucault's reading of Kant, he primarily argues that modernity "is best understood as an attitude of questioning the present."[54]

This perspective is an attempt to negate the inherent paradox of modernization that I discussed earlier. In opposition to marking space in hegemonically represented temporal terms (such as the words *backward* or *progress* imply), space is treated as a differential and productive constituent of modernity. Non-Western localities should be thought of as the site "where people 'make' themselves modern, as opposed to being 'made' modern by alien and impersonal forces."[55] If modernity is a "form of relationship to the present and to oneself" that emerges everywhere around the globe, then the analysis of modernity is based no longer on "sequential chronology" but on "coeval time."[56] Such a conception of modernity may have liberating effects, especially for non-Westerners. However, my contention is that within this framework, the theoretical and political problems that inflict the modernization approach are not totally resolved, if not simply reversed.

The effort to rethink yet maintain the distinction between "societal modernization" and "cultural modernity" along the axis of convergence/divergence remains highly problematic. Although divergence is thought to be possible within the limits of convergence, and divergence is treated as producing similarities at the limits, this framework does not really address the problem of the worn-out but still alive historical representations of modernity—not only in scholarly texts but in discourses that continue to justify power regimes in both the West and the non-West. The emphasis on coeval time and differential space reduces the power-stricken texture of history to a flat surface on which sameness and difference operate indefinitely. The implicit spatial factor in the linear-time model of modernization theories is, in a way, reversed. In the framework of multiple or alternative modernities, modernity appears to be a desired final destination the "latecomers" have their own creative ways of approaching. Yet one has to be sensitive to "the language and lessons of Western modernity" for a theory and practice of "creative adaptation."[57] Then, the chronology of Western modernity is not only assumed without questioning its historical construction and representation, but it is also implicitly taken as a model. The implicit chronology rendered invisible in the site-specific reading of modernity once again affirms the legacy and the model of Western modernity.[58]

The most intriguing question, however, for the specific problems raised in this article on the Turkish case is the question of the present. Modernity as an attitude or an ethos for interrogating the present runs counter to my argument so far, that the meaning of the present is displaced in Turkey. At this point, it would be worthwhile to look at how the framework of multiple modernities is applied to Turkey. Nilüfer Göle argues that there is an "indigenization of modernity" in Turkey and other non-Western contexts, which implies "a divorce of Westernization and modernization."[59] In her elaborate theoretical discussion on the problems and promises of multiple modernities, she rightly points to a new conceptual awareness in the effort to read non-Western modernities differently. According to Göle, postulates such as "1. Decentering the West; 2. Introducing coeval time; 3. Replacing the perspective of 'lack' with 'extra' modernity; 4. Dissonant traditions can provide some methodological foundations for an approach in terms of the non-Western modernities,"[60] may, to some extent, be meaningful in theoretically combating the oppressive model of Western modernity. Göle provides examples, especially regarding the Islamic experiences of modernity in Turkey, that point at the heterogeneity of "the modern." However, I would argue that the hybridity and heterogeneity of modern identities boil down to the historical markers of East and West to the extent that these identities are appropriated within the limits of national identity. Identities are always "hybrid" and "ambivalent" but they are, at the same time, totalized within boundaries and bear the violence and the burden of history as well as possibilities for resistance within themselves. Hence, the limiting and the totalizing hegemonic imaginary may not be at all congruent with the efforts of "creative adaptations" of modernity practiced by the heterogeneous social groups in the society. I contend that what is thought to belong to the past of Turkish modernity, and is assumed to be surpassed (i.e., the Western hegemony; the perspective of "lack"; the noncontemporaneous perception of time; the binary opposition of traditional/modern) is very much present in the hegemonic deployment of what modernity means. I have already discussed the present mode of discussing the EU membership in Turkey as a significant example of this.

Göle too easily equates the new theoretical awareness with the dissolution of the East-West divide. For example, she argues that decentering the West would replace the Western mirror of identity with one that "provides an opportunity to read our experiences in the reflection of each other's historical experience and social practice."[61] This immediately brings to mind the question of whether, in this case, the often-referenced Turkish-Greek enmity will be dissolved, and Turks and Greeks will read their experiences in the reflection of each other's experiences, which are historically intertwined. Many current examples, including the portrayal of the Greek and Turkish men in the "Europe Movement 2002 campaign" discussed earlier, make one think that "the West" is still a powerful mediator in the construction of national identities[62] that may encapsulate local experiences in a mythical time. What is called history is not easy to disentangle in theory, which is itself a challenge to theory.

The Mythical Time of Occidentalism

A new theoretical conceptualization is necessary in order to comprehend the historical interdependence between Turkey and the West without either collapsing particular differences into a dubious universalism or celebrating particularisms for their own sake.[63] This new perspective is especially relevant for Turkey, which has been regarded as an ideal space where East and West meet. But it was, at the same time, where the boundary between East and West was demarcated and consequently reproduced.[64] The history of Turkish nationalization/modernization/Westernization provides a rich account to study the persisting reproductions of the East-West divide. I will present snapshots from this history in order to illustrate the relevance of the theoretical framework of Occidentalism.

The late nineteenth century witnessed the rise of Turkish nationalism in the Ottoman Empire.[65] When the Empire was invaded and partitioned by British, Italian, French, and Greek forces after being defeated in the First World War, most of the Turkish nationalists who opposed the policies of the Ottoman government in Istanbul, and were "denounced as godless atheists waging war against the caliph,"[66] took refuge in Anatolia, where they participated in the "National Struggle." Halide Edip Adıvar, a rare female figure represented in the National Struggle, had been assigned the duty to visit different villages and report the violence done by the Greeks to Turkish populations.[67] She mentions, in her memoirs, a conversation with an old peasant woman at that time. The peasant woman complained to Halide Edip that her writing reports was in vain. She said, "Why do you write? What could writing mean for a people who are being slaughtered?"[68] Then she continued: "I have asked for pity from the Greeks. . . . They told us that they have been sent by Avrope [Europe; in Turkish, *Avrupa*]. So, my girl, please tell that man called Avrope to leave us alone, we didn't do anything bad to him, tell him not to disturb us."[69]

The old peasant woman's painful words on Europe give a sense of what the West or Europe could mean for the people of Anatolia during the imperialist invasion. It represented a threatening force that was involved in conspiracies striving to destroy the traditional order of things. But for Halide Edip herself, the writer, Europe always was an abstract concept, ambivalent in many aspects. While actually fighting the Western forces, Halide Edip and other Turkish intellectuals discussed and wrote on the possibilities of Westernization as a synonym of modernization. There was a wide gap between how the intellectuals and the local communities interpreted the "West."[70] The national discourse was not monolithic. It was produced and reproduced by continuous negotiations between the West and the Orient. Also, it was not a voluntarily created set of ideas, as the "imitation" problematic would say. Westernization and modernization had been brought on the agenda of the Turkish national elite by means of a threat, "by convincing Turks of past and present inadequacy."[71] The constitutive lack was there, right at the center of national identity.

The Turkish national identity propagated as the official identity of the new Turkish State after 1923 had to assume many dimensions that were thought to belong to the nation but were absent.[72] Turkish national discourse, as regulated and disseminated by the elite, was an eclectic mix of diverse elements: ideas taken over from past generations of nationalists; concepts, tools, and techniques borrowed from the West; unique solutions to deal with the pressing current political, ethnic, social, and economic problems; and much after-the-fact theorizing. Despite its pragmatic fluidity,[73] the consequent national discourse was structured in and through a fantasy. The diverse realm of relations with the Western countries was translated into a marker called "the West"; in a similar manner, the hetero-geneous realm of the population was signified as "the people," which repre-sented the Orient in terms of "backward" Islamic and Arabic influences.[74] The Occidentalist fantasy evoked a "lack" in "the people" upon which it orga-nized the "desire" to fill it. This was in close connection to the lack projected onto the Turkish by the Orientalist fantasy. They function in the same econ-omy of identity and desire.

If Orientalism is a representation that is informed by historical and material power configurations[75] but also conveys the desire of the Western subject, how the "Orientals" answered back to their representation by the West brings to view a complex field of subjectivity. Then, what is the subjec-tivity of the other? Furthermore, if "the creation of the Orient . . . signifies the West's own dislocation from itself, something inside that is presented, narrativized, as being outside,"[76] then what does the concept of "the West" produced by non-Westerners present and dislocate?

The concept of Occidentalism that I want to introduce is different from an idea of internalized Orientalism or a defensive reaction against the West.[77] Instead, it points to the specific mechanisms that "Orientals" employ to cre-ate their subject status (not at all a homogeneous entity) and also to the common sky that structures different horizons. The other is represented not only by the Western subject, as the theory of Orientalism would put it. Occidentalism also denotes the subjectivity of the other in relation to Ori-entalism. It opens a space for the positivity of the other—its experiences, utterances, and practices—instead of adopting the often negative definition of the other in theories of Orientalism. But it also shows how the subjec-tivity of the other is encapsulated in the discursive realm of the other that is denied the real thing of modernity. The other's inhabiting the space of the other and speaking for itself occurs in the same universe of signification. But the double reflection (the viewpoint of the Western representation— that is, how the non-Western imagines that the West sees itself—is incor-porated in the reflection on its own identity) complicates the identification process. Hence the critical study of Occidentalism not only deals with the ambivalent identity of the non-Western but also conveys that the imagined Western gaze is an integral part of this identity. It attends to how "center" and "periphery," or "model" and "copy," are already inscribed in the concep-tion of modernity.

I do not mean to suggest that Occidentalism represents the other, as such, as a unitary and separate entity; that it designates a (libertarian, or non-repressive and nonmanipulative)[78] alternative to Orientalism; or that it is merely a fictive representation of the other othered by Western domination. I argue that the term *Occidentalism* can be best understood as describing the set of practices and arrangements justified in and against the imagined idea of "the West" in the non-West. On the one hand, it signifies a projective identification with the threatening power of the West. On the other hand, it implies a demarcation of internal and external boundaries.

Westernization in Turkey cannot be understood as an objective process in which certain things, including manners, were imported from the West. Neither was it merely a subjective orientation that shaped events in line with the willpower of the ruling elite. It was a process in which the non-Westerners were othered and subjected to unequal power relations but also produced their subjectivity in that very encounter. *Occidentalism* refers to a field of social imagination through which those in power consume and reproduce the projection of "the West" to negotiate and consolidate their hegemony in line with their pragmatic interests. The hegemony operates by employing the mechanisms of projection that support the fantasy of "the West." Projection, in its psychoanalytical meaning, operates both as the displacement of what is intolerable inside into the outside world, thus as a refusal to know; and as introjection of what is threatening in the external world so as to contain and manage it. Therefore it designates at the same time what the subject refuses to be and desires to be. In Turkey, projection, in its double process, figures in the conception of "the people" on the one hand, and in the conception of "the West" on the other. Members of the national elite constituted their identity through a projection of the West in affirming their construction of a modern society. They organized the desire to be modern around the marker of "the West," which they claimed to possess. By doing this they introjected the imagined nation into their subjectivity. But they displaced what is disturbing for them, such as the threatening power of the West, by assuming a guardian role that modernizes but at the same time protects the "less civilized" and "infantile" population from the "dangers of too much Westernization." The virtual viewpoint of the West, which is the product of double projection, oscillates between recognition and rejection, leading to a series of splits.

It must be observed that Kemalists in early Turkish history were quite ambivalent about the possible impact of Westernization. While Western civilization was acknowledged as "superior" to the Ottoman heritage, it was, at the same time, despised for several reasons associated with its morality, the presence of "dangerous" class struggles and the existence of imperialist tendencies, and so on. It was seen as a source of both progress and threat. Civilization, in Mustafa Kemal's words, stands out as a fierce force that destroys those who resist or stay indifferent to it; it is aggressive, threatening, and all-powerful.[79] The feelings of panic raised by its progress and the fear of "being late" are accompanied by a feeling of inferiority inflicted on those who are not part of Western civilization. "The lethargic mentality of the past centuries" should be abandoned, said Mustafa Kemal; the new standards should be based on "speed and movement that define our century."[80] In a similar manner, the first sociologist of the nation, Ziya Gökalp, had said, "We shall skip five hundred years and not stand still."[81]

The impact of the West, therefore, was more than a mere import of concepts and techniques for Turkish nationalists. It was not just a movement of "modernity" in time and space. It was a performance for the imagined Western audience. It was also a totally new conception of time, which proceeded violently. It was a threat that the Turkish nationalists had to acknowledge and adapt to with "high speed." Şerif Mardin points to a feeling of urgency on the part of the Kemalists "to work for something which did not exist as if it existed and make it exist."[82] "Nation" and "Western civilization" were fundamental code words for this.

There is no need to say that Turkish economy, politics, and social life underwent major changes from the 1920s to the present. However, the mythical time of Occidentalism remains to this day without much alteration. *Mythical time* is the recurrence of the same appearing as new and desirable.[83] The past reappears as the desirable future in the Occidentalist fantasy. It is primarily a lack of historicity, a refusal to know the realm of forces that produce things as they are. It is a mode of representation of social reality reducing its complexity and heterogeneity in a national idiom that is captured in the timeless polarity of West and East. It is reproduced as long as it sustains its hegemonic power and sets the limits and terms of the subjectivities of various social groups in society.

The case of the present significations that restrict the EU debate in Turkey to timeless markers of East and West indicates that the Occidentalist fantasy is still at the heart of the hegemonic imaginary. I do not intend to underestimate the material interests in power struggles. But significations and representations also have a complex role in shaping power strategies. Just as the West always refers to the notion of the East to assert its hegemony, Turkey reproduces the reified images of the West to justify its regime of power in its boundary management of dividing spheres, regions, and people along the axis of East and West. Occidentalist fantasy nurtures power strategies. It is not simply an admiration for the West or hatred against it. The reified image of the West for Turkish in this context can have both positive and negative meanings. For example, a government in Turkey may bring the problem of human rights to the agenda with reference to the sensitivity of the West on this issue, as in the EU case. But when confronted with an accusation of human rights violations, the same government may warn people against the dangers of Western interference. Occidentalism makes the conflicting statements possible, justifying every act and statement with reference to an imagined Westernness. It should not be forgotten that Kenan Evren, the general who seized power after the military coup in 1980, commented that Turkey is an integral part of democratic and free Europe and intends to remain so. And he ironically objected to any Western criticism targeted to the military regime and massive human rights violations.

I have argued in this article that modernity is a historical construct, and its historicity is displaced in the polarity of East and West. Hence the historical path of modernity in Turkey, very much intertwined with the development of world capitalism, colonialism, and nationalism, remains unacknowledged. Instead a fantasy of the modern, as "the West," is replaced in the hegemonic imaginary. I have also argued that social theories such as modernization, by sustaining the polarity of East and West, have contributed to this fantasy. On the other hand, recent critical stances of alternative or multiple modernities miss the role of the fantasy by too easily dissolving the poles of East and West. I have suggested that one should address the symptoms of tension involved in the re-production of the polarity, in both its particular historical manifestations and "universal" relevance. Occidentalism provides examples of this tension. Occidentalism is an answering practice to the constructions of the West, which operates in the mythical time of reified representations. It may produce a resistance to Western power, but operates within its discursive terms to maintain a system of government that endorses its hegemony. The desire of the nationalist elite in Turkey to become both Western and anti-Western and Turkish resonates with the Western desire to see Turkey as a bridge that never crosses the distance between the West and the East. But Occidentalism also brings to light symptoms of mismatch and excess not pinned down in this timeless circularity. Therefore, a critical study of Occidentalism may illustrate how the projections of the West by non-Westerners hover over the universal principles of Western modernity as a deferred echo that challenges and alters its "universal" and "local" meanings.

I have also argued that the emphasis on speed in Westernization/modernization based on the idea of a time lag paradoxically blocks possible changes in the structure of social life in Turkey. It is in the notion of speed that the reified, thinglike character of modernity associated with the West is sustained. The idea of speed encapsulates energies that could otherwise be spent in dealing with frozen identities and problematics. The metaphor of "catching the train of Western civilization" both channels and frustrates the desires of the people to be modern. The anxiety of "being late" puts a barrier to critical and creative thinking that could have attended to the questions of the present. Most burning questions in Turkey today are deferred or made invisible by their displacement in Occidentalism, including human rights violations, gender inequalities, ethnic problems, and political Islam.

It is never easy to resist reification at either the level of the production of commodities or that of representations. But it is worth the effort. If we can understand and analyze the inner contradictions, the tensions of modernity that produce the intertwined histories of Orientalism and Occidentalism, then maybe we can revive the buried promise of modernity—the practice of critique. It is time that we reach out for the emergency brake[84] in the "train of Western civilization."

Notes

1   Turkey first became a candidate for membership in the EEC (European Economic Community) in the 1960s. After a long period of indeterminacy, Turkey was declared an official candidate for "full membership" to the EU (European Union) with twelve other countries in December 1999. Although most of the other candidates are proceeding toward a final decision in their negotiations with the EU, Turkey is the only candidate still waiting for approval from the EU to start negotiations for full membership.

2   In the Web journal *Enlargement Weekly* (December 17, 2002) the decisions of the Copenhagen Meeting of EU leaders December 12–14, 2002, are reported. According to these reports, not only is the starting date of the accession negotiations with Turkey postponed to 2004, but it is also made dependent on the fulfillment of certain conditions, which, this

time also include the "implementation" of legislative reforms. See www.europa.eu.int/comm/enlargement.

3 This metaphor has been widely used in Turkish media for years to point at Turkey's belated relationship to "Western civilization." Currently it has gained further prominence in the discussions over the question of the EU. For example, a distinctively pro-European newspaper, *Radikal*, has turned the phrase into a logo for its specific campaign for the EU: "AB Treni Kaçmasın" [Don't let the EU train run away].

4 The concept *hegemonic imaginary* is inspired by Cornelius Castoriadis's concept *social imaginary*. See Cornelius Castoriadis, *The Imaginary Institution of Society*, trans. Kathleen Blamey (Cambridge: Polity, 1987). *Hegemonic imaginary* refers to the realm of significations and representations that constitute and provide a historical mode of social being for individuals in the society. The imaginary is hegemonic to the extent that it is reinforced by power relations as the dominant mode of being and channels the desires of people to appropriate that mode of being. Turkishness in relation to the Western world is a significant element of the hegemonic imaginary in Turkey.

5 While *hegemonic imaginary* regards the significations and representations that provide the social mediation for being a social agent, *fantasy* refers to the psychopolitical dynamics in the constitution of subjectivities in a certain historical context. Postcolonial theory informed by psychoanalysis makes use of the concept to address the splits and projections in the processes of subject constitution and identification in a colonial and postcolonial situation. For significant examples, see Ashis Nandy, *The Intimate Enemy: Loss and Recovery of Self under Colonialism* (Delhi: Oxford University Press, 1994); Frantz Fanon, *Black Skin, White Masks*, trans. C. L. Markmann (London: Pluto, 1993); Homi Bhabha, "Remembering Fanon: Self, Psyche and the Colonial Condition," in *Colonial Discourse and Post-Colonial Theory: A Reader*, ed. P. Williams and L. Chrisman (New York: Columbia University Press, 1993). Mladen Dolar argues that fantasy is a "useless tool to explain its object." Yet it "can shed light upon its producers and adherents. It projects onto the screen of this distant Other our own impasses and practices in dealing with power, and stages them." Mladen Dolar, "The Subject Supposed to Enjoy," in *The Sultan's Court: European Fantasies of the East*, by Alain Grosrichard, trans. L. Heron (London: Verso, 1998), xiv.

6 In the 1830s August Comte wrote to the Grand Vizier Reşit Paşa: "The world has been divided into two oppositional worlds, Asia and Europe, for centuries; it is time that this opposition should be overcome; that there must be a common civilization in the world." Comte "regarded Turkey as the only country with the capacity, in historical and geographical terms, to realize the synthesis between the two worlds." Mehmet Kaplan, *Nesillerin Ruhu* (Istanbul: Hareket Yayını, 1967), 73.

7 A Turkish social scientist captures this structure of sentiment, which he, like most others, cannot manage to deal with critically: "Of all the nations in the world, Turkey is unique in having failed to forge a consistent image of herself. Is she of Europe or of the East? Is she a modern nation-state or a feudalist [sic] association wallowing in the Middle Ages? Is she a popular democracy or a camouflaged group dictatorship? Aware of their lack of articulateness in international discourse, the Turks blame themselves for the confusion."

Nuri Eren, *Turkey Today—and Tomorrow: An Experiment in Westernization* (London: Pall Mall, 1963), 249.

8   Clifford Geertz, *The Interpretation of Cultures* (London: Fontana, 1993), 14.

9   Nilüfer Göle, "Global Expectations, Local Experiences: Non-Western Modernities," in *Through a Glass, Darkly*, ed. Wil Arts (Leiden: E. J. Brill, 2000), 48.

10 Halil Nalçaoğlu, "Devrimci Öğrencilerin Özgül Fantezi Uzamı," *Toplum ve Bilim* 93 (2002): 142–72. See also Gregory Jusdanis's elaborate account of "belated modernity" in Greece: Gregory Jusdanis, *Belated Modernity and Aesthetic Culture: Inventing National Literature* (Minneapolis: Oxford, 1991).

11 According to Nalçaoğlu, the symptomatic significance of the train metaphor is not that we are late to it, but we are *always* late to it. Nalçaoğlu, "Devrimci Öğrencilerin," 146.

12 Ibid.

13 Peter Osborne dwells on the "temporal dialectic of modernity," arguing, "Insofar as 'modernity' is understood as a periodizing category in the full sense of registering a break not only from chronologically defined period to another, but in the quality of historical time itself, it sets up a differential between the character of its own time and that which precedes it. This differential formed the basis for the transformation in the late eighteenth century in the meaning of the concepts of 'progress' and 'development,' which makes them the precursors of later, twentieth-century concepts of modernization. For the idea of the *non-contemporaneousness* of geographically diverse, but chronologically simultaneous, times which thus develops in the context of colonial experience, is the foundation for 'universal histories with a cosmopolitan intent.'" Peter Osborne, *The Politics of Time: Modernity and Avant-Garde* (London: Verso, 1995), 16.

14 For a long time the debate centered on whether Turkey wishes to commit itself to the reforms required by the EU for membership, such as the ban of capital punishment and the right of Kurdish people to speak and broadcast in their mother tongue. It must be stated that no one party in the Turkish political arena was consistently for or against the reforms. The alliances on either front do not fit to the apparent political divisions in Turkey: while the big bourgeoisie, liberal intellectuals, Kurds, most Islamists, the new leftist movements, human rights activists, and those Kemalists that are devoted to Western civilization argue for the EU; the extreme right, the right conservatives, Turkists, radical Islamists and some Kemalists keen on national independence, leftist nationalists, and radical socialists argue against it. Oya Baydar, "Yalın Kılıç AB'ye Doğru," *Radikal*, June 16, 2002.

15 According to Ahmet İnsel, the ambivalent attitude toward the EU functions as a hegemonic power strategy that fixes Turkish society in a twilight zone, investing in hopelessness disguised as postponed hope. Even the leftist ÖDP (Freedom and Solidarity Party), he argues, is part of the hegemonic ideology, as its ambivalent attitude summarized in the slogan, "AB'ye Havet" [*Nes* to EU, *Nes* meaning a combination of yes and no] illustrates. Ahmet İnsel, "AB Kapısı Kapanırken," *Radikal*, June 23, 2002.

16 Mesut Yeğen, "AB Karşıtları: Sancılı Sağ," *Radikal*, July 7, 2002.

17 While the pro-European newspaper *Radikal* and the "Europe Movement 2002" celebrated their own contribution to "having a place in history," the newspapers, including *Radi-*

kal, continued to publish articles that emphasize the uncertainty of the present situation with reference to whether the recent legal initiative would be adequate for membership. While *Radikal* concentrated on the possible reactions coming from the EU, interestingly the Islamic newspaper *Yeni Şafak* introduced more radical questions regarding the meaning of the reforms and questions the link between modernization and Westernization often taken for granted. It argued that Turkey should get rid of its platonic love relationship with Europe and face its own identity as the other of the West, while getting ready to be a member of the EU. Yusuf Kaplan, "AB'ye Taraf Olarak Bertaraf Olmak mı; Yoksa Yüzleşerek Varolmak mı?" *Yeni Şafak*, August 4, 2002.

18   Avni Özgürel states that the debate over the EU in Turkey is informed by the question "What does Europe think?" By giving a historical account of the problem of the Western gaze, he argues that the question has a history of 250 years. Avni Özgürel, "Osmanlı'dan Başlayıp Bugüne Kadar Gelen 250 Yıllık Bir Soru . . . Avrupa Ne Düşünüyor?" *Radikal*, August 4, 2002.

19   For example, while the enactment of the reforms were celebrated, not much attention was paid to what will happen to the university students who have been penalized due to their demands of education in their "mother tongue," namely Kurdish.

20   The concept *civil society* gained prominence in Turkey in the late 1980s. Its meanings vary in different conceptions, from being associated with the "interests of the society" in opposition to the "state," to being positioned as the new agent of modernization. In most cases, *civil society* denotes the business and trade organizations, as in the case of "Europe Movement 2002." Tanıl Bora and Seda Çağlar critically discuss the role of the so-called civil society organizations as the new agents of modernization and Westernization in "Modernleşme ve Batılılaşmanın Bir Taşıyıcısı Olarak Sivil Toplum Kuruluşları," in *Modern Türkiye'de Siyasi Düşünce: Modernleşme ve Batıcılık*, ed. Uygur Kocabaşoğlu (Istanbul: İletişim Yayınları, 2002).

21   The campaign was specifically designed for creating a public opinion, especially on the need for enacting the reforms, as a condition for membership to the EU. However, it continued after the enactment of the reforms stressing the current problems that should be addressed in the process of becoming a member. The campaign had wide publicity in print media, as well as a Web site petition inciting individuals to enroll in the movement.

22   Greece and Turkey are not only engaged in a feud over territorial claims, such as in the case of the Aegean Islands or in Cyprus, they also compete for being considered Western. For example, when Greece was accepted in the EEC, a Turkish newspaper wrote: "They have become Europeans and we have remained Asians." The feeling of inferiority triggered by Greece's membership was addressed by Mümtaz Soysal, a Turkish academic and politician, in a significant remark: "This is the most opportune time to rid ourselves of the complex of 'being considered European.' . . . We are Turks from Turkey. Turkey is a country with one bank in Europe and the other in Asia. . . . We must realize this and accept this as such, and we must turn this embarrassment into a sense of superiority." David Kushner, "Westernism in Contemporary Turkey," in *Atatürk and the Modernization of Turkey*, ed. J. M. Landau (Boulder, CO: Westview, 1984), 234–40. On the other hand, Herzfeld points at the constitution of the Greek identity by inventing a Greek tradition that was supposed to be Western in opposition to the "foreign" local Turkish culture.

Michael Herzfeld, "Hellenism and Occidentalism: The Permutations of Performance in Greek Bourgeois Identity," in *Occidentalism: Images of the West*, ed. J. G. Carrier (Oxford: Clarendon, 1995).

23 In its press declaration on August 3, 2002, after the enactment of the reforms, IHD (Human Rights Organization) reiterated that "the ban of capital punishment cannot be regarded as a momentary decision. So many people have been struggling over decades for this end in Turkey, and they paid a price for it. Some were convicted and some were killed. So we should not forget the struggles that have been going on in the society by equating the recent reforms with the EU demands" (www.ihd.org).

24 Homi Bhabha argues with reference to Michel de Certeau's *The Writing of History* (New, York: Columbia University Press, 1988), "Beginnings can be the narrative limits of the knowable, the margins of the meaningful." Homi Bhabha, "The World and the Home," in *Dangerous Liaisons: Gender, Nation, and Postcolonial Perspectives*, ed. A. McClintock, A. Mufti, and E. Shohat (Minneapolis: University of Minnesota Press, 1997), 449.

25 Edward Said, *Orientalism* (London: Penguin, 1995).

26 The *London Times*, the *Economist*, and *Die Welt* have recently talked about Turkey as the "sick man" of Europe. The translated articles appeared in *Radikal* as part of the discussions on the EU membership. "Avrupa'nın Hasta Adamı," *Radikal*, July 6, 2002 (*London Times*, July 5, 2002); "Tükenmiş Başbakana Yer Yok," *Radikal*, July 6, 2002 (*Economist*, July 5, 2002); Dietrich Aleksander, "'Hasta Adam'ın Özgüveni Yerinde," *Radikal*, July 7, 2002 (*Die Welt*, July 1, 2002).

27 One comment, quoted from an Italian communist newspaper, *Manifesto*, clearly underlines the interplay of projections between Turkey and the West. The sarcastic comment reads, the "New Turkey is now 'like Europe.'" Nilgün Cerrahoğlu, "Türkiye'ye Evet Ama," *Cumhuriyet*, August 5, 2002.

28 For classical examples of modernization theory applied to Turkey, see Daniel Lerner, *The Passing of Traditional Society* (Glencoe, IL: Free Press, 1958); Bernard Lewis, *The Emergence of Modern Turkey* (London: Oxford University Press, 1968).

29 Enrique Dussell, "Beyond Eurocentrism: The World-System and the Limits of Modernity," in *The Cultures of Globalization*, ed. F. Jameson, M. Miyoshi (Durham: Duke University Press, 1998), 18.

30 Osborne, *The Politics of Time*, 17.

31 Osborne argues that "it is in the repressed spatial premises of the concept of modernity that its political logic is to be found." Osborne, *The Politics of Time*, 16.

32 This is due to the conceptions of space and time in hegemonic forms of modernity, in which time is associated with movement and politics and space is defined as stasis. Space and time opposition is also gendered along this axis; space is feminine, time is male. See Doreen Massey, "Politics and Space/Time," in *Place and the Politics of Identity*, ed. M. Keith, S. Pile (London: Routledge, 1993).

33 Said's account of Orientalism (in his *Orientalism*) illustrates this point. His path-breaking study illustrates how the Western scholars' attempt to travel to, to penetrate into, and to represent the Orient produced an objectified and essentialized Orient.

34 "Turkey today stands before important choices. It may choose, as some of its leaders would clearly prefer, to turn its back on the West and return to the Middle East, this time

not leading but following, in a direction determined by others. It may choose, as other Turkish leaders would clearly prefer, to tighten its ties with the West and turn its back on the Middle East, except for those countries that share Turkey's westward orientation and democratic aspirations." Bernard Lewis, *The Future of the Middle East* (London: Phoenix, 1997), 48. See also Lewis, *The Emergence of Modern Turkey*.

35 Lewis, *The Future of the Middle East*, 46.

36 Sibel Bozdoğan and Reşat Kasaba, introduction to *Rethinking Modernity and National Identity in Turkey* (London: University of Washington Press, 1997), 4.

37 The fact that Europe is already an example bound with the history of domination over others inscribes a hierarchy between the examples in Europe and those elsewhere. As Derrida puts it, "Europe has the privilege of being the *good example*, for it incarnates in its purity the Telos, of all historicity: universality, omnitemporality, infinite traditionality, and so forth; . . . The empirical types of non-European societies, then, are only *more* or *less* historical; at the lower limit, they tend toward nonhistoricity." Jacques Derrida, *The Other Heading: Reflections on Today's Europe*, trans. P. Brault (Bloomington: Indiana University Press, 1992), 115.

38 Keyder argues that "Turkish nationalism is an extreme example of a situation in which the masses remained silent partners and the modernizing elite did not attempt to accommodate popular resentment." Çağlar Keyder, "Whither the Project of Modernity? Turkey in the 1990s," in Bozdoğan and Kasaba, *Rethinking Modernity and National Identity in Turkey*, 43.

39 For example, Kadıoğlu, who makes use of Chatterjee's perspective to analyze Turkish nationalism, argues that "the emerging new Turkish identity . . . was distinguished by its manufactured character." Ayşe Kadıoğlu, "The Paradox of Turkish Nationalism and the Construction of Official Identity," in *Turkey: Identity, Democracy, Politics*, ed. S. Kedourie (London: Frank Cass, 1996), 188. Despite the fact that Partha Chatterjee insists on the colonial dynamics of imagining the nation in India, Kadıoğlu's statement reflects the exceptionalism that has been so widely internalized by the Turkish people. See Partha Chatterjee, *Nationalist Thought and the Colonial World: A Derivative Discourse* (London: Zed, 1993).

40 Kevin Robins, "Interrupting Identities: Turkey/Europe," in *Questions of Cultural Identity*, ed. S. Hall and P. du Gay (London: Sage, 1996), 67; emphasis added.

41 For example, Bhabha's concern is to overcome the given dichotomous model/copy or self/other poles of identity by pointing to the hybridity and ambivalence in colonial discourse. He argues that the narrative of colonial mimicry maintained a recalcitrant difference, "a difference that is almost the same but not quite," which is similar to the functioning of modernization narratives. Homi Bhabha, "Of Mimicry and Man: The Ambivalence of Colonial Discourse," *October* 34 (1985): 26. Bhabha thinks that the necessary heterogeneity in the narrative provides a medium of intervention. The "in-between" rewriting of the narrative, which produces not a copy of the original but a misappropriation of it, is capable of interrupting the hegemonic narrative and exposing its ambivalence.

42 Although Turkey does not really fit into a postcolonial model due to the fact it was never overtly colonized, and also because of the complications of its own colonial past, it is still possible to argue that it is more or less a proper object of study for postcolonial criticism if

we accept Bart Moore-Gilbert's broad definition: "In my view, postcolonial criticism can still be seen as a more or less distinct set of reading practices, if it is understood as preoccupied principally with analysis of cultural forms which mediate, challenge or reflect upon the relations of domination and subordination—economic, cultural and political—between (and often within) nations, races or cultures, which characteristically have their roots in the history of modern European colonialism and imperialism and which, equally, characteristically, continue to be apparent in the present era of neo-liberalism." Bart Moore-Gilbert, *Postcolonial Theory: Contexts, Practices, Politics* (London: Verso, 1997), 12.

43 For example, Gellner argues that the Turkish case is unique in that sense: "Turkey . . . can claim that its commitment to modern political ideas owes nothing to alien imposition, and everything to an endogenous development. Turkey chose its destiny. It achieved political modernity: it was not thrust upon it." Ernest Gellner, *Encounters with Nationalism* (Oxford: Blackwell, 1994), 82. For Gellner, the commitment to elective and constitutional government testifies for this. The military coups, in his view, although signs of not an "easy ride" in liberal democracy, were just necessary lapses in democracy, since they have always ensured that democracy is eventually restored. In this approach, the compromises in democracy, and a whole history of suffering that accompanied them, are shadowed as negligible while the commitment to Westernization is privileged.

44 Alain Grosrichard studies the European fantasies of the East focusing on seventeenth- and eighteenth-century writings on the Ottoman Empire. In *The Sultan's Court*, he analyses the Western image of "Oriental despotism" in terms of the Lacanian concept of fantasy. Mladen Dolar, in the introduction to the English translation of the book, states that "Said consciously limits himself to the Arab world, the Near East, while Grosrichard's sources mostly treat the Ottoman Empire (still a very real threat at that time)" (x).

45 Moore-Gilbert, *Postcolonial Theory*, 52.

46 Said, *Orientalism*, 248.

47 The power regime in the Ottoman Empire was highly centralized but flexible enough to hold different ethnic and religious communities over a large territory from Balkans to the Arabic peninsula under control by allowing some cultural autonomy to each community. The peculiar mechanisms and rationale of the Ottoman rule in its colonies is a vast subject for Turkish and Western scholars that lies beyond the scope of this article.

48 The Western capital infiltrated the Ottoman social, economical, and political life starting in the nineteenth century. The low tariff rates in trade during the Tanzimat era led to a flood of imported European goods, which dealt a blow to small craft industries. Şerif Mardin, *Türkiye'de Toplum ve Siyaset* (Istanbul: İletişim Yayınları, 1990), 89. Economic capitulations given to Western powers and the treaties that endowed European merchants with economic privileges "reduced the Turkish government to the status of the 'gendarmes of foreign capital.'" Feroz Ahmad, *The Making of Modern Turkey* (London: Routledge, 1993), 93. In addition to economic colonization, the social life was also colonized due to factors such as the constitution of Western schools and organizations, the invasion of Western technologies and ideas, and the political power enjoyed by Western embassies. See Ahmad, *The Making of Modern Turkey*, 41; Roderic H. Davison, *Essays in Ottoman and Turkish History, 1774–1923: The Impact of the West* (London: SAQI Books, 1990). Mete Tuncay makes the point that, despite the nationalist struggle against foreign privileges,

the position of "foreigners" in economic, social, and political life was not dramatically altered in the first ten years after the foundation of the Republic. Mete Tuncay, *Türkiye Cumhuriyeti'nde Tek-Parti Yönetimi'nin Kurulması* (Ankara: Yurt Yayınları, 1981), 198.

49   The only exception to this is a group of Kemalist intellectuals around the journal *Kadro*, which began publication in 1932 and was forced to suspend publication in 1934. According to Feroz Ahmad, their aim was the creation of "an ideology original to the regime." Ahmad, *The Making of Modern Turkey*, 65. Ahmad explains that they dwelled on the economic and political aspects of colonialism and reckoned their ideology to be useful for all colonies and semicolonies (a term they used to define the Turkish past) emphasizing the "original character" of the Turkish revolution. One of the prominent members of *Kadro*, Yakup Kadri Karaosmanoğlu, has continued to be an almost haunting critical voice of Kemalist reforms by evoking the self-deception of the cultural elite and their alienation from "the people" in his novels and essays.

50   Dilip Parameshwar Goankar, "On Alternative Modernities," *Public Culture* 27 (1999): 14. Goankar edited the *Public Culture* special issue on "Alter-native Modernities" in which different cultures in Asia, Africa, and Australia are analyzed with an alternative-modernities approach.

51   Ibid., 13.

52   From Charles Taylor and Benjamin Lee's working draft on the Multiple Modernities Project, cited by Göle, "Global Expectations," 42.

53   Goankar, "Alternative Modernities," 16.

54   Ibid., 13.

55   Ibid., 16.

56   Göle, "On Global Expectations," 46.

57   Goankar, "Alternative Modernities," 16–17.

58   "Those who submit to that rage for modernity are not naïve; they are not unaware of its Western origins, its colonial designs, its capitalist logic, and its global reach. In haphazardly naming everything modern, they are exercising one of the few privileges that accrue to the latecomer: the license to play with form and refigure function according to the exigencies of the situation. Thus, in the face of modernity one does not turn inward, one does not retreat; one moves sideways, one moves forward. All of this is creative adaptation. Non-Western people, the latecomers to modernity, have been engaged in these maneuvers for nearly a century." Goankar, "Alternative Modernities," 17.

59   Göle, "On Global Expectations," 40–42; see also Nilüfer Göle, *The Forbidden Modern: Civilization and Veiling* (Ann Arbor: University of Michigan Press, 1996); Nilüfer Göle, "Snapshots of Islamic Modernities," *Dædalus* 129 (2000).

60   Göle, "On Global Expectations," 45.

61   Ibid.

62   I have already cited Herzfeld and Jusdanis's research that points at the complexities of the Western mediation in the constitution of Greek national identity.

63   Deniz Kandiyoti makes an important point stressing how "revolving around two opposed narratives—two sides of the same discursive coin" brings us "full circle to posting notions of lost authentic 'indigeneity' and inviting forms of neo-Orientalism that are inimical to an understanding of complex historical processes." Deniz Kandiyoti, "Gendering the

Modern: On Missing Dimensions in the Study of Turkish Modernity," in *Rethinking Modernity*, 114.

64 Turkish national identity was constituted and continuously modified at the margin between being a "bad" and a "good" example of modernity. Islam has been a very important factor that contributed to the ambiguity. For Islam was seen to contradict Westernization and modernity, by both Westerners and Turkish nationalists who aspired to be Westernized. Yet, as Bobby Sayyid argues, Turkish nationalists, Kemalists, "found themselves in a paradoxical situation: to be western one had to reject the Orient," but "their rejection of the Orient relied on them being able to articulate and perpetuate an oriental identity . . . The only way to manage this paradox of westernizing and orientalizing was for the Kemalists to fix upon Islam the representation of orientalness." Bobby Sayyid, *A Fundemental Fear: Eurocentrism and the Emergence of Islamism* (London: Zed, 1997), 69. A group of people who call themselves "laicists" in Turkey today argue against the "Islamic fundamentalism" they think takes Turkey "backward" in modernity.

65 The rise of Turkish nationalism, the debates within its different advocates, and its connections to the rise of other nationalisms in and out of the former Ottoman Empire, such as Greek, Bulgarian, Serbian, Russian, Albanian, and Arab nationalisms, are extensively documented. References include Feroz Ahmad, *The Young Turks* (London: Oxford University Press, 1969); Suavi Aydın, *Modernleşme ve Milliyetçilik* (Ankara: Gündoğan, 1993); Uriel Heyd, *Foundations of Turkish Nationalism: The Life and Teachings of Ziya Gökalp* (London: Luzac and Co., Harvil Press, 1950); Ercümend Kuran, "The Impact of Nationalism on the Turkish Elite in the Nineteenth Century," in *Beginnings of Modernization in the Middle East: The Nineteenth Century*, ed. W. Polk and R. L. Chambers (Chicago: University of Chicago Press, 1968); Şerif Mardin, *The Genesis of Young Ottoman Thought* (Princeton: Princeton University Press, 1962); Ali Engin Oba, *Türk Milliyetçiliğinin Doğuşu* (Ankara: İmge Kitabevi, 1995); Osman Okyar and Halil İnalcık, eds., *Social and Economic History of Turkey: 1071–1920* (Ankara: Hacetepe University, 1980); Stanford Jay Shaw and Ezel Kural Shaw, *History of the Ottoman Empire and Modern Turkey*, vol. 2, *Reform, Revolution, and Republic: The Rise of Modern Turkey, 1808–1975* (Cambridge: Cambridge University Press, 1977); Eric Zürcher, *The Unionist Factor, the Role of the Committee of Union and Progress in the Turkish National Movement: 1905–1926* (Leiden: E. J. Brill, 1984).

66 Ahmad, *The Making of Modern Turkey*, 48.

67 Halide Edip is a significant figure in early Turkish literature. She wrote many novels and essays in Turkish, as well as in English. She was, at the same time, a militant nationalist who took part in the "national struggle" in the beginning of the twentieth century.

68 Halide Edip Adıvar, *Türkün Ateşle İmtihanı* (Istanbul: Atlas Kitabevi, 1994), 201.

69 Ibid.

70 Yakup Kadri, who also wrote on the war years in Anatolia, says: "The difference between a person educated in Istanbul and an Anatolian peasant is greater than an English Londoner and an Indian from Punjab." Yakup Kadri Karaosmanoğlu, *Yaban* (Istanbul: İletişim Yayınları, 1983), 53. The intellectuals felt that "as they went deeper into the country which they call their own, their alienation from their origins grew bigger." In return, the peasants labeled them as "strangers." Should the national struggle end in victory, said Yakup Kadri, then the intellectuals had "to make the nation" by bridging the gap.

71 Davison, *Essays in Ottoman and Turkish History*, 92.

72 The West, which had been a threatening force against the nationalist movements and reforms in the Ottoman Empire, was heralded as a natural ally. Ahmad, *The Making of Modern Turkey*, 41. The national dream was to bridge the gap between the West and Turkey, between the national elite and the local Muslim population, between the economic power concentrated in the hands of non-Muslim communities and the politics centrally controlled by the national elite, and between the authoritarian regime in practice and an image of a civilized democratic republic.

73 Hasan Ünder claims that the philosophy of Kemalism can best be described as pragmatism. He argues that pragmatism has been functional to maintain a distance against the Western techniques and principles that were instrumentalized in government, to sustain a position of being both Western and anti-Western. Hasan Ünder, "Türk Devriminin Felsefesi," *Mürekkep* 6 (1996): 31–48.

74 A Kemalist spokeperson wrote in his memoirs that "to be Westernized meant at the same time to escape from being Arabicized; it meant being Turkified." Falih Rıfkı Atay, *Çankaya* (Istanbul: Doğan Kardeş Basımevi, 1969) 446. Koçak dwells critically on this arguing that the "internationalization" of Turkey was an escape from the East to the West in order to guard against "Arabicization/Calibanization." Orhan Koçak, "Ataç, Meriç, Caliban, Bandung- Evrensellik ve Kısmilik Üzerine bir Taslak," in *Türk Aydını ve Kimlik Sorunu*, ed. S. Şen (Istanbul: Bağlam Yayınları, 1995), 239. The ethnic and religious minorities in the population, such as the Kurds, Armenians, Greeks, and Jews yet established another kind of other, which posed a threat to the idea of a homogeneous national unity.

75 Said, *Orientalism*, 23.

76 Robert Young, *White Mythologies: Writing History and the West* (London: Routledge, 1990), 139.

77 *Occidentalism* has been given different meanings by different scholars. Some employ the term to denote anti-Westernism. For example, in his afterword to the 1995 edition of *Orientalism*, Said talks about the reception of his work by some circles as suggesting anti-Westernism. Said disowns this stance, equating it with Occidentalism. On the other hand, Iranian historian Mohamed Tavokoli Targhi criticizes Said for contributing to the silencing of the other. He studies the self-fashioned experiences of modernity in Iran in the vein of postcolonial criticism. In this context Occidentalism is perceived as a means of reversing Orientalism. Mohamed Tavokoli Targhi, *Refashioning Iran: Orientalism, Occidentalism and Historiography* (Hampshire, UK: Palgrave, 2000). In a similar manner, Xiaomei Chen attends to the question of a "counter-discourse" in post-Mao China by utilizing the term *Occidentalism*. Xiaomei Chen, *Occidentalism: A Theory of Counter-Discourse in Post Mao China* (Oxford: Oxford University Press, 1995). Couze Venn's use of the term, Occidentalism, however, sets another, completely different example. Venn regards Occidentalism in relation to the process of "becoming-West of Europe and the becoming-modern of the world." Couze Venn, *Occidentalism: Modernity and Subjectivity* (London: Sage, 2000), 8. The conception of Occidentalism conveyed in the articles included in James Carrier's book comes closest to my understanding of the term. Carrier says that "Occidentalisms and orientalisms serve not just to draw a line between societies, but also to draw a line

within them . . . this process is likely to be particularly pronounced in societies that self-consciously stand on the border between occident and orient." James Carrier, introduction to *Occidentalism: Images of the West* (Oxford: Clarendon Press, 1995), 22–23. I have developed my framework of Occidentalism in Meltem Ahıska, "Occidentalist Fantasy: Turkish Radio and National Identity" (Ph.D. diss., Goldsmiths College, University of London, 2000).

78　Said, in his introduction to *Orientalism*, mentions his hope that there will be further research tackling those questions left beyond the scope of his own work. He says, "Perhaps the most important task of all would be to undertake studies in contemporary alternatives to Orientalism, to ask how one can study other cultures and peoples from a libertarian, or a nonrepressive and nonmanipulative, perspective" (24).

79　The imagery of Western civilization that appears in Mustafa Kemal's speeches is striking: "It is futile to try to resist the thunderous advance of civilization, for it has no pity on those who are ignorant or rebellious. . . . We cannot afford to hesitate any more. We have to move forward. . . . Civilization is such a fire that it burns and destroys those who ignore it." Mustafa Kemal Atatürk, *Atatürk'ün Söylev ve Demeçleri II* (Ankara: Türk Tarih Kurumu, 1957), 207–12.

80　Ibid., 277.

81　Ziya Gökalp's words are cited in Lerner, *The Passing of Traditional Society*, 136.

82　Şerif Mardin, "Religion and Secularism in Turkey," in *Atatürk: The Founder of a Nation State*, ed. A. Kazancıgil and E. Özbudun (London: C. Hurst and Co., 1981), 209.

83　Benjamin makes a connection between the myth of progress and the eternal recurrence of the new in commodity fetishism. I use the concept of mythical time evoking Benjamin's critique of progress. Walter Benjamin, *The Arcades Project*, trans. Howard Eiland and Kevin McLaughlin (Cambridge, MA: Belknap Press, 1999).

84　Countering Marx's idea of revolutions being the "locomotives of world history," Benjamin says, in his notes to "Theses on History," that "perhaps revolutions are the reaching of humanity traveling in this train for the emergency brake." Cited in Susan Buck-Morss, *The Dialectics of Seeing: Walter Benjamin and the Arcades Project* (Cambridge: MIT Press, 1999), 92.

Haldun Gülalp

Whatever Happened to Secularization?
The Multiple Islams in Turkey

Modernization was supposed to drive away religion, or at least its social and political role. Religion was supposed to become something private, between God and the individual believer. Although this never really happened, at least not uniformly, not everywhere the world, and not even across Europe,[1] it has always been treated as one of the most fundamental axioms of sociology. Moreover, the imaginary secularization experience of the West has also been treated as a normative standard against which the non-Western world has been judged and found wanting. According to Ernest Gellner, for example, unlike other religions, Islam is not conducive to secularization;[2] consequently, Islam has always occupied a central place in the lives of Muslim societies, so much so that "the hold of the religion over society seems interestingly independent of other aspects of society."[3] Likewise, according to Bernard Lewis, "if, then, we are to understand anything at all about what is happening in the Muslim world at the present time and what has happened in the past, there are two essential points that need to be grasped.

The South Atlantic Quarterly 102:2/3, Spring/Summer 2003.
Copyright © 2003 by Duke University Press.

One is the universality of religion as a factor in the lives of the Muslim peoples, and the other is its centrality."[4]

Turkey, however, is often considered as having passed the test of secularization. Thus, in Gellner's words, "Islam is unique among world religions, and Turkey is unique within the Muslim world. . . . Turkey [is] the exception within the exception."[5] Yet this truly exceptional model does not appear to be faring very well lately. The Islamist movement has been growing since the late 1980s, reaching a peak in the 1990s. In 1995, the Islamist political party (Welfare Party) won the general elections, making its leader, Necmettin Erbakan, the prime minister of the country for a period. It was only a short period, however, before the Islamist-led coalition government was removed from power through an indirect intervention of the military in 1997. This sort of intervention was not a new experience for Turkey. As Gellner himself has noted, the army, regarded by all as the guardian of Kemalism, does not seem to hesitate to step in every time a democratic election results in Islamist victory.[6] Hence secularization in Turkey seems to be a peculiar affair. While in the normative model, secularization is supposed to be associated with enlightenment and the freedom of thought, in Turkey it is imposed from above and protected in an authoritarian manner by state institutions, including the military.[7]

But perhaps secularization is not the correct concept to use here. Perhaps the whole discussion about the peculiarities of the Muslim people and of Islam as religion is based on a false premise. Perhaps the reason that Islam seems to play an important role in people's lives is not the centrality of *religion* in Muslim societies, but the role that Islam has historically played in signifying a social and communal identity. This identity aspect of Islam is something inherited by modern Turkey from the Ottoman Empire, notwithstanding the claims of the founding republican elite as to having severed all ties with the past and created a new national identity. It is certainly not unusual for religion to play an important part in the definition of any modern nation's identity;[8] and that Turkey's national identity contains a strong dosage of Islam is well documented.[9] In fact, this should also be clear to Bernard Lewis, who is certainly aware of the conflation between *Turk* and *Muslim* and who actually illustrates this by indicating how the Muslim citizens of Turkey do not even refer to the non-Muslim citizens as "Turks."[10]

But if this is the case, then the discussion ought to take a different direction. For, as a source of identity rather than religious dogma, Islam would normally be free to acquire any set of characteristics in the eyes of the beholder. Individual Muslims, who may even have no more than a superficial acquaintance with the tenets of the religion, may associate Islam with any set of values that they consider worthy—values that may come from identifiably non-Muslim (however that may be determined) material or philosophical sources, but values considered by that individual to be worthy of the social collectivity defined as the Muslim community. In other words, religion may (and often does) present itself publicly not really as religion as we know it (i.e., with its doctrine, rituals, institutions, clergymen, etc.), but simply as a cultural code for a way of life or a cultural frame of reference for a community of people that think of themselves as sharing a way of life.

At a general level, there really should not be much that is surprising in this. If, for instance, an average American refers in conversation to someone in an approving way by saying something like "Oh, he is a good Christian, you can always count on him," neither the listener nor the speaker, nor even the person referred to, has to be Christian (let alone a regular churchgoer) in order for this conservation to take place and for the cultural message to be understood. Or when someone exclaims, "Jesus Christ!" to express shock or reaction to a minor crisis situation, they do not really think that they can summon Jesus Christ to their aid (although that should normally be the aim of the exercise). Again, they do not even have to be Christian themselves in order to do so. At a more concrete level, however, the range of ideas that individuals may associate with Islam may be bewildering. In the same way as in the examples just given, many of the cultural references to Islam in Turkey have little to do with religion at all.

A close inspection reveals that in those cultural contexts in which people may cite Islam to make a statement about a this-worldly phenomenon, Islam may appear as a code for their own political ideas, their own personal philosophy about life in general, or an observation about their social status—in short, anything but religion. But the meaning of this code is usually clear only to them, or to those that they may routinely interact with, and may be completely foreign to an outsider—which may be one reason why Turks appear to be more devout than they really are. In what follows, I illustrate these points by citing examples from two interviews I have made in the course of my ongoing work on modes of secularization and political Islam.

Islam As Class

For the purposes of this discussion, a brief background on the two infor-
mants would suffice. A brother and a sister, whom I interviewed separately,
have both moved to Istanbul from a central Anatolian village. Their father
owned a modest amount of land, placing the family among the better-to-do
in this village that also had many landless peasants working as sharecrop-
pers. But the amount of land owned was not big enough to prevent them
from moving to Istanbul to look for work when their father died and the
land was divided among the many siblings. The mother and some of the siblings have remained in the village. Those who have moved to Istanbul still
benefit from the fruits of their small-scale landownership. My two infor-
mants, whom I will call Ali and Aliye, have both finished primary school
and attended privately organized religious education, a common experience
around the country, that was provided by the locally powerful religious order
(an offshoot of the Naqshibandi, in this case). Now in their midthirties, they
moved to Istanbul during the 1980s and 1990s. This was a period that may
without exaggeration be called the second "great exodus" from the country-
side, the first one having taken place in the 1950s. They did so mostly independently of each other, each with their own family and their own set of
priorities and projects—although, of course, they all link up in the big city,
not only with relatives but also with others from the same village.

I was told that about four hundred families from the same village
migrated to Istanbul within a few years, and they all had similar economic
trajectories. At first arrival, men typically find work as janitors in apartment buildings, which gives the family the opportunity to live in a basement
apartment without paying rent, and women find work as cleaning ladies
either in the same building or elsewhere through word of mouth. They may
move on to better paying (but still insecure) jobs, start their own little business enterprise (as Ali did, to be described later in this article), or remain
in the same job; but, in time, most of them save enough money to buy a
car and a unit in an illegally built apartment building (*gecekondu*) in one
of the working-class neighborhoods of the city,[11] and to send their children
to school, sometimes including university. Most children have ambitions
of upward mobility through education, although only a small fraction can
actually achieve it.

This group of people, including Ali and Aliye, have characteristics typical of the constituency of political Islam, although of course by no means are they all Islamist, nor do they invariably vote for the Islamist party.[12] Almost invariably, however, Islam and what they consider the Islamic way of life is an important part of their identity. Aliye, for example, admits, with some regret, but mostly with a matter-of-fact sense of resignation, that she does not practice Islam as she thinks she should. She only performs the ritual fasting during the month of Ramadan, which is a very popular activity in Turkey anyway, even among the nonbelievers, who sometimes think of it as a righteous method of losing weight. Still, with a tightly worn headscarf and overcoat, her appearance fits the profile of a devout Muslim (or even an Islamist activist), in terms of the prescriptive standards of Turkey's secular regime. From her point of view, however, her appearance is an expression of social identity. Although her husband has been a teacher of the Qur'an, as a qualified member of the religious order mentioned earlier, her own explanation of her appearance makes no reference to the husband's status. She simply says that this is who she is and has been, and that at her age it would be very difficult to change her appearance. Removing the headscarf would imply a radical change in lifestyle and identity and is therefore something she is not about to do, given her social background and community. This is completely understandable, of course, in the same way that it would be, say, for a man who has always worn a necktie at work to stop wearing it or sported a beard all his life to shave it off. But in her case, this mostly has to do with her class position. With that appearance, Aliye could not circulate in many of the public spaces controlled by the military or other bastions of secularism. But, normally, she would also not have any business in those places because of her class position.

This brings us to her use of Islam as a code for class, something she does completely unwittingly. Before explaining that, however, a few words are in order to describe the framework of the conversation. The Turkish Constitutional Court ruled to close down the Welfare Party in January 1998, less than a year after its removal from power by the military, throwing the Islamist political movement into disarray. The same ruling banned Erbakan, the legendary leader of Islamism since the early 1970s, from politics for five years. The Welfare Party was quickly replaced by the Virtue Party, led by people close to Erbakan, but the party was torn by internal fighting and weak leadership. After the Virtue Party as well was closed down by the Constitutional Court in the summer of 2001, the movement produced two new parties with no immediately perceptible ideological differences. The more traditional-looking Felicity Party is led by people who are in Erbakan's inner circle of friends and associates. The more eclectic Justice and Development Party has a younger leadership, with Tayyip Erdoğan at the helm. Erdoğan had become a legend in his own right after winning the mayoralty of Istanbul on the Welfare Party ticket in the 1994 municipal elections and then serving time in prison in 1999 for giving a speech that was deemed to incite hatred and conflict.

Aliye, like many others in her social class and status group, was originally drawn to the Welfare Party because of Erdoğan, rather than Erbakan. Erbakan had been active in politics since the 1970s, albeit without a large following. The Islamist party of the 1970s, the National Salvation Party, was created as an outcome of the conflict between the big industrial and other business interests in urban areas on the one hand and the traditional small-to-medium business sector in provincial towns on the other. The National Salvation Party's constituency mostly represented conservative followers of religious orders and these provincial small-scale business people. The Welfare Party, by contrast, was more radical than conservative, did not exclusively rely on support from religious orders, and had most of its support in big cities. Its constituency included segments of middle-class professionals and marginal workers in big cities, as well as small-scale businesses, which now constituted the most dynamic and export-oriented sectors of the economy.[13]

Moreover, Erdoğan's charisma mostly came from his working-class background, which, far from hiding, he had shrewdly turned into an asset. His background was completely different from Erbakan's. Erdoğan's senior by nearly thirty years, Erbakan was a popular professor of engineering at the prestigious Istanbul Technical University before he entered politics. Although he appeared to be a devout Muslim and a loyal follower of the Naqshibandi order, he also had a distinct taste for expensive clothes and the good life in general. For example, he would often make front-page news for such things as throwing an expensive party for his daughter's wedding. Clearly a very intelligent and knowledgeable man, Erbakan asserted his superiority to people around him. Therefore, an average follower might admire him but could not identify with him. Erdoğan, by contrast, was born to a migrant family in a poor neighborhood of Istanbul; went to a religious high school, which provided a relatively good education for students of humble background; and graduated from the economics department of a second-tier university in Istanbul.[14] Just as Erbakan always emphasized his superior educational credentials, Erdoğan always reminded you of his humble origins. Yet, his story was not one of upward mobility; on the contrary, he always claimed, and still claims, that he never left his working-class origins behind. He often expresses his original identity by explicit verbal reference to the neighborhood in which he grew up and, intentionally or unintentionally, in his implicit body language.

Knowing that Aliye had voted for the Welfare Party in the past and been a fervent supporter of Erdoğan, especially while he was in prison, I presumed that she would vote for him in the upcoming elections, now that he had his own political party and seemed to be doing exceptionally well in the pre-election opinion polls. "No," she objected, "I don't trust him anymore." She went on to explain that although he claimed to be a good Muslim, she was now convinced that he really was not; he was just dishonest. When I asked what led her to that conclusion, she pointed out that he was sending his daughters to the United States for their university education. Aliye's disapproval did not originate from an inherent objection to the United States, as one might be tempted to think (we shall soon see that Turkish Muslims can actually be quite fond of the United States); it rather had to do with Erdoğan's financial ability and willingness to send his children abroad. In response, I pointed out to Aliye that maybe he felt he had no choice, given the ban on the Islamic headscarf in Turkish universities. So maybe he was doing this *because* he and his daughters were good Muslims. In a logically rambling but culturally revealing explanation, Aliye told me why she thought I was wrong.

Her older sister's daughter had just finished university. She had had to face the same pressures because of her headscarf. But, surely, pressure or not, it had been possible for her niece, and many other girls in the same situation, to continue their education, sometimes slipping past the security staff at the university gates into their classes and sometimes wearing a wig over the headscarf to cover it from view (which actually became a common practice after the more strict enforcement of the ban in recent years). The niece had to struggle and it was not easy, but she got through it all and graduated. Yes, still wearing the headscarf, the niece was having problems finding a job now; and if Aliye had a daughter, she would certainly encourage her to remove the scarf, because that would be in her best interest. But what did it mean for Erdoğan to send his daughters to another country, instead of properly waging a political struggle right here to lift this ban for everybody's benefit? Sending his sons for their education might be understandable; but sending his daughters because there is a ban is nothing short of an individualistic solution to a social problem. Besides, where did he find the money to do so? When Aliye's family and other members of her community were faced with the same problem, could they send their kids abroad? This surely was not acceptable; Erdoğan could no longer be considered a Muslim.

In other words, *Muslim* in this context meant "one of us"—a member of our community, someone like us, someone who shares our problems and understands our suffering. *No longer a Muslim* in this context clearly meant a "sellout" in *class* terms. For Aliye, Islamic identity signified class position. She could no longer identify with Erdoğan, so in her eyes he was lying when he said he was a good Muslim. Therefore, she surely could not vote for someone who was lying like all the rest of them. We should also note here that the association between Islamic identity and class position is not a product of Aliye's idiosyncrasy. In a way, it sums up the cultural dimension of Turkey's modernization from above.

Turkey's modernization project aimed at a state-led emulation of Western social structures and cultural practices. The Kemalist leadership had declared the national goal to be the "achievement of contemporary civilization," a formula that equated modernization with Westernization. In this perspective, Islam was considered to represent "a set of traditions, values, legal rules, and norms which were intrinsically non-Western in character" and hence an inherent obstacle to be overcome.[15] In Turkish political culture modernization, development, Westernization, and catching up with global civilization are all interchangeable concepts. The assumption has been that along with economic development, and the urbanization and modernization of Turkish society, cultural practices of the people would evolve toward a Western lifestyle. That is, they would dress in Western garb, develop a taste for Western music, adopt Western architectural styles, read and write in Western alphabet, and so on. Accordingly, the history of the founding decades of the Turkish republic has been one of "state-led modernization," which included both an attempt at planned economic development and the hasty imposition of the above-mentioned cultural practices through government legislation and control.[16]

Moreover, in the Kemalist perspective, what is true for the nation as a whole also applies to the individuals. Thus, while it might be understand-able for "poor and ignorant" villagers to live in an "uncultured" manner, because they might still be under the influence of "tradition," it would be completely unacceptable for an urbanized and upwardly mobile individual to have nonmodern tastes and to pursue a traditional lifestyle, including the overt display of Islamic identity whether in clothing or in the public performance of religious rituals. The economic upward mobility, urbani-zation, and modernization of an individual are also expected to involve a Westernization (and de-Islamization) of his or her cultural tastes and prac-tices. It is on the basis of this rather naive assumption that the traditional-modern dichotomy is juxtaposed with the rural-urban and religious-secular dichotomies, leading to the oft-heard but false argument that political Islam is either a remnant of the backward-looking traditionalism of the country-side or an expression of the reaction of the rural masses to the strain and stress of modernization that they face when they migrate to the big city. In this reasoning, given enough time to adjust, the traditionalists will surely come around and internalize the secular principles of Kemalism.

If this were only a question of poor theory, hurting no one but the theorist, there would be no problem. However, state policy too is based on this mis-guided assumption; and it is this assumption that explains the intolerance of the "secular" regime for those university students who by definition ought to be modern, urban, enlightened, and upwardly mobile and yet wear the headscarf. In fact, it is not uncommon to find in those public offices where headscarves are officially banned, including universities, women workers with headscarves who do the cleaning or work in the kitchen, and so on. But they are tolerated because they are invisible—due to their class posi-tion. It is clear that the headscarf ban in Turkey has little to do with the usual claim that "secularism" requires the suppression of all overt signs of religious commitment in sites of public power, in order to avoid discrimi-nation against the non-Muslim or the nonbeliever. This would be a convinc-ing argument if the ban only applied to, say, professors at state universities. But the same reasoning cannot meaningfully account for the government-imposed ban, in both private and state universities, on a *student's* practice of wearing the Islamic headscarf.

Thus, according to official dogma, the nation's trajectory from Islamic traditionalism to Western modernity is to be replicated in the lives of indi-vidual Turks who come from rural backgrounds to the big city and aspire to upward mobility. As they move up the class ladder, they are supposed to shed their Islamic cultural traditions and become Westernized. Islam in this context stands in for class identity.

Sharia in America

Islam can also be a code for other things. In our first meeting, Ali was some-what apprehensive. Given the government's approach to "Islamism" as a security issue, he did not want to be categorized as an Islamist, which he thought was implicit in my wish to talk with him. Although not an activ-ist in any sense, as the term *Islamist* may imply, he is clearly more devout than his sister and also proud of his religious education. They learned their Qur'an and hadith very well, he explains to me, as young children back home. He has respect for teachers of religion; he still refers to his brother-in-law, Aliye's husband, as *hoca* (esteemed teacher), although the latter no longer serves in that capacity, having been displaced by the religious order for some wrongdoing. Ali further boasts that some of his friends from back then went on to study theology with success, implying that they were so well trained that he too could easily have done the same.

He never went beyond primary school, however, which is unfortunate, for he is clearly intelligent and articulate. The village had only a primary school. To be able to attend the middle and high schools in the nearby town, one needed relatives or family friends with whom one could live. It was also not common for villagers to send their children to school, because the purpose of education was to find employment in government bureaucracy (which actually has always been and still is the most secure, although not lucrative, career prospect in Turkey). Otherwise, the years spent studying were considered a waste. Ali did not need to do this because of the land that the family owned. He could easily earn a living working on the farm, and he did so for many years as a young man. Although he does not make a point of it, he clearly had some savings when he moved to the big city with his wife and children. All of his three children were born in the village; the oldest two also finished primary school there. The children have continued their education in Istanbul, and the oldest one is now preparing for the university entrance exam.

Soon after they came to Istanbul he bought a house in a *gecekondu* neigh-borhood, which he then rented out, and took a job as janitor that provided him a free basement apartment. This way, and with his wife working as a domestic cleaner, he was able to save some more money. He sold the first house that he had invested in and bought a new one in a better neighborhood, in which they now live. After working several years as a janitor, and again with the help of supplementary income still coming from the farm back home, he started his own business, which consists of a small truck with him in the driver's seat. A typical activity in the age of "flexible accumulation," this small business represents the merging of working-class status with entrepreneur status. He hangs out with other truck drivers in a designated location in his neighborhood, waiting for customers in need of moving household items or merchandise. Depending on the quality of the service these drivers provide, they may build a customer base and gain new ones by word of mouth. They are connected to that base through the mobile phones they all carry, now as ubiquitous an item in Turkey as in many parts of the world, yet another technological marvel enhancing "flexibility" in employment and business.

In recent decades, self-employment has grown in both the core and the peripheral areas of the world economy.[17] For example, subcontracting production to self-employed manufacturers, who are in effect workers in the guise of petty entrepreneurs, has become the chief method of achieving what is euphemized as "numerical flexibility," which really means the freedom to fire workers without suffering any consequences.[18] This new phenomenon in the labor market is part of a larger trend that has been described more generally as the rise of "network society."[19] The new trends in the global economy include such things as government deregulation; the breakup of large corporations into smaller and independent units; increased reliance on subcontracting for the production of both goods and services, often across national borders; and the revival of the precapitalist modes of organizing labor along artisanal and patriarchal lines.[20] Many of the recent immigrants into the big cities in Turkey have ended up as "petty entrepreneurs" because they could not find stable jobs in the formal sector. As I have argued elsewhere, political Islam has found a particularly fertile ground in the decline of traditional working-class politics and the rise of petty entrepreneurship.[21]

Given the historical link between big business and the state in Turkey that started in the founding stages of the nation-state and national economy and continues today, notwithstanding radical shifts in the orientation of the economy in the last couple of decades, including those from import substitution to export promotion, from inward orientation to opening up to globalization, and from protectionism to currency convertibility,[22] small-scale entrepreneurs understandably have always felt left out. As I indicated earlier, their reaction to government policy was an important source of support for the Islamist movement in the 1970s. Generally mistaken as a backward-looking response of the small independent businesses to the rapid industrialization process that threatened them with extinction,[23] the Islamist sentiment at the time really expressed a resentment by these businesspeople toward what they saw as unfair treatment. They complained about the channeling of government resources to large and well-connected corporations in big cities, demanding greater protection and support for themselves. They were not opposed to the state in general, or state intervention in particular; they just wanted some of the same for themselves. But in the 1980s and 1990s, the continued blatant reliance of big business on the state, despite the declared new orientation toward free markets, resulted in a clearer perception by the average citizen of the extent of corruption that was rampant among the political elite. Opposition to "corruption" has been a prominent theme in the Islamist political rhetoric and appealed to the religious sensibilities of the people.[24]

Ali, being more circumspect in our first meeting, complained much about corruption, but never linked this to any political view, other than stating more generally that faith and morals have always been important to him. On what at the time appeared to me to be an unrelated topic, he went into some detail explaining his thoughts about Turkey's prospects for membership in the EU. He expressed his belief that the EU did not really want Turkey as a member. He added that, although EU membership may be good for raising economic standards in Turkey, we should also be concerned about losing our culture and identity. He then continued at length about the significance of preserving authentic culture and Turkey's failure in this regard. He stated how the republican ideology had rejected the Ottoman past, resulting in cultural impoverishment. Many of these were ideas that I could hardly disagree with, although he could never elucidate why EU membership would lead to further loss of "authentic" culture. Finally, comparing the EU with the United States, he pointed out that the United States has always been friendlier toward Turkey and that the United States is at any rate superior to the EU. He said that the United States is more democratic and open-minded than the EU, because it is composed of people from many different nations. Moreover, he said, there is real meritocracy in the United States, and no favoritism or corruption.

Leaving aside the question of how accurate these observations were, I never really understood the point of the comparison between the United States and the EU until our second meeting, when Ali apparently felt more comfortable sharing his political views with me. Unprompted, he stated that the real Sharia order was in the United States. Flabbergasted, I asked what he meant by that. He explained that the United States is known for its respect for human rights, freedoms, the value of hard work, and meritocracy. He emphasized again that there is no favoritism or corruption there, but equality of opportunity. Prodding further, I suggested that this may be his own interpretation of the Sharia, which may be different from mine or others'. He readily agreed and offered that this may be one reason why Erbakan's Welfare Party appealed to so many different types of people with religious sensibilities. Everyone had their own conception of the Sharia, he affirmed. Some thought, he went on, that Erbakan was advocating the Iranian model, although Erbakan is too smart to want something like that; he was just going along with them, he explained, in order to capture their votes. So, what was Ali's choice among the political parties? Contrary to what might be expected, he did not support Tayyip Erdoğan. "I am a liberal democrat," he declared. Although he had not made up his mind yet, he was leaning toward the "Liberal Party"—which, as a matter of fact, is libertarian, rather than liberal democratic, and rather reactionary in its political philosophy.

Conclusion

When I asked Ali how significant he thought Islam was as part of his identity, he found the question rather incomprehensible. This reminded me of a sarcastic but angry remark that an Ethiopian colleague had made about how he found out that he was "black" after he began to live in the United States. Still, he added, he had no interest in joining any of the "black" organizations on campus—he could not identify with them. Clearly, self-perception may be very different from the perception of others. Although Aliye did not consider herself a religious person, her vocabulary was such that she expressed issues of community, class, and upward mobility in terms of religion. Ali, on the other hand, did consider himself a religious person, but did not see himself in a community with other Muslims. Turkey is often defined as a predominantly Muslim country; Islamists especially delight in repeating at every opportunity that 99 percent of Turkish people are Muslim. But this is mostly a definition given to them by the secular state. Unless declared otherwise, every child born in Turkey is registered as Muslim and this is clearly indicated in every person's government-issued identity card. Moreover, there is a limit to the choice of religions that could legally be stated in a person's identity card—only those religions officially recognized by the state are acceptable, identifying oneself as "atheist" or even just leaving that box blank is not. "Muslim" is evidently a social identity conferred upon the Turkish people by the "secular" state. These observations urge us to rethink the question of secularization.

Notes

1 See Jose Casanova, *Public Religions in the Modern World* (Chicago: University of Chicago Press, 1994).

2 Ernest Gellner, *Muslim Society* (Cambridge: Cambridge University Press, 1981).

3 Ernest Gellner, "The Turkish Option in Comparative Perspective," in *Rethinking Modernity and National Identity in Turkey*, ed. Sibel Bozdoğan and Reşat Kasaba (Seattle: Washington University Press, 1997), 233–34.

4 Bernard Lewis, *Islam and the West* (New York: Oxford University Press, 1993), 135.

5 Gellner, "Turkish Option," 233, 236.

6 Ernest Gellner, *Conditions of Liberty: Civil Society and Its Rivals* (New York: Allen Lane, 1994), 199–200.

7 Binnaz Toprak, *Islam and Political Development in Turkey* (Leiden: E. J. Brill, 1981); Nikki R. Keddie, "Secularism and the State: Towards Clarity and Comparison," *New Left Review*, no. 226 (1997): 21–40.

8 Benedict Anderson, *Imagined Communities* (London: Verso, 1991).

9 Toprak, *Islam and Political Development*; Baskın Oran, *Atatürk Milliyetçiliği: Resmi İdeoloji Dışı Bir İnceleme* (Ankara: Dost Yayınları, 1988); Etienne Copeaux, *Türk Tarih Tezinden Türk-İslam Sentezine* (Istanbul: Tarih Vakfı Yurt Yayınları, 1998); Kemal Kirişçi, "Disaggregating Turkish Citizenship and Immigration Practices," *Middle Eastern Studies* 36.3 (2000): 1–22.

10 Bernard Lewis, *The Emergence of Modern Turkey* (New York: Oxford University Press, 1968), 15.

11 Illegal construction has been a truly thriving sector in the last two decades. See Ayşe Buğra, "The Immoral Economy of Housing in Turkey," *International Journal of Urban and Regional Research* 22.2 (1998): 303–18.

12 See Haldun Gülalp, "Globalization and Political Islam: The Social Base of Turkey's Welfare Party," *International Journal of Middle East Studies* 33.3 (2001): 433–48.

13 For a comparison of these two periods of the Islamist movement, see Haldun Gülalp, "Political Islam in Turkey: The Rise and Fall of the Refah Party," *The Muslim World* 89.1 (1999): 22–41.

14 The growing literature on Erdoğan's biography includes Ruşen Çakır and Fehmi Çalmuk, *Recep Tayyip Erdoğan: Bir Dönüşümün Öyküsü* (Istanbul: Metis Yayınları, 2001); Muhammed Pamuk, *Yasaklı Umut: Recep Tayyip Erdoğan* (Istanbul: Birey Yayıncılık, 2001); Turan Yılmaz, *Tayyip: Kasımpaşa'dan Siyasetin Ön Saflarına* (Ankara: Ümit Yayıncılık, 2001).

15 Toprak, *Islam and Political Development*, 40. See also Oran, *Atatürk Milliyetçiliği*, 135–40.

16 Bozdoğan and Kasaba, *Rethinking Modernity*.

17 George Steinmetz and Erik Olin Wright, "The Fall and Rise of the Petty Bourgeoisie: Changing Patterns of Self-Employment in the Postwar United States," *American Journal of Sociology* 94.5 (1989): 973–1018; Stephen Crook, Jan Pakulski, and Malcolm Waters, *Postmodernization* (London: Sage, 1992).

18 Anna Pollert, "Dismantling Flexibility," *Capital and Class*, no. 34 (1988): 42–75.

19 Manuel Castells, *The Rise of Network Society*, vol. 1 of *The Information Age: Economy, Society, and Culture* (Oxford: Blackwell, 1996).

20 Bennett Harrison, *Lean and Mean: The Changing Landscape of Corporate Power in the Age of Flexibility* (New York: Basic Books, 1994); Gary Gereffi, "Capitalism, Development, and Global Commodity Chains," in *Capitalism and Development*, ed. Leslie Sklair (London: Routledge, 1994); David Harvey, *The Condition of Postmodernity: An Enquiry into the Origins of Cultural Change* (Oxford: Basil Blackwell, 1989).

21 Haldun Gülalp, "Globalization and Political Islam."

22 See Ayşe Buğra, *State and Business in Turkey: A Comparative Study* (Albany: State University of New York Press, 1994); Ziya Öniş, *State and Market* (Istanbul: Boğaziçi University Press, 1998).

23 See, for example, Ahmet Yücekök, *Türkiye'de Din ve Siyaset* (Istanbul: Gerçek Yayınları, 1983); Binnaz Toprak, "Politicization of Islam in a Secular State: The National Salvation Party in Turkey," in *From Nationalism to Revolutionary Islam*, ed. Said Amir Arjomand (Albany: State University of New York Press, 1984).

24 Ruşen Çakır, *Ne Şeriat Ne Demokrasi: Refah Partisini Anlamak* (Istanbul: Metis Yayınları, 1994); Mustafa Özel, *Refahlı Türkiye* (Istanbul: İz Yayınları, 1997).

Behiç Ak

Humoring the State

Every day during the past twenty years, Behiç Ak's cartoon strip in the daily *Cumhuriyet* has confronted the Turkish people with the paradoxes and absurdities of the lives they lead and the identities they try to inhabit. Ak defines humor as a way of positioning oneself against the existing order. His cartoons do this by producing laughter out of the logical distortions involved in behaving as though the existing order were natural and meaningful. His distinctly personal style combining wit and understatement gives expression to a penetrating critique of the deterioration of values evident in Turkish society during the period following the 1980 coup.

The *South Atlantic Quarterly* 102:2/3, Spring/Summer 2003.
Copyright © 2003 by Duke University Press.

"I'm reading Huntington these days. He says there will be a CLASH OF CIVILIZATIONS in the world. It's a good thing we're not a civilization."

"To tell you the truth, I'm more for Wallerstein's theses."

"Do you happen to have Turkish coffee?"

"I want to go to space when I grow up."

"Then you have to learn English."

"Look mom, an Ottoman!"

"So our Sabri is a Christian, huh? Where did you get that idea?"

"Don't you know? He died the other day, and they had his funeral in a church."

"I'm going through an incredible identity crisis these days. Am I a Turk? Greek? Arab? Or a Byzantian Jew?"

"How's your French? I have a wonderful article on this topic."

"My mother is a pure-blood Albenian."

"My father is a pure-blood Georgian."

"As for me, I am a pure-blood Turk."

"I am totally confused. My family will let me go to university only if I wear the headscarf, and the state will let me only if I don't."

"As a GERMAN NATIONALIST, I am against Turks' being accepted into the EU."

"And as a TURKISH NATIONALIST, I am against Turkey's entering the EU."

"I'm a nationalist, man. If somebody says, the strawberries in your country have hormones, I protest."

"Just as I protest when somebody says there's radiation in your tea."

"If someone says there are no human rights, I protest as well."

"If they say 'there's no law, there's no democracy,' I protest."

"So, isn't there anything you criticize in this country?"

"Of course there is! There's no democracy, the law doesn't work, everything is a pain, there are no human rights, and the strawberries have hormones."

Katherine Pratt Ewing

Living Islam in the Diaspora:
Between Turkey and Germany

Turkish immigrants constitute the largest
minority in Germany. Most first came to Germany as *Gastarbeiter* (guest workers) beginning
in the 1960s and have since established large
communities in many German cities and towns.
The vast majority of these immigrants are
Muslim, though many have an ambivalent relationship to Islam. Their ambivalence is largely
structured out of the particular (and in some
respects peculiar) position of Islam in the discursive construction of Turkey as a secularist,
modern nation. However, in the diasporic setting of Germany this ambivalence about Islam
also resonates in distinctive, surprising ways
with German concerns surrounding the maintenance of a democratic and free society. Public
statements by Germans about Turkish Muslim
practice tend to be shaped, I argue, not by specific threats to the German social and political
order, but rather by fears and polarizations stemming largely from political and social conflicts
within Turkey. These fears have been superimposed on phantasmic images of threats to German national identity that pre-date the arrival of
Turkish guest workers. The most prominent of

The *South Atlantic Quarterly* 102:2/3, Spring/Summer 2003.
Copyright © 2003 by Duke University Press.

these tensions shaping German discourse from within Turkey are based on images of the threat that Islam poses to *Turkey's* identity as a Western country, given that the large majority of all Turkish citizens are Muslim, if only by their cultural and family heritage. But these images of Islam, I argue, are taken up in German public culture and transferred onto Germany itself, so that the visible, practicing Muslim is constituted as a threat to the foundations of German democracy and the German constitution. The phantasmic nature of this sense of threat is suggested when we ask what, in practical terms, this threat could be, given that Germany is a historically Christian country that is now a dominant player in the Western world of democracy and freedom. How could a small Muslim minority undermine the foundations of the German state?

The association of Islam with threat is, of course, all too natural at the turn of the twenty-first century. Today much of the Western world, including some of its most influential leaders, recognizes "Islamic civilization" as the only serious challenge to the hegemony of "Western values," a view perhaps most vividly articulated in Samuel Huntington's vision of a "clash of civilizations," which collapses current tensions into an essentialized age-old struggle between Islam and the West.[1] The view of Islam as threat was dramatically reinforced by the destruction of the World Trade Center in New York, which demonstrated the power of certain Islamist groups to inflict real damage on the West. Practicing Muslims who live in diaspora communities in Europe and North America thus face an issue that most other minorities do not: the fear that they or some of their Muslim neighbors may be the powerful enemy within, a hidden threat to the basic values of democracy and freedom, and, especially after September 11, an immediate threat to the safety of everyday life. While many scholars have denounced Huntington's polarized view of the world and devote considerable effort to demonstrating not only the complex diversity of those who consider themselves Muslims but also the fact that Muslims are full participants in modern society, this view of Muslims as a dangerous enemy threatening the basic fabric of Western political and social institutions clearly affects not only the everyday treatment of Muslims but also the realm of what is an acceptable exercise of government power to curtail not only the activities of Islamist groups but even the rights of individual Muslims.

This all-too-real global threat has obscured and naturalized the peculiar contours of debate surrounding the integration of Turks into German society and the place of Islam in this integration process. In this article, I disentangle the multiple discursive strands that shape debates surrounding Muslims and Islam in Germany, foregrounding the specifically Turkish nationalist and German nationalist components and where they converge. I examine how these two discursive strands are naturalized by the global discourse of Islamic terrorism, and how they are rhetorically superimposed. I argue that despite the principle of religious freedom that Germans understand to lie at the heart of their political and social order, diasporic Turkish immigrants in Germany are constrained in the range of possibilities available to them for taking up or rejecting a Muslim identity. I approach this project by focusing on debates surrounding a specific Turkish "Islamist" group, the Islamische Gemeinschaft Millî Görüş (IGMG), which is said both by German officials and by leaders of IGMG itself to be by far the largest Islamic organization in Germany.

The Problem of Deceit and the Effects of September 11

One of the key terms in the debate is the trope of deceit, which holds that Islamists — defined by the German Ministry of the Interior as those who use Islam for political ends — are to be feared because they practice systematic deception concerning their goals and the activities they engage in to reach these goals.[2] Though this theme had already been prominent in German dealings with IGMG throughout its history[3] and is also a central trope in Turkish discourse about Islamists, it escalated in Germany following the attack on the World Trade Center and Pentagon and the realization that several of the perpetrators had been living unnoticed in Germany as students.[4]

Prior to September 11, I had understood my own project among members of Millî Görüş as an effort to interpret their activities in ways that disrupted the dominant German discourse grounded in the premise of a clash of civilizations. I have seen the frustrations many practicing Muslims face as they seek equal rights under the German constitution, laws, and policy, and I have seen misperceptions on the part of the German media and government as they seize upon issues such as the head scarves of Muslim women as evidence of IGMG oppression of women or the unfair refusal to allow Islamic education in the public schools, though Christian and Jewish education classes are offered.[5] I saw myself as being in a position to make visible to scholars and policy makers the efforts of this organization to modernize and integrate its members into Germany society, a role that members of the organization also saw for me. I was impressed by the knowledge and balanced perspectives of Mehmet Sabri Erbakan, the president of IGMG, and I had been sympathetic to his complaint, made when I met him in the summer of 2001, that the German Ministry of the Interior had kept the organization under surveillance for more than fifteen years, yet every year repeated only vague warnings that its members might be dangerous.

Everything changed after September 11, and I confronted the problem of truth and deception at two levels, the first being my own new questioning of what members of Millî Görüş communicated to me personally (and to German observers) and the second being how the German government and press, from their hegemonic position, used accusations of deception for their own political purposes. IGMG came under intense suspicion from the German government. At first I joined the chorus of people who urged that innocent Muslims must not be subjected to assault or discrimination and that most Muslims viewed the actions of these terrorists or the goals of Osama bin Laden as horrific and anti-Islamic. I was not surprised to receive email messages of condolence from people associated with Millî Görüş, including one from Mehmet Erbakan himself. I was also not surprised that the German government and media had included Millî Görüş in their operations to expose dangerous Islamist groups as an immediate threat. The result has been many newspaper articles, including a prominent article published in the major news magazine *Der Spiegel* in October 2001, presenting startling "revelations" of illicit Millî Görüş activities.[6] The article threw me into a serious dilemma: much of it focused on the Millî Görüş president himself and his "inner circle," accusing him of corruption and hidden motives linked to terrorism that contrast sharply with his public persona. Did this exposé undermine my whole perspective on IGMG and its goals? Even entertaining such suspicions changed my relationship to the predominant German perspective, which I have argued is based on a racist phantasm in which the Muslim is constituted as other. This perspective holds an unyielding suspiciousness of these "Radical Muslims."[7] This problem emerged with a sudden realization that my perspectives on IGMG may not have sufficiently taken into account the possibility that its leaders had systematically misrepresented the organization and its activities to me, given their abiding concern with managing the image of the organization in a German environment.

Since the postmodernist wave in the field of anthropology, anthropologists have been highly sensitive to their power and the effects of their actions and writings on the people they write about. Anthropologists have also become activists, often using their own power to further the political and economic interests of the marginalized people whom they typically study, often writing against governments and the forces of globalization in defense of local communities and indigenous practices. But this stance is more difficult to take for communities that are believed to have "real" power—the power to threaten Western states. My at least temporary solution to a basic disruption of my own moral positioning has been to allow space in my representations of Millî Görüş for the possibility of deception and to trace out the implications of this possibility without simply jumping to the other side and acknowledging that German suspiciousness is really justified. Rather, I examine the underpinnings of this suspiciousness—its genealogy in the discursive regime of the German state, on which is superimposed a structure of suspicion emanating from the discursive regime of the Turkish state, which claims common roots with modern Germany in its enlightenment values of freedom, secularism, and the individual.

With the rise of studies of postcoloniality and with the influence of Foucault, the relationship between power and knowledge has become a key issue.[8] When we foreground questions of power, the problem of lying and deception returns in a new guise: those strategically located speak authoritatively, constituting the truth and the legitimacy of their actions as they speak. From this perspective, "freedom and democracy" must be understood as truths articulated by and serving the interests of a hegemonic discursive regime.

German Discourse

The theme of deceit is particularly evident in concise form in a small pamphlet published by the Bavarian Interior Ministry and distributed to all school children in Bavaria following September 11. Entitled "Islamic Extremism," it was part of a series of pamphlets called "Protect Our Democracy."[9] The pamphlet features a large photo of Osama bin Laden with the logos of three Islamic groups superimposed on the photo, including that of IGMG pasted just beside bin Laden's eyes (see Figure 1). The pamphlet explains that there are seventeen Islamic groups in Germany under the surveillance of the Verfassungsschutz (literally, Protection of the Constitution),

algerischer Zweig der MB die „Islamische Heilsfront"
(FIS) und ihr militärischer Arm „Islamische Heilsarmee"
(AIS), die bis 1997 für zahlreiche Terroranschläge in
Algerien verantwortlich waren. Die „Bewaffnete Islami-
sche Gruppe" **(GIA)** verübt dort nach wie vor Massaker.

Türkische Islamisten

Die **Islamische Gemeinschaft Milli Görüs e.V. (IGMG)**
ist ein Sammelbecken von Anhängern der seit Juni 2001
in der Türkei verbotenen „Tugendpartei" (FP). Die IGMG
erhebt Anspruch auf gesellschaftliche Dominanz und
strebt nicht etwa eine friedliche Koexistenz, sondern die
Vorherrschaft des Islam an. Dazu betreibt sie derzeit
eine Kampagne mit dem Ziel, ihre Mitglieder zum
Erwerb der deutschen Staatsangehörigkeit zu moti-
vieren. Anders als in ihren offiziellen Verlautbarungen
bezweckt sie damit aber nicht die Förderung der
Integrationsbereitschaft ihrer Anhänger. Sie will viel-
mehr mit Hilfe eingebürgerter Muslime in Deutschland
eine eigene Partei gründen und damit islamisch-extre-
mistische Positionen, wie sie von der verbotenen FP
vertreten wurden, im politischen Spektrum der Bundesrepublik Deutschland dauerhaft verankern. Zwar betont
sie nach außen ständig, sie akzeptiere auch eine
nicht-islamische Gesellschafts- und Rechtsordnung;
ihr Leitfaden sind jedoch der Koran und die Scharia.

Der **„Kalifatsstaat" (Hilafet Devleti)** forderte eine
islamische Revolution in der Türkei nach dem Beispiel
des Iran. Mit Aufrufen zum gewaltsamen Vorgehen
gegen den türkischen Staat und zu militanten Aktionen
in der Türkei beeinträchtigte der Verband auswärtige
Belange der Bundesrepublik Deutschland. Kontakte
zur „Al Qaida" des Usama Bin Laden verwiesen auf
ideologische Übereinstimmung mit dessen gewalt-
orientierten antiwestlichen Positionen. Mit Nachdruck
wandte sich der „Kalifatsstaat" gegen die Integration
türkischer Staatsangehöriger in Deutschland. Der Verband wurde Ende 2001 vom Bundesministerium des
Innern verboten.

Emblem der MB

IGMG
Emblem der IGMG

Emblem des
„Kalifatsstaats"

Usama
Bin Laden

Figure 1. IGMG and bin Laden.

the name of an office of the government associated with the Ministry of
the Interior that functions at both federal and state levels and devotes itself
to tracking the activities of a variety of groups, ranging from neo-Nazis to
Scientologists to Islamist groups, regarded as threatening to internal security—and therefore threatening the principles of the post–World War II constitution itself. According to the pamphlet, the seventeen Islamic groups
tracked by the Verfassungsschutz have a total of more than 31,000 members, by far the largest among them being IGMG, with 27,000 members.

The pamphlet then goes on to describe just a few of these Islamic groups more briefly, dividing them into Arab and Turkish groups. A paragraph is devoted to IGMG, which I translate and quote in full because it embodies in concise form several of the discursive moves by which the German government locates IGMG as dangerous:

> The Islamische Gemeinschaft Millî Görüş e.V. (IGMG) is a reservoir of followers of the Virtue Party (FP), which was banned in Turkey in June 2001. The IGMG lays claim to social dominance and does not strive for peaceful coexistence, but rather for the supremacy of Islam. At present they pursue a campaign with the goal of motivating their members to acquire German citizenship. But in contrast to their official announcements, they do not aim at readying their members for integration by this means. Rather, with the help of Muslims who are citizens, they want to found their own party in Germany and by this means to anchor firmly within the political spectrum of the German Federal Republic the Islamic extremist positions that were represented by the banned Virtue Party. To be precise, they constantly stress outwardly that they also accept a non-Islamic social and legal order; their guides, however, are the Qur'an and Sharia [Islamic law].[10]

The structure of this paragraph relies for its impact on the prevailing Western discursive regime that pits the looming threat of Islam against a Western democratic principle: "They do not strive for peaceful coexistence." Here an implicit link with Islamic terrorism is drawn rhetorically, the opposite of peace being, of course, violence. In addition to this attribution of a basic motive to IGMG, there are four somewhat more specific accusations made against the organization. But when closely examined, it can be seen that these accusations are based not on the overt activities of the organization and its members, but rather on an attribution of their covert intentions and goals. Notably, there is no link drawn between IGMG and any of the Arab Islamic groups described as extremist in the pamphlet, aside from the visually powerful juxtaposition of the images of bin Laden and the group's logo.

The first of the accusations made in the paragraph quoted above is that "they strive for the supremacy of Islam." Striving for the supremacy of Islam sounds threatening, when located within a discursive regime in which the West and Islam are locked in a struggle for world dominance. But what does this mean specifically within Germany? Aside from the fact that IGMG has not been associated with any specific terrorist or violent activities, there is little evidence that members of IGMG devote much if any of their efforts toward converting non-Muslim Europeans to Islam, since they focus most of their attention on Turkish immigrants living in Germany and other parts of Europe. The threat to the Christianity of Germany is certainly not at issue. So where does the threat lie? The vast majority of these immigrants already have some sort of Muslim identity. Aside from the implied but never directly stated possibility of a link between IGMG and al-Qaeda, the locus of the threat lies in their growing influence over these Turkish immigrants living in Germany, especially the second and third generations. The key question is whether these second and third generations will retain a Muslim identity. I suggest that, in this discourse, a Muslim identity is seen as incompatible with a German identity. The threat for Germany is that if these Turkish Muslim youth become visibly Muslim, they will challenge Germany's ostensibly secular public sphere. Germany's large population of Turkish youth are safe only if they embrace a secular lifestyle. This logic is one aspect of a discursive regime that parallels the arguments made by Protestants against Catholics in the nineteenth century and against the Jews in the twentieth century.[11]

The second thing that IGMG is accused of is urging their members to acquire German citizenship. This passage represents a shift from prevailing German perceptions less than a year earlier, in the summer of 2001, when government officials I met with accused the IGMG of being unwilling to integrate by becoming citizens, despite what was to me clear evidence of citizenship drives sponsored by IGMG. The organization had created posters (see Figure 2) encouraging Muslims to apply for German citizenship. When I showed several German professional acquaintances one of these posters, most seemed surprised at first and then saw the poster as proof that IGMG is trying to prevent people from becoming German, because the young man pictured holding up his German passport had a full beard. The statement that IGMG members do not really strive for integration is undoubtedly based primarily on the more well-known fact that the organization supports and encourages the wearing of the head scarf by women, a visible marker of difference. This issue of deceptive citizenship has moved into political discussions, to the point of prompting the legal question of whether naturalization can be reversed. In December 2001, con-

Figure 2. IGMG poster encouraging members to adopt German citizenship.

servative Christian Democratic Union chair Angela Merkel publicly stated
to the newspaper *Bild* that "foreigners who adopted German citizenship
only in order to camouflage their membership in fundamentalist groups
should have their German passport taken away."[12]

By 2002, the IGMG citizenship campaign had been recognized, at least
by the Interior Ministry and the Verfassungsschutz, and it had been given
a sinister significance: IGMG seeks to control German politics by establishing an Islamist political party, the third accusation made against them.
Given the size of the Muslim population in Germany (approximately 2.9
million)[13] and the fact that IGMG is only one of several Turkish Muslim
organizations, each of which has a very different membership base and different political allegiances and agendas, religious and political orientations,
often with no sympathy for IGMG and its agenda, the threat of an Islamist
political party to the German state is hardly a credible one. Here we can see
clearly the specter of Turkish politics. The logic of this passage is that if the
secularist government of Turkey found the Virtue Party sufficiently threatening that it took the step of banning it, then people who support this party
and who are at the same time voting German citizens must by extension

be a threat to the liberal foundation of the German Republic. An implicit equivalence is made between the Turkish and German governments. The German government's basic identity is founded on the principle of liberal democracy, which stands as the antithesis of the organizing principles of the Third Reich. The government has banned neo-Nazi parties, justifying such a ban with the argument that the principles of such organizations are fundamentally illiberal and thus cannot be condoned because they are a threat to the Basic Law (Constitution). The passage implies that Turkey, too, is a liberal democracy and that if the Virtue Party has been banned, the ban must have been based on principles similar to those in terms of which Germany banned neo-Nazi groups; that is, the Virtue Party must be illiberal.

The possibility that Turkish government actions against the Virtue Party may themselves be an instance of the illiberal nature of the Turkish government is not prominent in German public discourse. In fact, secularists from Atatürk on have strived not for the peaceful coexistence of Islamic practices and institutions with those of a modernizing nation state, but for the dominance of secularist policies by any means necessary, including military intervention, circumvention of democratic processes, and total government control of religious institutions. This is in part because the principle of secularism (which in the Turkish case involves control of all religious activity) is confused with that of democracy, since both are seen as rooted in the Western Enlightenment. This confusion is reinforced by the fact that Islam and Islamists are painted as the threatening other. If both the Turkish and German governments fear the Islamists, then they have common interests and are somehow the same.

The fourth accusation in the pamphlet is that IGMG uses the Qur'an and Sharia as its guides. This is the final sentence in the paragraph and is presented as if it is the crowning proof of the threat to German democracy. The paragraph does acknowledge that the organization claims a willingness to live in a non-Islamic social and legal order, but asserts that this is a "false claim." IGMG extremism consists, "to be precise," in following the Qur'an and Sharia. The paragraph implies that living according to the Qur'an and Sharia is incompatible with living in a Western liberal democracy, thereby making its own interpretation of the Qur'an, based on the "clash of civilizations" model of Islam and the West. In this statement, the pamphlet actually goes further than secularist discourse in Turkey would.

Though secularists in Turkey also argue that a government based on Sharia is inconsistent with democratic principles, they would not go so far as to say anything against living according to the principles of the Qur'an itself, since to do so would be contrary to a Muslim identity at the most basic level.

Members of IGMG would certainly not deny that they seek to follow the Qur'an and Sharia, but neither would virtually all practicing Muslims. The real issue for the majority of Muslims is how these are to be interpreted in the modern world, and especially in a non-Muslim social order. Members of IGMG, ranging from the president of the organization down to young women who belong to IGMG youth groups, state that most of Sharia is actually consistent with German law. They further argue that some elements of Sharia as it developed in the four Islamic schools of law over the centuries may have been suitable for their times, but that living conditions are different today, making some of the principles of Sharia obsolete.

But it really doesn't matter what members of IGMG do or say because of the trope of deception that runs as a theme throughout the paragraph. It is assumed a priori that these people are dangerous, so that whatever they do that appears to further the integration of their members into German society must be a cover for more sinister activities. And they are seen as dangerous because they have connections with politics in Turkey, which necessarily makes them practitioners of "political Islam." Because of these political ties, which played a much more central role in the Millî Görüş agenda in their early years, during the 1980s, they came under the surveillance of the Verfassungsschutz. The Verfassungsschutz has uncovered no dangerous activities or rhetoric in more than a decade. Indeed, the 1998 Verfassungsschutz report states that the IGMG does not advocate the use of force: "The Islamistic group with the highest membership, the Islamic Community Millî Görüş e.V. (IGMG), is counting mainly on political activities to change the social system in Turkey."[14] Nevertheless, they remain under surveillance, and this fact in itself becomes proof to the German government and the German public that they are a dangerous group.

The Verfassungsschutz concern is with IGMG's social goals: "The IGMG and several other Islamist groups also try to establish a society based on the *Qur'an* and the *Sharia* for their sympathizers in Germany."[15] According to the 1999 report, adherents of Islam believe that their religion can be "freely practiced" only when the governing institutions of the society are themselves dictated by the Qur'an and religious law.[16] In the report's view, the claims by IGMG leaders that their freedom of religion is covered by the Basic Law are incorrect because the Basic Law only covers the freedom to practice religion within a society organized according to secular demo-cratic principles. The report implies that the IGMG's conception of reli-gious practice includes as an essential principle the replacement of secu-lar political institutions by new institutions controlled by Sharia, which is of course incompatible with Germany's liberal constitution. These asser-tions and implications, however, are presented without any evidence that the groups in question actually believe that religious practice necessarily involves a dismantling of democratic governing principles. Instead, the report assumes this to be true and interprets statements by IGMG func-tionaries, on their face identical to the assertions that Christian or Jewish groups might make (for example, "Muslims still have to fight before the courts to obtain basic rights especially as regards the free practice of reli-gion"), as implying this larger antiliberal, antidemocratic agenda. While these implications can be drawn from this quotation, the actual wording, which states that the IGMG is trying "to establish a *society* based on the *Qur'an* and the *Sharia*," (emphasis mine) actually says nothing about their political agenda, since it alludes to a social goal, not a political one. Repeated statements by IGMG functionaries that they do adhere to the democratic order are at least implicitly dismissed by the report. The report implies a conspiracy of silence by Islamic groups, as if they know that their true goals are illegitimate in a Western context and therefore dress these illegitimate goals in liberal Western garb. But what the writers of this report and many other Germans actually fear is that the Muslims will establish ghettolike communities in which they successfully resist complete assimilation into German social life. Members of IGMG argue that their own goal of retain-ing cultural distinctiveness and a Muslim way of life does not violate the German Constitution or laws.

The *Spiegel* Article

I turn now to the *Spiegel* article to demonstrate the logic that links decep-tion and terrorism and how this logic has been relegitimized in the wake of 9/11. The article, published in the October 10, 2001, issue, is a full two pages with pictures, including one of Mehmet Erbakan speaking to several

men in a mosque.[17] The picture itself, while not dramatic, was to me striking, primarily for the stark visual contrasts between Erbakan and the men
to whom he is speaking. The men are all wearing Muslim head covering
and have beards (two features that for the Western public are closely associated with bin Laden). They are all seated on carpets that cover the mosque
floor, shoes removed. The one young man in the photo is in Muslim garb,
while the others who can be seen are in casual clothes that a worker might
wear. Erbakan, in contrast, is in jacket and tie, standing on a low platform,
with no head covering, totally professional in appearance, the fact that he is
not wearing shoes made nearly invisible by an overlay in which Millî Görüş
corruption is diagrammed.

The text creates significance for this photo. It reiterates several times a
structure of stark contrasts between benign appearances and an underlying
reality that is dangerous and alien. It begins, in usual journalistic fashion,
with specific details of a mosque leader (not Erbakan) who feels slandered,
insulted, and deeply injured and wants to take a government official to court
because the official has not apologized for the conduct of the Verfassungsschutz. The article goes on to explain that the mosque had heard a secret
Verfassungsschutz report on Millî Görüş written after September 11. This
report claimed that, though Millî Görüş had outwardly expressed distress
over the attack, the "inner circle" of the group expressed undisguised joy
over the attack against the archenemy United States. After setting up this
dichotomy between outer appearances and inner reality, the *Spiegel* article
goes on to say that the German authorities have found Millî Görüş not
only extremist but extremely wealthy (the link between these two separate
issues being made through the repetition of the word *extreme* (*extremistisch*,
extrem) used in rather different senses. The bulk of the article is actually an
exposé of some shady financial dealings that Erbakan and other people associated with Millî Görüş seem to have been involved in, which were apparently detailed in the Verfassungsschutz report mentioned at the beginning
of the article.

The article tacks back and forth between allegations of terrorism and this
exposé. The next paragraph describes Erbakan (mentioning that he is the
nephew of Necmettin Erbakan, the former short-term Islamist prime minister of Turkey) and his efforts to assure the German government that he
would work with them against the Islamic terrorists. The following para-
graphs cite evidence from local Verfassungsschutz reports (at the level of

the German states) that "cast doubt on Erbakan's sincerity." One of them had reported a letter from a local Millî Görüş youth organization that invited "young mujahideen" to self-sacrifice and martyrdom according to the will of Allah, though it was not stated when this letter or report was produced or whether Erbakan or any other authority within the organization had approved of the letter. The other report, date also unspecified, stated that the "Islamic threat to Germany comes primarily from the political activities of IGMG and their influential and dominant organization." The article also quotes a politician who had stated that "Millî Görüş has systematically lied to the public for years about the real character of their organization and their connection to hundreds of disguised organizations." And then the article segues again into the opacity of their financial arrangements.

While it is true that Millî Görüş has created a number of independent organizations, the connections among at least some of these are known to authorities and are not particularly hidden. I often heard followers within the organization carefully distinguish activities of Millî Görüş itself from independent but linked organizations. It was obvious to me that much of this care to disassociate them was due to the heavy stigma surrounding Millî Görüş, and the network of linkages that I knew about were far from being a network of terror. The kinship tie between the two Erbakans, which has also been a target of controversy, is no secret. While Erbakan did not emphasize it in our conversations, he did not hide it.[18] The photo encapsulated the contrast that was being drawn between Erbakan's Westernized front and the organization's real underlying alienness, revealed not only in the contrast between his professional dress and that of the other men but in the fact that stockinged toes peaked out from behind the inset. Once I had recovered from the shock of the detailed financial exposé, I realized that there was nothing new or substantial in the linkages that both the Verfassungsschutz and the *Spiegel* article had rhetorically drawn between terrorism and deception.

What allowed me to take a position that distanced me from the rhetorical moves of the Verfassungsschutz and of the media reporting on them was the acceptance of the possibility of deceit, or, rather, the normalcy of deceit as a fundamental aspect of interpersonal relationships, especially when power negotiations lie at the heart of these relationships. I do not know whether the allegations of financial wrongdoing on the part of Millî Görüş leaders are accurate or not, and I do not know the extent of Mehmet

Erbakan's personal knowledge or even involvement. But I do know what the concrete effects of his leadership of the organization are, for example, on young women who are learning strategies for gaining independence in their marriages and developing professional careers. I find it difficult to construct a model of Erbakan and his goals in which this policy regarding the education of young women and support for the Taliban and terrorism can readily be juxtaposed. On the other hand, deceit regarding financial dealings is quite distinct and all I can say to this point is, who knows? When I returned to IGMG headquarters the following summer, I spoke with Erbakan and the head of IGMG's legal staff, which spends a significant portion of its time developing lawsuits against newspapers and magazines that slander the organization, which have increased in number since 9/11. The attorney claimed to have won virtually all of their suits thus far. But when I asked about this particular *Spiegel* article, he said that they had not sued because there weren't any specific accusations made in the article, that it was just all innuendo. Erbakan himself did not seem to know what article I was referring to, a response I had to take with a grain of salt.

In Germany, Turkish immigrants as a large population of foreigners play an important double role in current efforts to reconstitute a restored national identity in reunified Germany. First, the image of the Turk has been a target of neo-Nazi extremism, which official Germany, the media, and the general public loudly and visibly condemn, a disavowal that publicly and symbolically demonstrates German guilt and remorse for the inhumanity and racism displayed during the Holocaust. From this liberal positioning, politicians and scholars celebrate the evidence of progress toward assimilation of Turkish youth and debate the best strategies for further facilitating the assimilation process. But there is a second, disguised impulse, not overtly against Turks as a racial or ethnic minority, but against those Turks who are visibly devout Muslims.

The fear of the Millî Görüş has rested on vague images such as the idea that Islamist extremists are operating behind a screen of rhetoric about multiculturalism, human rights, and constitutionality, while they amass a following and resources that will allow them to control government decision making. In a rhetoric closely parallel to talk about the Jews during the National Socialist period, there is talk of Islamists, embodied in the Millî Görüş, infiltrating the spaces of everyday life, gradually corroding public order and space, ultimately imposing an alien totalitarian order in which women lose their equality and civil rights, in which all Muslims, whether believers or not, are subject to barbaric punishments stipulated in the Sharia. The uncanny, surreal nature of German images of the Islamist can be seen in German expressions of fear and suspicion, verging on paranoia, surrounding Islamist efforts to acquire rights from the German government.[19] In the aftermath of September 11, the result of such positioning is the construction of arguments and stories in which the discovery of any evidence of deception or untruth on the part of the other is proof of absolute otherness: members of Millî Görüş are really terrorists and, to quote from the *Spiegel* article, "the primary source of Islamic threat to Germany."[20]

Secularist Discourse in Turkey

As I have already suggested, the German Verfassungsschutz, as well as politicians, many in the media, and the general public are voicing fears that have been shaped by political struggles within Turkey, where secularists, supported by the military, have seriously worried about the possibility of Islamists coming to power through democratic elections. I argue that these struggles have spilled over from Turkey into the diasporic arena, so that the Germans generally sympathize with the Turkish secularists, who are presumed to be representative of Western democratic values.

Kenan Kolat, Executive Director of the Turkish Council Berlin-Brandenburg, in a talk to an American Fulbright Seminar in Berlin in July 2002, discussed the various organizations that work to help Turkish immigrants with integration into German society. Before the talk he was introduced by our German host as *"the representative of the Turks in Berlin."* After his talk, he was asked about the role of Muslim religious organizations in this process of integration and responded, "All the organizations with *Islam* in their titles are usually political organizations. They are not members of the Council—they cannot be members of the Council—though there are individuals who are privately religious who are in the Council. I am religious, but there is no room for an institution between God and me. Germans want a representative, someone they can talk to, but there is no such thing in Islam. The Islamic Federation has fought for the right to give religious classes in the schools, but it is an Islamist organization, dangerous when it comes to integration."[21] (The Islamic Federation is closely tied to IGMG but downplays this tie because of IGMG's status as a group under surveillance by the Verfassungsschutz.)

The model of religious practice that Kolat is publicly presenting here as his personal practice sharply distinguishes "political Islam" and "private" religion. It is also one in which there is no institutional structure at all. The argument that in Islam there is no such thing as a representative is a highly austere one, in the sense that it strips away centuries of Islamic institutional history in one stroke. This particular interpretation of Islam is characteristic of Turkey's secularist elite and is a reflection of the official interpretation of Islam that was developed as an important part of the ideological apparatus of the Turkish Republic.

As Talal Asad has argued in *Genealogies of Religion*,[22] the term *religion* as it is generally used today is a historically specific category that universalizes a Christian Protestant notion of religion. Within this tradition, religion belongs strictly to the private sphere, and people participate as a matter of individual choice. This process of secularization fosters the presumption that "politicized religions" threaten both reason and liberty and are diametrically opposed to the liberal political worldview of modernity. In response to this threat, those who claim a religious identity as a political act, as in the now-global phenomenon of "political Islam," may be accused of not "really" being religious, but rather of manipulating religious ideology for political ends. All of these elements can be seen in Kenan Kolat's response. In this discursive environment, asserting a "private" religious practice, as Kolat did, is itself a political act.

Among Atatürk's first moves as leader of the new Republic of Turkey in the 1920s was the recasting of Islam. During this period Kemalist intellectuals sought to rearticulate a sort of humanistic-nationalistic Islam that would be compatible with Western Enlightenment values and cultural practices. The Republicans explicitly sought to model their interpretation of Islam on the European Protestant movement, drawing "historical parallels, asserting that their revolution mirrors the Protestant battles against Papism in its dislike of intermediaries and direct access to the faith for all."[23] Though the Republicans ideologically advocated an Islam with no institutional mediation between God and the believer, and though they ordered the closing of the Sharia courts and the Sufi Brotherhoods and banned clothing styles associated with Islam (head scarves for women and the fez and full beard for men), they did not simply eliminate all institutional structures. Rather, they replaced the Ottoman Ministry of Religious Affairs with the little-publicized Directorate of Religious Affairs (Diyanet), which was established as a branch of the new government.[24] The Diyanet was and continues to be responsible for administering mosques and providing them with imams.

The paradox of an individual, private Islam in which people ostensibly are free to express their spirituality as they choose but that is administered and tightly controlled by a government department—an official Islam in a professedly secular state—is manifest in state efforts to maintain a kind of orthodoxy. As a result, the contest between Islamists and Secularists in Turkey has been extremely polarized, leaving little public space for an unpoliticized practice of Islam, though the government claims that over 90 percent of the population is Muslim.

Though many left-leaning academics have been critical of the authoritarianism of the Turkish regime, and some are critical of the Diyanet as a violation of the principle of separation between church and state, few question government teachings about the threat of Islamists to the secular state and government regulations such as the forbidding of head scarves in government buildings. When Muslims who support the right of women to wear the head scarf in universities and other government-controlled sites confront these intellectuals with arguments about religious freedom, the response is typically that the head scarf represents the oppression of women, which must be prevented. Most of the academics I have met in Turkey, as well as Turkish scholars living or doing research in Germany, also accept the secularist position that political Islam must be resisted in all forms and by any means.

In recent years the Islamists in Turkey have had considerable electoral success. Necmettin Erbakan, who first entered Turkish politics in 1969 and faced considerable obstacles in his efforts to establish an Islamist party, developed a general platform that he called *Millî Görüş* (national vision), a phrase taken up by the organizers of Millî Görüş in Germany, which eventually became the present organization Islamische Gemeinschaft Millî Görüş. In the 1980s and 1990s, Erbakan became the leader of the Islamist Welfare Party, established a new program, and presented himself as having a "progressive but distinctly Islamic point of view."[25]

In the face of the Welfare Party's overwhelming popular support and of the success of radical Islamist movements in countries like Iran and Afghanistan, the secularists, who had always seen political Islam as a basic threat to the Turkish Republic and its social and political order, were extremely threatened by the rise of the Welfare Party and feared that its goals were as extreme as those of the Taliban and of the Iranian Islamist regime. During Necmettin Erbakan's brief tenure as prime minister (June 1996–June 1997), the military became increasingly alarmed and repeatedly issued warning statements. Two of the steps the military urged for preserving democracy were a ban on propaganda on pro-Islamic television and radio and tighter restrictions on religious dress, an example of doublespeak that few secularist-oriented Turks questioned. Eventually the coalition collapsed under considerable pressure from the military, secularist politicians, and bureaucrats, forcing Erbakan to resign. Shortly thereafter, Erbakan's Welfare Party was banned altogether by the Constitutional Court.[26] The party was later reestablished as the Virtue Party, which was in turn shut down in June 2001.

Though most of Erbakan's and the Welfare Party's specific policies once in power were relatively moderate, Erbakan had been quite inflammatory in a number of his actions and statements as he sought to gain mass support from Turkey's large conservative population, much of which had moved into the major cities from rural areas, thereby changing the cultural and social orientations of the urban electorate. He blamed Turkey's economic condition on a global Zionist conspiracy, for instance, and he called for the harsh criminal punishments specified in the Sharia.[27] Positions such as these made many of the urban middle class, not to mention the secularist elite, afraid of the prospect of an Islamist state in which everyone would be forced to conform to a very conservative version of Islamic practice. In this situation the very meaning of "democracy" was stretched to its limit, with secularists, leftists, and much of the educated middle class being more comfortable with an authoritarian crackdown on Islamists that violated basic freedoms than with the prospect of another Iran or Afghanistan.

Secularists versus Islamists in Germany

This prolonged conflict between the Islamists and the secularists, with Necmettin Erbakan as the central actor, had a transnational dimension. Because of the large flow of Turkish guest workers into Germany and other European countries beginning in the late 1960s, the Turkish government decided to extend Diyanet activities into Europe, making it a transnational organization. A subdepartment of the Diyanet for religious services abroad (Turkish-Islamic Association for Religious Affairs, or DITIB e.V.) was founded in 1971, the beginning of an effort to "prevent opposition forces from exploiting the religious needs of Turkish migrants and mobilizing them against the interests of the Turkish republic."[28] DITIB came onto the European scene rather later than other Islamic organizations and after local Turkish guest worker communities had already established informal mosques and Qur'an schools. The Diyanet appointed its own imams to existing mosques when it could and established new mosques in areas where the Turkish population was growing. In many cases, DITIB has established a rival mosque within the same community as an IGMG mosque or has even managed to replace a Millî Görüş imam with one of its own imams, though the reverse also occurs. The Diyanet disseminates an ideology stressing a unitary Turkish national identity expressed in Islamic language. It presents versions of Ottoman and Turkish history stressing pride in a glorious past and downplaying the differences among the various sects of Muslims in Turkey, stressing that Islam is a religion of harmony and peace.

DITIB has become an umbrella organization that sponsors, finances, and staffs mosques and educational activities in cities with large Turkish populations throughout Europe. But DITIB faces a growing problem in its ability to reach out to the Turkish population in Europe: in contrast to IGMG imams and those of other nongovernmental Turkish Muslim groups, the leaders of DITIB in Germany, like all Diyanet imams sent to Europe, are Turkish government servants who serve in Europe for only a four-year stint and then return to Turkey. This arrangement, which ensures that the Diyanet imams retain their close ties to Turkey, worked well in the early years, when most of the attendees at mosques were Turkish-speaking first-generation immigrants who planned to return to Turkey. But it is now more problematic as the second and third generations grow up. The cultural and linguistic gap between the imams and the population they are trying to reach grows ever wider.

Why has the Turkish government manifested such concern for diasporic Turks and poured so many resources into these diasporic mosques? A key reason is that many political dissidents have fled to Germany and other European countries from Turkey. Because Islamist groups such as the organizations associated with the Welfare and Virtue Parties are tightly controlled within Turkey, many have focused their attentions on the Turkish populations of Europe, where they have had a freer hand to operate. Groups such as the precursor to IGMG initially had very close ties to groups in Turkey[29] and focused much of their attention on supporting political and religious groups back in Turkey. Members of IGMG, most of whom were guest workers who themselves intended to return to Turkey some day, made financial contributions intended to support the Welfare Party and its successor the Virtue Party back home.[30] The Turkish government felt that this powerful influence on Turkish politics had to be countered, and one way to do this was by developing a broad network of mosques itself.

The Diyanet organizations in Europe also seek to influence government policy in the host countries toward the suppression of groups the Turkish government sees as a threat, especially in countries with state-sponsored religious education. They have focused especially on blocking IGMG initiatives to have their Islam courses offered as an option in the German public schools,[31] since this is an activity that directly challenges the Diyanet and its efforts to propagate its specific form of Islamic education.[32] This policy is based on the idea that children are entitled to religious education in their own religious traditions. Diyanet imams have sought to control the content of this religious education for Turkish children and have even sought positions within the German schools. On occasion DITIB officials have also tried unsuccessfully to convince European governments that the other Islamic organizations operating within their territories should be illegal, something that did not actually come to pass in Germany until after the September 11 attacks, when Kaplan's "Caliph State" was banned. DITIB has also played a role in the pressure on the German government to ban IGMG as well, though thus far without success.

At the Intersection of Two Discursive Regimes

In Germany the forces of multiculturalism and human rights discourse have displaced the overtly racist principle of Germanness based on blood, resulting in a change in the citizenship laws, finally enabling people born in Germany whose parents or grandparents came from Turkey to become German citizens. As is the case with the Jews, liberals have managed to broaden the circle of who can be included as "us," extending it to include even assimilated Turkish immigrants. From this liberal positioning, politicians and scholars celebrate the evidence of progress toward assimilation of Turkish youth and debate the best strategies for further facilitating the assimilation process. Secularist Turkish-Germans and their emerging "hybrid" culture, which is often government-sponsored—for example, Turkish hip-hop and rap and youth centers[33] and a renaissance in German cinema spearheaded by German-Turkish directors—are celebrated in the media and taken as a demonstration of Germany's efforts to redefine itself as a multicultural nation. Many of Germany's Turkish youth have embraced this German youth culture that has little room for a Muslim identity. In their discussions of the Turks among them, most Germans are not concerned with the principle of freedom of religion, but concur with the application of an intense pressure to assimilate, viewing any other form of integration with extreme suspicion.

This fear of Islam has generated a collusion not only with Turkish secularists in Germany but also with the Turkish government, which operates directly on German soil through DITIB and its mosques. This collusion is manifested not only in a pervasive suspiciousness and condemnation of explicitly Muslim activities, but also in efforts to create silences that obscure the visibility and importance of Muslim communities and identity in Germany, even among scholars studying the Turkish diaspora and the process of integration into German society. These silences can be seen not only in the nature of research questions posed by scholars investigating immigration and diaspora issues, which tend to focus on problems of assimilation, but also in the explanations for why Muslims are asserting a distinctive identity through the use of visible signs such as the head scarf. These explanations tend to be reductive, explaining ostensibly "religious" practice in sociological terms.

Nevertheless, in a discourse that is reinforced by Turkish secularists and nationalists, who have established diasporic institutions that provide secularist representatives of the Turkish immigrant community who speak to the German press, serve as advisors to politicians, and even serve in local government, the phantasmic, abjected other is the ground on which "Germanness" rests. This other is the devout Muslim, especially the Muslim affiliated with an Islamic organization. This Muslim is seen to have no respect for democratic institutions or religious freedom, no idea of civil society founded on the principle that choice of religion is a private affair, no sense of the individual, and no loyalty to the German Constitution, which has become the object that, according to this discourse, Germans must protect at all costs if Germany is to remain intact. All of these threats to Germanness are thought to be hidden behind an elaborate web of deceit in which every visible activity of an organization such as IGMG has a hidden, sinister meaning.

Conservative politicians have used the visibility of Muslims who wear head scarves or recognizably Muslim dress as a political issue in ways that make particularly visible the precariousness of the notion of "German," its ambivalent links to a disavowed Nazi past, and the threat of the Muslim as the unassimilated other. During the winter of 1999–2000, a flurry of debate surrounded the idea of a German *Leitkultur* (leading culture), which was deployed by members of the CDU (Christian Democratic Party) as a concept intended to generate political support for a policy that would push immigrants toward a more complete assimilation to German cultural practices and ideals. Members of IGMG expressed considerable distress in their monthly magazine (a Turkish-language magazine published in Germany) over the introduction of this concept into political discourse.[34] Both Millî Görüş and liberal German writers have pointed out how empty of content the idea of *Leitkultur* is and suggested that the only content that could currently be attached to it is "multiculturalism." *Leitkultur* is a phantasmic image, embodying a movement of loss and failed or blocked recovery from the horror and guilt of the Nazi era.[35] Every effort to restore a lost Germanness by infusing *Leitkultur* with specific content was immediately repudiated by other Germans because of its association with Nazism and a nationalist identity that constituted the Jew as the enemy within.[36] IGMG leaders also drew immediate connections with Nazi ideology, arguing that this debate is one more manifestation of a discourse of racism. As fear of the Muslim other escalated after September 11, these echoes of the treatment of the Jews during the National Socialist period grew even louder.

This leaves Turkish immigrants with little leeway to practice their religion and few choices for how to maintain a Muslim identity. Most Germans who are not regular churchgoers still claim a Christian identity and many retain the possibility of being buried in the Church. They have Christian institutions to fall back on, including religious education in the public schools and a public organization of space and time that is implicitly Christian. For instance, one is not allowed to speak loudly or to run loud machines such as a lawnmower on Sunday mornings, yet church bells ring loudly all across town. And the church is an architecturally distinct form that is highly visible across the urban landscape.

In contrast, many Germans would prefer that Muslims have no visible religious institutions at all, and there have been various means taken to block them. As a result, Turks have lacked local accommodation of Muslim daily practices. An American reporter told me in 1999 that he had been planning to do a story on why there were no mosques in Berlin despite the large Muslim Turkish presence, but he decided against writing the story when he learned that there are actually many mosques, only they were invisible to the uninitiated observer, since they were located in old factories and warehouses.[37] The first "real" mosque in Berlin—that is, a domed structure with minarets—is currently under construction. It is sponsored by DITIB. Its builders faced considerable obstacles. Arguments against the mosque included objections that such a mosque would disrupt the Berlin skyline, being a constant and permanent reminder of the presence of foreigners in the heart of Germany. People were also concerned that Muslim practices associated with the mosque—such as the call to prayer—would disturb the peace. In Berlin, compromises on the height of the minarets and the volume of the call to prayer were reached, and construction has gone ahead. One of the compromises was on the location of the mosque. Instead of being located in a densely settled Muslim-majority neighborhood that would be easily accessible, DITIB was forced to build it in a relatively unpopulated area of Berlin, tucked between an airport and a large city park.

Reinforced by pressures and warnings from the Turkish government about the dire threat that the Turkish Islamist organization IGMG represents, the German government has operated under the idea that practicing Muslims threaten a secular public sphere. Yet the only specific content that the Verfassungsschutz reports have identified is that the goal of IGMG is to change the rules shaping the German public sphere so that Muslims have the freedom to live their own lives in a manner consistent with their interpretation of the Qur'an and Sharia. The imams of IGMG have issued fatwa-like rulings (i.e., interpretations of Islamic law for a specific situation not covered in the Qur'an or existing law) that clearly accommodate daily practice to the realities of the German lifestyle and the legal system. Though the Verfassungsschutz acknowledges that IGMG operates only through legitimate, nonviolent channels, the phantasmic fear is that IGMG will succeed in creating some kind of Islamic state in Germany.

The discursive formation which links fundamental but disavowed understandings of German racial identity with equally powerful fears of Islamic terrorism that are shared by many Germans as well as by many German Turks pervades everyday life in such a way that it hegemonically naturalizes difference and discrimination, making them nearly invisible even to those with liberal good intentions, in a manner analogous to ways that racial discrimination continues to be reproduced in the United States despite overt efforts to eliminate it.

Notes

I would like to thank the American Academy in Berlin and the Fulbright Commission for their support of the research on which this essay is based. I would also like to thank Yektan Türkyılmaz for his thoughtful reading of an earlier draft.

1　Samuel P. Huntington, *The Clash of Civilizations and the Remaking of World Order* (New York: Simon and Schuster, 1996).

2　The Federal Ministry of the Interior is loosely the equivalent of the American FBI or, perhaps more closely, of the new U.S. Department of Homeland Security. According to Interior Minister Otto Schily, the ministry's primary responsibilities are the protection of the Constitution and the prevention of crime. See www.eng.bmi.bund.de.

3　The first Millî Görüş organization was founded in the German city Braunschweig in 1976 under the name Türkische Union Deutschland e.V. After several restructurings, it was given the Turkish name Avrupa Millî Görüş Teşlikatleri (European National Vision Organization, or AMGT) and established its headquarters in Cologne in 1985. The name was changed to the half-German name Islamische Gemeinschaft Millî Görüş (IGMG) in 1995, when its extensive real estate holdings were spun off as a separate organization. See Eberhard Seidel, Claudia Dantschke, and Ali Yıldırım, *Politik im Namen Allahs: Der Islamismus—eine Harausforderung für Europa*, ed. Ozan Ceyhun (2000), available at www.aypa.net.

4　These students were Arabic-speaking members of al-Qaeda, which has to date no demonstrable links to the predominantly Turkish IGMG.

5　See, for example, Katherine Pratt Ewing, "Legislating Religious Freedom: Muslim Challenges to the Relationship between 'Church' and 'State' in Germany and France," in *The Free Exercise of Culture: How Free Is It? How Free Ought It to Be?* ed. Richard A. Shweder, Martha Minow, and Hazel R. Markus, a special issue of *Daedalus* 129.4 (2000): 31–54.

6　Michael Fröhlingsdorf, "Gold im Gepäck," *Der Spiegel*, October 10, 2001, 46–48.

7　Katherine Pratt Ewing, "Religion and Racism: 'Germanness' and the Islamic Threat As Phantasm" (paper presented to the Franklin Seminar, Duke University, May 4, 2001).

8　See Michel Foucault, *Discipline and Punish: The Birth of the Prison*, trans. Alan Sheridan (London: Allen Lane, 1977).

9　"Islamischer Extremismus," Schützt Unsere Demokratie: Bayerisches Staatsministerium des Innern, 2d printing, January 2002. The copy I have was given to me by an IGMG lawyer.

10　Ibid.; my translation.

11   See Ewing, "Legislating Religious Freedom," 39.

12   Merkel was quoted by Justus Leicht ("German Government Bans Turkish Islamist Group," World Socialist Web Site, www.wsws.org/articles/2001/dec2001/germ-d19_prn. shtml, December 19, 2001). Leicht, drawing out some of the implication of this statement, suggested that "either, for political reasons, legally recognized Germans could lose their citizenship, or that citizenship would come in two classes: one for naturalized foreigners and another 'genuine' form, i.e., those who are German through blood. Both alternatives recall the attitudes of the Nazi period."

13   Euro-Forum, Center for Strategic and International Studies (CSIS), "Islam in France and Germany," www.csis.org/europe/frm990412.html, March 6, 1999.

14   Federal Office for the Protection of the Constitution, *Federal Ministry of the Interior Annual Report—1998*, 102, available at www.eng.bmi.bund.de/downloaden/10269/ Download.pdf.

15   Ibid.

16   Bundesministerium des Innen, *Annual Report of the Office for the Protection of the Constitution: 1999*, available at www.eng.bmi.bund.ed/downloaden/10268/Download.pdf.

17   Fröhlingsdorf, "Gold im Gepäck."

18   In addition to this kinship tie to a prominent Turkish politician, Mehmet Erbakan's personal ties to Germany are unusually strong: both his mother and his wife are of German descent.

19   I hasten to add that analogous phantasms of Islamist terror can readily be seen in the United States, and in France and other European countries. But in each case, these images must be interpreted within the specific local and national contexts out of which they emerge.

20   Fröhlingsdorf, "Gold im Gepäck."

21   These comments were made in a talk to the Fulbright German Studies Seminar, "International Migration and National Identities," June 11, 2002, in Berlin. In most states of Germany, a choice of Catholic, Protestant, or Jewish religious education is offered in the public schools. Muslims are gradually winning the right in a few states to have Islam included in the curriculum.

22   Talal Asad, *Genealogies of Religion: Discipline and Reasons of Power in Christianity and Islam* (Baltimore: The Johns Hopkins University Press, 1993).

23   Shankland, *Islam and Society*, 23.

24   See Ronnie Margulies and Ergin Yildizoğlu, "The Political Uses of Islam in Turkey," *Middle East Report*, no. 153 (1988): 12–17. Even schools for training imams were closed until the late 1940s, when it became evident that the mosques, which were under government control, would eventually need replacement imams and that the government would need to provide schools for training them if religious practice and doctrine were to remain under government control.

25   Shankland, *Islam and Society*, 90.

26   Ibid., 111.

27   Necmettin Erbakan, *Adil Ekonomik Düzen* [The just economic order] (Ankara: Refah Partesi, [n.d.]), excerpted in Shankland, *Islam and Society*, 209–14.

28   Nico Landeman, "The Islamic Broadcasting Foundation in the Netherlands: Platform or

Arena?" in *Islam in Europe: The Politics of Religion and Community*, ed. Steven Vertovec and Cari Peach (London: Macmillan, 1997), 220.

29 In their early days they also had a more radical element, whose most visible faction was led by Cemaleddin Kaplan and split off in 1983 to eventually become the Caliph State (Federation of Islamic Associations and Communities [ICB]). This group renounced all ties with Millî Görüş and denounced the organization as infidels for their compromises with Western society. Following September 11, this group was banned in Germany and its members were threatened with deportation, though none had been charged with any specific crime.

30 One young man who was in high school in Istanbul during the mid-1990s when the Welfare Party was so successful in winning elections recalled to me how frightening it was to see TV images of what seemed to be huge numbers of Turkish workers living in Germany whom Millî Görüş had flown home just to vote. It indicated to him how fanatic and wealthy Millî Görüş was.

31 See Ewing, "Legislating Religious Freedom."

32 Ali Gitmez and Czarina Wilpert, "A Micro-Society or an Ethnic Community? Social Organization and Ethnicity amongst Turkish Migrants in Berlin," in *Immigrant Associations in Europe*, ed. John Rex, Daniele Joly and Czarina Wilpert (Aldershot, UK: Gower, 1987), 86–125.

33 Ayşe S. Çağlar, "Popular Culture, Marginality, and Institutional Incorporation: German-Turkish Rap and Turkish Pop in Berlin," *Cultural Dynamics* 10.3 (1998): 243–61; Levent Soysal, "Diversity of Experience, Experience of Diversity: Turkish Migrant Youth Culture in Berlin," *Cultural Dynamics* 13.1 (2001): 5–28.

34 Ayhan Candan, "Entegrasyonda İçi Boş Bir yeni Boyut: 'Deutsche Leitkultur" [A hollow new dimension in integration: German leading culture], *Millî Görüş Perspektive*, no. 72 (December 2000): 12–13.

35 Marilyn Ivy writes of an analogous phenomenon in Japan, where Japanese "traditions" are rediscovered as a way of constituting Japanese national identity following the ruptures of World War II. See Marilyn Ivy, *Discourses of the Vanishing: Modernity, Phantasm, Japan* (Chicago: University of Chicago Press, 1995).

36 For instance, *Heimat* (homeland) calls up images of forests and lederhosen, but these images readily translate into the trappings of neo-Nazism, as in the 1984 film *The Inheritors*, directed by Walter Bannert. An extended debate about *Leitkultur* can be found at www.leitkultur.de/main.html.

37 See Ruth Mandel, "A Place of Their Own: Contesting Spaces and Defining Places in Berlin's Migrant Community," in *Making Muslim Space in North America and Europe*, ed. Barbara Metcalf (Berkeley: University of California Press), 147–66.

Tanıl Bora

Nationalist Discourses in Turkey

October 29, 1995, Republic Day; Istanbul, the center of the celebrations and the scene for an "olympiad" of Turkish nationalism. In line with the Olympic creed, "The most important thing is not to win but to take part," all existing types of nationalism were present: under the umbrella of the governorship's organization (or "impresarioship") and to the familiar strains of the Tenth-Year March, the nationalism of the state. Caught between the choices of taking shelter beneath that umbrella or opening their own umbrella, turned upside-down, and getting soaked in the meantime, "Kemalist" "left-wing" nationalism, with its "ability to interpret," tries to find an eave under which it can give meaning to the "pomp" of the ceremony by calling it secularism. Idealist nationalism with its triple crescent flags and its wolf's-head signs, now mixes with any crowd.[1] "Neo"-nationalism, with its "modern" and ideology-free panorama, exhibits itself through the codes of the pop singer cult and the hedonism of urban youth. All these types of nationalism, since then, have increasingly interfused. In this article, I try to

The *South Atlantic Quarterly* 102:2/3, Spring/Summer 2003.
Copyright © 2003 by Duke University Press.

analyze the elements of this complexity, which ultimately reinforces the hegemony of nationalism.

Factors That Accelerated Turkish Nationalism in the 1990s

Turkish nationalism gained momentum in the late 1980s and early 1990s. This development took place parallel to the nationalistic wave rising throughout the world, and particularly in the triangle formed by the Balkans, the Middle East, and the Caucasus, of which Turkey is the point of intersection. Globalization, in a way that is actually not at all paradoxical, encouraged or incited nationalism: because altering frontiers and military conflicts became possible again after the collapse of bipolarization; because minorities and human rights have become diplomatic issues; because transnational processes of economic—and geographical—deregulation have upset the structures of the nation-state. These factors have affected the ideology of Turkish nationalism in a way that ratifies and contemporizes its reactionary patterns; for modern Turkey, established during a grave crisis in which its very existence was threatened,[2] has a nation-state tradition that subsequently perceived surrounding countries as a severe threat rectified by the Cold War. This condition regarding survival and threat had a considerable effect on the way in which Turkish nationalism and the Turkish national identity took shape. The fact that globalization challenges the nation-state can easily be perceived as the modern version of a centuries-old threat toward Turkey/Anatolia, thus reinforcing this mindset. The Kurdish issue no doubt plays the leading role in this perception of the challenge posed by globalization as a part of this ongoing process, which started with the Crusades and extended to the "Oriental Issue," the Western influence and Westernizing reform policies which caused the downfall of the Ottoman Empire, and the Treaty of Sevres, which—temporarily—buried the hope to found a new state that would rise from the ruins of the Ottoman Empire.

Another factor that afflicts the conscience of the Turkish nation is that the rise of the crisis regarding survival and threat occurred immediately after a course of self-confidence that was not properly enjoyed. Turkey had entered the 1990s with a boom of self-confidence. Capital accumulated thanks to the new right-wing economic policies in the 1980s, the progress made in merging with the flow of global capital, the fact that consumption had become modernized and widespread: all these fostered hopes of graduating economically to the "world's top league," as media commentators call it. By the end of the 1980s, when Turkey applied for full membership in the EU, the prevailing feeling was that the goal of attaining the "rank of modern civilization," cherished since the founding of the Republic, had finally been achieved—or at least this belief was shared by the pro-Western elite and the urban middle class. The neo-pan-Turkist perspective that focused on an economic "rationality" espoused by the Turkic republics, which had won their independence after the fall of the Soviet Union, reinforced this feeling.[3] The historical and cultural legacy of the Turkic republics, regarded as a hinterland from the point of view of official nationalism, were considered to be an additional guarantee for Turkey as it sought to bond to the West without losing its own authentic identity. Turgut Özal, prime minister of the "Motherland Party" ANAP's powerful liberal-conservative government of the 1980s, with a conception of a Turkish-Islamic-Western synthesis far more forceful than that of his predecessors, was also a symbol of the period's wind of optimism and self-confidence. Özal had the opportunity to repeat the Turkish right-wing politicians' buzzwords such as "great Turkey" and "powerful Turkey" in a relatively "realistic" context; at the beginning of the 1990s, an assertive catchphrase, "The twenty-first century will be the Turkish century," was added to these mottoes.

The Gulf War can be seen as a turning point, when the atmosphere of self-confidence and optimism started to fade and when the transition began. The Gulf War was experienced in Turkey alternating as, on the one hand, "national strategy" plans to "develop" in terms of influence, prestige, and geography and, on the other hand, the fear that the surrounding noose of threat would tighten and that Western hegemony, both in the region and in the country, would increase. The formation of a Kurdish state in northern Iraq after the war, and, moreover, the momentum of the Kurdish nationalist movement in Turkey proved the pessimists right and gave the fundamentalist/essentialist factions the opportunity to raise their voices. With Turkey's policies regarding the Kurdish issue restricted to the fanaticism of the "military solution"—while its entire "democratization" program remained under the embargo of these policies—the pressure it faced on the European platform was used by the radical nationalists to corroborate the argument that Turkey was confronted with a conspiracy.

Two other factors played a part in the eroding of Turkey's self-confidence and the increasing concern for the survival of the nation. One was the gradual revelation that the Turkic republics were not primitive and loyal states that considered Turkey to be their unconditional leader; that Turkey was equipped with nothing other than "Orientalist" prejudices in terms of knowledge about the Caucasus and Central Asia. The second was the spiral of economic crises that engulfed Turkey, now entirely dependent on the whims of free-flowing international capital, and that in 2001 brought the country to the brink of disaster comparable to that Argentina experienced. Eventually, as of the middle of the 1990s, Turkey, which had entered the 1990s with the slogan "The Twenty-First Century Will Be the Turkish Century," came face-to-face with the gravest depression in the history of the republic.

From the 1990s to the beginning of the twenty-first century, two dynamics were at play in the shaping of Turkish nationalism. One is a reactionary nationalistic movement that uses the theme of national survival in a dramatized way—this movement not only strengthens the opposing radical nationalistic movement, but also influences right-wing politics, and even, increasingly, the center-left-wing; furthermore, it dominates the army, above all, but also the state elite. The second is a pro-Western nationalistic movement (reminiscent of the nationalism of the late 1980s and early 1990s) which believes that the nation's best interest lies in merging with the globalization process and in harmonizing with civilization—in fact, its proponents are from the rising segments of the new urban middle class, the internationalizing sectors of big capital, and the media elite. In order to analyze the interplay between these two movements one must consider Turkish nationalism not as a homogenous discourse, but as a series of discourses and a vast lexis. I distinguish four main nationalist languages that speak using this lexis. The first is the language of the official Kemalist nationalism (ADD, or Atatürk nationalism), focused on the mission to build and perpetuate the nation-state; in one respect, this is the root-language of Turkish nationalism. The second, which can be considered a dialect of this root-language, is "left-wing" Kemalist nationalism (*ulusçuluk*).[4] The third, while being a liberal dialect of the Kemalist root-language, grows and develops under the spell of the promises held forth by the era of globalization; it is the language of a pro-Western nationalism advocating "civilizationism" and prosperity. The fourth, again a deviate dialect of the Kemalist root-language, is the language of the racist-ethnicist Turkish nationalism that derives from neo-pan-Turkism and from the reaction to the Kurdish nationalist movement. In the event that Islamism, which is currently expanding, merges with a nationalistic discourse, another dialect will be entering this family of languages. Below I discuss these four or five nationalistic dialects, as well as their verbal and visual elements.

Official Nationalism: Atatürk Nationalism

"Atatürk nationalism," the official nationalism of Turkey since the founding of the republic, is in a crisis due to the difficulty of balancing the tension between a "French-style" conception of nationalism, based on the principle of citizenship and territoriality, and ethnicist variations ("German-style" nationalism). Ziya Gökalp's synthesis, based on cultural identity, rested on an extremely delicate balance between a territorial conception of nationalism based on citizenship, handed down from Ottoman patriotism and the conceptions of nationalism that emphasize the nation's uniqueness and eternal existence. The official ideology may well be in line with nationalism based on the principle of citizenship; but in foreign disputes, in "national causes," and even, for instance, in the domains of popular culture such as international sports competitions, an ethnicist, "essentialist," aggressive language of nationalism can easily make itself felt. We can assume that the instinctive, if not conscious inclination to which the advocates of the official ideology are predisposed leans toward keeping the nationalistic model's duality latent, but keeping it all the same, for this duality and tension help extend their margin of political and ideological maneuvering.

Official nationalism, with its ideological ambiguity, thoroughly depends on the existence, power, and manifestations of the nation-state, its symbols and rituals, its pomp and omnipresence. The army, as the crystallized evidence of the existence, power, and manifestations of the nation-state, takes on a central role in the regeneration of official nationalism. Owing to the requirements of the ideology of vigilance and the automatic system of perceiving threat internalized by all armies, and specifically as a consequence of the "state-founding military" character of the TSK (Turkish Armed Forces), which are identified with Mustafa Kemal and his mission, the army considers itself to be the "true owner" and personified symbol of nationalism. Official nationalism, whose core is the army, has a mental perspective focused on the state itself and on populist attributions of heroism.

The definition of *nation* in a publication by the General Secretariat of the National Security Council as "one of the constituent elements of the state" and the expression "The state's indivisible identity with the country and the nation," a favorite among official refrains, both constitute avowals of the state-centered conception of nationalism. An important feature of the language of official nationalism is that its ritualism is far too rigid, cold, and stereotyped, and that its "enthusiasm" remains artificial. Official nationalism is "exhibitionist." It invades political rhetoric with its cliché vocabulary. In public life there is a frenzied consumption of symbols of the nation-state such as the national anthem, the effigy of Atatürk, the flag, and the star and crescent. Although this situation is not always directly related to the pressures or "incitements" of the state, it is at any rate encouraged by the rigid control the state has over civil society.

During the 1994 crisis, the symbols of the nation-state and the phraseology and images of official nationalism were diffused to an even greater extent. The Turkish flag was ubiquitous. People attached stickers of the Turkish flag to their license plates. Star-and-crescent-shaped necklaces and badges were especially popular. Certain singers and models decked their costumes with the star and crescent. Pretexts to sing the national anthem multiplied. While it used to be played in soccer stadiums only before games in which the national team appeared, the spectators started to stand and sing the national anthem before every league match. It could even be heard before pop concerts and at the opening of fashion shows in luxury hotels. Facing the economic crises of 1994 and 2001, both the government and business circles evinced a heroic nationalistic discourse: national-progressivist slogans were coined, such as "The Economic War of Independence," "All for Turkey," "Striving for Turkey," and "For Turkey, with a Good Will." The rise of the "Islamist" movement compelled official nationalism to emphasize the image of Atatürk in its repertory; and the portrait of Atatürk, which became a kind of logo, was displayed at every opportunity.

Kemalist Nationalism (*Ulusçuluk*)

Kemalism, which was questioned to a great extent among the leftist public opinion of the 1980s, flourished anew among the social democratic intelligentsia of the 1990s. The neo-Kemalism of the 1990s, besides constituting a reaction against the neo-right-wing hegemony and particularly against the

Islamist movement, had been incited by the anti-Kemalism these movements shared. Neo-Kemalism maintained that Kemalism had been cast out by the right-wing, who "watered it down" by putting their own people in permanent governmental positions after the September 12, 1980, coup, so that it was therefore no longer an official ideology. Thus, in the beginning, Kemalism stood relatively distant from the state and constituted a more "civil" tendency compared to what it had been in the 1960s. On the axis of this movement, which could be considered as the demand for a Kemalist revision, stood the secularist reaction opposing the rise of Islamism. During the last two years nationalism has come to the fore, with the realization that it could serve to popularize secularism, which is the chief cause. Because of the great disquiet that the neo-Kemalist movement felt in the face of the danger that the Sharia (the rule of Islamic law) would be reinstituted, the functionality of nationalism also depended on the need to seek support from the state and the army (on the "interest" certain of its elements would show anew in authoritarian state-controlled solutions based on the army). The fact that the Atatürk motif became incredibly widespread as official nationalism became excessively demonstrative gave rise to the hope of "transmitting" Kemalism by way of nationalism.

The nationalistic (*ulusalcılık*) discourse that the neo-Kemalist wave has acquired from the left-wing Kemalist discourse of the 1960s and 1970s is a version of ("Atatürkist") nationalism that claims to be left-wing. This claim is based on the neo-Kemalists' appropriation of the humanistic-universalist branch of Turkish nationalism, which is based on citizenship and territoriality. But it overlooks and cloaks the ambivalent character of Turkish nationalism; furthermore, to the extent that it insists on the dissimilarity of Kemalist nationalism from other nationalistic movements, it regenerates the nationalistic ideologies of essentialism and uniqueness. In the 1960s and 1970s, the chief principle of Kemalist nationalism, and the fundamental basis of its claim to be left-wing, were antiimperialism and the stand for independence. In the 1990s this was replaced by secularism, and at the beginning of the twenty-first century, the motifs of antiimperialism and independence once again became marked by the influence of the antiglobalistic discourse. This left-wing nationalistic discourse, while expressing its opposition to the Arabs and Iran, both of which it reduces to a symbol of political Islam, exhibits a stance that is racist, disparaging, and Orientalist. Bülent Ecevit, the prime minister of the "social-liberal-nationalistic" coalition government formed after the 1999 elections, typically represents the stance of proindependence left-wing nationalism; the anti-Western motifs, autarkist "national pride," and xenophobia in this posture are striking.

The Kemalist nationalistic discourse construes nationalism as the advocate of the process of secularization/modernization. And the fact that the term *ulusçuluk* is preferred to *milliyetçilik* is a part of the design that equates the concept with modernization and secularization. The term *millet* designates the religious community in the Ottoman language; the modern term for nation, *ulus*, prevents the connotations of belonging to the Muslim community (*ümmet*) that the Ottoman term implies. In building the nation-state in Turkey, nationalism has followed a course that aimed at taking over the monopolized sacredness of the nation-state and replacing religion with it. The efforts to "nationalize" religion are an even clearer indication of this desire; Kemalist nationalism, whether by recollecting the single-party Kemalist period when the call to prayer was given in Turkish, or by considering the Alaouite religion as a kind of "Turkish Islam," tends toward a kind of "Islamic-Lutheranism."

Liberal Neonationalism

Official nationalism has a strong modernist-Westernizing vein. Together with Kemalist nationalism, the movement I defined as "liberal nationalism" is also an offspring of this vein: this is a discourse that interprets modernization using the ideology of economics, and that emphasizes the progressivist-developmentalist aspect of the process of modernization. We can say that the ideology of liberal nationalism matured toward the end of the 1980s, through the progress of the capitalization/modernization process in Turkey.

The liberal nationalistic discourse defines national identity in terms of its fervor and ability to attain the level of the "developed" or wealthy countries of the world: the West. It explains "national pride" not through the nation's unique, authentic characteristics but through its capacity to harmonize with universal standards—the essentialist nationalistic discourse, of course, fancies this harmony to be an inborn trait "intrinsic to us." Such a nationalistic concept, which is tied to the Kemalist goal of "attaining the rank of modern civilization" and deems this vital for nationalism, was potentially present in the liberal and social democratic circles in Turkey.

The dazzling aura of the globalization discourse made this concept more manifest and turned it into an ideological discourse. The liberal nationalistic discourse emerged as the progression toward an oratorio after the self-confidence prelude mentioned at the beginning of this article. The most influential advocate of this discourse is the media, which is intertwined with big capital. Economics holds a privileged position in liberal nationalism. As is well known, creating the national market may be the most important function of nationalism; it is only natural that a liberal type of nationalism should emphasize this function. However, this is the "cold" and scheming aspect of nationalism, which really does not befit its enthusiastic character. As a matter of fact, even the National Economy movement, which emerged at the time the Turkish nation-state was founded, justified its goals through factors external to economics while completely transforming the economy into a vehicle. The economical dimension of nationalism has been able to become a verbal-visual entity through the populist progressivist discourse of the DP-AP (the Democratic Party and the Justice Party) tradition. As for a more weighty position, it has been able to acquire this only recently, as the ideology of economics became hegemonic, and also because Turkish capitalism's progress in interfusing with the global economy was "worked into" the collective consciousness as a national achievement. The liberal discourse can now speak with enthusiasm and pride of the "marketing and cultural unity of frozen foods, telephone ads and soccer games."[5] Now, the performance achieved in exports, the rise in consumption and standard of living, the fact that "our government bonds are eagerly bought on the Tokyo stock exchange"[6]—in short, the dynamism of the economy—are treated as the factors that most flatter our national pride. The incredibly enterprising energy of the "Turkish people," which was revealed with the liberalizing of the economy, is lauded as an extremely valuable national characteristic. Even the examples of anomie and vandalism generated by the inconsistencies of a sacralized economic entrepreneurship are sometimes tolerated because they are considered to be the side effect of a "healthy" potential booming with the desire to change and develop (a sort of "new blood").

A radical variation of liberal nationalism, interfused with the ideology of economics, is the neoliberal chauvinism of prosperity. This attitude, which violates the idea of social solidarity by its reluctance to share with "underdeveloped" regions or communities the prosperity it produces itself, is akin to "class racism," which excludes lower classes by viewing them as backward and "of no breeding" and branding them as a different race.[7] Certain symptoms of this variation of prosperity chauvinism and class racism can be seen in liberal nationalism in Turkey. Some examples are the Aegean businessmen demanding financial federalism in 1994 because they were unhappy about having "Ankara" "laying hands" on the wealth they were producing, or the villagers who owned land in the economically developing regions being the strongest advocates of privatization because they considered workers and civil servants "parasites," or the Europeanized urban upper middle classes (Euro-Turks) that have "caught up with the EU norms," educationally, professionally, and in terms of consumption, as well as with their good manners, cultural interests, and even "biological standards" (light complexion, tall stature, and other physical "acquisitions"), who distinguish themselves as the elite group that represents the nation's essence, as opposed to the impoverished lower classes, which they see as a hindrance to entering the EU. When the reactions of class egotism are shaped into nationalistic patterns, they can form the nuclei of the variation in question. The stance that sees "parasites" gnawing at economic prosperity, as personified by the Kurdish immigrants who come to the western regions for work and as refugees from the war, can easily ally the chauvinism of prosperity with nationalistic radicalism.

One very important source of pride for liberal nationalism is the degree to which the domestic market merges with the global market and becomes identical to world markets. This best manifests itself in the field of consumption. In this day and age, the indicator of the "rank of modern civilization" is consumer culture, which is also a sign of "universal culture." Neo-nationalism has buried the slogan of old-style nationalism, "Local goods are the goods of the Turks, every Turk should use them"; it takes pride in seeing in Istanbul "brands that are cousin to those one can see in Paris, in Washington, in Tokyo," in catching up with the universal "aesthetics of store windows and shopping."[8] It glories in providing, in tourism, "not just nature and history, as it did in the past, but also entertainment," and in having achieved an "international lifestyle" with credit cards, bars, discos, McDonald's, and international pizza chains—for these all mean that we are a "country that has attained a philosophy equivalent to that of the West, and a similar level of institutionalization."[9] This language of nationalism resembles that of advertising, which is a sine qua non rite of consumer culture.

The civilizationist discourse of liberal nationalism, which adapted to market fetishism the ideal of "attaining the rank of modern civilization" inherited from Atatürkism, defines a cultural identity in terms of its ability to "achieve" and "catch up with" the modern lifestyle. Such merits as being open to the world, enjoying the pleasures of life, and mastering the tools of the "information society" such as computers and the English language, are lauded as the values of the "new Turkish" identity. Hadi Uluengin extols the victory of the Efes Pilsen basketball team over Panathinakos in Athens because "basketball is without hesitation the sport of urbanites and of the cities." He believes "my country has cast off its *çarıks* [rawhide sandals], and become a dynamic society in basketball shoes; it has graduated from the stagnant soil to the swishing *basket.*"[10] The figure that acts as national hero for the "new Turk" or "Euro-Turk" (or the "white Turk," in the words of those who oppose this discourse critically) is youth—particularly urban upper- and middle-class youth. At any rate, urban youth is the most dynamic consumer of the modern/global lifestyle and of its distributor and simulator, the media. Urban youth is integrated with modern culture in Turkey as much as in the West—indeed, even more vigorously and creatively—and their physical appearance is a source of pride in the "new Turk." Ertuğrul Özkök, the editor-in-chief of *Hürriyet*, one of the mouthpieces of liberal neonationalism, is also the apostle of the good tidings that "the Turkish populace is becoming more comely."[11] Özkök, describing a soldier who lost his leg in the southeast, draws attention to "his very slender face set off by thin wire-framed glasses; the portrait of the changing, modernizing new Turkish youth."[12] He describes Sabahattin Öztürk, who won Turkey its first world championship in wrestling in twenty-three years: "Contemporary and good-looking. No mustache, strongly built, young and modern. . . . Our Sabahattin is more handsome, more modern, more contemporary than his counterparts in the West."[13] The civilizationist discourse of nationalism, which in its entirety is the "local" product of cultural discrimination or cultural racism as practiced in the West, will also lead to the eugenic tendency of neoracism in the event that it gets carried away by the enthusiasms embodied in the assertion "the Turkish populace is becoming more comely."

In a development parallel to the fact that consumer culture is the most valid indicator of "the rank of modern civilization," popular culture is replacing "high culture," as various forms of mass culture come to dominate "national culture." Liberal nationalism gives its due to this change occurring in the stock of nationalism's potential images; it transfers the "fervor" of nationalism to the world of popular culture. The position that Turkish pop music has acquired in the ritual economy of neonationalism reflects this tendency. The narcissism that manifests itself in the "I love you so much" messages that stars and admirers exchange as a kind of credo for pop music rites is transferred to a sort of national narcissism through the liberal nationalistic discourse. Narcissism intermingles with hedonism. Özkök, again advocating this neonationalism, preaches a "civil," entertaining national self-confidence that appeals to everyday life, and which has no truck with "gray colors, grave speeches," or politics: "Turkey's indestructible strength, its somehow persisting stability [which also manifests itself in pop music—T. B.] lies in this passion to live."[14] The liberal nationalistic discourse, with its narcissistic and hedonistic character, stands aloof from the rigidity of official nationalism on the one hand, and from the fanaticism of ethno-essentialist nationalism on the other. In contrast to the anachronisms of these types of nationalism, it presents itself as the nationalism of the twenty-first century: a sterile nationalism, without complexes, which isn't formalist, which has dissociated itself from populism and the rural world, and which does not transform national altruism into masochism. The leading exponents of this discourse support terminologies such as "constitutional citizenship" or "Turkish nationalism" that have nothing to do with the ethno-essentialist line; but while doing this, they take care not to depart from the aura of sacredness that is part and parcel of traditional nationalism. Özkök, for instance, has used the story of the guitarist of a heavy metal group from Istanbul who died while fighting the PKK in the southwest as proof that neonationalism is not at all lacking in patriotism. The liberal neonationalistic discourse is not only compatible with such causes and taboos of official nationalism, it can even transform and appropriate its basic themes. For example, the "renaissance of Turkish music," which pop music is believed to have achieved, is celebrated as the realization, in the dynamics of the market and on the "civil" level, of the Gökalpian East-West synthesis, something the state was not able to bring about with its cultural policies: "Turkey has finally found the magnificent synthesis that it had been looking for since the nineteenth century. We are discovering how to experience the East with the rhythm of the West."[15] Or, pop star Tarkan "is the first full-blown megastar of the East-West synthesis, uniting Turkish people of all ages. . . . The new music that gushes forth from Tarkan's unbuttoned shirt is the first sign that an exodus that had rejected the East without being able to set foot in the West, a mental migration, an aesthetic nomadism is achieving a transition to sedentary life."[16] The language of liberal neonationalism speaks a loose discourse; it is not yet articulate. For this reason, it can easily succumb to the hegemony of other nationalistic discourses. However, due to its capacity to address a large audience, it still has a chance to assert its domination in the modernization process. And Turkey's goal of entering the EU now introduces the necessary grounds to encourage the growth of this language of nationalism.

Turkist Radical Nationalism

Pan-Turanist/Turkist nationalism is a perverted branch of official nationalism. It is a fascist ideology founded by the Turkist intelligentsia, which has pursued the idea of the racist-ethnicist vein of Atatürk nationalism to its extreme. It departs from the patriotic/"Anatolianist" line of official (Atatürkist) nationalism in that it accepts the entire territory inhabited by people of Turkic descent as its homeland. In terms of the conception of an organic and authoritarian society, or of cultural essentialism (the ideal of becoming pure Turkish), one may say that the difference between this type of nationalism and the official nationalism of the period remains on a quantitative level (on a scale of moderateness-extremeness). As for a historical conception based on imagining an eternal national existence or the conception of a "national religion," these are the points where Turkism and official nationalism are able to agree. After the tension between the pan-Turanist/Turkist movement and official nationalism reached its peak during the World War II years, in 1944 Turkey joined the Western Alliance with "urgent haste" and the Turkist movement was reduced to an intellectual movement that could be considered marginal. In the 1960s, a new course was plotted by the idealist movement and the MHP (Nationalist Movement Party) formed by Alpaslan Türkeş, who merged the legacy of the Turkist movement with a nationalist-conservative reactionary potential created in the 1950s, founded on an anticommunist fanaticism. On the ideological level, racist motives lost ground and a new nationalistic discourse based on cultural-historical essentialism developed. This development, which intensified in the 1970s, in the late 1970s and early 1980s went so far as to assert that Islam is the primary and even principal element of national identity. Following the military coup of September 12, 1980, the dominance of Islamic identity increased to a great extent. Also questioned was the rationale whereby the state undertook the mission, prior to September 12, of acting as a de facto militia. During this period, pan-Turkist themes also became blurred.[17] With pan-Turkism becoming "rational," but especially with the reactionary nationalistic wave that arose against the Kurdish national movement, a new transformation took place in the 1990s. The idealist movement, both as original defender of pan-Turkism and by supporting the state morally and materially against Kurdish "secessionism," rehabilitated its relationship with official nationalism and drew closer to the political center. At the same time, it strengthened its cultural and popular ties.[18] By losing its "extremist" aspect it became "normalized." Within this development, the MHP rapidly grew stronger, increasing its votes from 2.9 percent in 1987 to near the 10 percent threshold required to enter the parliament in the general elections of 1995; finally, it took part in the coalition government by garnering close to 18 percent of the votes in the 1999 elections.

One aspect of the ideological change that the idealist movement went through with the transformation of radical nationalism in the 1990s was "re-Turkicizing." Pan-Turanist/Turkist literature, which had become marginalized since the middle of the 1970s, was revived during this period. References made to Turkish mythology and ancient Turkish history multiplied. The totem of original ("first") Turkism, the *bozkurt* (gray wolf), regained esteem both as a symbol and as the name of the young idealist movement, *Bozkurtlar* (the Bozkurts). Another development that occurred on the ideological level as a natural consequence of re-Turkicizing was the reduction of Islamism to the position of a subordinate/secondary component of national identity. Other factors of this transformation are as follows: the rivalry between the Islamic and the nationalistic movement became more severe because the Islamic movement grew and became a hegemonic power; the Islamic movement (and the Islamic countries) compete in the Turkic republics with the influence Turkey enjoys there; the MHP now echoes official nationalism and this draws it closer to a secular position. Even though the MHP did not strongly support the February 28, 1997, process in which the Islamic party RP (Welfare Party) was removed from (political) power through the initiative of the army, the MHP did give the state implicit approval with the aim of winning the trust of the regime. This approval reinforced the secular tendency of the MHP, which paralleled the MHP's adoption of Atatürk through depicting him as an uncompromising Turkish nationalist, and as a Turkist who was not loath to espouse the pan-Turkist utopia.

One very important development was that from the beginning of the 1990s the young idealist nationalistic movement, which had a fanatical, "harsh" character, reached out beyond the limits of its traditional constituency and began displaying its repertory of symbols outside of its inner circle. The movement started finding sympathizers among the young urban upper-middle-class constituency and reaching modern youth who listened to rock and pop music. The popularization of the idealist-Turkist symbols and the modernization tendency of the idealist movement's young constituency enabled links to form between this movement and the wind of liberal nationalism.

While this expansion opened a new field for the movement, it also constituted a problem for the MHP, because of the modernization of nationalism within its own constituency and the danger of the party's disarticulation. From the organizational point of view, it was difficult to absorb the conflicts between the traditional constituency, which has stronger religious proclivities, and the dynamics of the new urban-modern constituency. And from the ideological point of view, the party felt the anxiety that the rigid essentialism of the Turkist movement could be destroyed by the ways in which the identity of official nationalism and especially liberal nationalism were perceived. The latter they found to be more "lax," and they thought there was a risk it would shift toward cosmopolitism and become nonnational in character. The problems caused by this tension undoubtedly played a part in the MHP's poor showing in the 1995 general elections, in which it could not make the 10 percent threshold. After the death of Türkeş, whose emphasis of the "modernizing" image of his party had been somewhat exaggerated, Devlet Bahçeli took over the presidency of the MHP; his extroverted, relatively "moderate" image rendered the traditional proclivities of the constituency more harmonious and rehabilitated the internal relations of the organization; this paved the way for the success of the MHP in the 1999 elections.

In general the MHP showed a "low profile" during its coalitional governance from 1999 to 2002. It was important for the party to gain the confidence of the powers of the regime (the army, bureaucracy, big capital). In addition, anxious to "quietly" satisfy the mass constituency comprised mostly of the lower middle class, the party tried to expand its clientele. What is first striking in the ideological articulation of nationalism are the MHP ministers' sallies, which could be called naive and symbolic. Examples are statements about how "yogurt was invented by the Turks," the labeling of local plant and animal species with Turkish names, and the cool reception given to the foreign aid provided during the great earthquake of 1999, with the concern that it was a vehicle of "foreign interference" or even "espionage." Apart from this, two important matters that challenged the MHP's own specific conception of nationalism were whether the death sentence of the PKK leader Abdullah Öcalan would be carried out or not, and the legal measures necessary for Turkey to become a member of the EU. On the Öcalan matter, the MHP leadership supported the execution of Öcalan, because they see him as personifying the entire responsibility for the "Kurdish problem," which in any event they codified as the "problem of terrorism." Nevertheless, during their coalitional governance they consented to not having the sentence executed. This consent, which they justified in terms of not wanting "to put Turkey in a difficult position on the international front," was a part of the MHP's absolute loyalty to supraparty "state policies" and its strategy of earning trust in the eyes of the establishment. As for the goal of entering the EU, also designated by the establishment as a supraparty "national policy," the MHP does not oppose it; however, it interprets EU membership as a transitional step in Turkey's march toward the status of "great power" or "world power." The party insists, therefore, that the EU must not prevent Turkey from pursuing its aspirations of being an "eternal historical nation." On the other hand, the MHP spokesmen kept on interpreting the EU's supranational legal arrangements toward integration as undermining the foundations of the nation-state, and beyond this as a natural continuation of Europe's ancient plans specifically aimed at partitioning Turkey. As a matter of fact, in the summer of 2002, the MHP voted against the EU harmonization laws in parliament, going against the national left-wing/liberal-conservative majority of the government of which it is a part. The MHP's strategy on the eve of the November 2002 elections fit a reactionary and autarkist line opposed to integration with the EU.

Nationalism in Islamism

After the 1980s, Turkish modern Islamist intellectuals developed a radical criticism of the nation-state and of nationalism. In the traditional Islamist discourse the Muslim community (*ümmet*) stands above the nation. Still, one cannot overlook the strong nationalistic implications in the discourse at the center of the Islamist movement in Turkey, which includes the RP, MSP (National Salvation Party), FP (Virtue Party), SP (Happiness Party), and AKP (Justice and Development Party, or "white" party). The ideology underlying this type of nationalism envisages Turkey as the potential leader of the Islamic world and union. Within this context, the nostalgia for the Ottoman past can become a modern and nationalistic imperial (or irre-dentist) fantasy.[19] Anti-Western xenophobia is the common denominator of Turkist nationalism and Islamism. The specific point of Islamism is that it assumes religious identity to be the differentiating element, the back-bone of the nation and of "being national" (*millîlik*). In view of this, Islam (actually, "Turko-Islam") is viewed as the core of authenticity of the Turkish national identity.

Another ideological denominator linking the main Islamistic movement with official modernist nationalism is progressivism-developmentalism. The RP leadership, comprised of the Muslim technocratic elite and the new Muslim bourgeoisie, lauding "heavy industry" as opposed to "financial speculation," is a faithful disciple of the "cause for national progressivism." This vein creates the possibility for a bond to form between the national-istic elements within the RP-centered Islamist movement and the liberal nationalistic discourse.

Hybrid Languages and the Problem of Hegemony

Each type of nationalism involves articulations, osmoses, and syntheses alongside its "Eastern" and "Western," ethno-essentialist and civil aspects. In Turkey, in this ambiance where the nationalistic language and its differ-ent dialects are in progress, such cross-breedings prove to be fruitful and complex. Positions known as left and right can come together on the com-mon ground of nationalism. And the most striking "fusions" or meetings derive from the transfer of the verbal-visual universe of nationalism to the field of popular culture. Many national symbols become a kind of "pop" coat of arms, and thus can be worn relatively independent of a specific political meaning. National symbols become trademarks, and their consumption is engendered. Thus, a dual process begins. On the one hand, nationalistic "exhibitionism" dominates the everyday and public arenas, and on the other, by "becoming pop" it becomes tamed.

This broad and disorganized lexicon created by the plurality of nationalistic discourses gives rise before all else to a great swarm of words, a nationalistic hubbub. Nationalism's tyrannizing discourse dominates politics and everyday life. Nationalism's monopolizing logic expands to the utmost, generating an introverted fervor and violence, arousing hostility in the political opposition, insisting on national unity as a dogma that singles out political subjects, and turning the "shared good" into something otherworldly. And the struggle for hegemony, which arises in the different nationalistic discourses as they aim to show that they themselves are the "true" nationalism, above all reinforces the pressure of nationalism's structural logic.

Within the struggle for hegemony, because liberal nationalism is far from being complete ideologically and as a doctrine, it has a power that may not be visible but is actually very influential. This is why it covers most of this article; this dialect tends to form the dominant pattern of the Turkish nationalistic discourse. All languages of nationalism become apt to join this discursive system, regardless of the themes and material they use. But a handicap of the language of liberal nationalism is that it appeals to the "winners" of this process, and it is not likely that it can convince the "underclasses" during difficult economic situations; this is why it probably will find it necessary to join other nationalistic languages—by making concessions from its own discursive system. Under these circumstances, official nationalism and Turkist nationalism will continue to make themselves felt because they are more complete ("ready") discourses and because of the "maturity" of their reflexes in the face of burning national issues.

—Translated by Linda Stark

Notes

1   The nationalists who call themselves "idealist" (*ülkücü*) in Turkey are the radical right-wing pan-Turkist faction originating from the Idealist Hearths founded in 1969 by student supporters of the MHP (Nationalist Movement Party) to spread the nationalistic

consciousness and raise individuals committed to their race, religion, and culture. In this text, and whenever the "idealist nationalists" in Turkey are concerned, the word *idealist*, while bearing these connotations, should be thought of in terms of a highly enthusiastic attitude toward this pan-Turkist movement.

2 Tanıl Bora, "Turkish National Identity, Turkish Nationalism, and the Balkan Question," in *Balkans—A Mirror of the New International Order*, ed. Günay Göksu Özdoğan and Kemali Saybaşılı (Istanbul: Eren Yayıncılık, 1995), 101–20.

3 Tanıl Bora and Ömer Laçiner, "Die Turkrepubliken und die Turkei: Der zweite Anlauf," *Zeitschrift für Türkeistudien*, no. 1 (1995): 115–38.

4 There are two terms for *nationalism* in Turkish. *Milliyetçilik* derives from the Ottoman word for "nation" (and also for the religious community), *millet*; it is a more common equivalent. *Ulusçuluk* derives from the modern Turkish word for "nation," *ulus*, and is preferred by the left-wing nationalists. In this text, where Kemalist nationalism is concerned, the term refers to *ulusçuluk*; in all other cases the term *nationalism* refers to *milliyetçilik*.

5 Hadi Uluengin, *Hürriyet*, August 24, 1993.

6 *Hürriyet* headline, May 13, 1993.

7 See Etienne Balibar and Immanuel Wallerstein, *Race, Nation, Class: Ambiguent Identities* (London: Verso, 1991).

8 Ertuğrul Özkök, *Hürriyet*, December 19, 1993.

9 Güneri Civaoğlu, *Sabah*, August 13, 1993.

10 Hadi Uluengin, *Hürriyet*, November 27, 1993.

11 Ertuğrul Özkök, *Hürriyet*, November 4, 1992.

12 Ibid.

13 Ertuğrul Özkök, *Hürriyet*, August 29, 1993.

14 Ertuğrul Özkök, *Hürriyet*, May 30, 1993.

15 Ibid.

16 Ertuğrul Özkök, *Hürriyet*, July 3, 1994.

17 Tanıl Bora and Kemal Can, *Devlet Ocak Dergah* (Istanbul: İletişim Yayınları, 1999).

18 Tanıl Bora, "Der 'Nationale Reflex': Die fundamentalistische Disposition des Nationalen in der Türkei und der proto-faschistische Nationalismus der MHP," *Sociologus—Zeitschrift für Ethnosoziologie und Ethnopsychologie*, no. 1/2 (2001): 123–39.

19 Tanıl Bora, "Istanbul of the Conqueror: The 'Alternative Global City'—Dreams of Political Islam," in *Istanbul: Between the Global and the Local*, ed. Çağlar Keyder (Lanham, MD: Rowman and Littlefield, 1999), 47–58.

Ayşe Buğra

The Place of the Economy in Turkish Society

In the 1980s, Turkey, like many other countries similarly situated in the world economy,[1] had changed its economic strategy from a protectionist model characterized by heavy state intervention to a more outward-looking and market-oriented one. This change is often interpreted in terms of a basic dichotomy between the state and the market, and in this article I explore the changing place of the economy in Turkish society to highlight the limitations of the dichotomy in question.

"The place of the economy in society" is a phrase introduced and used by Karl Polanyi to investigate the basic coordinates of the livelihood of the individual in society.[2] For Polanyi, economy is "an instituted process," and the way it is instituted in a given society can be analyzed by looking at the relative importance played by the integrating principles of exchange, redistribution, and reciprocity in the allocation of resources. *Exchange* denotes the nonenduring and unbinding relations between anonymous individuals on competitive markets. *Redistribution* characterizes the role that the state plays in the economy via taxation and government spend-

The *South Atlantic Quarterly* 102:2/3, Spring/Summer 2003.
Copyright © 2003 by Duke University Press.

ing. Exchange and redistribution acquire their significance in the formal and legally binding context of market allocation and state intervention, while reciprocity is, in its nature, personal and informal. In general, relations of reciprocity follow the family metaphor in their different manifestations among fellow townsmen, neighbors, religious or ethnic community members, or within mafia-like organizations formed to realize illicit gain for their members.

This theoretical approach guides Polanyi's account of the nineteenth-century market economy as a unique and unnatural phenomenon incompatible with human society. This observation does not refer to the economic role played by markets in many different societies in history, but approaches the market society as one where the economy as a whole is instituted as a series of self-regulating markets. In an attempt to develop this idea, Polanyi highlights the qualitative difference between exchange on the one hand, and redistribution and reciprocity on the other. The supporting institutional patterns of the latter are not only, or primarily, economic in nature. Hence, the state and kinship or community exist prior to, and independently of, whatever economic roles they play. On the other hand, market, the supporting institutional pattern of exchange, is solely economic in function. In a setting where resource allocation takes place primarily in self-regulating markets, economy appears "disembedded" from society. Such a self-regulating market economy implies the commodification of land, labor, and money. This, for Polanyi, is an unusual state of affairs, which (a) could not spontaneously occur without deliberate intervention and (b) is bound to exercise a disruptive impact on the social fabric. Exchange, in other words, could hardly form the basis of social integration and should be complemented with either one or both of the two other integrating principles for the formation and containment of the market. On the basis of the nineteenth-century circumstances he has investigated, Polanyi mainly discusses the way redistribution has assumed this double task and reciprocity receives limited attention in this regard.

However, state intervention could at times leave a large area of regulation to networks of social relations, as in the case of many late-industrializing countries of the twentieth century. In this case, the principle of reciprocity indeed plays an important role in defining the place of the economy in society and shaping the nature of rights and entitlements of people, as illustrated by the Turkish case. But the case of Turkey also shows that reciprocity relations, where they play an important economic role, tend to permeate market exchange and state intervention, shaping the formal framework of the latter in conformity with their informal and personal character. In Turkey, in the post-1980 period, this particular way of instituting the economy has undergone a certain transformation without, nevertheless, leaving its essentially reciprocity-based character. What I am suggesting here is that the degeneration of state-business relations in this period, often explained by using terms such as *corruption* and *cronyism*, could be analyzed by observing the changing role of reciprocity relations in economic life. Especially after the financial crisis that hit the country in February 2001, the socioeconomic order in question has proven to be increasingly unsustainable. The discussion presented in this article develops this observation and highlights the obstacles faced by the attempts to build a formal redistributive framework in which people's entitlements would be redefined as citizenship rights.

Reciprocity As the Main Principle of Socioeconomic Integration in Turkey

In the 1980s, the emphasis of the problems engendered by heavy state intervention was central to economic policy debate in Turkey. Market reforms undertaken in this period had, as their main point of reference, the necessity of a new strategic orientation involving the retreat of the state and advance of the market. Yet, a closer look at the structure of employment and the nature of state involvement in the economy could easily reveal a different set of problems that the desired transition to a market economy had to address. For large segments of the population, it was neither their opportunities at the market place nor their rights as citizens, but their position in family or family-like relationships that defined the basic coordinates of economic life. In a parallel fashion, the role of the state in the economy had a personalized character, with rule-based, formal mechanisms of intervention often dominated by ones conforming to the informal principle of reciprocity.

In 1980, over 50 percent of employment in Turkey was in the agricultural sector, and small peasant holdings were still dominant. Hence, it was not agricultural workers but small peasants on family farms that formed the bulk of the workforce. Employment in the manufacturing sector was a mere 11 percent of total employment, and small firms played a very important role. Nearly one-third of manufacturing labor was in microenterprises employing less than ten workers. In commerce, the significance of micro-enterprises was even more important, with workplaces employing one or two workers constituting the typical business unit in this branch of activity.[3] The management of microenterprises, even when they do not actually use family labor, is significantly based on reciprocity. Consequently, not only do they typically exclude unionization, but they often exhibit tendencies to deviate from the rules regulating the labor market. In this regard, it is revealing that the State Institute of Statistics of Turkey currently estimates the scope of the informal sector on the basis of production and employment in microenterprises. However, references to labor market informality would not really be adequate to describe the society-specific setting of work relations in Turkey. In this setting, where wage and salary earners remained numerically much less important than the self-employed and unpaid family workers, labor did not really appear as a market commodity.

Limited commodification of labor also had to do with employment in state-owned enterprises (SOEs). From the early years of the republic to the 1980s, these enterprises remained an important instrument in the attempts to develop national industry. In this regard, underpriced industrial inputs supplied to private firms were of particular significance in the development of the private sector in Turkey. However, their role as an "employer of last resort" was also quite important. In the manufacturing sector, SOEs provided over 30 percent of employment.[4] Access to such public sector employment has often been contingent upon connections with political party circles, not excluding those at the lowest echelons of the party hierarchy. All types of institutions in which reciprocity relations are typically rooted, from family to ethnic or religious communities, have played a significant role in the access to political decision-making processes in the deployment of labor in the public sector.

State intervention, then, contributed to a setting where commodification of labor was limited. This was not achieved, however, by formal redistributive processes assuring the stability of employment and income as observed in the case of welfare state practices in developed Western countries. It was based, rather, on the basis of the principle of reciprocity, with the state both taking part in a reciprocal exchange of votes for favors and helping to sustain family and family-like relations in their significance for the economic life of the individual.

Agriculture constitutes an important area where the state has contributed to the survival of economic relations based on the principle of reciprocity. Historically, in many high- and middle-income countries, taxes imposed on agriculture, along with the state support given to infrastructure and technology development, have led to the concentration of land holdings and elimination of small peasantry. In Turkey, we see a rather different development. One of the first economic policy decisions, and probably the most important one, taken by the founders of the Turkish Republic was the elimination of the tax in kind on agricultural produce. The enormous loss of public revenue implied by this decision was not really compensated by other taxes later imposed on the sector, given the exemptions accorded to small producers.[5] The Land Reform bill enacted by the parliament in 1946 consolidated the status of small farm holdings, and in the following decades, the distributional conflicts between small peasants and large landowners have invariably taken place in a political environment favorable to the small peasants.[6]

In the meantime, agriculture was supported by subsidies. While the burden these subsidies place on the state budget is often emphasized in the current policy debate, the general level of subsidies has remained quite low, at least until the 1980s, compared to those in most OECD (Organization for Economic Cooperation and Development) countries. Moreover, contrary to the situation prevailing in the OECD region, the burden of agricultural subsidies fell not on the taxpayer, but on the consumer.[7] In Turkey, then, it was largely a policy of leaving agriculture outside the state redistributive system that has prevented the disappearance of peasantry and has kept a large portion of the workforce employed in small farms.

The commodification of labor was limited not only by keeping people employed in agriculture. As long as small peasants were not forced to sell their land, rural-urban migration has not necessarily implied a total rupture from the countryside. Hence, new immigrants in urban centers could continue to rely on in-kind, if not pecuniary, income supplements received from their relatives who had remained in the village. Small landownership has also created a situation where urban workers could seasonally leave their jobs to participate in agricultural production on their family farms.[8] Livelihood in the urban environment, in other words, has not been fully determined by the logic of the labor market.

The fact that economic survival in the city has not depended entirely on labor market relations relates to another aspect of the society-specific role of the Turkish state in the economy. Housing constitutes a very important problem that social policy is often in a position to address in the course of industrial development. In Turkey this problem, too, has not been handled through formal redistributive processes. Nevertheless, *gecekondu* (irregular housing) has appeared as a crucial mechanism of integration in the urban society. While such irregular settlements are found in many other countries of Asia, Africa, and Latin America, the state has played a much more significant role in the development of *gecekondu* in Turkey, through the vast supplies of public land in and around the cities. Neither privatized nor used for social housing projects, these vacant public plots of land have been treated as "commons" and appropriated by successive waves of immigrants from rural areas. This situation has provided ample room for the reciprocal exchange of entitlements to invaded public property with votes. In this process, the *gecekondu* has ceased to be the site of the precarious existence of marginal segments of population and has become the typical form of popular housing in the country. Moreover, the irregular settlements built on individual plots of land could expand or be converted into apartment buildings. They could thus constitute a mechanism of supporting future generations by providing them with a place to live or a source of rental income for the family.[9]

The "employer of last resort" role played by the SOEs, agricultural policies that have contributed to the survival of small family farms, or the *gecekondu* solution to the urban housing problem do not, of course, constitute a formal policy of income and employment comparable to standard welfare state practices in the West. Yet they have been quite successful in keeping unemployment and worse forms of poverty under control. They have also kept in place a socioeconomic order where family solidarity could compensate for the absence of a formal social security system that could effectively deal with risk situations such as unemployment, sickness, or old age.

Changing Character of Reciprocity Relations in the 1980s

In the 1980s, when a neoliberal agenda for market reform was set, there was little room in it for social security provisions. Neither was there much concern for a restructuring of the redistributive system in conformity with social and economic objectives. The objective of reform was simply defined in terms of radically reducing the economic role of the state to make the unregulated market the main mechanism of resource allocation. That this was not such a smooth process could be realized only a decade later, after many unexpected and undesired developments.

As in many countries similarly situated in the world economy, structural adjustments in Turkey involved price deregulation, especially the deregulation of major macroeconomic indicators such as the foreign exchange rate and the rate of interest, as well as attempts to privatize the SOEs, trade liberalization, elimination of barriers against foreign direct investments, and, finally, elimination of controls against international capital movements. While the ideological environment in which these policies were implemented was hostile to employment and income support policies, it was not unfavorable to measures taken to support private sector development. Hence, outward-looking international trade policies involved not only the elimination of barriers against imports but also significant subsidies provided to exporters of manufactured products. Other than exporters, real estate developers and investors in tourism benefited from diverse types of preferential treatment.

Since 1980, agriculture has ceased to be the leading export sector in the country, while the manufacturing sector has come to account for over 75 percent of the country's exports.[10] Improving agricultural productivity had never been a policy priority in Turkey. But agriculture was hit especially hard by economic and political developments in the last two decades, and it has become increasingly difficult to keep the majority of people employed in peasant holdings. The developments in question pertain, first, to liberalization of imports of agricultural products, particularly meat imports, which had an important negative effect on the sector. Second, in the 1980s, when tourism and real estate appeared as the main engines of growth, the most fertile plots of land in the western and southern regions of the country were sacrificed to tourism or real estate developments for summer residences. Then came the devastating impact of the war with Kurdish nationalist forces in the southeast. At the end of the 1990s, the result of these developments could be easily seen in agricultural productivity. In fact, Turkey is one of the few countries in the world where there have been no productivity improvements in agriculture between the early 1980s and the late 1990s.[11]

The dissolution of the countryside has also manifested itself in the rural-urban migration trends. Between 1980 and 1999, urban population has increased dramatically, with the number of people living in urban areas increasing from 44 to 74 percent of the total population.[12] Many of these migrants had to leave their villages in eastern and southeastern Turkey because of the military conflict in the area. For them, as well as for the rest of the new immigrants, "push factors" such as the threat of violence or complete loss of livelihood, rather than the attraction of urban opportunities, were behind the decision to come to the city. Unlike the earlier immigrants, they did not necessarily come to established networks of family or fellow townsmen that could help them find work and shelter.

Shelter, in particular, has become a problem for all new immigrants. By the end of the 1980s, the *gecekondu* had lost its basis of legitimacy as the society-specific form of social housing. Appeal to the indisputable need for shelter no longer seemed sufficient to morally justify the invasion of public land or self-built houses on peripheral land without regular construction permits. Irregular construction activity has not been limited to popular dwellings; it significantly extended to middle-class residential areas. This, however, has not helped generate more sympathy for the urban poor in need of shelter. On the contrary, the poor have found themselves in intense competition over urban land with real estate developers catering to the middle-class housing market. With the geographic expansion of the cities and the new popularity of suburban middle-class residences, irregular access to peripheral land has become increasingly difficult for the new immigrants.[13]

At the same time, working conditions in the industrial sector have undergone a radical change. After the military coup in 1980, the activities of labor organizations have been significantly curtailed and the most radical labor union confederation, DISK, was closed.[14] As a result, industrial wages fell steadily until 1988, when political life was, at least to a certain extent, normalized. Soon after the reversal of the downward trend in wages, however, a new trend, in conformity with the characteristics of flexible production, set in, controlling labor in a much more effective fashion than mere political repression could. Relations of subcontracting and outsourcing have led to a further shift of employment away from large enterprises to smaller firms. Piecework allocated to women working at home on a totally informal basis and for extremely low wages has also become very significant. In other words, adoption of a market-oriented strategy in Turkey has not resulted in the formalization of labor relations but has led, on the contrary, to a situation where employment in the formal manufacturing sector has shrunk in size.[15] This has resulted in a massive informalization of the labor market. Even official statistics, which always underestimate the extent of labor market informality, indicate that irregular work now extends to well over half of the total labor force. While deregulation has thus come to characterize the employment scene, production relations reflect less the principle of market exchange than the family metaphor. Reciprocity relations, in their personal and informal character, define the conditions of access to employment and determine the rhythm and remuneration of work both at home and in small enterprises.

While reciprocity relations remain important for employment, recent demographic trends indicate that the family, the typical institutional context of such relations, today appears to be under considerable pressure. While politicians still like to refer to the "young and dynamic" population of the country, statistics show declining fertility rates and an aging population. The observed decline in fertility rates leads to two developments, both with serious implications for social policy. First, the number of people in the labor force—people between fourteen and sixty-five years of age—continues to increase. Second, the number of those above sixty-five is also increasing.[16] These trends place a double burden on social policy given both the pressing need to create jobs for a growing labor force and the measures needed to care for the elderly. In the meanwhile, the nuclear family has become the norm and family solidarity hardly covers the extended family anymore. Under these circumstances, it ceases to be realistic to expect family support and care to continue to substitute for formal social safety nets.

We observe, in other words, a certain change in the role of reciprocity relations in defining the coordinates of the livelihood of the individual. As family ceases to be an effective mechanism of social protection, its role in the unregulated context of flexible production is enhanced. A parallel change could also be depicted in the ways in which reciprocity relations infiltrate redistributive processes to shape the character of state intervention in the economy. I have discussed how the informal mechanisms through which the Turkish state has traditionally attempted to sustain need satisfaction began to be abandoned in the 1980s. This has not led, however, to a formalization of state-society relations in line with the formal and impersonal character of the principle of redistribution. Instead, the decade has witnessed an intensification of particularist relations between the state and private sector actors with claims on public resources. Exporters who were supported by tax rebates, investors in tourism and real estate benefiting from preferential credits, and the bidders for public sector enterprises in privatization deals have all appeared as important actors in newly emerging networks among public authorities and private businessmen. Liberalization and deregulation have provided ample opportunities for the mobilization of such networks for private gain, and what was critically labeled populism has given way to downright corruption.

As a result, through the 1980s, while many steps were being taken toward liberalization and deregulation, government spending increased considerably. The budget deficit, which was 1.8 percent of GNP in 1981, had reached 5 percent by the end of the decade.[17] Internal borrowing was financed by issuing government bonds and treasury bills, which, unlike the case in most high-income market economies, had higher returns than bank deposits or private securities. At the end of the 1980s, 90 percent of the transactions on the Istanbul Stock Exchange involved government securities.[18] After a decade of market-oriented structural adjustment and stabilization efforts, the presence of the state in the economy appeared as the most significant factor explaining chronic double-digit inflation in a highly unstable macroeconomic environment.

Economic Crisis in the Absence of Social Protection

It was in this environment that capital account was fully liberalized in 1988. As several economists have since remarked, financial liberalization before achieving fiscal restraint could only be a recipe for further instability.[19] Financial crises that hit many Latin American and Asian countries in the 1990s have shown that unregulated short-term capital flows could cause instability even in the absence of fiscal imbalances such as the ones characterizing the Turkish economy.[20] However, the society-specific dynamics of the crisis, which hit Turkish economy in February 2001, were clearly related to the factors that link a practically bankrupt state to a poorly regulated and irresponsible banking sector.

Since the decision to liberalize the capital account, productive activity in the manufacturing sector has been significantly dominated by financial operations. While foreign direct investment has remained negligible,

Women waiting in line to receive free food from the municipality. Photo by Arif Aşçı.

portfolio investment has grown considerably.[21] Financial liberalization has also enabled the banking sector to incur external borrowing in order to invest in public securities. The latter had very high rates of return reflecting the increasing public sector borrowing requirements. Consequently, lending to the state was more attractive than financing productive investment. Throughout the decade, credits extended to the government have increased much faster than total bank credits and appeared, by the end of the decade, the largest item in the assets of commercial banks.[22] Turkish banks have, in other words, given up their natural function of investment finance for a much more profitable financial operation that could be carried out at a very large scale thanks to the possibility of foreign exchange borrowing in a policy environment of full capital account liberalization. In Turkey, highly profitable arbitrage operations, through which the banks financed their high-interest government security holdings by foreign exchange borrowing, had made both the banking system and the economy extremely vulnerable to foreign exchange rate and interest rate fluctuations.[23]

This vulnerability led to a major economic crisis in February 2001. It was triggered, like other financial crises of our contemporary world economy, by the outflow of short-term speculative capital. In spite of the efforts of the Central Bank to counter the speculative attack against the Turkish lira, it was not possible to maintain the value of the currency in conformity with the stabilization program then in implementation. The lira was left to float, with an initial loss of value of about 40 percent. This was the end of the IMF-backed stabilization program launched in December 1999 to fight the chronic double-digit inflation Turkey has been living with since the 1970s. In July, there was a new wave of capital outflow causing further interest rate hikes and currency depreciation. Since then, major financial turbulences were avoided, but the economy is under close supervision by the IMF authorities.

The dimensions of social and economic problems associated with the crisis were enormous. The exact figure for bankruptcies is still not known. In those manufacturing firms that could avoid bankruptcy in 2001, employment fell by 18.7 percent in small enterprises, by 8.4 in medium-sized ones, and by 4.4 in large establishments.[24] The decline in employment in the manufacturing sector could give only an incomplete idea about the aggravation of the problem of poverty already threatening a large segment of the population in the environment of social transformation before the crisis. Especially in urban areas, increasing visibility of the poor has recently generated a concern with the danger of "social explosion" and led to policy suggestions to at least complement informal solidarity mechanisms with more formal mechanisms of social integration. Yet these policy suggestions coexist with pleas for deregulation of labor and capital markets, which render the establishment of formal safety nets practically unfeasible. While it is increasingly clear that poverty is a serious social problem, which has reasons beyond the control of the poor, policy failure to deal with poverty is justified with reference to the imperatives of insertion in the global market.

Given the contemporary realities of the international system, integration of a national economy in the world system takes place, first and foremost, through the flow of financial capital. Starting in the 1970s, the world economy entered into a phase of financial expansion, with the volume of short-term financial transactions exceeding the volume of trade at an accelerating rate.[25] According to some estimations, at the end of the 1990s, the former was over fifty times the latter.[26] In this environment, economic crises are triggered by the immense volatility of short-term capital flow. Yet the same volatility also makes it necessary to define policy priorities in terms of enhancing investor confidence by strengthening the financial sector. This explains why the banking sector, which had a central role in the unfolding of the crisis in Turkey, cannot be asked to assume the burden of the highly profitable risks it had taken before the crisis.

Through the bankruptcies that have affected thousands of small- and medium-sized firms and their employees and the massive layoffs in other enterprises, an overall sum of $45 billion was transferred to the banking system, in cash and government paper. Moreover, through a swap operation realized in June 2001, short-term, Turkish-lira-denominated government debt held by banks was converted into longer-term, foreign-exchange-denominated debt. The following depreciations of the lira have thus provided another mechanism of transferring public resources to the banking sector. While this article was being written, the government was preparing to transfer another $5 billion to the sector. Hence, a total sum of $50 billion, roughly equal to one-third of the country's predicted GNP for 2002, will have been used for financial system rescue operations, excluding the sum involved in the above-mentioned swap operation.[27]

Compared to the magnitude of these resources used to bail out banks, those devoted to the so-called real sector remain pathetic. In fact, the absence of a serious effort to deal with unemployment and poverty is clearly reflected in the composition of the government budget. Debt service payments now constitute the largest item in the budget and have recently reached over half of total government spending.

Before the last crisis, the Turkish government had made some attempts at an overall social security reform, mainly to reduce the burden of the system on the public budget. Much of the reform debate centered on the need to increase the age of retirement. Yet the enacted reform bill also included certain measures to increase job security and introduce an unemployment insurance scheme. Laid-off workers who had been paying social security premiums during the last three years have recently begun to receive an unemployment benefit for a maximum period of ten months, limited by the amount of the prevailing minimum wage, now about $125 per month. This new institutional arrangement, like the measures directed at enhancing job security, is hardly the answer to the current problem of poverty, given the extent of informal labor practices that the crisis is clearly rendering even more widespread. Workers desperate to find jobs or keep the ones they have are obviously in no position to demand social security coverage from employers who amply use the crisis as a pretext to justify informal employment. In fact, the Union of Turkish Exporters has even attempted to launch a nationwide campaign for the reemployment of laid-off workers without social security coverage. This idea, enthusiastically supported by the media, was nevertheless rejected mainly because of the ILO conventions ratified by Turkey.[28] However, there is reason to believe that through the media coverage of the proposal, many enterprises have laid off their workers only to rehire them without their former social security benefits.

While there are practically no attempts to devise enterprise support policies conditional on formal employment generation, policies that accelerate the dissolution of the country's informal, reciprocity-based system of social protection continue at full speed. Dependence on sources of foreign credit, which the economic crisis has enhanced, renders the state totally unable to resist the demands of international financial organizations in this direction. Hence, the World Bank–assisted agricultural liberalization program, with its special emphasis on the replacement of subsidized product prices with direct income supplements dissociated from production, is discussed as an integral component of the agreements with the IMF, among other conditionalities.[29] Subsidies provided to agriculture are now being cut in a way to reduce the area of cultivated land and aggravate the problems caused by rural dislocation, regardless of the already alarming dimensions of urban unemployment.

Employment in SOEs has ceased to be an instrument to deal with the problem of unemployment, especially since privatization attempts have gained a new impetus to generate public funds to be channeled to debt service payments. Public land in the cities is also viewed as a resource that could be used to alleviate the burden on the government budget. Attempts are currently being made to sell public plots in order to generate income necessary for the bankrupt state to meet its obligations to its creditors. In the meantime, there is not even any discussion on the necessity of social housing projects to replace the informal solution that *gecekondu* could, through several decades, present to the problem of integrating immigrants into the urban society. While everyone recognizes that the social exclusion of uprooted peasants constitutes a serious social problem beyond the control of the individuals involved, the "unavoidable necessity" of structural adjustment and financial stabilization dominates this type of social concern.

Charity food handout to the poor. Courtesy of *Cumhuriyet*.

Conclusion

In this article, I have tried, first, to elucidate the nature of society-specific arrangements, which, until recently, were able to prevent the worst forms of social exclusion and poverty in modern Turkey. I then argued that neither the state nor the family, as two pillars of the socioeconomic order characterized by these arrangements, is now able to carry the burden of leading the society through its current market-oriented transformation. However, the contemporary policy environment allows only very limited room for the creation of formal employment opportunities and welfare provision. In a setting where structural adjustment policies for the establishment of a self-regulating market system restrict the scope of industrial policy and push countries like Turkey with abundant cheap labor resources to compete with each other on markets for manufactured exports, compensating the effects of deruralization with the dynamics of rapid industrialization does not seem easy. Meanwhile, in an international economy dominated by unregulated capital flows, the prerogative of assuring the stability of the financial system places an overwhelming burden on public funds and limits the scope of social spending for the establishment of formal safety nets.

In *Shame and Necessity*, Bernard Williams discusses Aristotle's approach to slavery.[30] The discussion shows the futility of Aristotle's attempts to legitimize slavery as a "natural" phenomenon based on natural characteristics of slaves. While such an approach to other manifestations of hierarchy and subordination could have a basis, as in the case of justifications of the inferior status of women, for example, it could hardly hold in the context of Greek slavery. Slaves came from different ethnic and social groups, and they were often born free. Williams argues that the arbitrariness and violence involved in the process of becoming a slave were not overlooked by ancient Greeks. Thus, unlike Aristotle, they did not try to legitimize the phenomenon but accepted it as a necessity for the best development of their cherished social life. Economic and cultural necessity, along with individual bad luck, seemed sufficient to explain the slave's status. Williams writes that the distance between ancient Greece and our modern times does not only consist of our rejection of necessary identities, but also of the attempts to control necessity and chance with a view to reduce their effects on the individual and to show that what cannot be reduced is not unjust. "However," he continues, "we shall not know how great our distance really is from the ancient world until we are in a position to claim, not merely that there is this task, but that we have some hope of carrying it out."[31]

The discussion presented in this article indicates that in contemporary Turkey this hope is not completely lost, since the need to replace traditional solidarity mechanisms with formal social safety nets is still emphasized in social policy debate. Yet the appeal to "necessity" is disturbingly present in contemporary attempts to justify the transfer of the bulk of public funds to the financial sector. "Necessity" also dominates the determined efforts to rapidly dismantle the country's traditional reciprocity-based system of social protection, which, with all its problems, has proven effective in controlling social exclusion. Nevertheless, it might still be possible to argue beyond necessity, by problematizing the pace of socioeconomic transformation and by questioning the priority given to the financial sector over all social and human concerns. This could only be possible through an attempt to reinstitute the economy with a more important role assigned to the formal principle of redistribution.

Notes

1 Terms such as *developing, periphery, Third World, newly industrializing,* or *less developed,* which one could use to situate Turkey in the world economy, all reflect different ways of conceptualizing international economic order with their respective shortcomings. The World Bank presents a fourfold categorization based solely on income per capita levels: high-, higher-middle-, lower-middle- and low-income countries. With a GNP per capita of U.S.$2,900 for 1999, Turkey is situated in the lower-middle-income country category in the last World Development Report. See World Bank, *World Development Report 2000/2001: Attacking Poverty* (New York: Oxford University Press, 2000–2001). After the economic crisis of February 2001, this figure has fallen to U.S.$2,160, in part because of the considerable depreciation of the lira against the dollar. UNDP (United Nations Development Program), on the other hand, classifies countries on the basis of a more sophisticated measure of "human development" by taking into account achievements in health and education along with per capita income. According to this basic human development index compiled by UNDP, Turkey is situated in the medium human development category. See UNDP, *Human Development Report 2001* (New York: Oxford University Press, 2001).

2 Karl Polanyi, *The Great Transformation* (Boston: Beacon, 1944); Karl Polanyi, "Economy As Instituted Process," in *Trade and Market in the Early Empires,* ed. Karl Polanyi, Conrad M. Arensberg, and Harry W. Pearson (Chicago: Gateway, 1957), 243–69; Karl Polanyi, *The Livelihood of Man* (New York: Academic, 1977).

3 Tuncer Bulutay, *Employment, Unemployment, and Wages in Turkey* (Ankara: International Labor Office and State Institute of Statistics of Turkey, 1995), 196–97.

4 Ibid., 191.

5 İzzettin Önder, "Aşar'ın Kaldırılması ve Tarım kesimine Uygulanan Vergiler," in *75 Yılda Köylerden Şehirlere* (Istanbul: Türkiye Ekonomik ve Toplumsal Tarih Vakfı, 1999), 67–74.

6 Çağlar Keyder, "The Genesis of Petty Commodity Production in Agriculture: The Case of Turkey," in *Culture and Economy: Changes in Turkish Villages,* ed. Paul Stirling (Huntingdon, UK: Eothan, 1993), 171–86.

7 Haluk Kasnakoğlu, "Agricultural Policy Reform in Turkey in the Light of International and National Developments: Options and Prospects" (unpublished paper, 2001).

8 Çağlar Keyder, "Social Structure and the Labor Market in Turkish Agriculture," *International Labor Review* 128 (1989): 731–44; Keyder, "The Genesis of Petty Commodity Production."

9 Ayşe Buğra, "Immoral Economy of Housing in Turkey," *International Journal of Urban and Regional Research* 22 (1998): 303–17.

10 World Bank, *World Development Report 2000/2001,* 312.

11 Ibid., 288–89.

12 Ibid., 277.

13 Ayşe Öncü, "The Politics of the Urban Land Market in Turkey: 1950–1980," *International Journal of Urban and Regional Research* 12 (1988): 38–64; Buğra, "Immoral Economy of Housing."

14   DISK could resume its functions only in 1992, after a long series of legal and political struggles.

15   Fikret Şenses, "Labor Market Response to Structural Adjustment and Institutional Pressures: The Turkish Case," *METU Studies in Development* 21 (1994): 405–49.

16   TÜSİAD, *Türkiye'nin Fırsat Penceresi: Demografik Dönüşüm ve İzdüşümleri* (Istanbul: TÜSİAD, 1999).

17   TÜSİAD, *1989 Yılına Girerken Türk Ekonomisi* (Istanbul: TÜSİAD, 1989), 34; TÜSİAD, *1991 Yılına Girerken Türk Ekonomisi* (Istanbul: TÜSİAD, 1991), 41.

18   Ibid., 80.

19   Yılmaz Akyüz, "Financial System and Policies in Turkey in the 1980s," in *The Political Economy of Turkey*, ed. Tosun Arıcanlı and Dani Rodrik (London: MacMillan, 1990), 98–131.

20   Ilene Grabel, "Rejecting Exceptionalism: Reinterpreting the Asian Financial Crises," in *Global Instability: The Political Economy of World Economic Governance*, ed. Jonathan Michie and John Grieve Smith (London: Routledge, 1999), 37–67.

21   In 1999, foreign direct investment flows constituted 0.4 percent of the GDP while other private flows of a financial character reached 4.2 percent. See UNDP, *Human Development Report 2001*, 192.

22   Erinç Yeldan, *Küreselleşme Sürecinde Türkiye Ekonomisi: Bölüşüm, Birikim ve Büyüme* (Istanbul: İletişim, 2001), 144–45.

23   Emre Alper, "The Liquidity Crisis of 2000 in Turkey: What Went Wrong . . . ," *Russian and East European Finance and Trade* 37 (2001): 51–71.

24   İstanbul Sanayi Odası, *Ekonomik Durum Tespiti Anket Çalışması Sonuçları 2001–2* (Istanbul: İstanbul Sanayi Odası, 2002), 17.

25   Giovanni Arrighi, *The Long Twentieth Century* (London: Verso, 1994).

26   John Gray, *False Dawn* (New York: New Press, 1998), 62.

27   It is interesting that a clear and explicit statement on the magnitude of banking system rescue operations and the burden they placed on the economy was made by a member of the board of directors of a private bank in the course of an interview given to a daily newspaper. The interviewee thought, not surprisingly, that this was the outcome of a no-alternative policy decision. See *Radikal*, February 4, 2002.

28   *Radikal*, December 8, 2001.

29   See the letters of intent of the Turkish government to the IMF, available at www.treasury.gov.tr.

30   Bernard Williams, *Shame and Necessity* (Berkeley: University of California Press, 1993), 103–29.

31   Ibid., 129.

Bruce Kuniholm

Turkey and the World in Twenty-Five Years:
Thinking about the Future

This article explores Turkey's future and its
relations with the European Union (EU), the
United States, and the world. While the fault
lines that help to frame the tectonic shifts in
Turkey's evolving identity are unquestionably
being redrawn and will have a critical bearing on
how Turkey positions itself relative to the rest
of the world, it is my belief that the importance
of the Turkish state in the geopolitical world
will not diminish and that Turkey will play an
increasingly significant role in world affairs.

It has become commonplace to argue that
in an era of globalization the state system has
become less relevant; that economic, cultural,
and other dimensions of human existence, to
the extent that they transcend traditional boundaries, have opened the way to an international
identity crisis where people throughout the
world are struggling to think about how they
define themselves outside the boundaries of the
state system; and that the major questions they
confront involve how they want their countries
to position themselves relative to these forces.
Evidence of this phenomenon was apparent in
the debates over Maastricht and NAFTA. In spite

The *South Atlantic Quarterly* 102:2/3, Spring/Summer 2003.
Copyright © 2003 by Duke University Press.

of the importance of these forces, however, it is my contention that the demise of the state system is vastly overstated, and that geopolitical factors, *together* with these forces, will continue to be critical in defining the Turkish state's important role in world affairs. This article offers an educated guess as to what the geopolitical world might be like twenty-five years from now, speculates on Turkey's place in that world and its relationship with the EU and United States, ponders the current implications of regional dynamics and Turkey's struggle to define itself, and suggests some of the critical choices that will affect Turkey's future.

Thinking about the Future: The Primary Power Configurations

How can we determine whether a projection of future developments or a policy that is based on certain assumptions about the future is reasonable? The short answer is that, before these assumptions are tested, we can't. One way to address the problem, however, is to judge both projections and policies not on *how* they turn out but on *the quality of our thinking about how they might turn out*. One way to facilitate meaningful debates when making judgments is to spell out available alternatives, to explore their feasibility, and to speculate on their wisdom and efficacy in light of reasonable projections of what might happen. Historians rarely do this. Policy makers generally do—or *should*, because for them the question is not just academic; they are held accountable for how things turn out and they know it. If future projections are a function of the relationship between an evolving present and the future, changes must be incorporated into one's thinking and, as a result, conceptions of the future must *constantly* evolve (to reflect the implications of those changes) if they are to be useful. The trick is to remain flexible and adapt as circumstance requires.

Let us try to imagine the future. Turkey's role in the world in the next twenty-five years will be a function not only of critical geopolitical developments, which it is part of my task here to speculate about, and Turkey's capacity to adapt to them, but also of the policies and choices Turkish governments make at home. Let us try to imagine what some of Turkey's tough choices may be by first looking at the world in which they will take place.

Twenty-five years from now the critical power configurations among those with an interest in Eurasia are likely to be: (1) the United States, (2) a united Europe, (3) China, and (4) Russia. The critical question, as Zbigniew

Brzezinski has noted in his thoughtful book *The Grand Chessboard*,[1] which has helped inform my thinking, is which combination of these powers will dominate Eurasia, which holds 75 percent of the world's population, produces 60 percent of its GNP, and has 75 percent of its energy resources.

The United States. Let us look at the United States first. The United States, in my judgment, will continue to remain a global power, although it will be increasingly reluctant to exercise that power unless there is a clear threat to its security interests, as was the case in Afghanistan after the attacks of September 11, 2001. Aside from the ongoing war on terrorism, its goal will be to safeguard its security interests on the periphery of Eurasia—which are to make sure that no hostile power dominates. It will do this through its alliances with NATO, Japan, and Korea—not an unreasonable strategy. I believe that the NATO alliance will hold—giving the United States and its NATO allies a powerful foothold in Europe, and in this endeavor the relationship with Turkey is particularly important to both the United States and the EU.

One of the U.S. concerns will continue to be Russia (discussed below). More problematic for the United States may be the Far East. The unification of Korea—which could happen in the next twenty-five years, as the regime in the North mellows or is co-opted, or collapses (you have to imagine the possibility)—would probably result in Korea gravitating into China's sphere, because unification would not happen without Chinese acquiescence. The question then would be the extent to which the balance of power in eastern Eurasia would be upset by divisive U.S.-Japanese relations over a continued U.S. presence in Japan, or upset by rearmament of Japan, or stabilized by improved Korean and Japanese relations. A lot depends on how the process plays out.

A United Europe. The question of whether the EU, as a united power, becomes more integrated or fragments is anybody's guess. I think the former, at least economically, although the critical questions will be the extent to which the Franco-German relationship holds as a united Germany's leadership begins to dominate, and, as the EU's enlargement progresses, whether, eventually, the EU will include Ukraine, Turkey, and possibly even Russia.

On the military front, one has the sense that the EU's military arm, the Western European Union (WEU), or, depending upon how it develops, the European Security and Defense Policy (ESDP), will lack the financial resources to develop the kind of military capability that will permit it to operate out of area to any significant extent (its performance in the Balkans was dismal, and its lack of funding, which has necessitated a greater reliance on NATO, has mired it in the complexities of Greek-Turkish differences). For that reason, the EU's relationship with the rest of NATO and the United States will continue to be important, but its independent military capabilities will be limited. It is likely to respond to serious military threats outside of Europe only in conjunction with NATO and the United States.

China. China will develop into a regional economic power, but the extent to which free trade and the free market, with their requirements of openness, will change the system of government as they did in the Soviet Union remains to be seen. China's joining the World Trade Organization is a step in this direction. The critical geopolitical questions for China concern the manner in which Hong Kong is handled, settlement of the Taiwan question, changes in the power balance in east Asia if and when Korea becomes unified (with all that implies for the U.S.-Japan relationship), and China's relationship with Russia (with all that implies for its relationships with Central Asia and the Middle East). At the very least, China will be a regional power with an increasing interest in Central Asia (and its oil), where it will be a player, and hence of possible interest to Turkey.

Russia. Russia is the great unknown because what it decides to do and how it decides to do it will determine its capacity to ally with or oppose (and be opposed by) either the EU and NATO or China. The extent to which economic reforms are able to take place, the extent to which Russia is included or excluded from an enlarged EU and, even if the economy does improve (as development of its oil resources and its new economic policies suggest it will), the extent to which it will choose democratic reforms over empire are still open questions. The verdict is still out on the leadership of Russian president Vladimir Putin. Putin's statements prior to being elected president were contradictory (e.g., publicly raising the prospect that Russia might someday join NATO, and then asserting that Russia had no hope of doing so and didn't want NATO on its borders),[2] and his policies after his election have provided observers with an equal measure of hope and concern. Observers are hopeful in the sense that he has taken a pragmatic, pro-Western approach toward the economy, sought closer cooperation with the EU, and conceived—with Duma backing—a strong liberal market-oriented economic program. He has fostered close personal ties with President Bush, been supportive of U.S. policies in the aftermath of 9/11, and on May 24, 2002, together with Bush, signed a nuclear arms reduction treaty that marked a new strategic relationship between the United States and Russia.[3] Most recently, on August 22, 2002, U.S.-Russian cooperation and collaboration made possible the removal of weapons-grade nuclear material from a research reactor in Yugoslavia.[4]

But observers also remain concerned about tendencies toward political authoritarianism that were evident in Putin's earlier attacks on freedom of the press; in his efforts to obtain de facto control of Gazprom, the biggest company in Russia; and in his efforts to put through a law making it possible to dismiss elected regional governors from the upper chamber of Parliament in order to strengthen the Kremlin's control.[5] At the summit of the Commonwealth of Independent States (CIS) countries in June 2000, Putin's goal of reinforcing a presence in Central Asia was evident in his initiative to adopt a three-year CIS antiterrorism program that would authorize Russian operations in the CIS and in his efforts to create a South Caucasus regional security forum, made up of Russia, Georgia, Armenia, and Azerbaijan, that would overshadow other forums such as GUUAM in which Western countries have influence.[6] In spite of Putin's positive support for the U.S. war on terrorism in the aftermath of 9/11, Russian operations in Georgia, Russia's closer relations with Iraq (a $40 billion trade and infrastructure deal) and Iran (a $10 billion nuclear reactor program), and the continuation of military hardware sales to China all have raised questions about the future direction of Russia.[7]

Turkey's Real Choice

Turkey, in thinking about its place in the world twenty-five years from now, will have little to say about how the great power configurations discussed above develop, except, perhaps, down the road in Central Asia. It will have a lot to say about how it positions itself *relative* to these great power configurations and a lot to say about regional stability in Central Asia, the Balkans, and the Near East. In that context, Turkey's choices when it comes to alignment are complicated but clear: (1) closer ties with the larger pan-Turkic community in the Caucasus and Central Asia, (2) closer ties and coordination with the Islamic Middle East and all that they imply about Turkey's identity, and (3) continued and even closer partnership with the EU, with all that it implies about democratic development and a free market, and close security ties with NATO in general and the United States in particular. These choices are complicated because they are not mutually exclusive, but they are clear, because which one Turkey chooses and how it chooses to pursue it will have a lot to say about the thrust of Turkey's future identity, its future foreign policies, its relationship with the United States, and its place in the world.

Reviewing the Options. Looking at the first choice, I do not see the pan-Turkic route as a real choice—at least for the period under examination. In the years since the collapse of the Soviet Union, realism has tempered initial romanticism. Great progress really has been made—especially in opening new markets, communications, and education—but many countries of the former Soviet Union continue to look to the West instead of south, and at some point there are limits to Russia's tolerance of rivals in what it still sees as its sphere of influence—as demonstrated by its policies toward the CIS. Turkey's serious economic problems, meanwhile, at least for the time being, will put constraints on what is possible, as will other dynamic factors within the region. It is true that the Central Asian states have fairly well-established secular (if not democratic) rule and Turkic-speaking populations. Turkey clearly shares a common cultural heritage with them, and Russia fears the ethnic ties that draw the Central Asian states elsewhere, particularly since almost ten million Russians live in those states; it also fears the Islamic component, which draws them closer to the Middle East, and which resonates with twenty million Muslim citizens in Russia. But there are also many complicated and sometimes counterintuitive ties in the region. Iran, for example (for internal concerns related to its northwest province), finds greater affinity with Armenia than with Azerbaijan, and (for legalistic reasons relating to sectoral divisions of the Caspian) on occasion finds greater affinity with Russia than with the other Central Asian powers of the Caspian. The possibility of a closer relationship between Russia, Iran, and Iraq cannot be dismissed—even, as we have seen, under Putin—and especially if someone like Yevgenniy Primakov again comes to power.[8]

Examining the second choice, I see strong political ties between Turkey and the Middle East and the Muslim world as problematic. Economic ties, yes, especially if regional tensions ease. Cultural ties, yes, particularly since the election of November 2002 resulted in the triumph of the Islamist-rooted Justice and Development Party (AKP) at the polls. But the Arab Middle East, for all the rhetoric about being Islamic brothers, does not look kindly on its former Ottoman rulers, any more than Russia's "Near Abroad" looks kindly upon Moscow; and whether undermined by the machinations of Saddam Hussein or support for Islamic fundamentalism from Saudi Arabia and the Arab heartland, close political ties (as opposed to cultural ties) with the Middle East, in my judgment, are more a fantasy than a reality, however much a small segment of the population in Turkey may believe it. It is significant that even the AKP supports Turkey's accession to the EU.

Turkey's third choice, and in my judgment the only real choice, is a tough one. Why? It is the only choice because neither Russia nor China is a realistic partner. It is a tough choice because however much many of us support Turkey's membership in the EU—and I have done so since I wrote an article in *Foreign Affairs* in 1991[9]—I do not think Turkey will become a member of the EU much before 2020 (in this case, foresight is 20:20). It could, of course, and I would like to imagine it. But Turkey must first get its act together, particularly in the very near future, and until it does, it will not become a member of the EU. This will hurt Turkish pride; it will also be seen as direct assault on what Turks feel they have rightfully earned through their long and important role in NATO.

It is true that there is prejudice against Turks and Muslims in the EU. Recent remarks by former French president Valéry Giscard d'Estaing to the effect that Turkey was "not a European country" and that including Turkey in the EU's enlargement "would be the end of Europe" have underscored this judgment.[10] But it is also true that there are other, real issues, some of which are economic, and which were articulated by the European Community (EC, precursor to the EU) commission in December 1989 (when it pushed back the date for considering Turkey's application to be a candidate for accession to the EC) that bolster that prejudice: Turkey's large size, large population, and low level of development; high inflation and high unemployment; a purchasing power that is a third of Europe's; the large percentage of its population in agriculture; and problems associated with the access of Turkish labor to European markets.

Political questions are even more difficult. The EU's announcement at the

Helsinki summit in December 1999 that Turkey, finally, was a candidate for full membership may be seen as a turning point in the EU's attitude toward Turkey, but the political criteria for accession that are spelled out in the 1999 Regular Report from the Commission on Turkey's Progress toward Accession[11] make clear that until major questions are resolved—questions that involve civilian control of the army, human rights, and democratic practices, including a civil, nonmilitary solution to the Kurdish question—accession will not take place. And then there is the Cyprus problem. The EU's formal endorsement of the Accession Partnership Document (APD) in December 2000 was held up by the question of whether it would include two preconditions relating to Turkey's accession: a solution to (or serious effort to solve) the Cyprus problem; and a resolution of (or serious efforts to resolve) differences between Greece and Turkey over the Aegean. The final document, which was characterized by the French foreign minister as having been crafted with the intricate care it takes to do wood inlay, did not solve the problem; rather, it only postponed it.[12]

In spite of the EU's concerns about such political questions, the Turks have persevered in their desire for accession to the EU—a goal that polls suggest is supported by nearly 70 percent of the population.[13] Anticipating the EU's draft report in October 2002 on Turkey's progress toward accession, and knowing that the EU expects to complete enlargement talks with ten candidate countries in December 2002, the Turkish parliament, after an emergency all-night meeting, passed a fourteen-point reform package on August 3, 2002. This package constituted a significant step toward the reforms required for accession, including abolition of the death penalty in peacetime, legalization of the teaching of Kurdish in private schools, expansion of freedom of expression (e.g., ending punishment for criticizing the armed forces), and amending regulations governing the police.[14]

The executive commission of the EU reacted guardedly to this positive development, suggesting that careful analysis and monitoring of the reforms' practical implementation would be required to address its impact.[15] The *New York Times*, meanwhile, reported continuing doubts among the member states of the EU that Turkey "belongs in the club," citing their doubts that it had "the collective will to adopt the common practices of the European Union," especially since the Nationalist Action Party, or MHP (one of the coalition partners in former Prime Minister Bülent Ecevit's government), clearly intended to fight the reforms.[16]

Implementation of the reforms requisite to Turkey's accession to the EU will be a difficult task, even under the new government, which, after winning 34.28 percent of the votes, has majority control (363 of 550 seats) in parliament. But what are Turkey's other options? Could Turkey turn toward Central Asia and focus on that connection, as some supporters of the MHP (which received only 8.34 percent of the vote and failed to meet the 10 percent threshold for representation in the new parliament) would have liked? In the long run, that may be a possibility. For now, that is not an option that either Turkish resources will permit or (if Turkey had the resources) that the Russians are prepared to accept, although a more modest relationship is reasonable, especially if Turkey is given leverage through support from its Western Allies. If there is a road to Central Asia, it will be through Europe.

Could Turkey turn toward the Middle East? To Islam? It could happen, of course. Some in an earlier government of former Prime Minister Necmettin Erbakan (where the Welfare, or Refah, Party, which was shut down by the military, was a precursor of the AKP) undoubtedly imagined that it could. Secular governments and the Turkish military have warned that it could, especially if Turkey is spurned by the West, and the Erbakan government's behavior in 1996–97 does not give one confidence that it couldn't. Influential Turks, in a fit of pique at their love-hate relationship with Europe, have even suggested more drastic alternatives. On March 7, 2002, General Tuncer Kilinc, secretary-general of the National Security Council, in light of what he characterized as the EU's negative view of the problems that concerned Turkey, suggested that Turkey search for new allies such as Iran and Russia (taking care not to disregard the United States).[17] But that, in my humble opinion, would not help to solve Turkey's problems, nor is it likely to happen, at least not as long as the door to the EU is still open.

In my judgment, the third option—to remain oriented toward Europe—is Turkey's only real option. As mentioned earlier in this essay, polls suggest that almost 70 percent of Turks support this orientation. But it requires swallowing one's pride, acknowledging that not all the problems impeding Turkey's accession to the EU stem from prejudice, and putting Turkey's own house in order to do what is in Turkey's best interests. What does putting one's own house in order mean? I think it means addressing up front the half-empty part of the proverbial glass and doing what it takes to meet the Copenhagen political criteria (established in 1993 as conditions for formal accession talks), not only by passing new reforms and laws such as those passed by parliament on August 3, 2002, but also by implementing them. When we look at the past, it is easy to talk about the half-full glass. In the last seventy-five years, Turkey's progress has been extraordinary, and its leaders have overcome monumental obstacles. If Turkey had some of the natural resources—like oil—that the Soviet Union squandered during its existence, it would be in a very different place today. The important resource Turkey does have is the energy and work ethic of its people—a work ethic destroyed by communism in Russia. So Turkey's glass is half full. But we have to look at both halves, and in the context of the future, the question is, What needs to be done to fill the rest of it?

I should be clear that I don't presume to have the answers as to how Turkey should solve its problems, which I see as largely internal. Ultimately, only the Turks can answer them, and I realize that developments in my own country and our failures to address similar questions adequately put me in no position to be giving gratuitous advice.[18] But I have been asked to share my thoughts about the future of Turkey, so I will. In my judgment, Turkey's place in the world twenty-five years from now and its interaction with the various power configurations in Eurasia will be determined in part by the power configurations (discussed earlier) that are likely to be dominant; in part by how it handles its neighbors (discussed below) in what everyone acknowledges is a very rough neighborhood—made even more dangerous in the future by the proliferation of weapons of mass destruction; and, most importantly, by how it deals with important internal questions (discussed at the end of this article). The imperatives of survival in the region, meanwhile, to the extent that they require a more activist policy by the Turkish government and affect democratic practices regarding a range of issues of interest to the EU (civilian control of the army, freedom of religious expression, and a civil, nonmilitary solution to the Kurdish question), will continue to create tensions between Turkey and the EU and complicate Turkey's accession to the EU.

An Emerging Regional Alignment

Since the Gulf War, and in the context of what it has seen as an increasingly hostile post–Cold War regional environment, Turkey has undertaken a number of activist initiatives toward its neighbors that are uncharacteristic of its prior, more conservative foreign policies.[19] As deputy chief of staff

General Cevik Bir observed in 1997, some of Turkey's neighboring states continue to claim Turkish territory (one could cite Armenia, Syria, and Greece), some try to export their regime contrary to Turkey's constitutional order (one could cite Iran), and some have supported terrorism against Turkey (one could cite Russia, Syria, Iraq, Iran, and, relatively recently, even Greece).[20]

Turkey's response to these threats, based on the notion that one's enemies determine one's friends, has been reinforced by a sense that in spite of recent developments, many Europeans fundamentally oppose Turkish membership in the EU. The EU decision at the Luxembourg summit in December 1997 to exclude Turkey from the list of the next potential candidates to join the EU caused Prime Minister Mesut Yılmaz to react angrily, freeze ties with the EU, and rethink Turkey's foreign policy. His reaction, which was widely shared, explains, in part, the more independent foreign policy currently being pursued by Turkey, even as the decision of the EU at the Helsinki summit in December 1999 unlocked the door to the EU and the Accession Partnership Document in December 2000 opened it. Turkey's foreign policy, Foreign Minister Ismail Cem told Stephen Kinzer of the *New York Times* in December 1997, was no longer fixated on Europe. The fall of the Soviet Union, the creation of the newly independent states, and a growing consciousness of Turkey's European and Asian identity, he observed, had provided Turkey with a new approach. The fixation on Europe had been the result of a limited outlook, he noted, of a feeling that Turks had to resolve a conflict over whether they were European or Asian. Culturally, historically, and geographically, Turks were becoming aware of the fact that they didn't have to choose and that they were a global state.[21]

The result of this line of thinking, reinforced by Europe's response to the Öcalan affair and Turkey's need to develop friends and allies, has been to find common ground with a de facto network of friendly states (a "pro-Turkish" group, which includes Azerbaijan, Georgia, and Israel) bound by common interests and antipathies in the Balkans, the Caspian Basin, and the Middle East, while being more guarded about its relationships with another de facto network of states (an "anti-Turkish" group, which includes Russia, Armenia, Iran, Iraq, Syria, Greece, Cyprus, and Serbia) whose interests are often at cross-purposes with Turkey and whose antipathies are often directed toward Turkey.

The United States supports Turkey because of its strategic importance in the Caucasus, the Middle East, and the Balkans, and because it sees Turkey as a secular democratic model for the region. Unlike its European allies, the United States very early condemned Kurdistant Workers Party (PKK) leader Abdullah Öcalan and, apparently with Israel, helped the Turks to capture him. In spite of powerful anti-Turkish lobbies in the U.S. Congress,[22] the United States has been supportive of Turkey's relationship with Azerbaijan (to include support for the Main Export Pipeline [MEP] from the Caspian Sea through Azerbaijan, Georgia, and Turkey, to the Mediterranean) and supports the emerging strategic relationship between Israel and Turkey. The Bush administration, with its need for allies in the war in Afghanistan, and its growing focus on Iraq, continues to give Turkey its strong support. Turkey's "friends" in the region (the pro-Turkish group) have been supportive of a pro-Western policy in general (e.g., they all supported the NATO bombing of Serbia), while those whose interests are often at cross-purposes with Turkey (the anti-Turkish group) often have opposed such policies.

Clearly, relations among these countries—both as individual countries and as de facto blocs—are much more complicated than the stark separation indicated here.[23] But the relationships (however changing and dynamic they may be) indicate a general and meaningful inclination toward or away from Turkey. They suggest that Turkey's strategic importance (as opposed to its political orientation) is shifting from Europe (where its importance in the Balkans undoubtedly played a role in the EU's decision on Turkey's candidacy for accession), back to the Middle East (where it is even more important), and, now, Central Asia; and that, in giving NATO an out-of-area capacity that has been of significant benefit since the Gulf War, it is increasingly valuable (particularly to the United States, with whom it has a good relationship). The EU, constrained by institutional impediments in addressing collective responsibilities, absorbed by the difficulties of establishing its collective identity, divided over the best means to secure its defense interests, and influenced by a postcolonial attitude toward regions on the periphery or outside of Europe, is more ambivalent.[24]

The sets of relationships described here, meanwhile, may also indicate why the countries that can be described as anti-Turkish, all of which hold territory once possessed by the Ottoman Turks, all but one of which are not members of the NATO alliance, most of which have troubled relations with the alliance, and some of which retain historical animosities toward Turkey, may be interested in blocking Turkish interests and, in some cases, undermining Turkey's ability to govern. They point to the fact that, even with the Helsinki decision and the APD, because Turkey feels less welcome in the West, and because the reciprocal ties that bound Europe to Turkey during the Cold War have been loosened, Turkey may also feel less constrained by NATO (but especially by its EU members) than in the past to pursue its own international agenda and follow a more activist course in safeguarding its security interests. Clearly, as the process of accession to the EU evolves, tensions between a closer relationship with the EU and the imperatives of survival in a tough neighborhood will continue to exist. The necessities of state—whether they involve limits on how far the government can go in addressing the EU's concerns about Cyprus or how far it can go in implementing internal reforms that are seen as inviting international interference and threatening Turkey's cohesion—may well impede, delay, and even halt the process of accession.

The Struggle for Turkey's Soul

Turkey's place in the world twenty-five years from now, however, even if contextualized by geopolitics and the dynamics of regional alliances discussed earlier in this essay, will be determined more by how it answers the following questions, which are at root internal and related primarily to the struggle over the soul of Turkey and its identity.

1. *The political question.* How can Turkey find the leadership to clean up its corrupt patronage system and transcend the feuding among the secular, democratic parties who represent a majority of Turks, but who, instead of working together, work at cross-purposes, letting less representative parties rule by default? The mandate given to the AKP in November 2002 is a result of these feuds. Whether the AKP can learn from the failure of the Welfare Party in 1997 and follow the example of the Christian Democratic parties in Europe remains to be seen.

2. *The economic question.* How can Turkey address an increasing disparity in income distribution, institute tax reform, make privatization really work, build a safety net, and address the host of economic problems that, without solution, risk turning the country over to demagogues?

3. *The Kurdish question.* How can Turkey find a way to accommodate legitimate Kurdish cultural aspirations while maintaining its integrity

as a state and functioning democracy? Turkey has not found a way to accommodate those legitimate rights, and until it does, Turkey will not have taken the steps it needs to take to be a truly civil society—or, one might add, a member of the EU.

4. *The role of Islam.* What role will Islam play in Turkish political life? To the extent that the success of political Islam can be explained in part as a protest against the corruption and ineptitude of Turkey's traditional parties, or in part as a response to successive religious parties' capacities to deliver municipal services, or in part as providing an inner need for meaning not satisfied by Turkey's secular political culture, the solution may be not to ban parties like them, but to encourage the AKP to follow the model of Europe's Christian Democratic parties, to encourage the traditional parties to act more responsibly and to rely less on the military as a deus ex machina to save them from their irresponsible behavior.

Turkey's place in the world twenty-five years from now will largely be determined by how it handles these internal questions. We could quarrel over which problem is paramount, because they are all important and intricately related. But I would argue that solving them, while no easy matter in light of regional threats, will be at least as important as the larger geopolitical framework that constrains Turkey's choices in the twenty-first century. If over the next twenty-five years it can solve the tough questions and make the trade-offs that I have outlined, Turkey, a hundred years after the Treaty of Lausanne, will be a Western-oriented model to emulate throughout much of the world; and, with leverage from its relationship with the EU, for much of Central Asia, where we could see the flowering of what President Turgut Ozal, when he came to Duke University to talk to faculty and students in 1991, called the "Turkish Century." But a new generation of Turkish youth has to *imagine* it, as opposed to other, *alternative* futures, and then do what it takes to get there.

Postscript

Many of the issues discussed in this essay (and all four of the critical problems mentioned at the end of the essay) were at play in February 2003 as the Turkish government confronted the U.S. request to deploy 62,000 ground troops and 320 planes and helicopters in Turkey in preparation for a U.S.-

led war against Iraq. With its NATO allies split and Turkey's geopolitical role in making possible a second front against Iraq at center stage, the Turkish government found itself on the horns of a very difficult dilemma.

On the one hand, the AKP had many reasons to reject the U.S. request. Roughly 90 percent of Turkey's population opposes what they see as a war against a Muslim neighbor, a war that risks the wrath of a tyrant who possesses weapons of mass destruction and who has sworn to retaliate against those who assist the United States. Turks remember that in 1990–91, President Turgut Ozal took the unpopular position of closing Iraq's oil pipeline through Turkey, allowing the United States to use the Incirlik air base for bombing Iraq, and forcing Iraq to contemplate the possibility of a second front. While Turkey subsequently received some assistance from the United States (Congressional opposition prevented the government from honoring all of its commitments) as well as from other foreign governments, this assistance in no way covered the costs resulting from the war of 1990–91: revenue lost from closure of the pipeline, reduced trade and tourism. More problematic was the influx of 500,000 Kurdish refugees from northern Iraq, the costs of which not only disrupted Turkey's economy (whose growth rate was reduced from 5 percent to 1 percent), but also complicated its internal attempts to cope with the Kurdish question. In the current crisis, Germany and France, whose support will be critical in the EU's decision regarding Turkey's accession to the EU in 2004, are opposed to U.S. policy in Iraq. Along with Belgium, they vetoed the deployment of NATO defensive equipment (AWACS surveillance aircraft, Patriot Missiles, and antigerm and antichemical warfare units) to Turkey until the rest of Turkey's NATO allies prevailed and found a mechanism (NATO's Defense Planning Committee, from which, years before, France had withdrawn) to circumvent French opposition.

On the other hand, there were good reasons to acquiesce to the U.S. request. The United States, since World War II, has been Turkey's best and most important ally. It supported Turkey defense against the Soviet Union in 1946 and its accession to NATO in 1951–52. Where the EU had been lukewarm-to-cold toward Turkish efforts to deal with the Kurdish terrorist problems of the 1980s and 1990s, the United States had been far more understanding of Turkey's problems (even helping the Turks catch Abdullah Öcalan, the leader of the separatist and terrorist PKK). The United States also had given strong support to Turkey's desire for accession to the EU, and had been instrumental not only in facilitating IMF assistance that helped to address Turkey's recent economic crises, but also in meeting a request for NATO support when Turkey had asked for it under Article IV of the North Atlantic Treaty. The United States, moreover, sensitive to Turkey's difficult financial situation, and after prolonged negotiations, was prepared to provide it with a reported six billion dollars in grants (two billion dollars in military assistance, and four billion dollars in economic assistance), the economic portion of which would leverage additional loans that would help the Turks withstand the affects of a war that would otherwise devastate its economy. The United States had also worked out with the Turkish government an understanding that would address Turkey's concerns for protecting its borders (Turkish troops would deploy in a twelve-mile buffer zone along Iraq's northern border). Understandings regarding the role of the Iraqi Kurds in the war, the distribution and collection of weapons to Kurdish forces, and the occupation of Kirkuk and Mosul were designed to assuage Turkish fears that an autonomous Kurdish entity, nurtured by UN funds over the last year, and benefiting from a fragmented postwar Iraq, would seek independence and, through its attraction to Kurds in Turkey, threaten the integrity of the Turkish state.

Under these circumstances, the government of Prime Minister Abdullah Gul recommended parliamentary approval of the U.S.-Turkish agreement. Given the importance of the issue, however, and perhaps because key officials in the party, overwhelmed by their new responsibilities (which also included the possible endgame to the Cyprus issue), were not fully aware of parliamentary rules, AKP did not enforce party discipline (AKP controlled 363 of the Grand National Assembly's 550 seats). While the vote in parliament was 264–250 to approve the deployment, 19 abstentions meant that an absolute majority (267) of the 533 delegates present (as required by Article 96 of the Turkish constitution) had not approved, forcing the government to reject the U.S. request to use Turkish bases in a second front against Iraq. Among the factors that affected the votes of those who opposed their own party were antipathy for joining a war against an Islamic neighbor (particularly when not supported by the legitimacy of a UN Security Council vote), a sense that Iraq (which had begun to destroy some of its Al-Samoud 2 missiles) was cooperating with UNMOVIC, resentment over U.S. pressure for a quick decision, and a negative reaction to the stereotypical characterizations in the U.S. press of Turks as rug merchants who could be bought off.

In the aftermath of the decision, a sobering reassessment of the real and potential costs to Turkey of not supporting U.S. efforts, coupled with a public statement by the chief of the Turkish general staff General Hilmi Ozkok (who had hitherto refused to offer any public comment on the crisis) that backed the parliament's reconsideration of the resolution, appeared to change the attitudes of some of those who had voted against the government's recommendation. On March 9, the election to parliament of the charismatic Recep Tayyip Erdoğan (former mayor of Istanbul and de facto leader of the AKP) paved the way for formation of a new AKP government and a reconsideration of the resolution. Erdoğan had supported the AKP's endorsement of the U.S. deployment, but had been prevented from running for and holding public office (until his party, elected in November 2002, amended the constitution) because in 1998 he had recited a poem that was alleged to have incited religious hatred. With the UN Security Council vote on the U.S./UK/Spanish resolution now a dead letter, and President Ahmet Necdet Sezer questioning the legitimacy of U.S. actions in Iraq, Erdoğan's new government acted more cautiously. It recommended, and parliament approved by a vote of 332–202 with one abstention, that Turkey allow U.S. warplanes only to use Turkish airspace in its war with Iraq. As a result of this more limited mandate for U.S. forces, the quid pro quo was significantly reduced. President Bush requested a one-billion-dollar aid package from Congress that could be leveraged into eight billion dollars in loan guarantees to help Turkey cope with its anticipated economic difficulties.

In light of developments related to the war in Iraq, it is clear that politics as usual in Turkey has undergone a sea change. There is no doubt that the strategic partnership between the United States and Turkey will be carefully reconsidered by both parties, even if it is also clear that the two will have continuing mutual interests. Turkey will also have to cope with a number of problems that began to surface almost simultaneously with the impending war in Iraq: the failure in early March of UN-sponsored settlement talks on the Cyprus problem; the March 12 judgment of the European Court of Human Rights that the trial of Abdullah Öcalan was unfair; and the questions raised by French and German opposition to NATO's responsibilities when it came to the defense of Turkey. But the fact that the military allowed the government to function as it was supposed to, and that the Grand National Assembly's decision was consistent with popular sentiment, even if it was not as responsive as it could have been to Turkey's military establishment and the country's economic interests, meant that, whatever the outcome of the war in Iraq, democratic governance in Turkey was the better for it.

Notes

An earlier draft of this article was presented in November 2000 at a conference at Ankara University.

1 Zbigniew Brzezinski, *The Grand Chessboard: American Primacy and Its Geostrategic Imperatives* (New York: Basic Books, 1997).

2 Michael Wines, "Putin Has a Big Lead, but Few Know Where He's Going," *International Herald Tribune*, March 23, 2000.

3 See http://usinfo.state.gov/topical/pol/arms/start/homepage.htm.

4 See Scott Peterson, "U.S.-Russia Ties Jolted by Crisis in Georgia," *Christian Science Monitor*, August 26, 2002.

5 See various articles by David Hoffman in the *International Herald Tribune*, March 28, June 29, July 8–9, 11, 2000.

6 GUUAM is a political, economic, and security alliance of Georgia, Ukraine, Uzbekistan, Azerbaijan, and Moldova that, with U.S. support, seeks to create a legal framework and infrastructure for economic activity such as the Europe-Caucasus-Asia Transportation Corridor, sometimes dubbed the "new Silk Road." See Malcolm Gray, *Calgary Herald*, June 5, 2000; Igor Torbakov, "Putin's Threats to Bomb the Taliban Meant for Central Asian Ears," posted June 13, 2000, www.eurasianet.org; Vladimir Socor, "Holding the Line at the CIS Summit," *Wall Street Journal*, June 23, 2000.

7 See, for example, Peterson, "U.S.-Russia Ties."

8 See Bruce Kuniholm, "The Geopolitics of the Caspian Basin," *Middle East Journal* 54.1 (Fall 2000): 546–71.

9 Bruce R. Kuniholm, "Turkey and the West," *Foreign Affairs* (Spring 1991): 34–48.

10 BBC News, November 8, 2002: www.news.bbc.co.UK/2/hi/europe/2420697.stm

11 This document is available on the EU's Web site: www.europa.eu.int/comm/enlargement /pas/turkey.htm.

12 Part of this discussion is drawn from Bruce Kuniholm, "Turkey's Accession to the European Union: Differences in European and American Attitudes, and the Challenges for Turkey," *Turkish Studies* 2.1 (Spring 2001): 25–53.

13 According to "Turkey-EU Agenda 2002," a survey carried out by the Turkish-European Foundation with the support of Taylor Nelson Sofres–PIAR Research Institute, and which surveyed 1,886 people in seventeen cities, 68 percent of the Turkish public want Turkey to become an EU member. See www.flash-bulletin.de/2002/eFebruar21.htm (visited August 3, 2002).

14 "Turkey Abolishes Death Penalty," *Guardian Unlimited*, August 3, 2002.

15 See Claudia Parsons, "Turkey Passes Rights Reforms in Step towards EU," http://asia. news.yahoo.com/020803/reuters/asia-118605.html (visited August 3, 2002).

16 Daniel Simpson, "Turkey and EU Hesitate to Tie the Knot," *New York Times*, August 5, 2002.

17 See the Center for Strategic and International Studies, "Turkey and the European Union: Heading for a Break?" March 8, 2002, www.csis.org/turkey/TU020308.htm.

18 Witness the fact that the United States has always had serious racial and ethnic problems, fought a bloody civil war with separatists over their right to secede, and itself continues to abuse human rights, as evidenced by harsh annual reports from Amnesty International. See their Web site at www.amnesty.org. When one talks about a half-empty glass, there is a lot to talk about in the United States, where today we have more than two million people in jail. Another interesting comparative statistic is that since 1984 no one has been put to death in Turkey; in the United States, by contrast, since 1984, 763 people have been executed; and in August 2002, the national death row population stood at 3,718. See www.deathpenaltyinfo.org/dpicexec.html and www.deathpenaltyinfo.org/DRowInfo. htm11#year. One wonders if the United States would pass muster before the EU.

19 The discussion in this section draws (in considerably shortened form) from Bruce Kuni-holm, "Security and Identity: The Evolving Strategic and Political Significance of Turkey's Relationship with NATO," in *A History of NATO: The First Fifty Years*, ed. Gustav Schmidt (Macmillan: London, 2001). For a good discussion of Turkey's more adventurous foreign policy in general and the Turkish-Israeli relationship in particular, see Alan Makovsky, "The New Activism in Turkish Foreign Policy," *SAIS Review* 19.1 (Winter–Spring 1999): 88–119.

20 For a shortened version of his presentation to the National Defense University in November 1997, see General Cevik Bir, "Turkey's Role in the New World Order," *Strategic Forum*, no. 135 (February 1998).

21 Stephen Kinzer, "Turkey Turns Away from Europe toward New Strategic Relationships," *International Herald Tribune*, December 29, 1997.

22 The pro-Israeli lobby, it should be noted, has been very supportive of Turkey.

23 Turkey, to cite one example, is a NATO ally of Greece (with whom relations have improved markedly since the earthquake in 1999) and has recently signed two major multi-billion-dollar deals with Iran and Russia for natural gas.

24 These and subsequent questions discussed in the remainder of this essay are elaborated on in much more detail in Bruce Kuniholm, "Turkey's Accession to the European Union: Differences in European and American Attitudes, and the Challenges for Turkey," *Turkish Studies* 2.1 (Spring 2001): 25–53.

Levent Soysal

Labor to Culture: Writing Turkish Migration to Europe

The New Topography of Migration

"Migration, together with the enunciation of cultural borders and crossings," as Iain Chambers affirms, "is deeply inscribed in the itineraries of much contemporary reasoning."[1] From popular fables to intellectual discourses on the meaning of life, from policy documents to commercial advertisements on the techniques of living, the talk is about movement, going to places, being displaced, and re-membering anew. The tendency is "to adopt," as organizing guides and protocols, "metaphors of movement, migration, maps, travels and sometimes a seemingly facile tourism."[2]

Not that migration—the movements of peoples and goods—is a novel phenomenon. People have perpetually and inevitably moved, traveled, and relocated. The anthropological and political histories of trade and exchange, invasions and conquests, and quests for dreams and the good life are in effect chronicles of long-distance ventures and displacements.[3] However, to affirm the historical salience of movement

The *South Atlantic Quarterly* 102:2/3, Spring/Summer 2003.
Copyright © 2003 by Duke University Press.

and migration is not to render their significance incidental either to the contemporary configuration of the world we inhabit or to the popular and intellectual imaginary of that world, for the world we "imagine"[4] is now "global" and connected in tangible and elusive ways. The movement of peoples and goods is no longer confined to binary itineraries between proper units of the Inter-*national* Order put in place at the turn of the twentieth century. It is more and more difficult to isolate a rupture in the global order of things; a financial crisis here and a refugee crisis there are experienced worldwide, albeit differentially. The direction of the movement is not simply from peripheries to centers, from Third Worlds to the First. The citizens of the Third World are everywhere (Pakistanis in Japan, Indonesians in Malaysia, Zimbabweans in Botswana, and so on). The citizens of the First World are seeking fortunes in Third Worlds (the British in Hong Kong, Berlin, and Dublin, Americans in Mexico, and so on).[5]

In the contemporary topography of the "global," as Chambers puts it, "migrancy involves a movement in which neither the points of departure nor those of arrival are immutable or certain."[6] This does not mean that movements and itineraries are unidentifiable and unconditional. The migrations are patterned and regulated, following economic, political, and historical trends and exigencies.[7] Neither does it mean that the proper units of the Inter-*national* Order, the nation-states, are discharged of their task to control and manage movement. The movements of peoples and goods do cross nation-state borders and obey ordinances of sovereignty.

In Chambers's becoming assertion, however, we find acute trends flowing from contemporary migrations. As exemplified by the uneventful disappearance of the distinction between "*e*-migration (out-migration)" and "*im*-migration (in-migration)" from our vocabularies, migrations are less and less about origins and destinations—leaving homes and arriving in foreign places for permanency. Contemporary migrations are about "border crossings,"[8] "multi-connectedness,"[9] having simultaneous presences, and being both permanent and in flux. The possibility of concurrent flux and permanence in migrancy derives from the gradual but eventual reconfiguration of "the *national* order of things."[10] In other words, behind the difficulty in dictating the role of the migrant as native or alien lie macroshifts in the politics of sovereignty, citizenship, and culture, all of which have been defined and are realized within national units but increasingly exhibit a dissociation from the national.[11]

Despite the changes occurring in this *trans*national geography and the imaginary of migrancy, and almost four decades after its arrival in our scientific and everyday lexicons, the term *Gastarbeiter* continues to captivate our scholarly and popular imagination. It has been almost a customary sign of credibility to make a reference to the guest worker when writing about migrants in Germany and Europe. Even those who set out to evidence the "changes" in the status of migrants find it hard to refrain from the practice. In our narratives, migrants, and Turks in particular, appear as perpetual guest workers, arrested in a state of cultural and social liminality.

I counter this seemingly intuitive convention with a critical view to the migration stories—namely, stories of labor and culture—recounted in our analytical and empirical narratives. Like the immigration literature at large, much of the work on migration to Germany and Europe takes as its vantage point the delineation of cultural and ethnic formations. This undue emphasis on the culture paradigm confines the study of migration to habitual accounts of marginalization and integration of foreigners, who are said to form cultural islands within the modernity of the host society. In public, popular, and scholarly discourses, Turkish migrants appear, at best, as relentless advocates of revitalized Turkishness or Islam, or, at worst, as essentially unassimilable agents of foreignness. Furthermore, this attribution of radical otherness, in cultural or ethnic variety, sets the migrants apart from public spaces in their country of residence, renders their participation invisible, and presents their situation as anomie.

In this essay, I recapitulate and critique the prevalent migration stories of labor and culture, starting with the story of the five hundred thousandth Turkish worker on his way to Germany, traversing the chronicles of cultural odysseys in *Ganz unten*, and ending with the new plots of transnational movements and excursions. In so doing, my aim is to assert that European migrants do not simply react to alien landscapes by reviving essential ethnicities (Turkishness) or religions (Islam). Rather, as participants at several social and cultural borders, they generate their visions of culture and belonging drawing upon the discursive repertoire of contemporary politics and citizenship, through processes of selection, modification, and enactment. I particularly emphasize the affinities of transnational cultural flows and local social spaces, which engender their presence in the public spaces of Berlin, Germany, and Europe, and complicate "national" configurations of belonging and conventional conceptions of otherhood.

My related goal is to locate the end(s) and infirmities of migration stories. I do not intend to set the record straight but to suggest an end to the migration story as we know it and as we theorize it. Needless to say, the end(s) contain and prelude beginning(s) — beginnings of stories traversing specific itineraries, say between Turkey and Germany, but taking place in the (dis)continuous geography of Europa and within the enfolding (in)consonant politics and economies of Europe.[12] I start with the re-rendition of the migration story, as we know it, in an attempt to recapture its end(s) in the present tense of a near-past. It is a story that has been tirelessly enacted and fictionalized.

The Story of the Worker As *Gastarbeiter*

The story begins with a black-and-white photograph in a newspaper from 1972. The photograph is part of a newspaper story inscribing "social scenes" from "Turkey in the '70s" and depicts a man with short hair and an imperceptible moustache, wearing dark pants, a lighter colored jacket, presumably a white shirt with no necktie. He walks in between two official-looking men in dark suits and, in his hands, holds two neatly wrapped packets. They are walking toward the camera. The caption reads: "The 500,000th worker is being sent with wishes of a safe journey, and with gifts given to him for this occasion."[13] The accompanying news story identifies Turkey's then–minister of labor Ali Rıza Uzuner and Germany's general consul, Dr. Adolf Sonnenhol, among the official farewell committee.

This is the beginning of my version of the migration story, captured in a personal archive of newspaper clippings and literary journals from the summer of 1972. This migration story, according to an article in the literary journal *Yeni a Dergisi* [The new A journal], entitled "Photograph of a Worker," begins in 1964, more or less when the labor migration to Europe had begun.

Meet Necati Güven, an unskilled worker, on his voyage to become a slave in a factory in a foreign land. He is a peasant on the way to becoming a worker, a family man on the way to the lonely state of singlehood, and a rural native on the way to facing urban foreignness. In this story, Necati Güven is also on a journey to separation, going away from home to a foreign place. The emotional burden of the separation is underscored by a pair of poetic signifiers, *gurbet* and *sıla*, the customary vocabulary of folk songs and laments of the longing for home. In the songs and laments, one moves into the vast unknown of the *gurbet* as soon as one leaves the known limits of the *sıla*, usually the village where home is located. In other words, *sıla* marks a discrete point of departure, whereas *gurbet* is nondescript, as in anywhere away from home. When presenting the migration of the worker, the story remaps the poetic convention, marks the worker's home as his country of origin, and names his foreign destination, another country. Hence, in the persona of Necati Güven, a labor migration story is set to motion, a story with a binary itinerary, between Turkey and Germany.

The first wave of the social-scientific versions of the migration story strongly resonates with the literary kind exemplified in the pages of *Yeni a Dergisi*. While the sociological and economic narratives of migration are about labor market demands, surplus workforce in sending countries, and labor shortages in host countries, the anthropological narratives follow the paths of peasants-turned-workers from their villages to the workers' quarters in the urban centers of the West. The protagonist in this story is the categorical international migrant worker, primarily taking part in institutionalized worker exchanges, known as guest-worker programs. The movement of labor is between countries at the industrialized center of Europe (i.e., Austria, Belgium, Germany, France, the Netherlands, Sweden, and Switzerland) and the countries at Europe's southern periphery (i.e., Italy, Spain, Portugal, Greece, the former Yugoslavia, Turkey, and Morocco). The direction of the movement is from the latter to the former, from periphery to the center. Also in movement toward the center (Britain, France, the Netherlands) in this period are migrants from (former) colonies (India, Pakistan, the Caribbean, Algeria, Surinam, Indonesia).[14]

The formal policies of labor recruitment in Europe ended in the mid-1970s (in Germany in 1973). By this time, the presence of foreign populations in Europe had risen substantially. In 1976, there were about 12 million foreigners in the above-mentioned European countries, whereas in 1960 this number had been only 5 million. Germany's share in the number of foreigners in 1976 was close to 4 million, about 6.4 percent of the total population of what was then the Federal Republic. The end of formal recruitment did not mean the end of migration. Mainly through family reunification programs and political asylum, the influx of foreign populations persisted throughout the 1980s and 1990s, with occasional drops fueled by restrictive legislation and promotion of return migration. By 1990, the foreign populations in Europe had reached 14.5 million.[15] In Germany, the number of foreigners amounted to 7 million in 1994, 2 million of which were from Turkey.[16]

In the two decades following the end of labor recruitment, the foreigners in Europe have been solidly "incorporated" into the available legal, political, economic, and social structures and institutions in their host countries.[17] They have become part of the labor and investment markets, education and welfare systems, and policy discourses and regimes, as well as entering as formal categories in national and European statistical schemes. They have attained and exercised *as foreigners* rights and privileges that are conventionally considered to be in the proprietary domain of *national* citizenship. They have been extensively involved in public life through associational activity, union membership, party politics, electoral practices, and arts and literary production. They also have been part of *extant* regimes of income inequity, social differentiation, and ethnic and racial discrimination. In short, the foreigners are *subjects* in a complex terrain of exclusions and inclusions, contention and accommodation, and disenfranchisement and membership.

Odysseys in *Ganz unten*: From Labor to Culture

"Man hat Arbeitskräfte gerufen und es kommen Menschen" [We called for labor and came human beings]: Max Frisch's legendary expression sums up more than anything the turn of tide in migration story, a turn that resignifies the guest *worker* as a *person*, a total being with feelings and needs. Compared to the immigration classics of the 1970s that focus primarily on labor struggles, class structures, and the plight of workers, the social science of the turn testifies to the permanence and personhood of the "guests who stayed" and were "here for good."[18] The story is no longer simply about incomes, numbers, and policies, but about conditions of migrants, understanding migration, and (anthropological) trials and rituals of moving and settling. In addition, the new version of the migration story differentiates its subject, the migrant, along gender and ethnic lines; Women, Turks, Portuguese, and Others do not appear simply as categorical entries in statistical tables but become legitimate topics of inquiry in their own right.

In this version, the emergence of the Turk as subject follows a dramatic, nonacademic path. In 1985 Günter Wallraff, a prolific investigative journalist, published *Ganz unten*, the story of the Turkish migrant Ali's struggle for survival at the bottom of the German social ladder.[19] The book immediately attained the status of best-seller and was translated into other languages with similarly striking titles—in the following year, into Turkish as *En Alttakiler*, into French as *Tête de Turc*, and into English as *Lowest of the Low*. In the story, Ali frequently changes jobs, working one day as a construction worker, the next day as a part-time janitor at McDonald's, and, expectedly, is exploited. He lives in dire conditions, experiences oppression, and feels discrimination in the lowest, and strongly segregated, echelons of Germany. From the cover of the book, a picture of Ali stares at the reader, an image Arlene Akiko Teraoka describes thus: "[In] torn clothing and a construction hat from Thyssen, the figure of the Turk presents his familiar face—the hair, the eyes, that moustache."[20]

Ali's picture and story convey a starkly different impression than the solemn images of absence inscribed into the migrant photos that beautify the artful pages of John Berger's *A Seventh Man*, written a decade ago.[21] There, Berger's lyrical commentary marks the migrant in disturbing absences of speech and gesture. There, the migrant is not heard and seen, remaining invisible beyond walls that separate him from European imagination. In Wallraff's story, the migrant enters the world of European economy and imagination. He has a place, at the bottom, and he speaks as a member of the dispossessed and underprivileged. Wallraff's story has a twist, though. Ali is Wallraff, disguised as Ali and uncovering the experience of the Turkish migrant, captured ironically through "teilnehmende Beobachtung" (participant observation).[22] Ironies and epistemic quandaries aside, the story of Wallraff's Ali (or Wallraff as Ali) identifies a presence, reconfigures statistical evidence as experiential narrative, and accords a blueprint for the habitual stories of Turkish *Gastarbeiter* experience to come, *ganz unten* and with nowhere to go.[23]

I take Wallraff's story as a marker, signaling the end of the labor story of migration. After *Ganz unten*, the migrant is neither a guest nor a worker. That is to say, after the mid-1980s, the predominant mode of writing migration is to narrate culture and identity stories. At this stage, labor statistics no longer dominate the migration texts but attribute credence to identity stories. The protagonist of the story is the Turk (the Other), whose identity is analyzed vis-à-vis the German (the native)—within the conventions of cultural otherness and difference. As for disciplinary prowess, anthropology and literary/cultural studies take over the task of writing migration, which thus far has been subject matter for sociology and economics. Relieved from the social analysis of labor markets, sociology revives studies of citizenship, a historical concern of the discipline, which is apparently amplified by massive migrations and foreignness within nation-states.[24]

In the same period, policy debates move away from the economics and logistics of labor importation and focus on nebulously defined integration and factual border controls. Border controls regressively concern limiting further *im*migration into the nation-states that comprise Europe, while integration involves the "adjustment" of those who are already in. The formal integration policies, if they do exist, are documents that reiterate purported "integration problems," which are never defined but circularly deployed as proof for the need to integrate migrants to their new society — seasoned with occasional statistics about the number of German friends a migrant has, and the obligatory recitation of cultural differences such as being Muslim or Turkish.

This shift in the story of migration conveniently coincides with "the cultural turn" in social sciences, a new era of social thought in which "culture is broadened from being the traditional consequence of social determination to include the processes of determination"[25] and "culture does not just provide the meaning of experience but is also the terms of that experience."[26] In other words, culture affords not only a framework to understand, and explain, social formations and productions but also becomes those forms and products through which individuals and collectivities live and experience social life and signification. What is crucial here is that, with the turn to culture, culture simultaneously occupies the domains of the explanation and the explained, becoming the primary tool of meaning making for both the social scientist and social actor. For the story of migration I am narrating, it suffices to note that the turn to culture lends a new narrative fabric to migration.

If the connection of the new migration story and the turn to culture is one of conjunction, the relation of this culture- and identity-oriented story of migration to incorporation is one of disjunction. As I have argued above, the incorporation of migrants into legal and societal institutions, regimes of rights and membership, and economies of ownership and inequity in Europe has proceeded rather rapidly and without exceptional controversy.[27] This is a seemingly paradoxical outcome, given the amplifying talk about integration, or rather, its lack thereof, on the part of the keepers of the nation (and its state). The key to unravel the paradox is the disparity between the premise of the nation-state, that is, congruence of the membership in a state and nationality, and the growing populations of foreigners within nation-state borders in Europe. If I were to paraphrase Mary Douglas here, foreignness constitutes the paramount *anomaly* "in reference to a total structure of thought [and action] whose key-stone, margins and internal lines are held in relation" by nation-based notions and units.[28] In the world we live in, foreignness confuses this classificatory order of nationness, threatens its rule, and enables transformations, albeit still within the same classificatory schemes and at times creating further aberrations.[29]

The amplified talk about integration is, then, more about maintaining the categorical integrity of national order than remedying empirical inequalities, which are more often than not subsumed under the foreignness of migrants and erased from social agendas of policy-making and academic writing. The periodic amnesties to regularize the status of "illegal aliens" and the efforts to expand citizenship to foreigners, as well as prohibitive measures to limit border crossings, are all attempts to contain foreignness within the nation-state paradigm. However, the signs that point in the other direction are also in place: the degree and terms of incorporation; the high rates of preference for dual citizenship on the part of migrants; the reluctant yet implicitly or explicitly accepting stances toward dual citizenship on the part of nation-states; and, last but not least, the newly emerging transnational formations of membership such as European citizenship. These developments all compound, in the words of Zygmunt Bauman, the "tendency toward 'denationalization of the state,' 'privatization of nationality,' or more correctly, toward separation between state and the nation."[30]

The cultural story of migration disregards the processes of incorporation, the augmenting obstacles to national narratives, and the difficulties of maintaining foreignness. Instead, the narrative wanders the terrain of "culture" and renders an elementary story of exclusion and inclusion, in which the parameters that make difference and identity are taken to be national/ethnic—Turkishness, Germanness, and Islam being three principal ones. Rather than attending to the complex layering of exclusions, inclusions, inequities, and connections within and without the nation-state, the migration story relies on the empathy generated by obligatory references to the plight of *Gastarbeiter*, almost two decades after its drop from official use and after it has lost any bearing to the legal and empirical condition of migrants. In the end, "ironically, as guestworkers are increasingly incorpo-rated into the membership schemes of European host polities, the debate over how well they 'adjust' intensifies, and their cultural otherness is accen-tuated. Guestworkers become *symbolic* foreigners" in migration stories.[31]

As guest workers are progressively rendered into symbolic foreigners, in an inverse movement to the normalization of their status, the foreigner has assumed the guise of the Turk. Into the 1990s, the migrant in Europe has been named "the Turk." In public and private conversations of the jour-nalistic, academic, and official kind, the opening "as the Turks in Europe (or more commonly in Germany)" has attained an explanatory inertia of its own. The narrative that follows this epigram is in need of not so much substantiation as mere articulation. That narrative is already imbued with a mélange of migrant places, circumstances, and allusions: "Gathering on the edge of 'foreign' cultures; gathering at the frontiers; gatherings in the ghettos or cafés of city centers; gathering in the half-life, half-light of foreign tongues, or in the uncanny fluency of another's language; gathering the past in a ritual of revival; gathering the present. Also the gathering of people in the diaspora: indentured, migrant, interned; the gathering of incriminatory statistics, educational performance, legal statuses, immigration status."[32] These, according to Homi Bhabha, make up "the genealogy of that lonely figure that John Berger named the seventh man."[33]

What is notable in Bhabha's gatherings, which he relates to his own experiences in "that moment of scattering of the people that in other times and other places, in the nations of others,"[34] is the end point in the geneal-ogy of migration. The circle of migration story closes when the seventh man returns—and the seventh man of migration is none other than the Turk. Embodied in this figurative design of displacement and inert gathering, the Turk arrives as the ultimate signifier of migrancy:

> His migration is like an event in a dream dreamt by another. The migrant's intentionality is permeated by historical necessities of which neither he nor anybody he meets is aware. That is why it is as if his life were dreamt by another. . . . The body loses its mind in the gesture. How opaque the disguise of words. . . . He [the Turk] treated the sounds of the unknown language as if they were silence. To break through his silence. He learnt twenty words of the new language. But to his amaze-ment at first, their meaning changed as he spoke them. . . . Is it possible to see the opaqueness of the words?[35]

Thus Bhabha echoes Berger, and this is the end of the cultural story of migration. At this end, the act of writing is not there to register silences of migration; it is not in silences that the cultural stories of migration are written. Silence becomes the story—the story of the Turk, the migrant, at the pinnacle of his tropical presence in the real and imaginary topography of migrancy.[36]

In Conclusion: Transnational Plots and Movements

In drawing up this conclusion to the cultural story of migration, I have turned to Bhabha and Berger not so much to dispute the lyrical collection of gatherings in Bhabha's intimation to migrancy or to question the sudden silences and momentary opaqueness of words so evocatively pictured in Berger's *A Seventh Man*. An itinerary of gatherings and silences do play out in migrancy. What I have chosen to accomplish instead is to uncover the concealed yet recognizable texture of the cultural stories of migration—an inescapable and placid speechlessness, frailty, and boundedness. The migrant is tied to an unyielding past, the past of his home and culture, and a persistent present, the present of his host place, his bureaucratic shackles, and his otherness. He is bounded by his nation in nations of others and in this boundedness he lives diasporas. Lost are futures, dreams, and competencies, along with possibilities for enacting agency, achieving more homes than one, and living without nations. Are all stories of migration about nations, homes, pasts, and tedious repetitions of the present? Do all migrations end in one place and then conjure incessant longings for loss? Is contemporary migration simply a cultural economy of movement between peripheries with Edenic pasts and centers with affluent presents, or between the nothingness of underdevelopment and the wealth of advancement?

These are vexing questions in search of a new narrative. This new narrative is in formation in the stories of migrants who traverse the world in inordinate numbers, as (il)legal aliens, and burdened with inequities of travel regulations, market demands, and fortunes and desires. We encounter their stories in unlikely places, the places we hardly associate with migrancy—Belize, Malawi, and Sierra Leone, for instance. Their numbers overburden international statistical exercises beyond recognition. Their movements confuse migration geographies that are mapped into nation-states.

As a way to identify the coordinates and scope of the new narrative, I will cite three seemingly disparate items from the contemporary inventory of migrations. My first illustration regards the volume of movement in the postwar period. Based on statistics kept by the German state, between 1954 and 1994, about 21.9 million foreigners entered and 15.6 million left the country.[37] Taken in terms of conventional migration narrative, these numbers translate into a net *im*migration of 6.3 million. If looked at from another interpretive frame, the numbers highlight a movement involving 37.5 million people in a span of forty years. This other story is about a movement that goes far beyond the simple net immigration number registered in statistical accounts, expeditiously affecting the people on the move, their families, and their towns, at the point of both departure and destination. The geography, as well as social and economic design, of this movement covers and transforms places within and without Europe. The simplicity of the net immigration figure only reveals the inadequacy of the national account of migrancy in capturing the complexity and density of the movement, and its human condition.

Second, I exemplify an annual movement between Berlin and Bahadın, a small town in central Turkey. Every year in Berlin, following the customary speeches of the union leaders, the May Day Parade turns into an impressive street festival. The participants leisurely walk through a variety of stands selling books, handicrafts, and food, enjoying the festivities. In 1996, one of the most successful food stands was operated by the Bahadın Association of Berlin. In their makeshift stand, they were busy baking and selling homemade foods. These "authentic" food items were drawing record numbers of customers willing to wait at least fifteen minutes in line. The members of the association were giving their time and labor to raise money for the annual festival they organize every summer in Bahadın. For the contingency of foreigners around the Bahadın Association, the festival had a significant place in ordering their year-round activities in Berlin. The festival aimed to bring together progressive and popular artists and Alevi singers from Europe and Turkey in Bahadın for a week.[38] Its progressive orientation usually generated frictions with the local state administration in Turkey. The festival, rather than being a sign of their nostalgic orientation to their past "home," was at the focal point of Bahadınlıs' relation to both Berlin and Bahadın. It allowed them to have a concurrent settlement in two "homes," enabled by a vigorous participation in the economies and social life of both places. The level and scope of their participation first and foremost was subnational in that it primarily concerned Berlin and Bahadın, as well as spanning the spaces of progressive and Alevi politics in Europe and Turkey.

Finally, let's sample a youth festival called STREET '94: The Posse Effect and staged in Kreuzberg, Berlin. In the spring of 1994, publicity posters and graffiti on walls in Kreuzberg radiantly displayed the mottos of the festival: "TO STAY HERE IS MY RIGHT" and "WE ALL ARE ONE." The festival revolved around a street art exhibition, dance parties with rap, reggae, and ethnopop bands, and open-air screening of the films such as *Juice*, *New Jack City*, *Menace II Society*, and *Boyz 'N the Hood*.

STREET '94 was organized under the auspices of NaunynRitze, a youth center in Kreuzberg, and funded by Kreuzberg's municipal government, Berlin's Ministry of Youth and Family, and various private corporations. It was officially part of another Berlin-wide youth project staged by (former East) Berlin's Akademie der Künste: an upscale "Youth Art+Culture" project called X '94, with the subtitle *50 DAYS TO BLOW YOUR MIND*. In the grand design of X '94, STREET '94 represented the cool art of the street, subcultural undercurrents of the metropolis, and the raw skill of ghetto boys and girls. And, true to its projected image, STREET '94 was located in Kreuzberg, the ghetto, with a touch of hip and avant-garde.

During the festival, various rap and graffiti workshops took place, attracting renowned local street artists and numerous rappers and writers-to-be. Also present were the prominent graffiti writers from other metropolitan centers, such as T-KID from New York and JAY-ONE from Paris. As invited artists, they stayed with their hip-hop brothers, exchanged views on aesthetics and style, and told tales of their fortunes. At workshops and performances, the hip-hop community was heralded as a multicultural community, extending beyond borders and delivering the message of peace and brotherhood. In the "imagined"[39] world of hip-hop, graffiti paintings on the walls were artistic expressions and messages addressed to society at large. Styles were many and varied, and so were the cultures and writers; the writers and rappers were innovators of style and meaning. Their enactments of hip-hop community were not, however, rudimentary imitations of the ghetto bravado of other places. With resourcefulness, they appropriated styles and discourses and invaded the scenes of youth culture in Berlin. More importantly, with their "Posse," they intervened in civic spaces and claimed their right to stay, whoever they were and from wherever they were, disrupting the monolithic narratives of a second generation lost and stranded in between Turkishness and Germanness.[40]

When considered worldwide, the expanse, density, and character of the new migratory movements are indicators of the transnational turn in migrancy, a new complex of movement underwritten by multireferential orientations and economies located in subnational, national, and global terrains.[41] Oblivious to this new topology of movement in transnational spaces, our current language of *im*migration still privileges nation and nationness and confines migrancy to a movement from peripheries to centers—Europe, the United States, and Canada. Moreover, in narratives of integration and diasporic cultures, the dominant language of *im*migration (in)advertently "valorizes centers" and "evicts" migrants from centers. For, as Sassen asserts, being "installed" outside the center is de facto devaluation.[42] To redress this devaluation requires not sentimental acts of valorizing "migrant stories and cultures" but frameworks attentive to the transnational dimensions of contemporary migrancy. Only such frameworks are capable of capturing the new story of movement and transformation in which migration, and the migrant, are simultaneously present and absent, free and constrained, beyond the nation but within states, which persistently conserve the "nation" as part of their definition and operation.

The contemporary stories of migrants cross multiple borders, expand beyond topographies of national order, and disrupt the hegemony of prosaic labor-culture stories. So should our narratives.

Notes

An earlier version of this essay was published in German as "Kultur als Fiktion: Forschen über (türkische) Migration nach Berlin, Deutschland, Europa," in *Inspecting Germany: Internationale Deutschland-Ethnographie der Gegenwart*, ed. Thomas Hauschild and Bernd Jürgen Warneken (Münster: LIT-Verlag, 2002).

1   Iain Chambers, *Migrancy, Culture, Identity* (London: Routledge, 1994), 2.

2   Ibid., 3.

3   For historical accounts of the movements of peoples and goods, see Klaus Bade and Myron Weiner, eds., *Migration Past, Migration Future: Germany and the United States* (Providence, RI: Berghahn, 1997); Stephen Castles and Mark J. Miller, *The Age of Migration: International Population Movements in the Modern World* (New York: Guilford, 1998); and Saskia Sassen, *Guests and Aliens* (New York: New Press, 1999).

4   Benedict Anderson, *Imagined Communities* (London: Verso, 1983).

5   On ways of imagining and theorizing the world as "global," see Arjun Appadurai, *Modernity at Large: Cultural Dimensions of Globalization* (Minneapolis: University of Minnesota Press, 1996); Zygmunt Bauman, "Modernity and Ambivalence," in *Global Culture: Nationalism, Globalization and Modernity*, ed. Mike Featherstone (London: Sage, 1990) and *Globalization: The Human Consequences* (New York: Columbia University Press, 1998); Ulf Hannerz, *Transnational Connections: Culture, People, Places* (New York: Routledge, 1996); Roland Robertson, *Globalization: Social Theory and Global Culture* (London: Sage, 1992); and Saskia Sassen, *Globalization and Its Discontents* (New York: New Press, 1998).

6   Chambers, *Migrancy*, 5.

7   Saskia Sassen, *Losing Control? Sovereignty in an Age of Globalization* (New York: Columbia University Press, 1996).

8   Renato Rosaldo, *Culture and Truth: The Remaking of Social Analysis* (Boston: Beacon, 1989).

9   Yasemin Nuhoğlu Soysal, "Changing Parameters of Citizenship and Claims-Making: Organized Islam in European Public Spheres," *Theory and Society* 26 (1997): 509–527.

10 Liisa H. Malkki, *Purity and Exile: Violence, Memory, and National Cosmology among Hutu Refugees in Tanzania* (Chicago: University of Chicago Press, 1995).

11 See Bauman, "Modernity and Ambivalence," Sassen, *Losing Control?*, and Yasemin Nuhoğlu Soysal, *Limits of Citizenship: Migrants and Postnational Membership in Europe* (Chicago: University of Chicago Press, 1994).

12 I take *Europe* to denote not a cultural or geographical area but a set of nation-states and regional entities connected through various institutional arrangements and organizations, international treaties and agreements, and cultural and sports connections. In this sense, Europe is not one but many, depending on the countries and regions included in the permutations of arrangements, treaties, and connections. In varying degrees, Turkey belongs to this multifaceted Europe as a member of institutional structures and as a signatory of treaties. For an extensive review of the formal relations of Turkey with Europe and the European Union, see Canan Balkır and Alan M. Williams, eds., *Turkey and Europe* (London: Pinter, 1993), and Meltem Müftüler-Bac, *Turkey's Relations with a Changing Europe* (Manchester: Manchester University Press, 1997). For a critical anthropological account of the origins of Europe, see Michael Herzfeld, *Anthropology through the Looking-Glass: Critical Ethnography in the Margins of Europe* (Cambridge: Cambridge University Press, 1987).

13 Turhan Ilgaz, "70'ler Türkiyesi: Toplumsal Görüntüler," *Cumhuriyet*, August 19, 1972.

14 For a sample of the early social-scientific works on migration, see Nermin Abadan-Unat, ed., *Turkish Workers in Europe, 1960–1975: A Socio-Economic Reappraisal* (Leiden: E. J. Brill, 1975); Stephen Castles and Godula Kosack, *Immigrant Workers and Class Structure in Western Europe* (London: Oxford University Press, 1973); Ali S. Gitmez, *Dışgöç Öyküsü* (Ankara: Maya Matbaacılık Yayıncılık, 1979); and Hans-Joachim Hoffmann-Nowotny, *Soziologie des Fremdarbeiterproblems: Eine theoretische und empirische Analyse am Beispiel der Scweiz* (Stuttgart: Ferdinand Enke Verlag, 1973).

15 Soysal Nuhoğlu, *Limits of Citizenship*, 22–23.

16   Rainer Münz and Ralf Ulrich, "Changing Patterns of Immigration to Germany, 1945–1995," in *Migrants, Refugees, and Foreign Policy: U.S. and German Policies toward Countries of Origin*, ed. Rainer Münz and Myron Weiner (Providence, RI: Berghahn, 1997), 84, 93.

17   In *Limits of Citizenship*, Soysal Nuhoğlu defines incorporation as "a process whereby a guestworker population becomes a part of the polity of the host country" and elaborates that independently of the degree of the individual migrant's adaptation "to the life patterns of the host society, [guestworker populations] do become incorporated into its legal and organizational structures and participate in various activities of the host society" (30). She also shows that the incorporation of migrants is primarily dependent on host-country structures and institutions, on the one hand, and world-level universalistic discourses of personhood and human rights, on the other. My assertions in this essay follow her analysis.

18   Stephen Castles, *Here for Good: Western Europe's New Ethnic Minorities* (London: Pluto, 1984) and "The Guests Who Stayed: The Debate on 'Foreigners Policy' in the German Federal Republic," *International Migration Review* 19 (1985): 517–34.

19   Günter Wallraff, *Ganz unten* (Cologne: Verlag Kiepenheuer and Witsch, 1985).

20   Arlene Akiko Teraoka, "Talking 'Turk': On Narrative Strategies and Cultural Stereotypes," *New German Critique*, no. 46 (1989): 104–28.

21   John Berger, *A Seventh Man: A Book of Images and Words about the Experience of Migrant Workers in Europe* (Baltimore, MD: Penguin, 1975).

22   Teraoka, "Talking 'Turk,'" 105.

23   Wallraff's book is not a first in its genre of realistic ethnography/ethnographic novel. Wallraff is not the most prolific writer of this genre, either. I privilege Wallraff's account because of its best-selling status and international acclaim. For a critical account of the genre, see Teraoka, "Talking 'Turk'" and "Turks As Subjects: The Ethnographic Novels of Paul Geiersbach," in *Culture and Contexture: Essays in Anthropology and Literary Studies*, ed. E. Valentine Daniel and Jeffrey M. Peck (Berkeley: University of California Press, 1994).

24   In the past two decades, there has been an explosion in migration studies, covering all continents of the world and focusing on numerous ethnic groups, their movements, and cultures. Among this corpus, the literature devoted to studying Turks in Europe is rather significant in terms of both its topical and theoretical expanse and representativeness of the field. For a sample of studies on migration, culture, and identity regarding Turks in Europe, with varying degrees of emphasis on, and analytical significance attributed to, culture, see Ayşe Çağlar, "Hyphenated Identities and the Limits of 'Culture,'" in *The Politics of Multiculturalism in the New Europe: Racism, Identity, and Community*, ed. Tariq Modood and Pnina Werbner (London: Zed, 1997) and "Popular Culture, Marginality, and Institutional Incorporation: German-Turkish Rap and Turkish Pop in Berlin," *Cultural Dynamics* 10.3 (1998): 243–61; Thomas Faist, *Social Citizenship for Whom? Young Turks in Germany and Mexican Americans in the United States* (Aldershot, UK: Avebury, 1995); Deniz Göktürk, "Turkish Delight, German Fright: Migrant Identities in Transnational Cinemas," in *Mapping the Margins: Identity Politics and the Media*, ed. Deniz Derman and Karen Ross (Creskill, NJ: Hampton, 2002); Wilhelm Heitmeyer, Joachim Mueller, and

Helmut Schoereder, *Verlockender Fundamentalismus: Türkische Jugendliche in Deutschland* (Frankfurt am Main: Suhrkamp, 1997); David Horrocks and Eva Kolinsky, *Turkish Culture in German Society Today* (Providence, RI: Berghahn, 1996); Riva Kastoryano, *Négocier l'identité: La france, l'Allemagne et leurs immigrés* (Paris: Armand Colin, 1996); Ayhan Kaya, *"Sicher in Kreuzberg": Constructing Diasporas. Turkish Hip-Hop Youth in Berlin* (Berlin: Transcript Verlag, 2001); Ruth Mandel, "A Place of Their Own: Contesting Spaces and Defining Places in Berlin's Migrant Community," in *Making Muslim Space in North America and Europe*, ed. Barbara Daly Metcalf (Berkeley: University of California Press, 1996); Werner Schiffauer, *Die Bauern von Subay: Das Leben in einem Türkischen Dorf* (Stuttgart: Kleff-Cotta, 1987) and *Die Migranten aus Subay: Türken in Deutschland, eine Ethnographie* (Stuttgart: Kleff-Cotta, 1991); Levent Soysal, "Beyond 'Second Generation': Rethinking the Place of Migrant Youth Culture in Berlin," in *Challenging Ethnic Citizenship: German and Israeli Perspectives on Immigration*, ed. Daniel Levy and Yfaat Weiss (New York: Berghahn, 2002) and "Diversity of Experience, Experience of Diversity: Turkish Migrant Youth Culture in Berlin," *Cultural Dynamics* 13.1 (2001): 5–28; Hermann Tertilt, *Turkish Power Boys: Ethnographie einer Jugenbande* (Frankfurt am Main: Suhrkamp, 1996); Jenny White, "Turks in the New Germany," *American Anthropologist* 99 (1997): 754–69; and, Barbara Wolbert, *Der getötete Pass: Rückkehr in die Türkei* (Berlin: Akademia Verlag, 1995). For a more extensive bibliography, see Levent Soysal, "Projects of Culture: An Ethnographic Episode in the Life of Migrant Youth in Berlin" (Ph.D. diss., Harvard University, 1999).

25 David Chaney, *The Cultural Turn: Scene-Setting Essays on Contemporary Social History* (London: Routledge, 1994), 23.

26 Ibid., 182.

27 Here I particularly refer to governmental policy and action. Aside from its solid place in racist politics of right-wing parties and organizations, immigration primarily becomes a powerful rhetorical device and issue of controversy in electoral politics. The exploitation of immigration in electoral politics, on the other hand, does not follow a consistent path — at one moment overburdening the electoral agendas with images of immigrants swarming the economy and culture of the host nation-state, and at another moment completely and conveniently forgotten as an electoral strategy. Despite controversies, restrictions, and reversals, it can be safely said that the policy decisions regarding migration in Europe in the last three decades have been consistently expansive.

28 Mary Douglas, *Purity and Danger: An Analysis of the Concepts of Pollution and Taboo* (London: Ark, [1966] 1988), 41.

29 See Akil Gupta and James Ferguson, "Beyond 'Culture': Space, Identity, and the Politics of Difference," *Cultural Anthropology* 7 (1992): 6–23; Malkki, *Purity and Exile*; and Soysal Nuhoğlu, *Limits of Citizenship*.

30 Bauman, "Modernity and Ambivalence," 167. See also Eric J. Hobsbawm, *Nations and Nationalism since 1780: Programme, Myth, Reality* (Cambridge: Cambridge University Press, 1990); Sassen, *Losing Control?*; and Soysal Nuhoğlu, *Limits of Citizenship*.

31 Soysal Nuhoğlu, *Limits of Citizenship*, 135.

32 Homi K. Bhabha, *The Location of Culture* (London: Routledge, 1994), 139.

33 Ibid.

34 Ibid.

35 Ibid., 165. Bhabha indicates that he has "composed this passage from quotations that are scattered through the text" of Berger's *A Seventh Man* (268 n. 59). Here I cite a slightly compacted version of Bhabha's composition.

36 See Göktürk, "Turkish Delight, German Fright" and Leslie A. Adelson, "Opposing Oppositions: Turkish-German Questions in Contemporary German Studies," *German Studies Review* 17 (1994): 305–30. Both Göktürk and Adelson also criticize the taken-for-granted incommensurability of communication and translation in Bhabha's rendition of the "Turkish migrant" as speechless and inarticulate.

37 Münz and Ulrich, "Changing Patterns of Immigration," 92.

38 Alevis are members of a religious(-cultural) minority group from Anatolia. In very broad terms, as a belief system Alevism is a variant of Sufism, which has affinities with, but is not congruent with the Shia branch of Islam. Since 2000, mainly because of political differences among Bahadınlıs in Berlin and changes in the political composition of the municipal government in Bahadın, the festival is not taking place.

39 Anderson, *Imagined Communities*.

40 STREET '94 was not the only megashow put on by the migrant youths in Berlin under auspices of NaunynRitze. There was MAPP (Multinationales Anti-rassistiches Performance Project) in 1995 and POW (Personen Ohne Wohnung [People without homes]) in 1996. For a comprehensive account and analysis of the production and enactments of migrant youth culture in the social spaces of Berlin, see Soysal, "Projects of Culture."

41 As the social science literature stands, transnationalism is generally an undertheorized field of study. While anthropological theorizing emphasizes the multireferentiality of transnational movements, sociology and political science literatures tend to conceptualize transnationalization as binationalization. On transnational movements from sociological and political science perspectives, see Peggy Levitt, *The Transnational Villagers* (Berkeley: University of California Press, 2001); Alejandro Portes, "Divergent Destinies: Immigration, the Second Generation, and the Rise of Transnational Communities," in *Paths to Inclusion: The Integration of Migrants in the United States and Germany*, ed. Peter H. Schuck and Rainer Münz (New York: Berghahn, 1998); and Susanne H. Rudolph and James Piscatori, ed., *Transnational Religion and Fading States* (Boulder, CO: Westview, 1997). For ethnographic and cultural accounts of transnational movement of peoples and goods, see Appadurai, *Modernity at Large*; Linda Basch, Nina Glick Schiller, and Cristina Szanton Blanc, *Nations Unbound: Transnational Projects, Postcolonial Predicaments, and Deterritorialized Nation-States* (Langhorne, PA: Gordon and Breach, 1994); Donald Martin Carter, *States of Grace: Senegalese in Italy and the New European Immigration* (Minneapolis: University of Minnesota Press, 1997); Roger Rouse, "Questions of Identity: Personhood and Collectivity in Transnational Migration to the United States," *Critique of Anthropology* 15 (1995); 351–81, and Hannerz, *Transnational Connections*.

42 Saskia Sassen, "Analytic Borderlands: Race, Gender, and Representation in the New City," in *Re-Presenting the City: Ethnicity, Capital, and Culture in the Twenty-First-Century Metropolis*, ed. Anthony D. King (New York: New York University Press, 1996).

Hülya Adak

National Myths and Self-Na(rra)tions:
Mustafa Kemal's *Nutuk* and Halide Edib's
Memoirs and *The Turkish Ordeal*

Mustafa Kemal (1881–1938), the commander-in-chief of the Nationalist Army in the Indepen-dence Struggle of Turkey and the first president of the Turkish Republic, delivered his seminal speech entitled *Nutuk* [The speech] in 1927 in Ankara to the Congress of the Cumhuriyet Halk Fırkası (Republican People's Party).[1] *Nutuk* was epic in proportion and content. Delivered by Mustafa Kemal over six days for a duration of thirty-six hours and thirty-one minutes (Octo-ber 15–20, 1927), *Nutuk* described the heroic accounts of the Independence Struggle of Turkey against the Allies (1919–1922), particularly the military leadership of Mustafa Kemal during the Struggle, with much hyperbole. The speech fore-grounded the role of its narrator in Turkish his-tory at the expense of defaming or ignoring the Ottoman Sultan-Caliph, the roles of the leading figures in the nationalist struggle and the estab-lishment of the republic. Such figures included former leaders of the Terakkiperver Cumhuriyet Fırkası (Progressive Republican Party), the oppo-sition party to the Republican People's Party, such as Kazım Karabekir, Ali Fuat Cebesoy, Refet Bele, Caffer Tayyar Eğilmez, Hüseyin Rauf

The *South Atlantic Quarterly* 102:2/3, Spring/Summer 2003.
Copyright © 2003 by Duke University Press.

Orbay, and Dr. Adnan Adıvar. *Nutuk*, a vindication of the closing of the Progressive Republican Party and the establishment of Mustafa Kemal's single-party regime, was also a justification of the acts of the Independence Tribunals, which, in 1926, ordered the arrest and/or execution of former PRP members (and prominent surviving Unionists) after the attempt to assassinate Mustafa Kemal, regardless of whether the accused were plotters or not in the assassination.

Immediately after the delivery of *Nutuk*, a number of letters of defense and alternative autobiographies were written by some of Mustafa Kemal's political opponents, including Kazım Karabekir Paşa, Ali Fuat Cebesoy, Dr. Rıza Nur, and Halide Edib Adıvar. After 1925, however, not only the political opposition but also its press was silenced, so that these articles did not enjoy publicity in Turkey. Some of the autobiographies were not published in Turkey until the 1960s, while some were published only recently.[2] With alternative accounts of the history of the period silenced, for decades *Nutuk* monopolized the writing of the history of the Independence Struggle of Turkey as well as the establishment of the Turkish Republic.

One autobiography written as a response to *Nutuk* was by a prolific woman writer and political figure, who, at the time *Nutuk* was delivered, was, with her second husband Dr. Adnan Adıvar, in self-imposed exile in the United Kingdom. This woman writer, Halide Edib, had been influential in the Turkish nationalism movement a decade before the Independence Struggle. In 1910, Edib, who had embraced Turanism, was called "The Mother of the Turk" among the pan-Turanistic organizations Türk Ocakları (Turkish Homelands). Her early novels — *Raik'in Annesi* [Raik's mother] (1909), *Seviyye Talip* (1912), *Yeni Turan* [New Turan] (1912), *Handan* (1912), *Son Eseri* [His/Her last work] (1913), *Mev'ut Hüküm* [The decree] (1917–1918) — some explicitly narrating her Turanist ideology (*Yeni Turan*), others dealing with different facets of women's issues in Ottoman society, such as polygyny, had been received with wide acclaim.[3] At the end of World War I, Edib vouched for the American mandate for the Ottoman Empire, arguing that this was the only solution if the territories held by the Ottoman Empire were not to be compromised. Further, the American protectorate would entail, according to Edib, siding with a stronger power than Europe, which would protect Turkey from the threats of the Christian minorities who were being empowered by the Allies.

In March 1920, Adnan and Edib, convinced that the only solution for the salvation of the Ottoman Empire lay in armed resistance against the Allies, secretly escaped from Constantinople to Anatolia to join the Nationalist Army.[4] During the Struggle, Edib worked as public speaker, journalist, translator, writer, editor, nurse, and soldier. As recompense for her services, she was promoted to sergeant-major in the Nationalist Army. In 1922 and 1923 respectively, Edib published two of the most famous Turkish nationalist novels, *Ateşten Gömlek* [The shirt of flame] and *Vurun Kahpeye* [Thrash the whore], relating the struggles of Kuvayi Milliye (Nationalist Army) against the Allies and against the Islamic fundamentalists in Anatolia.

In 1925, Edib was chosen as candidate to be a member in the republican parliament by the Turkish women's organizations. However, republican Turkey did not grant women political suffrage until 1934, and Edib herself was not to become a member of parliament until 1950.[5] In 1925, when the Progressive Republican Party was closed,[6] Adıvar, one of the founding members of the party, and Edib left Turkey, not to return until 1939.[7] In 1926, the first volume of her autobiography, *Memoirs of Halide Edib*, was published in London. One year after *Nutuk* was delivered in Ankara, in 1928, the second volume of her autobiography, *The Turkish Ordeal*, which complemented the narration of the national struggle in *Nutuk*, was published.

The Turkish Ordeal, narrating Edib's pivotal role in the nationalism movement and particularly in the Independence Struggle, was a text of self-defense written as a response to *Nutuk*, which dismissed Edib's role in the Independence Struggle entirely and characterized her as "mandacı-traitor"[8] of the Turkish National Struggle, based on a letter Edib sent Mustafa Kemal in 1919 vouching for the American mandate. *Nutuk* presented the issue of the American mandate not in its historical context, but as a choice Edib had allegedly made over national independence.[9] As was the case with other political opponents of Mustafa Kemal, Edib's defense did not enjoy much publicity in Turkey. Her articles were not published in Turkey between 1927 and 1935, and it was not until 1962 that *The Turkish Ordeal* was translated into Turkish as *Türk'ün Ateşle İmtihanı* and published with certain modifications. Until recently, she paradoxically remained the writer of the most important works of Turkish nationalist literature, *Ateşten Gömlek* and *Vurun Kahpeye*, but a "mandacı-traitor" of the Turkish nation nonetheless.

This article aims to revise and historicize Halide Edib's position in Turkish history through an analysis of her autobiography. Concomitantly, the monopoly of *Nutuk* over the narrative of the Turkish nation will be explored, through which the definition and parameters of national myth in the Turkish context is outlined. The import that *Nutuk*-as-myth held for decades in Turkey implied simultaneously that the autobiographies of the political opponents of Mustafa Kemal were to be banned or ignored. This case illustrates the necessity of an understanding of the significance of the reception of works, particularly the *credibility* and *authority* of texts in the way some texts were valued and given credibility in Turkey, while others, lacking such credibility and authority, were dismissed. An analysis of such autobiographies, however, which lack the same credibility and authority as *Nutuk*, particularly Edib's *The Turkish Ordeal*, will lead us to analyze challenges to *Nutuk*-as-myth and to the monopoly of *Nutuk* as narrative, both structurally and in terms of content.

Taxonomy of Narratives

The respective contents of Mustafa Kemal's *Nutuk* and Halide Edib's *Memoirs* and *The Turkish Ordeal* are similar, narrating the writers' accounts of the Ottoman Empire, the history of the Turkish nationalist movement, the Independence Struggle of Turkey and, at a superficial level, the foundation of the Turkish Republic. However, classifying both writers' works according to their content or according to the generic category of memoirs or autobiography would be naive at best. On the one hand, *Nutuk* was produced not only as a political but also a historical document, which, since 1927, has been received as the "sacred text" of the Turkish Republic. The prophetlike qualities of the author (Mustafa Kemal) of this sacred text are eulogized in the preface to the English translation of *Nutuk*: "[*The Speech*] reveals the activity of the speaker from the time when he first felt himself called upon to take the leadership of his nation into his own hands and guide it from shame and threatened ruin to freedom and power."[10]

On the other hand, Edib wrote the *Memoirs* and *The Turkish Ordeal* to record her version of the events of the Turkish nationalist struggle but without the pretense of producing a "historical record [or] a political treatise," rather seeking to make a "human document" about men and women during her lifetime.[11] Both the reasons for producing the respective texts of *Nutuk* and *Memoirs/The Turkish Ordeal* and the texts' receptions differed significantly. In contrast to the "sacred text" of the Turkish Republic, *Memoirs* and

The Turkish Ordeal are the memoirs of a woman writer, whose role in Turkish history was the subject of much controversy and whose credibility in the context of Turkey was minimal until recently.

The difference in the particular taxonomy of the works in Turkish history and literature necessitates the consideration of not only the "content" and "genre" of narratives, but also the "claims" narratives make and the way in which the texts "interact with their readers." *Nutuk* and Edib's autobiography can be contextualized with the help of a taxonomy of narratives categorized according to claims made by their narrators and the ways in which those claims are received by their audiences.

Three narratives make truth-claims: *Myth* and *history* are those narratives that have credibility, while *nonfiction* is the term used for a narrative possessing credibility but not to the extent of history and/or myth. Narratives that do not make truth-claims are called *fiction*. It is noteworthy to add that, in the production of the work, even if truth-claims are not made, the audience may give credibility or authority to the narrative. The distinction between myth and history is that myth, as not only a "model of" but also a "model for" reality, is laden with authority in a given society while history is not. Bruce Lincoln explains the authority of myth as "akin to that of revolutionary slogans and ancestral invocations, in that through the recitation of myth, one may effectively mobilize a social grouping." Myth, the essential fabric in the construction of a given society, is also "a discursive act through which actors evoke the sentiments out of which society is actively constructed."[12]

Thus myth establishes and determines the foundations of the very being, system of morality, and values of a particular collectivity or nation. Myth, in the words of George Schöpflin, "creates an intellectual and cognitive monopoly in that it seeks to establish the sole way of ordering the world and defining world views. For the community to exist as a community, this monopoly is vital."[13] Through this monopoly, myth not only defines a given collectivity but also draws a boundary around that particular collectivity, distinguishing it from any other collectivity.

In general, many scholars draw a strict line between myth and untruth or deception, arguing that myth need not rely on truth because its historical truth/fact is not sought, that myth is altogether separate from historical fact and historiography. However, in the Turkish case, *Nutuk*-as-myth actually makes a claim to history and historiography. Indeed Mustafa Kemal expostulated that his aim in writing *Nutuk* was to facilitate the writing of Turkish history.[14] *Nutuk*'s claim to history was supported by the incorporation of a plethora of historical documents within *Nutuk*, and for decades, the "interpretation" of documents by the narrator of *Nutuk* was taken as synonymous with historical fact.

Thus, a traditional categorization of narratives told from the perspective of the first-person narrator cannot simply be categorized as memoirs or autobiography because reception plays a crucial role in the categorization of narratives. As such, *Nutuk* was and is a very significant part of the Turkish (Kemalist) nationalist myth. Edib's *Memoirs* and *The Turkish Ordeal*, on the other hand, were not translated into Turkish till the 1960s. The Turkish translations, *Mor Salkımlı Ev* and *Türk'ün Ateşle İmtihanı*, would at best be categorized as nonfiction in the context of Turkish society.

It is noteworthy to add that reception is a concept that should not be reified, but instead analyzed over different time periods and within particular social and cultural contexts. For instance, *Nutuk*, whose status as myth and history was widely accepted during the 1920s and 1930s in Turkey, is challenged by scholars today. Likewise, Edib's *Memoirs* and *The Turkish Ordeal* gained more credibility in Turkey with the revision of Edib's position in Turkish history and literature. The social and cultural contexts of the works are also important. In a given time, a text may be contextualized and received differently by two different societies or cultures. Such was the case with *Memoirs* and *The Turkish Ordeal*, which were received as historical documents within the United Kingdom,[15] but denied reception in Turkey.

Nutuk As Plethoric Myth

Nutuk is the self-narrative of the "new individual," who represented the history of his life by inscribing it in the narrative of the nation. In the Ottoman context, the new individual was a Napoleonic figure, with the aim of bringing his nation to the zenith of "(European) civilization" and "progress." The first example of this heroic Ottoman "new individual" was Reşid Paşa, minister of foreign affairs under Sultan Abdülmecid, who brought the *Tanzimat* (reorganization reforms) in 1839. Şinasi's *kasides* (commemorative poem) in *Divan-ı Şinasi* honored Reşid Paşa like a prophet; the bible of his religion was the *kanun* (law), that is, the reforms he brought with the *Tanzimat*.[16]

A new concept to the Ottoman literati in the nineteenth century, the "new individual" has many antecedents in the male autobiographies produced in the Western autobiographical tradition. Within this tradition, the writing of history and narrative, the representation of the growth of nations, temper of the times, political and cultural zeitgeist, and the "exemplary man" all form a mutually reinforcing network of identity. All judged progress by the "making of it" that was profoundly self-centered—a tradition of self-aggrandizement in men's autobiography that could be called "The Lives of Famous Men," exemplified in such works as Rousseau's *Confessions* and Goethe's *Dichtung und Wahrheit*. Hence, the man in these texts is the mirror of his times, and history could be told as the story of this self.[17]

Structurally, *Nutuk* differs from the Western autobiographical tradition that began in the eighteenth century. In the eighteenth-century Western context, human reality was seen to be profoundly historical, which necessitated an analysis of the self as an analysis of how the self became what it was. Often, history was associated with a story of progress; the self experienced a "development or Bildung," moving from childhood or naïveté to gradual maturation.[18]

Nutuk, on the other hand, is a linear, progressive account of historical events beginning in 1919, but not the narrative of a self experiencing an evolutionary process toward maturation or development. Rather *Nutuk* is a cyclical and repetitive account of a self with a prophetlike calling to rescue the nation. This self's others, the Ottoman Sultan-Caliph and the political opponents of Mustafa Kemal, are likewise denied development or maturation and remain unchanged as the self's others throughout *Nutuk*. The self of *Nutuk* had a priori knowledge on how history would unravel—that is, the fact that the nationalist struggle would end with victory and "the self" would establish a republic in 1923—even before historical events took place. The transcendent, unchanging self of *Nutuk* is prior to and above history and does not undergo linear historical development during the 1919–27 period *Nutuk* narrates.

The transcendent, unchanging self of *Nutuk* points to one of the most foregrounded myths in *Nutuk*, the myth of the narrator of *Nutuk* as the unique/sole hero or secular prophet in Turkish history. Besides this particular myth, *Nutuk* is a composite of several others, such as the myth of *Nutuk*-as-history discussed earlier in this essay, the myth of rebirth, the myth of military success, the myth of sacred territory, and the myth of nation-as-family and shared descent.

As a myth of rebirth, *Nutuk* is a foundational myth in which the Independence Struggle is depicted not as a struggle to claim parts of the Ottoman Empire but as a struggle to establish the Turkish Republic.[19] This myth of rebirth takes its zero-point or naissance not as Mustafa Kemal's biological birth in 1881 but as May 19, 1919, the day Mustafa Kemal set foot on Anatolian soil, in the city of Samsun, and started working for the national cause. Hence, the famous first line of *Nutuk*: "I landed in Samsun on the nineteenth day of May 1919."[20] In *Nutuk*, in May 1919, the naissance of the unified and atomistic self of Mustafa Kemal is conjoined with a unified depiction of the nation—a depiction not only anachronistic but also paradoxical, considering that *Nutuk* starts with a description of the lack of ideological and strategic consensus among the variety of organizations throughout Anatolia and Constantinople trying to defend their territorial rights from the Allies and establish political rule. This unified nation and the unified self are presented in *Nutuk* as interchangeable and intertwined; in general, the nation is denied an autonomous existence extricated from the I of the narrative. Thus the self of *Nutuk* could more accurately be termed the "I-nation." The I-nation's naissance in May 1919 comes at the expense of the historical significance and existence of the Ottoman Empire. In *Nutuk*, the more the I-nation is praised for the victory in the Independence Struggle and success in securing political autonomy, the more the I-nation is separated from the Ottoman Empire as its legacy and sultans are debunked. Thus, the day that the I-nation was born in Samsun, he was presented as distinct from the historical conditions that came into being before the zero-point of Turkish history.

In *Nutuk*, this myth of rebirth is linked with the narrative of discontinuity, a narrative of distinct separation from the Ottoman Empire. This narrative of discontinuity distanced the Turkish Republic from the Ottoman Empire on several different levels. First and foremost, the Sultanate and the Caliphate are presented as useless and backward institutions that cannot be reconciled with modernization.[21] The argument for the abolition of both the Sultanate and the Caliphate (in 1922 and 1924, respectively) was made through the individual acts of treachery of Sultan Vahdeddin, who vouched for the British mandate and, during the Independence Struggle, actively struggled against the nationalist forces in Anatolia. In *Nutuk*, not only the *last* Ottoman Sultan Vahdeddin but all Ottoman Sultans are degraded as "a bunch of madmen," "moronic and ignorant" "animals."[22]

The narrative of discontinuity also promotes, in lieu of the multiethnic configuration of the Ottoman Empire, a strictly ethnic nationalism.[23] Ethnic nationalism was reinforced with the aid of the myth of the nation-as-family that was to become a significant part of the Kemalist national myth in the 1930s.[24] Thus, the Turkish nation was seen as one family, whose father was Mustafa Kemal. This paternal role was underscored in 1934 when Mustafa Kemal instigated the "Last Name Law," whereby all Turkish citizens had to take last names, and claimed the name of *Atatürk*, which literally meant the "Father of the Turk," for himself.[25] The descendants of the "Father of the Turk/Atatürk" were the Turkish youth; *Nutuk* ends thus with Mustafa Kemal's inheritance passed on to the future generations of the Turkish nation-family.[26]

It should be noted that *Nutuk*'s I-nation is, as transcendent construct, prior to language, which means that it is above the problematics of narrative representation. Thus, the I-nation of *Nutuk* is conjoined with the historical self of Mustafa Kemal, presenting a certain I-nation speaking without the artifice of fiction. This one-on-one correlation between the I-nation of *Nutuk* and the historical self of Kemal was imposed after *Nutuk*'s delivery. The "book," "man," and "nation" trinity came to bear on logocentric authority, which was secured on the grounds that they shared the same proper name, "Father Turk." Thus the proper name of the author conjoined the text and the self, so that the untouchable status of the author dictated the untouchable status of the book. In this sense, *Nutuk* was doubly untouchable, since in the context of *Nutuk*, who touched the man touched the book and touched the nation, where the unified I-nation united the self of Kemal with the unified nation or the recently and painstakingly reclaimed "sacred land" of Turkey, whose borders, claimed in the Treaty of Lausanne in 1924, were inviolable and whose various ethnic groups were united under the roof of ethnic/Turkish nationalism. The myth of sacred territory and the myth of nation-as-family were intertwined in the presentation of Anatolia as the motherland of the Turks and the Independence Struggle as synonymous with the quest for the establishment of the Turkish Republic.

Consequently, the self of *Nutuk* sought credibility by justifying the credibility of his story with the biographical fact of Mustafa Kemal's success. The fact that Mustafa Kemal, as commander-in-chief of the Nationalist Army, was victorious in the Independence Struggle and became *Halâskar Gazi*

(the savior and conqueror),[27] the fact that he became president and his political opponents and the Ottoman Sultan-Caliph were eradicated from the
annals of Turkish history, meant that this I-nation was the sole hero who
had foreseen particular historical events and how history was to shape itself,
while the enemies of the I-nation had been proven wrong and treacher-
ous (the Ottoman Sultan-Caliph, Mustafa Kemal's political opponents). The
I-nation then is not only prior to language but also prior to history, which
in *Nutuk* is a narrative serving the I-nation's ends, unraveling only to prove
the accuracy of Kemal's judgment and decision making. Further, *Nutuk* dictates that the I-nation's position of transcendence (over language and history) be accepted as historical fact. Consequently, because of the logocentric authority invested in the man-book-nation trinity through the 1990s in
Turkey, mainly due to the authority and prestige of the author, it has been
difficult to analyze *Nutuk* and the way it narrates its "objects of contemplation" as a nexus of history and fiction, rather than as direct unmediated
historical fact.

Halide Edib's *Memoirs* and *The Turkish Ordeal*:
The Self/Selves Inscription of the "Mandacı-Traitor"

The two separate volumes of Halide Edib's autobiography, *Memoirs* and *The
Turkish Ordeal*, show remarkable differences in terms of content. *Memoirs*
narrates Edib's childhood years during the Ottoman Empire. Underscored
in the account are reminiscences of the multiethnic, multireligious character of the empire and the different phases of Turkish nationalism before
1918. The second volume of Edib's autobiography, *The Turkish Ordeal* exclusively narrates the events of the Independence Struggle of Turkey, fore-
shadowing the early years of the Turkish Republic, 1923–27. *The Turkish
Ordeal*, I argue, was written as a response to the narration of the self and
the nation in *Nutuk*. Thus, I focus on *The Turkish Ordeal*, with sporadic references to the *Memoirs*.

   Both volumes of Edib's autobiography closely follow the Western autobiographical tradition. Edib's autobiography narrates the development of a
"self" moving from *childhood* or *naïveté* to *gradual maturation* with particular sensitivity to different phases of being of the self as the self matures.
The difference between the mainstream Western autobiographical tradition
and Edib's autobiography lies in her persistent exploration of interpersonal

identity.[28] This is such a prominent trait in *The Turkish Ordeal* that the volume could equally and simultaneously be categorized as Edib's autobiography and a biography of Mustafa Kemal. *The Turkish Ordeal* is an attempt to inscribe Edib's involvement in the Independence Struggle into Turkish history and literature while expounding on Kemal's involvement and position in the Struggle. In this respect, the text concentrates almost equally on Edib's and Kemal's roles in the Struggle.[29]

Nevertheless, *The Turkish Ordeal* does not concentrate solely on Kemal and Edib. Even when *The Turkish Ordeal* asserts individuality and tries to foreground the roles of Edib, Kemal, and other leaders of the Struggle, it simultaneously denies the concept of individuality in its attempt to give agency to the people of Anatolia. From the point of Edib's Sultan Ahmet speech (June 6, 1919) to the end of the Struggle (1922), when the Nationalist Army marched into Izmir, Edib strips herself of the individuality of the I: "I suddenly ceased to exist as an individual: I worked, wrote, and lived as a unit of that magnificent national madness."[30]

This "national madness" entailed the foregrounding of a collaborative effort in lieu of particular individuals leading the effort. *The Turkish Ordeal* depicts negatively all characters who tried to foreground their roles in the Struggle, Kemal chief among them. This interpersonal depiction of character entails interdependence. For instance, *The Turkish Ordeal* underscores the fact that the nationalist movement in Anatolia began not with Kemal but under the leadership of Kazım Karabekir in the East[31] with the collaborative efforts of the Karakol organization, Kara Vasıf Bey, and Major Kemaleddin.[32]

Although the zero-point of Turkish nationalist history according to *Nutuk* is underlined in *The Turkish Ordeal* as a turning point in the nationalist movement, it was not a turning point prepared solely by Mustafa Kemal but rather was staged concomitantly by the leadership and strategic planning of Ali Fuad Pasha, Kazım Karabekir Pasha, Rauf Bey, Colonel Refet, and Colonel M. Arif.[33] According to *The Turkish Ordeal*, the early phases of the nationalist movement in Anatolia were spearheaded by the sagacious Kazım Karabekir Pasha, who possessed "vision and the ability to act promptly." It was Kazım Karabekir Pasha who assembled the Erzurum Congress in July 1919 for a "more legal pretext to pass into action." It was yet again Kazım Karabekir Pasha who appointed Mustafa Kemal Pasha as leader of the nationalist movement.[34]

The Turkish Ordeal's account of the Sıvas Congress held in September 1919 empowers the names *Nutuk* tried to dismiss. For instance, Halis Turgut Bey is presented in *The Turkish Ordeal* as the most able and enthusiastic supporter of the representative body at the Sıvas Congress, endangering his life by supporting the representative body and breaking from the government in Istanbul.[35]

Drawing on names integral to the Nationalist Struggle in Anatolia and depicting their importance and collaboration, *The Turkish Ordeal* emphasizes the network of identities, the interdependence of leaders and people in the Struggle. Such a depiction of interdependence contrasts with the myth of the sole hero, the prophet of the republic, instead describing the Struggle as a collaborative effort. In this contrast, the impermeable boundaries between the atomistic I-nation of Mustafa Kemal's *Nutuk* and the I-nation's others, particularly the political opponents of Mustafa Kemal (1923–26) become blurred.

This method of delineating characters and the Struggle interpersonally does not entail merging characters or denying the importance or role of one character at the expense of another. Rather, in Edib's work, the self is not interchangeable with the nation as was the case in *Nutuk*. The "I" in *The Turkish Ordeal* was separated from the "nation/people" even though during the Struggle, their goals were the same. The "narrating self" in Edib's autobiography manifests the permeability of its ego boundaries as it tries to give existence to other selves in its description of her self. For example, before Edib gave her nationalist speech in Fatih in 1918, she realized that she shared the same goals as the people: "*I* realized that *their* supreme demand was identical with *mine*. *We* all longed for hope, for absolute belief in our rights and in our own strength, and *I* gave them what *they* wanted."[36] In the particular example of the Fatih speech, as well as in the narrative overall, Edib makes a constant attempt to give agency to the "people."

This determination to give agency to the people is most evident in the separation of Mustafa Kemal from the nation and the national cause. What was most indicative of this split was the dialogue that took place between Kemal and Edib during the Struggle—a dialogue that motivated Edib to start writing her memoirs:

> "What I mean is this: I want everyone to do as I wish and command."
> "Have they not done so already in everything that is fundamental and for the good of the Turkish cause?"

He swept my question aside and continued in the same brutally frank manner.

"I don't want any consideration, criticism, or advice. I will have only my own way. All shall do as I command."

"Me too, Pasham [my Pasha]?"

"You too."

His absolute sincerity deserved a reciprocal frankness.

"I will obey you and do as you wish as long as I believe that you are serving the cause."

"You shall obey me and do as I wish," he repeated, ignoring the condition.

"Is that a threat, Pasham?" I asked, quietly but firmly.[37]

As is evident in this excerpt, the "Halâskar Gazi of *Nutuk*," whose military leadership is praised in certain sections of *The Turkish Ordeal*, is nonetheless extricated from the "national cause" in Edib's autobiography to illustrate that his interests did not always overlap with those of the "nation." Hence, the less the selves of the nationalist leaders asserted themselves, the more agency was given to the people, leading from the beginning of the Struggle to its victorious end, from the beginning of *The Turkish Ordeal* to its climactic epilogue: "All through the ordeal for independence the Turkish people itself has been the supreme hero."[38]

Moreover, as *The Turkish Ordeal* incorporates an intersubjective/interpersonal exploration of Kemal, whose goals did not overlap with those of the nation, who was significant, yet one among several leaders of the Struggle, the work relieves the burden that the I-nation in *Nutuk* imposes on the Anatolian people. Whereas the I-nation of *Nutuk* encumbers the people of Anatolia by demanding obedience from them on the grounds that the I-the-Savior-and-Creator-of-the-Nation (*Ben-Halâskar Gazi*)[39] served and rescued them from being exterminated by the Allies, *The Turkish Ordeal* empowers them and the leaders of the Struggle by giving recognition to their sufferings and struggles for national liberation.

The Self/Selves Moving through History and History Moving through the Self/Selves

Halide Edib's *Memoirs* and *The Turkish Ordeal* manifest an awareness of the *plethoric reflexive pronoun* "I,"[40] that is, the different moments of being of the "I" in line with historical change. Edib, in order to record every single instance of the remembering and nonremembering self in her autobiography, delineates the early sections of the *Memoirs*, depicting her childhood as flashes of memory, fragmented in structure. The narrating self gives particular attention to shifts between degrees of consciousness and understanding between the various phases the self went through as her life unraveled. The early phases of Edib's childhood are related referring to the autobiographical self as "she" to record the distance between the writing self and the experiencing self. When the "self" reaches a higher degree of consciousness and understanding of the world and events unraveling around her, the self appropriates the story as the narrator remarks that she decided to pass from writing of herself in the "she" to the "I": "The story of the little girl is my own henceforth."[41]

The changing "I" of *Memoirs* and *The Turkish Ordeal* also serves as a narrative technique to parallel the multiplicity of roles Edib assumed during the Turkish nationalist movement and the Independence Struggle, including public speaker, journalist, writer, editor, nurse, and soldier. As the writing self, she becomes a spectator at times to the variety of roles she enacted. For instance, chapter 8 of *The Turkish Ordeal* begins: "A small figure in a nurse's uniform walked from the Eskişehir Station to the Red Crescent Hospital. It was I."[42] Likewise, this is how "the writing self" (1926–27) assesses "Corporal Halide" (1921–22): "Corporal Halide is almost a stranger to me now. I often turn her soul inside out and stare at it hard. . . . Where did she find the strength to endure the sights of so much human suffering?"[43] Hence, whereas the "unified self" of Mustafa Kemal's *Nutuk* was narrated as a continuum of consciousness, a never-forgetting, all-remembering self, which never erred, the "self" in *Memoirs/The Turkish Ordeal*, in an attempt to represent accurately the biographical fact of the "I" at different times, forgets, remembers, and reports the events forgotten as well as the ones remembered in order to enable biographical specificity and historical change to mold narration of the self.

Likewise, *The Turkish Ordeal* presents the prophetlike and unchanging self of *Nutuk* as one undergoing change according to historical exigencies. For instance, at the beginning of *The Turkish Ordeal*, while the nationalist movement is in progress in the East, Mustafa Kemal Pasha, as an influential leader in the army, tries to persuade the sultan to close the parliament to inaugurate a regime of absolutism so that Mustafa Kemal Pasha himself can become the minister of war.[44] The image of Mustafa Kemal in *The Turkish Ordeal* stands in stark contrast to the self of *Nutuk* who has severed all ties with the Ottoman Sultan-Caliphate and has a calling to found the republic as early as 1919.

Further, *Nutuk* controls not only historical memory but also "historical progress," as the temporal hegemony it sets up prioritizing its own history (over the history of the Ottoman Empire) precludes it from imagining a better future. *Nutuk* defines "national liberation," the ultimate goal of the nation, as "a thing of the past," synonymous with reclaiming Anatolia and Constantinople from the Allies and becoming "politically autonomous," and, as such, as goals that have already been achieved. The only mission left for future generations is to preserve this fixed and unchanging entity, the nation and the name of its creator/father, "Atatürk."

In *Nutuk*, the constant, unchanging, static "I" secures his immortality by passing on the republic, its most unique creation, to the youth of Turkey. *Nutuk* ends with the self entrusting the Turkish youth with the mantle of guardianship of the Turkish Republic (alongside the honorable name of the "man" and his "book"): "This holy treasure I lay in the hands of the youth of Turkey. Turkish Youth! Your primary duty is ever to preserve and defend the National Independence, the Turkish Republic. . . . The strength that you will need for this is mighty in the noble blood which flows in your veins."[45] Whereas *Nutuk* underscores reification and preservation, *Memoirs* and *The Turkish Ordeal* underscore historical progress. Denying the myth of rebirth and the narrative of discontinuity, Edib's autobiography depicts the variegated stages of "Turkish nationalism" as it does the Independence Struggle beginning in the mid-nineteenth century, indicating that Mustafa Kemal's role in the Independence Struggle made up one phase of a roughly seven-decades-long process.

Similarly, *The Turkish Ordeal* emphatically foregrounds "historical progress," which permeates the text as a move toward the gradual attainment of national liberation: "My nation has earned her independence by an ordeal which will stand out as one of the hardest and the noblest in the world's history. But she has another ordeal to pass through . . . called the Ordeal for Freedom. . . . in the unending struggle for freedom there can be no real individual symbol, no dictator."[46] Liberation in the sense of military victory is achieved, and Edib's autobiography, while criticizing some flaws, underscores Kemal's leadership qualities in the Struggle. However, according to

Edib, the goal of the Turkish nation was not completed with the military victory in the Struggle. Hence the title *The Turkish Ordeal* signifies not only an ordeal of the past—the Independence Struggle—but also one of the future, a process of democratization, which had yet to be achieved in the 1920s in Turkey.

Potential Resistance Unrealized

The narrative of the Turkish nationalism movement and the early years of the republic in *The Turkish Ordeal* is far from unproblematic. The autobiography excludes details of the events after the military victory in 1922, although its epilogue hints at problems in Kemal's rule after 1923. In addition, the reader is left uninformed about the "writing self" of Halide Edib, her political convictions regarding the issue of the Sultanate, the Caliphate, the political beliefs that precluded her and Dr. Adıvar from collaborating with Kemal and the Republican People's Party, and the reasons behind her self-imposed exile. Also, without expounding upon the period between 1922 and 1927 and providing particulars about the Kemalist regime, *The Turkish Ordeal* seems to suggest that the personal flaws of Mustafa Kemal the narrator encounters during the Independence Struggle[47] prepared the scene for the "dictatorship" in the 1920s.[48]

Further, the resistance of Edib's autobiography to the Kemalist national myth should perhaps be recast as "potential resistance," as yet to be realized, not only because the text was translated into Turkish only in the 1960s, but also because the text was modified immensely when it was translated. Instead of criticizing the self of *Nutuk* and the assertions regarding Turkish history writing in *Nutuk*, as was the case in *The Turkish Ordeal*, the translation of the text into Turkish showers the self of *Nutuk* with compliments. The appeal to the ordeal for liberation and democracy is dismissed in the translation; even the title, translated as "Türk'ün Ateşle İmtihanı" [The Turk's ordeal with fire] loses its dual meaning, referring exclusively to the Independence Struggle, an ordeal overcome through the charismatic leadership of Mustafa Kemal during the Independence Struggle. Thus, rather than challenging the Kemalist national myth as expounded in *Nutuk* through strategies employed in *The Turkish Ordeal*, such as the historical and intersubjective exploration of the self and other, *The Turk's Ordeal with Fire* paradoxically endorses the Kemalist national myth.

Notes

1   In 1925, after the instigation of *Takriri Sükun* (law on the maintenance of order), which ensued in the closing of the opposition party and the silencing of its press, the Republican People's Party became a "power monopoly" as the Kemalist regime became an authoritarian single-party regime. With the exception of one more experiment with an opposition party, Turkey did not have a legal opposition until after the 1940s. Erik J. Zürcher, *Turkey: A Modern History* (New York: I. B. Tauris and Co., 1998), 184.

2   For instance, Kazım Karabekir's autobiography, prepared in 1933, was burned before it was published. In 1960, Kazım Karabekir's *İstiklal Harbimiz* [Our independence war] was published, but the published copies were collected because the autobiography violated the law against defaming Atatürk, and as such, was a serious case of *lese-majesty*. *İstiklal Harbimizin Esasları* [The facts of our independence struggle] was not published in Turkey until the 1990s. Kazım Karabekir, *İstiklal Harbimizin Esasları* (Istanbul: Emre Yayınları, 2000.)

3   Some of Edib's novels received international acclaim, and *Handan* was translated into several languages.

4   The first night of the occupation of Istanbul, British soldiers began a search to arrest nationalist leaders, including Dr. Adnan because of his affiliation with the Struggle. Halide Edib, *The Turkish Ordeal: Being the Further Memoirs of Halide Edib* (New York: Century Co., 1928), 67–69.

5   In 1950, Edib became MP from İzmir for the Democrat Party led by Adnan Menderes; she resigned from the political arena altogether in 1954, accusing the Democrat Party of tending toward a dictatorship. See Orhan Koloğlu, "Halide Edib, Fevrimler ve Demokrasi" [Halide Edib, revolutions and democracy] *Tarih ve Toplum Dergisi* [Journal of history and society], no. 177 (1998): 181–87.

6   The Progressive Republican Party was closed because the Independence Tribunals found the party complicit in the Kurdish rebellion of 1924 and accused the party of using religion for political purposes. Zürcher, *Turkey*, 180.

7   Halide Edib visited Turkey briefly in 1935, to see her grandson for the first time.

8   *Mandacı* refers to the person who advocates the mandate of a foreign power over national and political autonomy.

9   See Gazi Mustafa Kemal, *Nutuk-Söylev*, 2 vols. (Ankara: Türk Tarih Kurumu, 1984), 4, 17, 49.

10 Mustafa Kemal, *A Speech Delivered by Ghazi Mustafa Kemal, October 1927* (Leipzig: K. F. Koehler, 1929), 1.

11 Edib, *Ordeal*, 190.

12 Bruce Lincoln, *Discourse and the Construction of Society: Comparative Studies of Myth, Ritual, and Classification* (New York: Oxford University Press, 1989), 24–25.

13 George Schöpflin, "The Functions of Myth and Taxonomy of Myths," in *Myths and Nationhood*, ed. Geoffrey Hosking and George Schöpflin (New York: Routledge, 1997), 19.

14 Hıfzı Veldet Velidedeoğlu, "Doğumunun 100. Yılında *Söylev*'in 9. Basısı Üzerine" [One hundred years after his birth, on the ninth edition of *The Speech*], in Mustafa Kemal, *Söylev* [The speech], 3 vols. (Istanbul: Can Matbaa, 1988), 30.

15   For instance, in the *Times Literary Supplement*, *The Turkish Ordeal* was described as a "history written by the novelist who helped to make it history." John Murray, "*The Turkish Ordeal*," *Times Literary Supplement*, November 29, 1928.

16   Ahmet Hamdi Tanpınar, *Ondokuzuncu Asır Türk Edebiyatı Tarihi* [History of nineteenth-century Turkish literature] (Istanbul: Çağlayan Kitabevi, 1988), 200.

17   See Leigh Gilmore, "Autobiographics: Women's Autobiography and the Poetics of Identity" (Ph.D. diss., University of Washington, 1988), 69.

18   Further, in the eighteenth century, the notion of self-conception came to be synonymous with individuality. For instance, according to Goethe, "individuation" was a constant interaction of a maturing self with a changing world configuration. Such "an interlinked coexistence" between the gradually changing self interacting with the gradually changing world was how the self experienced history. Karl Weintraub, *The Value of the Individual: Self and Circumstance in Autobiography* (Chicago: University of Chicago Press, 1978), 336.

19   Zürcher, *Turkey*, 183.

20   Kemal, *Nutuk*, 2; my translation.

21   See Kemal, *Nutuk*, 21, 1105, 1185.

22   Kemal, *Nutuk*, 21, 319, 321.

23   For instance, even though the Independence Struggle was a struggle fought by the Muslim community of the Ottoman Empire, namely the Kurds and the Turks, *Nutuk* portrays the struggle as one fought exclusively by Turks. This myth of rebirth and narrative of discontinuity was highly influential in the writing of republican history, especially the distancing of the Ottoman Empire from the Turkish Republic. Republican historians vouched for the "discontinuity thesis" mostly because of the significance of religion in the Ottoman Empire that secular republican intellectuals did not want to embrace and also because of the ethnic heterogeneity of the Empire that was modified with the ethnic nationalism of the Turkish Republic. Büşra Ersanlı, "The Ottoman Empire in the Historiography of the Kemalist Era: A Theory of Fatal Decline," in *The Ottomans and the Balkans*, ed. Fikret Adanır and Suraiya Faroqhi (Boston: E. J. Brill, 2002), 135.

24   The Kemalist national myth includes *Nutuk* but is not synonymous with *Nutuk* itself. I see the Kemalist national myth as a composite of myths including not just *Nutuk* but also other speeches made by Mustafa Kemal, as well as the "Westernizing" reforms and laws.

25   *Ata* also means "ancestor." In vernacular, *ata* is interchangeable with *Atatürk*.

26   Even though Atatürk was not a title Mustafa Kemal held in 1927, when *Nutuk* was delivered, his paternal role in the Turkish national family was foreshadowed in the depiction of the "self" of *Nutuk*. In general, the narrator of *Nutuk* and the nation formed one composite entity, but at those exceptional instances when they were separated, it was only because the nation had not matured into the same consciousness as the all-knowing "I/we" of the narrative. For instance, according to the narrator of *Nutuk*, in May 1919, the nation was not at a state of maturity to judge the outdatedness of the institutions of the Sultanate and the Caliphate. Kemal, *Nutuk*, 15. The narrator of *Nutuk* had to lead the nation to this state of maturity. Hence, the "I" of *Nutuk* solved problems that the nation was not prepared for, and as such, acted the role of the protector, the father figure for the nation.

27 *Gazi* was a title Mustafa Kemal inherited from the Ottoman Sultans who, as Gazis, were holy warriors bound to prove their military power against the Christians.

28 Transnationally and transhistorically speaking, the interpersonal exploration of identity might be a trait common to women's autobiographies. See *The Female Autograph: Theory and Practice of Autobiography from the Tenth to the Twentieth Centuries*, ed. Domna Stanton (Chicago: University of Chicago Press, 1984).

29 Thus, *The Turkish Ordeal* could be located at the nexus of autobiography and biography, between Phillippe Lejeune's autobiographical pact (author is/is not the narrator is the protagonist) and the biographical pact (author is/is not the narrator is not the protagonist). Philippe Lejeune, "The Autobiographical Contract," in *French Literary Theory Today*, ed. Tzvetan Todorov, trans. R. Carter (Cambridge: Cambridge University Press, 1982), 204–5.

30 Edib, *Ordeal*, 23.

31 Ibid., 14.

32 Ibid., 20–21.

33 Ibid., 42.

34 Ibid., 45.

35 *The Turkish Ordeal* pointed out that after the establishment of the republic, Halis Turgut Bey supported the opposition to the Republican People's Party and was executed in 1926 although he was not complicit in the assassination attempt. Ibid., 48.

36 Ibid., 26–27; emphasis added.

37 Ibid., 188.

38 Ibid., 407.

39 After the victory of the Independence Struggle, Mustafa Kemal had become *Halâskar Gazi* (the savior and conqueror), a title he was determined "to use . . . to consolidate his position in the post-war era." Zürcher, *Turkey*, 166.

40 This phrase is borrowed from James Olney's analysis of Samuel Beckett's *Watt*. See James Olney, *Memory and Narrative: The Weave of Life-Writing* (Chicago: University of Chicago Press, 1998), 229. I use the phrase to refer to a changing "I" in line with historical change. It may be added that the "I" is not even reflexive because whenever the "I" returns to or refers to itself, it is not or no longer the same "I."

41 Halide Edib, *Memoirs* (New York: Century Co., 1926), 32.

42 Edib, *Ordeal*, 261.

43 Ibid., 311.

44 Ibid., 12.

45 Kemal, *Söylev*, 724–25.

46 Edib, *Ordeal*, 407.

47 See ibid., 127, 136, 141, 158, 166, 167–68, 183, 384.

48 Ibid., 407.

Necmi Zeka

A Prisoner of Language: The Strange Case of Modern Turkish Poetry

I came to Istanbul to look at the past, not at the future—since the latter doesn't exist here: . . . Here there is only an unenviable, third-rate present of the people, industrious yet plundered by the intensity of the local history. Nothing will happen here anymore, apart perhaps from street disorders or an earthquake."[1] These rather harsh remarks belong to the Nobel Laureate Joseph Brodsky, who paid a short visit to Turkey in the 1980s in order, among other things, to see the city where his "favorite poet" Cavafy had once lived. Even though one has to admit that Brodsky might be right about the "street disorders" and "earthquakes," one cannot help but wonder, from a literary point of view, why such a well-read poet showed no interest at all in the poetry of a country that prides itself on producing many world-class poets.

Indeed Turkey is a country well deserving to be called a nation of poets, if not necessarily poetry readers. Despite incredibly low sales of poetry volumes, every month the number of unsolicited poems submitted to literary journals is easily double, even triple, the journals' circulation figures. One can safely argue that poetry

The *South Atlantic Quarterly* 102:2/3, Spring/Summer 2003.
Copyright © 2003 by Duke University Press.

in Turkey is the most favored form of personal expression, with perhaps just one possible exception: love letters. More than this extraordinary popularity, however, what strikes one as peculiar is the firm conviction shared by both ordinary readers and professionals about the allegedly worldwide superiority of the poetry written in Turkish. In fact, the majority of Turkish poets seriously believe in their capacity to revitalize world poetry, which they assume to be a dying form of art outside of Turkey. For instance, İsmet Özel, one of the leading contemporary poets and political thinkers, recently posited that modern Turkish poetry should be considered Turkey's most significant contribution to modernity in general.[2] What makes this claim sound rather naive is, of course, the fact that hardly any international student of modern world poetry seems to be aware of, let alone acknowledge, such a contribution. Actually, it is even quite unlikely that an average European or American poetry enthusiast could name a Turkish modern poet other than Nazım Hikmet, the exiled "romantic revolutionary" who is usually ranked with poets such as Pablo Neruda or Louis Aragon.

What causes many magnificent Turkish poets to remain unnoticed in the Western world? For years, Turkish intellectuals have been struggling to find a plausible answer to this question. Leaving aside ludicrous conspiracy theories arguing that the international literary establishment deliberately ignores this powerful poetry because it would threaten its hegemony, the most favored explanations center upon the lack or insufficiency of publicity and marketing efforts by both state officials and academic institutions. Recently, a new dimension has been added to this idea, emphasizing the fact that Turkish poets' lack of interest in contemporary poetry written abroad might be a contributing factor to their own poetry's nonpresence outside of Turkey. Enis Batur, one of Turkey's most prolific poets and vigorous publishers, uses the monetary term *convertibility* to illustrate this idea. According to Batur, "To understand the *right quota* of the poetry written in Turkey, to discover its depth from a universal perspective, it is sine qua non to get to know world poetry thoroughly."[3]

However, Turkish poets display such a high degree of self-esteem, bordering on vanity, that, even after increased transactions with world poetry circles, an adjustment in their self-perception looks quite doubtful. In other words, Turkish poets with their current disposition would most certainly continue to regard their achievements as being superior in every aspect to those of their foreign contemporaries. The argument developed below can be seen as an attempt to highlight some of the underlying reasons for this unshakable conviction of literary greatness.

Obviously, one is inclined to relate this idiosyncratic state of mind to the existence of a very old poetry tradition. The six-centuries-old Ottoman verse, and the folk poetry schools going even further back, one can argue, entitle Turkish poets to act as presumptuous inheritors of an enormous fortune. Especially compared to prose writing, where Turkish people of letters have long suffered from latecomer shortcomings, poetry is regarded as the truly indigenous, and thus easy to master, form of art. "If we enter any discussion of Turkish poetry today, we will sooner or later, however briefly, become involved with its long and complex history."[4] This viewpoint, articulated by the poet Güven Turan in his introduction to a recent anthology of contemporary Turkish poetry, is indeed very common. Yet, as Turan indicates, one should be cautious about taking this history per se as a well-established tradition, since it underwent many radical interruptions and redefinitions, most notably during the nation-building efforts at the beginning of the last century. For many decades, Turkish intellectuals' attitudes toward past achievements in poetry have been problematic and, to a large extent, overburdened with ideological issues. The emergence in 1923 of the Republic of Turkey, which enforced fundamental modernization measures, most drastically the change of alphabet, is usually taken as the trigger of a massive cultural alienation process. Within the Western-looking revolutionary climate of the Republic, it became customary to dismiss classical poetry as reactionary, or at least difficult. Victoria Rowe Holbrook, who discusses the modern reception of Ottoman verse in detail, writes: "Turkish revolutionaries found it necessary, for the survival of a Turkish state, to submit Ottoman poetry to orientalization. 'Difficulty' is a euphemism for that surrender, by which statements about Ottoman poetry became allusions to the Ottoman State, and literary criticism became a field for the articulation of Turkish nationalism."[5]

One should also note that the unsettled relationship with the past cannot be reduced solely to the cultural reorientation that began with the republic. During the nineteenth century, dissatisfaction with classical poetics gave rise to many renewal attempts accompanying social and political reforms. As Nermin Menemencioğlu rightly asserts: "Modern Turkish poetry does not conveniently begin with the Republic, but some hundred years earlier, with the rejection of the notion that a poem consists of individual lines (*mısra*), not necessarily related in meaning, and strung together on a rhyme scheme like the pearls of a necklace."[6]

Thus, it seems worthwhile to investigate the development of modern Turkish poetry within the framework of a long quarrel between attitudes considered old and new. Critic Orhan Koçak's analysis of Nazım Hikmet's poetry with reference to the antagonism between "memory" and "freedom," the latter incorporating not only the revolutionary urge for a new start but also the "rejection of influence,"[7] can be regarded as a useful model and applied to modern Turkish poetry in general. The history of modern Turkish poetry is in fact full of many real, and sometimes imaginary, cases of rejection, verifying Harold Bloom's thesis, "True poetic history is the story of how poets as poets have suffered other poets, just as any true biography is the story of how anyone suffered his own family—or his own displacement of family into lovers and friends."[8]

Surprisingly, however, Turkish poetry still lacks extensive reevaluations of the old masters, even though the questioning of the ideological denial of the prerepublican past has been strengthening since the late 1960s. Following Bloom's terminology, one can argue that modern Turkish poets have been acting reluctantly to produce "misinterpretations"—neither "giving birth" to their fathers nor "inventing" new ones.

So the heritage itself can only partly explain modern Turkish poets' unsubstantiated claim for superiority. To provide a better answer, one should perhaps look at another peculiar, less explored aspect of modern Turkish poetry, which can be summarized as the glorification of the Turkish language.

As T. S. Eliot points out, poetry has a "social function" of "preserving" and "developing" "the beauty of a language."[9] Without rejecting poetry's language dependency, one can argue that modern Turkish poets' trust in their language exceeds these ordinary concerns and serves, so to speak, as a mythical basis of justification for their poetic endeavors. Apparently, their insistence on the importance of the poetic tone or voice can also be regarded as part of this language glorification. Relying upon the same ideal of tonality in fact seems to be a common trait shared by generations of poets despite drastic changes in the Turkish language.

Well-known utterances by the two giants of modern Turkish poetry might help illustrate the point. The novelist and critic A. H. Tanpınar tells us that one day he witnessed a rather ridiculous question put to the great poet Yahya Kemal about the exact time he had begun to consider himself a poet. Yahya Kemal replied: "It was the day when I felt the Turkish language."[10] In a similar vein, Fazıl Hüsnü Dağlarca states that he writes poems in order to show that "Turkish is the greatest language on earth."[11]

These utterances, emblematic of a widely shared conception of poetry in Turkey, are also echoed in the critical discourse with popular phrases of appreciation for poets such as *söz kuyumcusu* (jeweler of words) or *Türkçe'nin yüzakı* (the pride of Turkish). Accordingly, all major turning points of modern Turkish poetry, even Nazım Hikmet's politically oriented realistic poetry, are usually analyzed in terms of their mastery of Turkish. For instance, the leading poet of the Second New Movement, Turgut Uyar, commenting on Nazım Hikmet pursues a similar line of thought. He claims that Nazım Hikmet "is the man who would invent or discover poetry if it did not exist—he would do that especially in Turkish and with Turkish."[12]

Thus, in an ironic way, modern Turkish poets tend to consider themselves fortunate for being able to use such a sophisticated language, yet at the same time think that the uniqueness, and therefore the unavoidable difficulty, of Turkish prevents their poetry from being translated and read extensively.

However, taking refuge in an idealized language not only gives rise to unjustified grandiosity, but also often leads Turkish poets to work with a limited number of obsolete ideas and worn-out sentimentalities. In particular, when most Turkish poems are translated into other languages, that is, when their linguistic properties are stripped away, they disclose a certain imaginative and intellectual narrowness. One can hope, though, that Turkish poets will eventually free themselves from the limitations caused by their obsession with language, or at least avoid using it as an excuse for their lack of inventiveness. Developing a more relaxed relationship with Turkish will also enable them not only to make use of the huge possibilities offered by Turkish history and geography, but also to capture more easily the distinctive voices of the Turkish language. In addition to the increase in the number of female poets, the flourishing of Turkish prose that used to be considered a slow developer will certainly contribute to the enrichment of Turkish poetry both in subject matter and language usage.

Referring to a statement made by Derek Walcott in his Nobel Lecture that "poetry is an island that breaks away from the main,"[13] we may conclude that Turkish poetry will somehow manage to break away from the main of the language and, using its resourcefulness, will give European poetry a new creative vitality.

Notes

1   Joseph Brodsky, *Less Than One* (London: Penguin, 1987), 444.
2   İsmet Özel, "Modern Türk Şiirinin Savunması," *Parşömen Kültür Edebiyat Dergisi* 2.1 (2001): 28–40.
3   Enis Batur, *Smokinli Berduş* (Istanbul: Yapı Kredi Yayınları, 2001), 79.
4   Güven Turan, "The Adventure of Modernism in Turkish Poetry," *Agenda* 38.3–4 (2002): 9.
5   Victoria Rowe Holbrook, *The Unreadable Shores of Love, Turkish Modernity, and Mystic Romance* (Austin: University of Texas Press, 1994), 31.
6   Nermin Menemencioğlu, introduction to *The Penguin Book of Turkish Verse*, ed. Nermin Menemencioğlu and Fahir İz (London: Penguin, 1978), 48.
7   Orhan Koçak, "Yahya Kemal'le Mayakovski Arasından Nazım Hikmet," *Hece Aylık Edebiyat Dergisi*, no. 53–55 (2001): 162–72.
8   Harold Bloom, *The Anxiety of Influence*, 2d ed. (New York: Oxford University Press, 1997), 94.
9   T. S. Eliot, "The Social Function of Poetry," in *On Poetry and Poets* (London: Faber and Faber, 1957), 22–25.
10   Ahmet Hamdi Tanpınar, "Şiire Dair," in *Edebiyat Üzerine Makaleler* (Istanbul: Dergah Yayınları, 1992), 24.
11   Quoted by Tacettin Şimşek, "Masaldan Destana: Dağlarca'nın Şiiri," *Hece Aylık Edebiyat Dergisi*, no. 53–55 (2001): 185.
12   Turgut Uyar, *Bir Şiirden* (Istanbul: Ada Yayınları, 1983), 70.
13   Derek Walcott, *What the Twilight Says* (New York: Farrar, Straus, and Giroux, 1998), 70.

Jale Parla

Car Narratives: A Subgenre in Turkish Novel Writing

It is possible to talk about a literary preoccupation with cars, along with other vehicles such as carriages, buses, and tractors, in the Turkish novel from its very beginnings. These vehicles, whether carriage, train, bus, tractor, or van, appear as tropes rather than means of transportation. The generic term for vehicles that run with engines is *makina* (machine) in Anatolia. *Makina* also refers to all machines. Thus, the trope of the car becomes important in at least two ways: in its relationship to the machine and in its signification of a particular kind of space that has become meaningful in Turkish modernization.

In terms of both plot and character, the theme of automation and its primary motif, the car, seem to have inspired many a fabulation in the Turkish novel. Each execution of the theme is related, first and foremost, to that inexhaustible subject of Turkish writing, the effects of Westernization and modernization. But this is not all. As the car stories are plotted in different periods of the Turkish novel by different novelists, these stories, which begin with the seemingly innocent acquisition

The *South Atlantic Quarterly* 102:2/3, Spring/Summer 2003.
Copyright © 2003 by Duke University Press.

of cars, grow into enigmatic narratives of possession and dispossession, empowerment and loss of power, function and dysfunction, maturation and infantilism, narcissism and fetishism, fragmentation and self-destruction, not to mention a whole century of estrangement and a feeling of inferiority inspired by the contact with the West.

When a certain theme becomes periodically charged with a new motif, as is the case with the theme of the car in the Turkish novel, one might be justified in suspecting the presence of a subgenre. Such, for example, are the subgenres in the Western tradition of the novel of the Bildungsroman, the Künstlerroman, the novel of bourgeois tragedies, and so on. Car novels, which we see appear at every significant turn of the sociohistorical process in Turkey, and which are undertaken by major Turkish novelists, constitute an important subgenre of the novel in the Turkish language.

If the Word Must Represent the Thing . . .

The Turkish novel's preoccupation with cars and carriages begins in the *Tanzimat* period, with Recaizade Ekrem's *Araba Sevdası* [The carriage affair].[1] The theme of *Araba Sevdası* is nothingness. Among the other novels of the *Tanzimat*, Ekrem's novel occupies a unique place: it displays its writer's awareness of the cultural chaos of his age and represents Ekrem's perception of the dark space at the meeting of two different epistemologies where literary representation became practically impossible.[2] The novel is composed as a parody of futile writing and reading activities, as futile as the rounds made by the fancy carriages of Westernized beaus in the fashionable Çamlıca.

Bihruz Bey of *Araba Sevdası* is one such beau whose one fad in life is a carriage that he flaunts as he rides dressed in the most elegant and fashionable manner—without regard to the weather. (So he might be wearing a coat under the hot sun and a silk shirt on a cold day, but that does not bother him so long as his attire is European.) During one such excursion, Bihruz Bey catches a glimpse of a beautiful woman in another carriage and instantaneously becomes enamored, believing such beauty in such an elegant carriage must be a Western-educated young girl from a respectable family. (The truth is that Periveş, the woman in the carriage, is one of the best-known courtesans in town and the carriage is a rented one.) Bihruz's obsession with this woman complements his craze for the carriage. The two

Photo by Arif Aşçı.

become one in his deranged mind as Ekrem depicts Bihruz's confusion in a dream:

> The carriage of Perives speeds so fast down the slope that leads to Beylerbeyi that the wheels do not touch the ground. The fantastic animals that pull the carriage do not look like horses. . . . Bihruz Bey, riding a steed, follows the carriage but cannot catch up. He spurs his horse, drives it on, but just as he is about to catch up, his horse begins to run backward. Bihruz Bey turns around to find out that an old woman (perhaps Madame Pierre) is hanging onto the tail of his horse and pulling the horse back! In the meantime, M. Pierre, wearing a long robe de chambre and a woman's hat adorned with colored feathers, with a Bordeaux bottle of wine under each arm, appears. Mme. and M. Pierre jump and dance as they sing: "Que est-ce que l'amour? C'est un tambour! C'est un tambour! Mais mon cher chevalier! J'ai vu enfin que le beau sex vaut mieux qu'un lapin!" And as they jump, they turn the carriage over. From within the carriage rush out a couple of turtles and a little dog. And then Bihruz Bey's steed frees itself and flies into the

air, the turtles begin to dance, and the little dog barks the tunes of the opera *La Belle Helene*.[3]

The dream is no sillier or more pathetic than Bihruz's idolatry of Western manners, nor is the love letter that he tries to compose in the ludicrous mixture of Turkish and French more absurd, in sense and sound, than the tunes of the opera barked by a dog. The writing of this letter is a masterpiece of satire and irony that targets the ravings of a poorly educated young Ottoman man who is cut off from his own culture and caught up in miserable ignorance. The most critical part of Bihruz's futile search for self-expression comes when he tries to translate a poem from French to Turkish. The attempted translation reads as the following:

> I name a rose
> That woman who confuses my mind
> If the word must represent the thing
> That woman deserves that name of beauty
> Like a rose.

In this poem, the one line that makes absolutely no sense to Bihruz Bey is "If the word must represent the thing." Bihruz's total helplessness to conceive the relationship between the word and the thing provides the major irony of the book: the fruitlessness of Tanzimat writers' labors to represent and communicate. Bihruz Bey's poorly composed, incomplete, and unread epistle, therefore, signifies the mimetic crisis that Ekrem perceived was engendered by the cultural and linguistic chaos of his times. Among other factors that contributed to this chaos, one was especially relevant to writing and representation: the clash between the empirical, realistic epistemology of the Western novel and the aprioristic and idealistic epistemology that the first Turkish novelists were reluctant to give up. Ekrem held undigested "over-Westernization"[4] responsible for aggravating the epistemological clash and producing the follies that reigned in the intellectual as well as the creative spheres. He chose the carriage, the vehicle that takes its rider nowhere but makes its perennial rounds in circles that close on themselves, to represent the cultural as well as the textual ineffectiveness of the whole enterprise of Westernization. Ekrem's text offers no solution for this miserable state of things except for the estranged apology that ends the novel in a French word: Pardon!

Dulce et Utile!

During the decade 1920–1930, the founders of the Turkish Republic launched industrialization projects whose priority was the mechanization of manufacture and farming. The machine, therefore, signified progress and was celebrated as such in Nazım Hikmet's poetry. This occasion was one in which Nazım's ideal of progress, which was orthodox Marxist, corresponded to that of the founding fathers of the republic. Although the famous poem by Nazım, "I want to become a machine" with its easily sung rhyme of the "trum trum trak / trak tiki tak" became a motto of the new zeal for automation, Nazım's poetry went further than just a nursery rhyme in cultivating the idea and the imagery of the machine. The *835 Satır* [835 lines] of 1920–30 abounds with such imagery, which Nazım put into unprecedented use, formally as well as thematically. He sited a visionary geography of a land tilled by tractors, rebuilt by steel beams, traveled by "iron horses running on iron tracks," navigated by motor boats "that race with the wind," a land where the sound of turbines and dynamos resonated, a land lit up by "the fire of the lightning of the steel-toothed wheels."[5]

Nazım's enthusiasm for the machine was naturally related to the Communist project of industrialization in the Soviet Union under the Stalinist regime. It reverberated, however, in the Turkish republican project of progress, and so was appropriated later by the leftist writers of Anatolia, graduates of the *Köy Enstitüleri* (Village Institutes) who launched a campaign under the dissident motto "The land belongs to whoever tills it."[6]

One such writer was Talip Apaydın, who wrote an agenda novel entitled *Sarı Traktör* [The yellow tractor] that exemplified the proper attitude that had to be taken toward the machine.[7] Even in this novel, however, where the tractor is desired for the efficiency it will provide for harvesting, the *makina* still figures as a foreign object that threatens the villagers by planting the seeds of snobbery and rivalry in a way menacing to solidarity and community feeling. Apaydın, therefore, looks for a strategy to rub out this sinister potential of the machine that has crept into his writing almost despite himself. He achieves the erasure by bestowing priority on the human over the machine. When at the end of the novel Arif, the protagonist, finally gets the tractor of his dreams, he finds that he will not be able to drive it into the village because of the snow that has blocked the roads. Unable to delay the gratification of having his tractor right in front of his house, Arif impatiently shovels the snow with superhuman effort before the puzzled eyes of his watching villagers. When he finally succeeds in this almost impossible task, he is praised and acquires the nickname "Yellow Tractor." The human thus valorized over the machine, community feeling is restored and the threat of the machine is wiped away; only its subdued utility remains.

Sinister and Futile

The fascination with the machine that was inspired by Nazım's poetry and found some resonance among the progressive writers of Anatolia was short lived. The machine as a sinister theme returned with a backlash in Ahmet Hamdi Tanpınar's fiction. His two enigmatic novels, *Saatleri Ayarlama Enstitüsü* [The clock-setting institute] and *Mahur Beste* [Mahur music] represent the author's overarticulated reaction to the machine—especially the clock.[8] As for *Saatleri Ayarlama Enstitüsü*, that novel seems to have been germinated in a short story Tanpınar wrote in 1949, in which he portrays the Sani Bey of the family house in Acıbadem in his compulsive relationship with the machine.[9]

The house in Acıbadem is an old house with many mirrors, gilded old furniture, and heavy dark curtains. The narrator regards this house both as the site of his early childhood fantasies when he lost himself in dreams in the shadowy depths of the mirrors and as the site of a turning point in his life because he witnessed an eccentric uncle's crazy experimentations with machines.[10] Although the narrator remembers the uncle and the house as constituting the most formative experiences of early childhood, the uncle, Sani Bey, is not much more than a second child in the house. The other members of the family humor his crazy inventions because, like a spoiled child, he cannot be opposed.[11] Sani Bey, a retired engineer, has the hobby of collecting pieces of machinery and hoarding them in a basement, where they await their turn to be used in an invention like, for example, the bathing apparatus he installs in the house. If the basement is the site of the unconscious, as Gaston Bachelard maintains in *The Poetics of Space*,[12] these bits and pieces of motors and engines stand for the fragmented consciousness of Sani Bey or correspond to the fragmented image he has of his own body.

That uncanny bathing apparatus, which the narrator remembers as an upright stove that resembled a locomotive, becomes the end of Sani Bey who dies by burning himself while taking a bath, and yet dies happy. Sani

Bey's passion in life is a four-stage process of engineering that consists of *icat* (invention), *islah* (improvement), *tadil* (modification), and *ikmal* (completion). This four-phase passion is always accompanied by an aesthetic ambition, for Sani Bey is never content with just the utility of the machine — he wants the *dulce* as well as the *utile*. This ambition leads him to his greatest invention and the story's climax.

Sani Bey gives his son a bike as a graduation present. However, as he contemplates the bike, it occurs to him that this great giaour invention needs improvement and modification. It should protect the rider from rain and sun. So he sells his horse (old Derviş, almost a member of the family) and starts working on the carriage to turn it into a bike. He succeeds, only to discover that everything works well until the vehicle has to climb a slope — then somebody has to get off and push it. To improve on that fault of his modified carriage, he gets old Derviş, the horse, harnessed to the new vehicle, thus completing the process of invention, improvement, modification, and completion.

Carriage turned bike, and then again carriage, continues the theme of futility that surrounds certain Westernization efforts as elaborated by Recaizade Ekrem in *Araba Sevdası*. This theme of the absurd reappropriation of everything Western is, once more, related to the theme of artistic expression. Whereas, in Ekrem's novel, the theme had been affixed to the epistemological gulf that the Westernized writer did not know how to bridge, in Tanpınar's short story, it is intricately connected to the sociohistorical and individual-pathological, for the irony of the last stage, completion, does not only target society but also exposes the pathological state of immaturity that Sani Bey will never outgrow. We can say, then, that the uncle Sani Bey, the second child in the house, is actually the child-narrator whose growth was arrested at an early stage of childhood, that he never proceeded beyond the mirror stage of his development, and that Sani Bey's "happy" death by accident (brought about by his own invention) is an escape from the painful recognition of incompletion, a lack that the child narrator will later try to fill by the art of writing.

Hayri İrdal of *Saatleri Ayarlama Enstitüsü* is a character similar to Sani Bey. He, too, is an artist manqué who has tried his luck, like Wilhelm Meister, in the theater, but who has managed to realize his artistic intentions only by getting involved in a fantastic quackery, led by the novel's Mephistophelian figure, Halit Ayarcı. The master and the novice launch a grotesque project of regulating the clocks in the whole country so as to instill in the people the value of time and punctuality—note the jab at modernism. And they are very successful until, not content with their political achievement, they decide to crown their accomplishment with an aesthetic touch. They want to construct a building for the Clock-Setting Institute designed in the shape of a clock. Hayri İrdal, the novice, starts a search to find the right shape. He roams in Istanbul, Bursa, and Konya (all centers of classical Ottoman architecture) to find the ideal model for the construction. For inspiration, he studies the mosques and the various details of their architectural grandeur. Finally, however, he abandons this aesthetic search and decides to model his plan on the old clock in the house, Mübarek. The incongruity between the antique clock and a modern building, the unbridgeable gap between the private clock and the public building intensifies the absurdity of the whole undertaking.

One reading of the finale of that enigmatic novel of machinery, *Saatleri Ayarlama Enstitüsü*, will therefore involve a multilayered signification of the clocks as metonyms of incompletion and lack, on the personal-psychological level as well as the cultural-aesthetic. For in the end of that novel, Halit Ayarcı, the hegemon of the institute, is frustrated by the architectural designs in the shape of clocks commissioned for the institute's building. He cannot see any originality in these designs and asks, in frustration: "How are these any different from an ordinary building? How are they modern? Where does one see the clock in these?" Annoyed by the lack of creativity he witnessed in the contestants, Ayarcı insists on the spirit of the competition: "We want to see the idea of the clock penetrate into the constitution of the building."[15] If we supply the missing *n* (which, by the way, in Turkish also means "what") to the insistent questions of Ayarcı ("where does one see the clock in these?") the word *clock* (*saat*) will read *art* (*sanat*). Then what is missing from the word *saat* is that *n*, the addition of which will turn it into *sanat* (art). *Saat* (clock) is *sanat* (art) minus the *n*. A person whose aesthetic development is curtailed becomes a *saat* just as a society that lets its culture be led by charlatans (like Halit Ayarcı) will turn into a clock-setting institute instead of an oasis of cultural regeneration. All that kind of society will get, then, is a hegemon, a totalitarian leader who will manipulate it as Halit Ayarcı manipulates the whole system. By the same token, one who allows oneself to become the clock will suffer the authority of the father from which one cannot free oneself but will sink into further automation by giving up creativity. The missing *n* that turns the word *sanat* (art) into *saat* (clock) stands for lack of maturity, lack of art, lack of self-actualization, and the Lacanian desire for completion.[14]

Mercedes, the Betrayer

The next appearance of the car in a major Turkish novel is in 1975 with Adalet Ağaoğlu's *Fikrimin İnce Gülü* [The slender rose of my thought]. The 1970s were the years when the effects of capitalism were felt in the growing passion for commodity fetishism. A Mercedes that a Turkish guest worker, Bayram, drives from Germany to his village is the symbol of the machine-God that he has worshiped since he was a boy. His tragedy began when, as a child, he experienced a violent break from nature (and the natural) when he saw a Ford automobile come to his village. Ağaoğlu describes the child's awe of the machine in terms of a ritualistic sacrifice that ingrained the hegemony of the machine in the boy's subconscious.[15] Bayram's development seems to have been arrested at that moment of sacrificial offering, for, afterward, he never stopped worshiping the machine-God until their mutual destruction.

The car, the Mercedes Bayram comes to possess after hard work and at the cost of selling out everything — friends, family, even the girl he loves — represents, on the surface, status and power. As a village boy, Bayram was bullied wherever he went — in his village by the elders, in the military service by the police, in Germany by his employer. He chooses to compensate for these humiliations by bullying people weaker than he is. This is one way in which hegemony circulates in Turkish culture: the bullied, intimidated by his superior, becomes the bully by intimidating his inferior. Bayram, therefore, is the victim who will not miss a chance to become the victimizer to heal the wounds of his crippled ego. On another level, Bayram exemplifies the fate of the peasant caught up in the process of the transformation from the agricultural to industrial society who becomes a misfit in both. This Ağaoğlu depicts with the symbol of the apricot seed, the tree under which Bayram and Kezban (the sweetheart Bayram leaves behind) met, and the stars under which Bayram slept. As another star, the steel-star emblem of the Mercedes, replaces all these natural symbols, Ağaoğlu gets the chance to making her statement: industrialization is achieved at the cost of breaking people away from nature, which is the same thing as eradicating their natural goodness. On a further and more directly psychological level, the road novel portrays the gradual fragmentation of Bayram's self, so that at the end of his journey all he arrives at is homelessness: "At the end of the road, there, no one was waiting for Bayram."[16]

Bayram begins his journey from Germany and drives his Mercedes in cocky pride, wearing a Franz Lehar shirt and a green hat. Bihruz-like, he reenacts the clownish infatuation with Westernization until he begins to experience the series of mishaps that gradually turn his brand new Mercedes, his Balkız (honey maiden), into a raped and defiled woman (these are Bayram's terms) and himself into a ragged man. The gradual disintegration of the car parallels the spiritual disintegration of Bayram, so much so that by the time the car and the man arrive at the village, both of them are a wreck. Bayram's village, Ballıhisar (honey castle), which Bayram thought was awaiting the arrival of the knight accompanied by the honey maiden, becomes the destination of a degraded quest of a problematic hero in auto-mated homelessness—to modify Georg Lukacs' well-known definition of the quest of the hero in a capitalistic system.

Because of his feminine fragility, Bayram was nicknamed "Incegül" (slender rose) in his village. He becomes the slender rose of Ağaoğlu's thought as she contemplates Bayram's condition. What happens to a village boy, an orphan, who is bullied, harassed, and teased by the authoritarian, masculine Turkish culture? What happens when such beginnings are reinforced by the institutions of a military-police regime? What happens when such a boy is plunged into the clutches of the capitalist system that came upon and was adopted by an authoritarian military regime? What happens to a village boy when he, from a very early age, experiences the desire for empowerment and tries to realize it within the system Ağaoğlu describes in the terms I tried to portray here. Answer: the slender, fragile rose of the village, bullied by his own people, becomes the slender rose of contemplation of the novelist and culminates in her condemnation of commodity fetishism. Mercedes, as the symbol of that fetishism, stands for betrayal—of others as much as of one's own self.

Volvo, the Fratricide

When Latife Tekin's *Sevgili Arsız Ölüm* [The dear unabashed death] exploded on the Turkish literary scene in 1983, everybody knew that here was genuinely new stuff—new in characterization, narration, freshness of vision, strength of conviction. The book won unanimous acclaim as the portrait of the artist as a young girl. *Sevgili Arsız Ölüm* finishes with the artist's exile from home, symbolized by her poetry breaking free from the rooftop of her house to fly over the city. Leaving home, the risk every artist has to take, became a haunting motif in Tekin's writing following this first novel, and the theme of rooflessness preoccupied her writing afterward.[17] In her third novel, *Gece Dersleri* [Evening classes], which followed *Berji-Kristin Çöp Masalları* [Berci-Kristin garbage tales], we find that the theme of wordlessness is added to the theme of worldlessness Tekin had worked on in her first two novels. The wings of words that carried her writing over rooftops in the finale of her first novel are soon broken and her utterances fall, shatter, break into pieces, and even freeze—a despairing immobility and paralysis are what she gets from those evening classes she attends with the leftist youth of the 1970s. The automobile of *Gece Dersleri*, the black Fiat driven in the sky by her dead mother, will now and then descend upon the daughter, almost in mockery of the latter's plight, her immobile speechlessness.

In her fourth novel, *Buzdan Kılıçlar* [The swords of ice], the downpour of the magical narrative style that colored her first three novels recedes to the background as Tekin experiments with speechlessness.[18] This time it is a Volvo that seduces the main character of the novel, Halilhan Sunteriler, into believing that by possessing the Volvo he will achieve a threefold empowerment: he will share something with the inhabitants of that city which he watches from afar, from the outskirts where his bidonville is located; he will own the highest status symbol in his community; he will be Westernized. When a woman who calls herself Julie and claims her cat is from China gets into his car, Halil sees this as an undeniable sign of the cosmopolitanism he has attained thanks to his Volvo. (The woman is actually Turkish and her real name is Jülide. As for her cat, that is no more a Chinese cat than the woman is an English lady.) More significant than these Bihruz-like self-delusions of Halilhan, however, is the fact that the Volvo becomes the instrument for Halilhan, who is another impostor with his fake projects, of exercising verbal control over his brothers and his friend Gogi to enforce them into passivity and acquiescence.

And yet Halilhan never feels that he is in full possession or control of the Volvo. The car will sometimes act in a funny way and just go wherever it wants to go despite its driver's efforts to steer it toward a certain destination. When, it is wrecked in an accident, it will not hold *sente*—that is, like its driver, who is in the process of losing his balance because of his fruit-less effort at empowerment and the consequent estrangement from family and community, the car refuses to hold balance. Halilhan tries yet another way of possessing the car by imagining it as a creative product and by try-ing to envision the engineer who designed it, but that effort is mocked by the absurd treatise on New Automobilism and its chapter called "The Auto-mobile and Dream" penned by a military officer. It is almost as if Tekin is reviewing the ways in which the theme has been dealt with in the Turk-ish novel before she abandons its representation by depicting Halilhan in complete speechlessness.

Halilhan's relentless flow of words does not stop until speechlessness comes with fratricide. He, who used to mesmerize his brothers and friend Gogi by his orations, finds out that they are breaking free from his rhetorical power. So he tries to reassert his lost hegemony by challenging his brother to a beer-drinking contest. During this contest, Halilhan kills his brother by accidentally running over him with his Volvo. Was it an accident? Was it Halilhan who was driving it? Or did the Volvo assert its autonomy again to show its driver what an autonomous automaton is capable of doing? What-ever answer the reader chooses will not break the absolute silence of the end, Halilhan's steel speechlessness as he views the city from the hill and feels nothing.[19]

Chevrolet, the Suicide

In *Mach I'dan Mektuplar* [Letters from Mach I], Sevim Burak wrote to her son Karaca about her passion for cars, especially racing cars.[20] She also told him that she was planning to write an astounding story about a car, one with which she hoped to shock her readers with her originality and courage. The result was her novella, *Palyaço Ruşen* [Ruşen, the clown], which has a Chevrolet as its protagonist and a Ford Mach I as the antagonist. The two cars represent the psychic division of Sevim Burak; her writing is aleotary, surrealistic, even rhyzomatic. In its self-reflexivity, the novella is symptom-atic of the apolitical atmosphere of the 1980s marked by the unprincipled, liberal Özalization that followed the military coup of 1981.

The characters in *Palyaço Ruşen* include an Alfa Romeo, a Cougar, a Ferrari, and an Austin Maxi, all cars of the affluent. They all hate the Chevrolet (the car driven by taxi drivers in Istanbul) and are hated in return. So the conflict between the Chevrolet and all the other cars stems from a class conflict but develops into one of gender before it finally destroys the antagonist, the Chevrolet.

We are first introduced to the atmosphere of mindless snobbery of the luxury cars of Bagdat Street.[21] As they belittle, harass, and patronize the poor Chevrolet, the scene focuses on the latter as it sits by the sidewalk, smokes a cigarette, and then falls asleep. In his dream we enter the hidden, psychic life of the Chevrolet/the clown. Although the Chevy-clown hates all the cars, its real enemy is a Ford Mach I. As the dream unfolds, the reader becomes aware of a certain masculinity attributed to the Mach I and femininity to the Chevrolet. Obviously, among other things, the two cars also stand for a troubled relationship between a man and a woman—the enmity, therefore, involves class as well as gender.

The Chevy-clown works in a circus and entertains people at the cost of its own tears, the proverbial clown image. The spectators are unfeeling, but it is certainly the Mach I that is responsible for the greatest pain that the Chevrolet suffers, for it is as the result of the seduction and abandonment by the Mach I that the Chevrolet is reduced to clowning in a circus. The Ford Mach I, tantalizing at the same time as it is cold and cunning, is an unbeatable victor of all the encounters with the Chevrolet and plays with it as a cat plays with a mouse. The last act and the final encounter come with a dance of seduction and rejection between the Ford Mach I and the Chevrolet. It culminates in the suicide of the latter by blowing its tank.

Conclusion

In this ride through Turkish writing, I attempted to follow what I call the subgenre of the car novel from its first appearance in the *Tanzimat* period up to its recent surrealistic executions. In *Araba Sevdası*, the craze for the luxurious carriage, which results in the financial ruin of its owner, Bihruz Bey, stems from a sense of inferiority and the accompanying desire for power and status. More important, however, is the fact that the theme is located in the epistemological impasse and the cultural impoverishment that Ekrem depicted in this pioneering novel of modernization.

Seemingly the most straightforward of the car novels we have discussed, Ağaoğlu's *Fikrimin İnce Gülü* makes its statement on two levels: the road

stands for society (and social change), and the car is identified with Bayram as the author holds a mirror to the road and lends an ear to the front
seat of the Mercedes to record Bayram's thoughts in a skillful application of
indirect free discourse.

Still, there is a crucial question that must be asked and answered. Why
the car and not any other machine? Why did the Turkish novelists choose
the car to represent the psychic responses of their protagonists to the changing times?

One obvious answer is that industrialism entered Turkish life with vehicles and only afterward with manufacturing machines; that is to say, people
were riding in cars and carriages long before the factories were set up. A
less obvious reason might be that the car provided the Turkish psyche with
something it desperately needed through all the stages of modernization
from 1880 to 1990. For Turkish women and men reluctant to leave the private space of their homes to confront the demands of the public space, such
as individuation, anonymity, efficiency, self-reliance, and self-discipline, the
car provided the semiprivate space with its blurred boundary between the
home and the street. Moreover, as the car was metaphorically identified with
the novels' protagonists, when it became the extension of their bodies, it signified the linguistic site where the conscious and the unconscious met. For
the man-child Sani Bey of Tanpınar's short story, the effort to turn the bike
into a carriage is actually an attempt at a reconciliation of the id and the ego.
Down in the basement he collects his materials, bits and pieces of machinery; up in the street he puts them together but shelters them in a carriage.
After all, was it not because the bike was open on all sides that he decided
to improve and modify it? The semiprivate space of the carriage (just as the
semiofficial space of the Clock-Setting Institute) is the topos from which
Tanpınar debates the artistic and the cultural issues of his time, as well as his
characters' bizarre fixations, "without coming up into the open," so to speak.

Cars replace the homes that the protagonists of these novels leave, or
have to leave, one inescapable imposition of modernity. The compromise
involves settling for the semiprivate, semi-intimate space. The car is the
extension of the house into public space; it is both outside and inside; it
brings the individual into contact with the world at the same time as it shelters the individual from rooflessness, from perfect anonimity, or cold formality. One can embellish one's car as one can embellish one's house, and
still keep it as an alternative space to the house.

As a setting from which the authors debated the issues of moderniza-tion, the car epitomizes the mental and psychic confusion of the novels' characters. That confusion ranges from stupid ignorance to suicidal defi-ance. Accordingly, the narrative mode of the subgenre runs the gamut of styles from the comic and the ironic to the satiric and the tragic. All of the protagonists of the car novels are antiheroes, as befits the modern novel. With antiheroes, the adoption of the satiric and the ironic tone is easier, but such heroes have the disadvantage of turning the story into a superfi-cial one. The authors of the car novels have circumvented that disadvantage by portraying these antiheroes within the particular space of the car, the blurred space that is neither totally inside nor outside, neither totally pri-vate nor public. In this space, the protagonists need not wear the masks of pretense they put up in the public sphere, nor are they allowed to be the uninhibited and uncensored selves they are in the privacy of the home. The space of the car, in one sense, is a space of escape where it is easy to indulge in illusion and self-delusion. That is perhaps one other reason that the car turned into a fad so easily and the car novels became a subgenre as the novel-ists exploited what they saw hidden inside the car. It was also from that space they chose to debate the various aspects of Turkish modernization by unfolding its ironies, unmasking its delusions, holding its fads up to ridi-cule, and relinquishing its aspirations to bathos—in short, laying bare its clichés and exposing its false promises.

Notes

I thank friends who brought to my attention certain works by Turkish authors about cars: to Ayhan Aktar for Sevim Burak's *Mach I'dan Mektuplar,* to Süha Oğuzertem for Ahmet Hamdi Tanpınar's *Acıbademdeki Köşk,* to Ayse Buğra for Tarık Buğra's *Mavi Doç* [The blue Doç], to Fatih Özgüven for Ömer Seyfettin's *Nezle* [The cold], to Zeynep Ergun for Peride Celal's *Jaguar.* Some of these works that I had to omit in this essay, for considerations of space, will be included in a longer investigation of the topic. I also wish to thank the Rockefeller Center at Bellagio for providing the opportunity of a fourteen-day stay, during which this article came to be put down on paper, doubtless owing to the inspiration of the beautiful Como.

1   Recaizade Mahmut Ekrem, *Araba Sevdası,* ed. Seyit Kemal (Istanbul: İnkılap, 1985).
2   Jale Parla, *Babalar ve Oğullar: Türk Romanının Epistemolojik Temelleri* [Fathers and sons: The epistemological foundations of the Turkish novel] (Istanbul: İletişim, 1990), 105–24.
3   Recaizade Mahmut Ekrem, *Araba Sevdası,* ed. Seyit Kemal (Istanbul: İnkılap, 1985), 54.
4   Şerif Mardin, "Tanzimat'tan Sonra Aşırı Batılılaşma," [Over-Westernization after the *Tan-zimat*], in *Türk Modernleşmesi* [Turkish modernization] (Istanbul: İletişim, 1971), 21–76.
5   See the poems "Rodos Heykeli," "Berkeley," "Nikbinlik," "Yanardağ," "Sanat T elâkkisi,"

"Yeni Sanat," "Gözlerimiz," "Yalnayak," "Güneşi İçenlerin Türküsü," and "Grev," in *835 Satır* (Istanbul: Adam Yayınları, 1973.)

6   The project of the Village Institutes adopted the principle of practical education for the villagers with a view to improving the living conditions of the rural population. The project was led by İsmail Hakkı Tonguç, who believed that the modernization movement had to be undertaken by the peasants at the same time as it was adopted by the urban intelligentsia. Osman Kafadar, "Cumhuriyet Dönemi Eğitim Tartışmaları" [Debates on education in the Republican period], in *Modernleşme ve Batıcılık* [Modernization and Westernism], ed. Uygur Kocabaşoğlu (Istanbul: İletişim, 2002), 351–81.

7   Talip Apaydın, *Sarı Traktör* (Ankara: Başak, [n.d.]), 201. First published in 1957.

8   See Süha Oğuzertem, "Fictions of Narcissism: Metaphysical and Psychosexual Conflict in the Stories of Ahmet Hamdi Tanpınar," *Turkish Studies Association Bulletin* 14.2 (1990): 223–33.

9   Ahmet Hamdi Tanpınar, *Acıbademdeki Köşk* [The House in Acıbadem] (Istanbul: Dergâh, [n.d.]), 95–109.

10 Oğuz Demiralp, *Kutup Noktası: Ahmet Hamdi Tanpınar'ın Yapıtı Üzerine Eleştirel Bir Deneme* [The polar point: A critical essay on Ahmet Hamdi Tanpınar's work] (Istanbul: YKY, 1993), 15–35, and Nurdan Gürbilek, *Yer Değiştiren Gölge* [The moving shadow] (Istanbul: Metis, 1995), 11–23.

11 The name "Sani" means "the second."

12 Gaston Bachelard, *The Poetics of Space*, trans. Maria Jolas (Boston: Beacon, 1969).

13 Ahmet Hamdi Tanpınar, *Saatleri Ayarlama Enstitüsü* (Istanbul: Dergah, 1998), 287.

14 Completion in Tanpınar's fiction is an impossible dream, the impossibility of which he expresses by the symbol of machines (motors, engines, cars, and clocks) in his novels, and the notion of the unreachable-inconceivable undivided time in his poetry.

15 Adalet Ağaoğlu, *Fikrimin İnce Gülü* (Istanbul: Remzi, 1977), 85–89.

16 Ağaoğlu, *Fikrimin İnce Gülü*, 325.

17 Sibel Irzık, "Latife Tekin'de Yersizliğin Mekanları" [The sites of placelessness in Latife Tekin] (paper presented at the symposium on Turkish women novelists and short story writers, Bilkent University, Ankara, April 8–10, 1999).

18 Nurdan Gürbilek, *Ev Odevi* [Home work] (Istanbul: Metis, 1998), 35–58.

19 Latife Tekin, *Buzdan Kılıçlar* (Istanbul: Metis, 1989), 141.

20 Sevim Burak, *Mach I'dan Mektuplar* (Istanbul: Lagos, 1990), 145–46, 153–54, 159.

21 Sevim Burak, *Palyaço Ruşen* (Istanbul: Nisan, 1993), 49–61.

Sibel Irzık

Allegorical Lives: The Public and the Private in the Modern Turkish Novel

In *Lying Down to Die* [*Ölmeye Yatmak*], Adalet Ağaoğlu's first novel, published in 1973, the protagonist Aysel, a university professor who has slept with her student and experienced a second bleeding of the hymen after many years of marriage, makes a somewhat tongue-in-cheek attempt at willing herself to die. In the anonymity of a hotel room and the nakedness of her body, Aysel tries to withdraw not only from the socially scripted roles and imposed identities she has so far assumed, but also from the discourses that have infected and inhibited her voice. It is in the course of this experiment that she has a dream worth quoting at length. Here it is:

> I have found the most definitive formula to develop and save Turkey. I am in a place that resembles a wax museum. Two guards from Victorian England stand before a high gate. They don't move. Confidently, I walk through this gate. I seem to know that the guards will not stop me because they are made of wax. Having walked through the door, I find myself in a long and narrow hall. A long, narrow table is placed across the hall. And beyond the table

The *South Atlantic Quarterly* 102:2/3, Spring/Summer 2003.
Copyright © 2003 by Duke University Press.

are a series of cloaked men with green faces. They, too, are motion-less. But I am certain that right after I present my dissertation they will come to life. . . . Their green faces will go from pink to white as they cheer "Viva! Viva!" Atatürk will then kiss me on the forehead, I tell myself. He will point with the index finger of his right hand and just as he had said "Armies! Your first destination is the Mediterranean. Advance!" he will say: "Turkish nation! Your destination is to follow the road that this woman shows, advance!" . . . But, just as I am stand-ing there before Atatürk and the other old professors, I find myself at ten years of age. . . . I worry about my outfit for they might think of me as a little coquette. . . . Lame, I try to run here and there. Dragging my lameness, I try to find something. At that moment, the head of the fox fur collar hanging around my neck comes to life. The mouth of the fox keeps biting my chin. I cannot talk. The fox's mouth prevents me from expressing myself. I try to shove it off, but it won't go. Then, as I struggle on the broken high heel of my shoe with the fox's head, Ata-türk suddenly moves. He waves the leather glove he is holding in his left hand to my face. . . . His face looks as if he is blowing on the ashes of a furnace. As he blows, he keeps asking, "Where is your disserta-tion? Let us see your dissertaion. Show it." As I hold the fox's head with one hand, I search the pockets of my school uniform with the other. Then the huge volumes in the hands of the six green-eyed professors on my right and the six green-faced professors on my left turn out to be forks and knives. They all sit around the table. They beat with their knives and forks. "Bring your thesis! Bring your thesis!" And I am not aware that I have placed a whole pot of *dolma* [stuffed grape leaves] in front of them instead of my thesis. I suddenly realize that what I have put before them is not my thesis but a whole pot of *dolma*. I am very embarrassed, especially because I am in Atatürk's presence. But I can-not see Atatürk. The person I thought was Atatürk turns out to be a hunter. He is trying to shoot the fox around my neck. He is aiming at it with a hunter's gun. I try to say, "It is not a real fox. Only a stage accessory! Only a prop!" But I can't find my voice.[1]

Commenting on this dream, Jale Parla points out that "the confident and determined walk with which Aysel walks through the big gate of Western civilization is undermined by her lame helplessness; her intellectual product turns out to be a pot of *dolma*; her asexual composure is threatened by the bite of the fox (obviously symbolizing sexual seduction and violation); and her libidinal energy is suppressed by the aiming of the father in the person of Atatürk turned hunter." She goes on to conclude that "regressive, infantalized, and fearful, vacillating between over confidence and angst, the dream stands for the subconscious of the whole Turkish nation."[2]

If this is true, then the dreamer, an isolated individual on the verge of suicide and struggling to wake up from "the nightmare of history," must stand for the whole Turkish nation. What, then, would it mean for a nation to be represented in the figure of a woman ridden by sexual guilt and a keen sense of a failed social mission? Why does this failure find its supreme expression in the transformation of the program for national salvation into a pot of *dolma*, the demotion of the dreamer from public intellectual to housewife? How should we interpret this sudden fall from the sublime to the ridiculous, a fall caused by the unwelcome intrusion of "home, which waits for us over there, right after great ideas, great passions, right after everything great and beautiful, embarrassing us with its mundane details when we least expect it"?[3] What can one make of the "libidinal energy" of a nation "suppressed by the aiming of the father"?

Atatürk as the father of the nation seems to be quite a permanent feature of many a character's dreams or nightmares in the Turkish novel. Neither is the suicidal bent of pained and playful gestures of self-irony and self-authorization unique to Adalet Ağaoğlu's *Lying Down to Die*. Oğuz Atay's 1972 novel, *The Disconnected [Tutunamayanlar]*,[4] for instance, is dominated by a voice from the grave. In this uncompromisingly ironic bildungsroman depicting the "sentimental education" of Turkish intellectuals, Selim Işık, whose name could be translated as "benign light," has already committed suicide when the novel begins. But the novel articulates a very similar nightmare of frustrated idealism and claustrophobic national history through the texts Selim leaves behind and the echoes of his voice inside other characters' minds. Both Turgut and Selim, the double protagonists of the novel, have several dreams featuring not only Atatürk, but also such unlikely figures as Sultan Abdülhamit. In a rather extreme example of this mania for historical nightmares, Selim has, or claims to have had, a dream in which his supposed unconscious stage-manages a congress of fifty "great Turks and Ottomans." The congress takes place in his own childhood home and brings together Hitler, Abdülhak Hamit, Maksim Gorki, Alpaslan, Fuzuli, Baki, Namık Kemal, Nedim, "the prime minister of the day," and others. Not surprisingly, the debate is about the meaning of Turkishness and how to save Turkey, and again not surprisingly, it disintegrates into chaos and absurdity as soon as it starts.

These narratives, which stage comical invasions of the characters' unconsciouses by public figures and exhibit a disturbing entanglement of the private sphere of experience with a variety of public rituals and discourses, seem to be perfect illustrations of what Fredric Jameson has dubbed "national allegory," the defining mode of Third World literature. In his much debated essay "Third-World Literature in the Era of Multinational Capitalism," Jameson defines *national allegory* in the following notoriously clear-cut terms:

> All third-world texts are necessarily . . . allegorical, and in a very specific way: they are to be read as what I will call *national allegories*, even when, or perhaps I should say, particularly when their forms develop out of predominantly western machineries of representation such as the novel. . . . Third-world texts, even those which are seemingly private and invested with a properly libidinal dynamic, necessarily project a political dimension in the form of national allegory: *the story of the private individual destiny is always an allegory of the embattled situation of the public third-world culture and society.*[5]

It is not possible to do full justice here either to Jameson's entire argument or the various criticisms that have been directed to it, most notably by Aijaz Ahmad in "Jameson's Rhetoric of Otherness and the 'National Allegory.'"[6] I will concentrate instead on a less-debated but certainly central thesis of his essay: the proposition that Third World novels display a *salutary* lack of the crippling bifurcation between the private and the public. In other words, according to Jameson, the allegorical structure of Third World novels both results from and offers "a possibility of grasping the social totality." This is a social dimension denied to modern and especially postmodern Western texts populated with and expressive of "fragmented subjectivities." Through the notion of national allegory, Jameson aims "to stress the loss of certain literary functions and intellectual commitments in the contemporary American scene," and "to dramatize that loss by showing the constitutive presence of those things—what I called narrative allegory (namely the coincidence of the personal story and the 'tale of the tribe,' as still in Spenser) and also the political role of the cultural intellectual—in other parts of the world."[7]

Jameson's approach is in many ways a corrective to standard conceptions of the novel that marginalize examples such as the Turkish novel by defining the genre in terms of the construction and elaboration of an interior, psychological self and the emergence of an autonomous aesthetic divorced from the political. The Turkish novel has seen itself as a means of social critique and mobilization ever since its beginnings during the last decades of the nineteenth century. It has always exhibited a preoccupation with social and historical themes, ranging from the first novels' warnings against excessive Westernization to the romantic depiction of the spirit of the Anatolian people in the so-called village novels of the early years of the republic, or the criticism of class oppression and state corruption in the social realist novels of the 1950s. Even in the modern Turkish novels that place themselves more squarely within the mainstream Western novelistic tradition of narrating the evolution of an "authentic" subjectivity, politics is never a "pistol shot in the middle of a concert."

The question, however, is whether Jameson is justified in proceeding from this prevalence of politics and allegory to a healthy lack of a split between the public and the private, an essentially unproblematic, positive consciousness of collectivity built into the telling and understanding of individual lives in Third World literature. Since Turkey fits Jameson's characterization of Third World countries as those "which have suffered the experience of colonialism and imperialism,"[8] since it has clearly not recovered, economically or culturally, from its contact with the capitalist West, the combination of overtly political themes with unmistakable allegorical structures in a broad range of Turkish novels should be seen as a confirmation of Jameson's theory. However, a number of major late-twentieth-century Turkish novels, including the two I have already referred to, provide reasons to think that the notion of national allegory is not so much in need of confirmation as it is in need of complication, and even, in a certain sense, reversal and irony.

My main reason for thinking so is already apparent in nuclear form in Aysel's dream. The very fact that it *is* a dream, and that it is a dream in which the "manifest content" is quite explicitly "national" while the "latent content" seems to be predominantly sexual, casts some doubt on the validity of Jameson's shorthand for the distinction between Western and Third World literatures: "Freud versus Marx." But, more important, the humor and the horror of the dream result from the dramatization of the distance between the role and the actor, the costume and the body, the ideal and the *dolma*. In other words, what makes the dream both comical and psychologically revealing is the *awkwardness* of the assumed or demanded coincidence between individual and national destinies, the burden of feeling obliged to achieve such a coincidence, and the pain of failing to do so, of being "unmasked" as a particular individual.

In both *Lying Down to Die* and *The Disconnected*, the "historical" dreams do not simply present characters and situations that demand allegorical interpretation. They are, rather, tragicomic representations of the compulsion to allegorize. They clearly reflect the anxiety and paralysis created in the dreamers by the sense that they are dwarfed by the figures populating their unconscious and the sense that they will never be able to live up to the expectations of those figures. As such, the dreams are very much like the novels in which they occur. In many modern Turkish novels, the characters are portrayed as having been condemned to lead allegorical lives. They are haunted, frustrated, and paralyzed by the sense that they must somehow be representative of things larger than themselves, bearers of meanings and destinies imposed on them by what is referred to in *Lying Down to Die* as "the hand that has remade history" (83).

One of the most comical examples of the pressure placed upon a character by these imposed sociohistorical meanings occurs in Ahmet Hamdi Tanpınar's *The Clock-Setting Institute* [*Saatleri Ayarlama Enstitüsü*],[9] serialized in 1954 and first published in book form in 1962. As a result of several coincidences and misunderstandings that lead to legal prosecution, Hayri İrdal, the somewhat impotent protagonist of this novel, finds himself in compulsory analysis with psychiatrist Dr. Ramiz, freshly back from his training in Vienna and employed in the Department of Forensic Medicine. Dr. Ramiz embodies, if you will, another and more literal conflation of "Freud" and "Marx." He is deeply concerned with social matters, viewing psychoanalysis not merely as a method for curing patients but as a vehicle for reforming the world, as what Hayri İrdal calls "that unique path toward salvation found only in religions."[10] Psychoanalysis is *his* "definitive formula to develop and save Turkey." He is understandably frustrated and disappointed because he has not been given the power and opportunity "to

make the entire country shift axes by using this miraculous instrument"
(85 [104]).

Dr. Ramiz's diagnosis for Hayri İrdal is that he is suffering from a typical case of a "father complex." He has unconsciously rejected his father,
but instead of placing himself in the position of paternal authority, he has
been engaged in an endless search for the father, thus failing to achieve
adulthood. According to Dr. Ramiz, this complex is widespread, even natural, in our society today "because socially, we are all suffering from this
disease. Just look around you; we are all complaining about the past, we
are all obsessed with it. We want to transform it from within. What is the
meaning of this? Is it not a father complex? Child or adult, aren't we all
engaged with it? What is all this affection for the Hitites, Phrygians, I know
not what tribes? Is it anything other than a father complex?" (95–96 [115]).
Having thus satisfied himself with a psychosocial diagnosis in which Hayri
İrdal's alleged father complex becomes an instance and an allegory of the
embattled relation of Turkish society to its Ottoman past and to its history
in general, Dr. Ramiz expects his patient not only to accept this diagnosis
but also to have dreams that corroborate it: "I want you to have dreams that
are more suitable to your disease. Do you understand? Make every effort to
have such dreams!" (98 [118]).

Indeed, Dr. Ramiz's contribution to the science of psychoanalysis is his
invention of a new method of cure: "The method by which, after making
a diagnosis on the basis of previously dreamt dreams, the patient is cured
through a strict control with which his later dreams are administered."
Hayri İrdal's failure to have the prescribed dreams makes Dr. Ramiz indignant: "Even though you are the one who inspired this method, you now
don't make any effort. What kind of person are you? Don't you have any willpower?" (99 [119]). When Hayri İrdal tells him about a dream in which he
saw a lion that frightened but did not touch him, Dr. Ramiz is very disappointed. "You should have made the lion eat you," he says, "Or you should
have killed it and worn its skin. In short, you should have been lost in it and
reborn from it. Haven't you ever noticed it in fairy tales? They always get
lost. To get lost, that is to die, then to return to life . . . There is no surer way
of getting rid of a complex. You failed to do it . . . You failed . . . You missed
an opportunity!" (100 [120]).

The Clock-Setting Institute is, in fact, the story of Hayri İrdal missing
the opportunity to live out and tell his own story, even though he is the

first-person narrator of the novel. Süha Oğuzertem has commented on "an inability on Hayri İrdal's part to conceive separateness, to regulate his boundaries in relation to others, to have an identity of his own."[11] Whatever the psychoanalytical bases and implications of this inability are, its primary manifestation is Hayri İrdal's helplessness as he gets inserted into "grand narratives" of social significance, especially the one constructed around Halit Ayarcı's (Halit the Regulator's) insanely successful project of social engineering, the Clock-Setting Institute. There is a rather short distance between sharing one's psychological hang-ups with an entire society, or being diagnosed as doing so, and having one's dreams, or one's life, administered with a view toward a social cure.

The position of authority that Dr. Ramiz, a doctor in the Department of Forensic Medicine, occupies in relation to Hayri İrdal is, of course, a significant barrier against any attempt on Hayri İrdal's part to construct an alternative self-representation. Similarly, it is wealth, status, and especially his close ties to government circles that authorize Halit Ayarcı, the founder of the Clock-Setting Institute, to force and to seduce Hayri İrdal into submitting to the role assigned to him in the ridiculous national modernization script the institute enacts. Throughout his association with Halit Ayarcı and the institute, Hayri İrdal finds that he is "a lie made up by others, . . . a serialized lie," that he has become "the pivot of a large organization after having been created in one man's imagination piece by piece."[12] Moreover, given this pivotal position and the already written, institutionally sponsored historical script about the Turkish nation's insatiable desire and unique capacity for modernization, even he, Hayri İrdal, can create a person in his imagination, authoring a socially significant and representative life. Temporarily empowered by financial success and social status, he writes the biography of a nonexistent but exemplary figure, Ahmet Zamani Efendi (Ahmet the Temporal), a great seventeenth-century Ottoman scientist and clock-maker.

This issue of power is essential for understanding that the problematization of the relationship between the private and the public in these novels is not simply a return to the rather exhausted theme of the tension between individual and society, between desire and responsibility. Even more explicitly than *The Clock-Setting Institute*, both *Lying Down to Die* and *The Disconnected* dramatize the drive toward reading individual destinies in terms of social, especially national narratives. They mark this drive as a repressive, inhibiting demand coming from the sites of power. As presented, resisted, and parodied in these novels, the tendency to allegorize originates not in some situational, materialist consciousness of community, but in the official ideology itself, in its need to mobilize individual lives in the process of imagining the nation in its own terms.

A rather literal illustration of this process is found in "The Dawn of the Ideal," an early chapter in *Lying Down to Die*. This chapter describes the graduation celebrations, held on the day of the fifteenth anniversary of the republic, at the protagonist Aysel's provincial primary school. As part of this event, the emergence on the stage of a portrait of Atatürk, "in which the Great Leader's face is like a sun rising over us,"[13] is followed by the performance of *The Professions*, a play authored and directed by the idealist teacher of the graduating class. The play introduces the main characters of the novel as the soldiers of the new nation's army of enlightenment, an army in which each is assigned a very clear position, rank, and duty directed toward a particular kind of contribution to the future already charted out by the light radiating from the Great Leader's face. Thus, dressed in borrowed adult clothes, featuring such emblems of future careers as injectors, hoes, chalk, swaddled dolls, and others, the children reluctantly appear on stage as representatives not only of different professions, but also of different classes, gender roles, and cultural backgrounds, each child's role in the play corresponding quite strictly to his or her family's social status. During the entire performance of this allegory of the Turkish nation boldly entering the civilized world, the awkwardness that ill-fitting costumes, stuck stage curtains, forgotten lines, and sheer embarrassment produce on the stage is matched by the discomfort in the audience caused by the incomprehension and the disapproval of various groups of parents.

The rest of *Lying Down to Die* retains something of the naïve theatricality of this initial school play, while the characters retain something of the sense of inadequacy and helplessness that comes from having been cast for a part one cannot quite fill. The playful artificiality of the narrator's language evokes, in syntax and tone, the language of stage directions for a play. All the chapters except those consisting of Aysel's interior monologues have titles that quote and highlight phrases or slogans from within the passages they introduce, much in the way of Brechtian stage legends. And even though much that could not possibly have been included in the initial scenario occurs in these lives, just as it does in the life of the nation, the parts the children play in this Republic Day performance seem to have a fateful influence on their futures, most of them ending up in the professions predicted for them and continuing to feel the burden of a vaguely comprehended ideal they are supposed to be embodying.

It is not a coincidence that Aysel's nightmare articulates her sense of failure as an intellectual by taking her back to that early memory of a stage upon which she stood in shoes that were too big for her. The theatricality of the impersonal narrator's voice, its imitation of the idealist, collectivist rhetoric of official republican discourse as it stage-manages the predetermined lives of the characters, brings out its complicity with the forces that infantalize through allegorization. The quiet authority of Aysel's interior monologue and her deliberate rejection of every costume and stage prop as she lies down to die are designed to contrast with this authoritarian theatricality. Her attempt to strip off every prop of social identity, to invest her life with the authority of a self-consciously achieved conclusion, could be seen as the answer of a modernist aesthetics of self-making to the dwarfing discourse of modernization in the early stages of fashioning the Turkish citizen.

In Orhan Pamuk's most recent and overtly political novel, *Snow* [*Kar*], the theater takes on a surrealistically sinister aspect as it becomes the setting not only of the type of crude national allegory exemplified by the school play in *Lying Down to Die*, but also of the naked and deadly exhibition of the connection between such allegory and power. Set in the eastern city of Kars in contemporary Turkey, *Snow* is the story of a "theater coup" orchestrated by a former leftist activist who is now a Kemalist playwright and actor, the owner of a third-rate theater company touring Anatolian towns, offering cheap entertainment along with political enlightenment.

The coup begins with the performance of a long-forgotten play from the 1930s: *The Motherland or the Veil*. Although most of the dialogue becomes inaudible because of the cheering and the protests from the audience, especially the big crowd of students from the Islamic training school, the play has "such a solid dramatic structure that everything in it could be understood even by the deaf and mute":

> 1. A woman in a pitch-black veil was walking in the streets, talking to herself, thinking. For some reason, she was unhappy.
> 2. The woman declared her freedom by taking her veil off. She was now unveiled and happy.

3. Her family, fiancée, relatives, and some bearded Muslim men were objecting to this freedom for various reasons and attempting to make her put the veil back on. In response, at a moment of rage, the woman burned the veil.

4. The bearded religious fanatics with rosaries in their hands reacted to this rebellion with violence and just as they were about to kill the woman, whom they were dragging by the hair . . .

5. The young soldiers of the Republic saved her.[14]

The actual unfolding of this solid dramatic structure does nevertheless give rise to several moments of surprise, awkwardness, and downright commotion, reminiscent in some ways of the mishaps during the Republic Day performance at Aysel's school, even though the circumstances are drastically different and the irony seems to have reached a deadly dose. For instance, the fact that the woman emerging from under the veil is not the usual innocent village girl wearing glasses and thirsting for knowledge but a dexterous belly dancer displaying plump naked arms and a beautiful neck causes difficulties in interpretation for a large part of the audience. Because not much care has been taken with stage props, the woman is taken to be laundering her veil while she dabs it with gasoline and this increases the surprise effect when next the veil is in flames. By the time the woman gets a chance to clarify the message by delivering her speech about how, for nations as well as for individuals, the essence is in the spirit and not in attire, how we must rid ourselves of such symbols of backwardness as the veil and run toward Europe to join the civilized and modern nations, the hall is too noisy for anyone to hear anything being said on the stage.

It soon becomes clear, however, that the ultimate effect of the play does not depend on the audibility of its words or the clarity of its message. The "theater coup" gets under way when the "young soldiers of the Republic" who come on stage to save the unveiled woman from the fanatics begin to shoot at the audience with what are only later understood to be real bullets. During the next few days, the snowbound city of Kars becomes the scene of continuing violence and a Kemalist dictatorship, with a would-be artist as dictator. This phantasmic political experiment comes to an end as the snow melts and the city once more becomes accessible to law and order on a national scale. Its end is marked by yet another theatrical performance, *Tragedy in Kars*, inspired by Thomas Kyd's *Spanish Tragedy*, written and directed by Sunay Zaim, the ex-communist/Kemalist/artist/public intellectual/entertainer/dictator.

In many ways, *Tragedy in Kars* is a more refined repetition of the first allegory, *The Motherland or the Veil*, this time involving Kadife's (Velvet's) publicly removing her headscarf and her heated defense of her decision to commit suicide as an assertion of autonomy. Kadife is a prominent public figure in Kars. She is a revered symbol of political Islam in the city, an object of sublimated desire for the young Islamist men, and the girlfriend of the enigmatic underground Islamist leader Lacivert (Navy Blue). Moreover, her defense of suicide makes her a representative and a spokesperson for the several young girls, mostly wearers of the headscarf, who have committed suicide within the past year, apparently as a result of an epidemic of female suicides that started in another Anatolian city and spread to Kars.[15] It is the dictator Sunay Zaim, however, who ends up committing suicide on stage as part of this "Turkishized" tragedy, repeating the same trick of real bullets in a stage gun, this time fired by Kadife.[16]

The point of this series of fatal entanglements between fiction and life, art and politics, is not, of course, that there is a sense in which political allegory kills either art or life or both. Or rather, it is not merely that. In *Snow*, as in the other novels I have already referred to, parodies of "solid dramatic structures" are not simple warnings against the authoritarian and paternalistic potential of allegory, although that is certainly part of the story. They are also not simply the novels' defenses against being reduced to allegories by a readership with a long-standing tradition of doing so, although that too is certainly part of the story. In all these novels, the obsessive return of a theatricality that robs characters of "authentic" lives has the function of exhibiting and exorcising the narrative's own compulsion toward political allegory. It is a way of acknowledging but also attempting to overcome the contortions that language, narrative, and individual lives have to go through under social conditions that provide neither a protected private sphere within which individuals can have at least the illusion of sovereignty and freedom, nor a public sphere in which their demands for sovereignty can be freely negotiated.

Snow makes this explicit by duplicating many features of the two plays in its own narrative strategies. The characters' names are often obtrusively emblematic, although it is not always clear of what. The plot seems to render the boundaries between fiction and life almost as permeable as

Sunay Zaim's scenarios do, not only by including actual political figures and events, but also by using metafictional techniques such as the admission of the author himself into the "scene of the crime." The omniscient narrator habitually addresses the reader directly, sometimes referring to his own task as a sort of stage-managing. The main cast of characters has been carefully selected to represent different sections of the society, different shades of religious and political belief, opposing positions in the Islamist-secularist or East-West debate. All the chapters have titles and subtitles, some of which sound like signposts for the correct allegorical interpretation: "Negotiation between Life and Play, Art and Politics." The bizarreness of the theater coup as the main premise of the plot smacks of the same lack of concern for verisimilitude evident in the staging of the plays.

In the midst of all this, however, the vision of another kind of art is inscribed into the narrative in the form of a lost text.[17] This is the manuscript of a book of poems written by Ka, who returns to Turkey for a brief visit after many years of political exile in Germany and goes to Kars with hopes of romance and marriage with İpek (Silk), a beautiful former classmate who has recently been divorced. He is reluctantly drawn to the center of the events during the bizarre snowbound days in Kars, and struggles desperately to resolve and/or manipulate the political conflicts in such a way as to be able to return with İpek to what he imagines as a blissful private existence in Germany. However, a political betrayal causes him to lose İpek and later his life.

The poems that are lost after he is murdered in Germany by Islamist terrorists punishing his betrayal of their leader come to him effortlessly, almost miraculously in Kars, at different stages of his desperate negotiations between private and public roles. His notes about the lost poems that were meant to be collected in a book titled *Snow* explain that they are arranged according to the model of a snowflake, each poem located at some particular point upon the star-shaped snowflake made up of the axes of reason, imagination, and memory: "He had thus marked upon a snowflake not only the structure of his new book of poems, but also everything that made him Ka. . . . According to Ka, there was a map like this and a snowflake behind everybody's life, and one could prove by analyzing every individual's own snowflake, how different, strange, and incomprehensible were the people who looked alike from a distance."[18] Reading the novel *Snow*, one gets the distinct feeling that the narrative is both amused and horrified by the pull Sunay Zaim's "national allegories" exert upon it. While recording this pull, it also rejects it, hopelessly striving to achieve instead, the form of the lost text "Snow," the map of a perfect correspondence between poetry and a unique life.

The Disconnected is an even more radical refusal to construct a life story that could be appropriated and articulated into a national narrative. This refusal takes the form of taking the allegorical impulse to a parodic extreme. Selim's supposedly autobiographical poem, "Yesterday, Today, Tomorrow," for instance, is surrounded with a mock commentary consisting of a perverse proliferation of ridiculous life stories inserted into ridiculous historical narratives. The absurd abundance of biographies, identities, and histories creates a constant background noise which interferes with even the most serious attempt to find the essence, the proper meaning of an individual life, as in Turgut's search for the truth Selim's life and death are supposed to represent. Oğuz Atay's characters are dispossessed not only of possessions and status, but also of allegorizable lives. They are disconnected not only from the comforts of bourgeois existence, but also from the "grand narratives" of the nation.

There is, then, a certain repressive conflation of the public and the private that the political allegories in several Turkish novels parody and resist even as they self-consciously reproduce it. In different ways, these novels use a strategy Neil Larsen observes in certain Latin American novels: "An almost conscious decision to create *only* characters whose national-allegorical representativity is so complicated and ironized as to be made virtually impossible."[19] This does not mean that these texts long for experiences of privacy uncontaminated by political involvement, or for the fragmented subjectivities of Western postmodernity. They illustrate, instead, a dialectics of the public and the private helpfully outlined by Thomas Keenan: "Publicity does not befall what is properly private, contaminating or opening up an otherwise sealed interiority. Rather, what we call interiority is itself the mark or the trace of this breach, of a violence that in turn makes possible the violence or the love we experience as intersubjectivity."[20]

Fredric Jameson's definition of Third World literature in terms of the relationship between the public and the private is a very important insight. But it is too simplistic to see this relationship as simply a lack of differentiation. One must instead ask how the modalities of the public and the private change in different social contexts, how the boundaries between them are drawn differently under different local pressures. Such an approach enables one to notice, for instance, that the figure of the political intellectual in the Turkish novel has typically served as a means of constructing a private space for the flourishing of a complex and isolated subjectivity. It enables one to understand the somewhat paradoxical way in which subjectivity, individuality, and privacy come to be defended against the encroachments of the state and the community through the cultivation of the properties that distinguish the intellectual—oppositional politics and the production and appreciation of art. Similarly, seeing Third World texts as not only consequences but also problematizations of specific modalities of the public and the private reveals the complex ways in which these texts both fulfill and nullify the allegorical impulse. It makes greater sense of the "multiple polysemia of the dream"[21] quoted at the beginning of this article, or of Saleem Sinai's ambivalence in Salman Rushdie's *Midnight's Children* when he says: "I had been mysteriously hand-cuffed to history, my destinies indissolubly chained to those of my country."[22]

Notes

1 Adalet Ağaoğlu, *Ölmeye Yatmak* (Istanbul: Yapı Kredi Yayınları, 1998), 272–74.

2 Jale Parla, *Don Kişot'tan Bugüne Roman* [The novel from *Don Quixote* to today] (Istanbul: İletişim Yayınları, 2000), 313.

3 Nurdan Gürbilek, *Ev Ödevi* [Home work] (Istanbul: Metis Yayınları, 1999), 105. In this book, Gürbilek traces in several modern Turkish novels the theme of "home" as the site of the realities of everyday life that prove to be inassimilable by ideals and aesthetics. She also mentions Aysel's dream of the *dolma* as an instance.

4 Oğuz Atay, *Tutunamayanlar* (Istanbul: İletişim Yayınları, 1992).

5 Fredric Jameson, "Third-World Literature in the Era of Multinational Capitalism," *Social Text* 15 (1986): 69.

6 Aijaz Ahmad, *In Theory: Class, Nations, Literatures* (New York: Verso, 1992), 95–122.

7 Fredric Jameson, "A Brief Response," *Social Text*, no. 17 (1987): 26.

8 Jameson, "Third-World Literature," 67.

9 Ahmet Hamdi Tanpınar, *Saatleri Ayarlama Enstitüsü* (Istanbul: Dergah Yayınları, 1987). Recently published in English as *The Time Regulation Institute*, trans. Ender Gürol (Madison, WI: Turko-Tatar Press, 2001). All translations of quotations are mine. The corresponding page numbers in the published translation are provided in parentheses.

10 Tanpınar, *Saatleri Ayarlama*, 85 (104).

11 Süha Oğuzertem, "Unset Saats, Upset Sıhhats: A Fatherless Approach to *The Clock-Setting Institute*," *Turkish Studies Association Bulletin* 19.2 (1995): 10.

12 Tanpınar, *Saatleri Ayarlama*, 217 (238), 194 (215).

13 Ağaoğlu, *Ölmeye Yatmak*, 7.

14 Orhan Pamuk, *Kar* (Istanbul: İletişim, 2002), 147–48.

15 Like many other incidents in the novel, this epidemic of female suicides alludes to an actual event that received much media coverage and caused heated debate about issues of class, gender, and ethnicity.

16 One could see the preoccupation with suicide that runs through all these novels as yet another striking instance of the volatility of the distinctions between the public and the private, their almost paradoxical entanglements and permutations. Suicide seems on the one hand to be the most private act possible, an act of taking absolute control of one's own private destiny. On the other hand, it is inescapably symbolic, an act of investing an individual death with external meaning, turning it into a kind of public performance. The talk of an "epidemic" of suicides is especially interesting in this context, reminding one of the "collective dreaming" that takes place in several magical realist novels as well as in a coffee house frequented by spiritualists in *The Clock-Setting Institute*. The following passage from *Snow* is notable for linking the question of privacy to suicide: "What led Ka to feel an odd despair in relation to all these stories was that the suicidal girls could barely find the privacy and the time they needed for suicide. The girls who committed suicide with sleeping pills were sharing their rooms with others even while secretly dying. Having grown up reading Western literature at Nişantaşı in İstanbul, Ka, whenever he contemplated suicide, felt that he would need plenty of time and space to do it, that he would need to have a room on whose door nobody would knock for days." Pamuk, *Kar*, 21–22.

17 See Parla's *Don Kişot'tan Bugüne Roman* for an illuminating discussion of lost texts that interrupt and enable novelistic narratives.

18 Pamuk, *Kar*, 377.

19 Neil Larsen, "Imperialism, Colonialism, Postcolonialism," in *A Companion to Postcolonial Studies*, ed. Henry Schwartz and Sangeeta Ray (Oxford: Blackwell, 2000), 38–39.

20 Thomas Keenan, "Windows of Vulnarability," in *The Phantom Public Sphere*, ed. Bruce Robbins (Minneapolis: University of Minnesota Press, 1993), 134.

21 Jameson, "Third-World Literature," 73.

22 Salman Rushdie, *Midnight's Children* (London: Vintage, 1995), 9.

Orhan Koçak

"Our Master, the Novice": On the Catastrophic Births of Modern Turkish Poetry

> A hastening world, this one; everything is too early,
> And everything too late. The sun will go into eclipse
> while we are asleep.
> —M. C. Anday, "Faltering Night"

My subject is the "Second New," a group of poets who entered the Turkish poetry scene in the early 1950s and had mostly exited it by the end of the 1980s. Over these forty years, the reception they had would move from total bewilderment to outright rejection to an all too ready acceptance—with little sober assessment in between. But perhaps sobriety was altogether out of the question: they tantalized the less obdurate of their peers and immediate followers, rather than delivering them to their own powers. No, they did not lack followers or imitators, although in the end it was mostly the Second New poets themselves who would have a mute but sharp intimation of the fact that they had pushed poetry to an intolerable edge, that their late-won acceptance had a ring of futility about it, that in repeatedly overturning and outdoing their own previous performances, they had also undone themselves as poets. The one thing

The *South Atlantic Quarterly* 102:2/3, Spring/Summer 2003.
Copyright © 2003 by Duke University Press.

no Second New poet could bring himself to acknowledge, however, was also the movement's supreme, perverse achievement: not only had they drawn many of the poets of the preceding generation into their own force field, but by their action, they had also compelled at least three of them to become more consummate poets than themselves. Cemal Süreya, a leading protagonist of the Second New, in an essay written just a year before his death in 1990, would call attention to the group's influence on its predecessors:

> There are two movements in the history of Turkish literature that have influenced earlier generations, or at least imbued them with fresh passions: The *Servet-i Fünun* [The Riches of Learning—a group of writers and poets that had been active at the end of the nineteenth century and were so labeled in reference to the journal that published their works] and the Second New. That a generation exerts some influence on the succeeding ones—this is only natural. But the reverse must be something rarely encountered.... There were as many poets who were influenced by [us], as those who were not. But on the whole, this: When the Second New appeared, some of the artists who had been writing for some time went into action in their own direction.[1]

What really happened was even more complicated than Süreya's ambiguous account allows. Not "some," but only the major poets were influenced; they prevailed as major poets by letting themselves be influenced; they did not "go into action in their own direction," but were stopped short and led astray; and by going astray became still stronger poets than the ones who had thrown them off their course. The Second New poets had overwhelmed their predecessors and effectively nullified the poetry of the 1940s, but even as images of the phoenix began to frequent their poems more and more, they found themselves watching the three elders move to an infinitely hardened poetry. The epigraph above belongs to one of the latter.[2]

But, as many a Turkish studies scholar around the world may have wondered, how to write about a subject practically nonexistent for a non-Turkish-speaking audience? The main body of work by these poets still awaits translation, which greatly hinders any attempt at pertinent commentary.[3] But this may still be regarded as only an end result, the range of difficulties starting with the marginalized status of Turkish literature itself, with the fact of its effective isolation from any kind of international discursive setting. Turkish literature was written off as a literary phenomenon almost concurrently with the establishment of a specifically *literary* Orientalism at the end of the nineteenth century, and the most unequivocal pronouncement to this effect came from none other than E. J. W. Gibb, the author of the first comprehensive study of Ottoman poetry to be published in any language. "In all literary matters," Gibb would write for a posthumous 1911 *Encyclopedia Britannica* article, "the Ottoman Turks have shown themselves a singularly uninventive people, the two great schools, the old and the new, into which we may divide their literature, being closely modelled, the one after the classics of Persia, the other after those of modern Europe, and more especially of France." However much the British Orientalist's judgment may have been concerned only with *Ottoman* literature, combined with similar statements in his authoritative six-volume history,[4] it would still work to make all Turkish literature, past, present, and future, a nonobject for any disinterested scholar abroad. Hence the necessarily embattled preambles of some recent studies in the field:

> In a world where critical thought frequently applies itself with minimal personal and institutional self-awareness to the problematics of the great master narrative of "World Literature," someone outside of a small coterie should have long-since asked "what ever happened to Ottoman literature?" The Ottoman Empire, singularly and without question, represented *the great Muslim "Other"* from approximately the time of Columbus to the end of the First World War. It had profound cultural influences on a vast number of people from North Africa to the Middle East to Eastern Europe and Central Asia. Yet it is unquestioningly and all but universally assumed that this major political, economic, social, cultural entity had no literary culture worthy of notice, despite the fact that poetry was a major activity at all levels of Ottoman society. . . . What has, of course, happened is that the literature of the Ottoman/Muslim "enemy" has been written out of the master narrative.[5]

The fragmentary state of the translations and the lack of preliminary studies may well hamper any contemporary critic wishing to make a case for modern Turkish poetry, but measured against the Ottomanist's thankless task— that of hauling back a past literature from the state of limbo to which it has been relegated—the critic's job would still seem easier (if not already prescribed), because just pointing at that modern poetry's relative isolation from an international audience is already saying something specific about it—which is not the case with Ottoman literature, declared defunct long before the advent of the idea of an international audience or an international canon. The Second New, by contrast, emerging at a time when most Third World cultures had long since felt the brunt of European literature, and emerging precisely on account of the disenfranchisement visited upon the Ottoman literary tradition, can serve—can be made to serve—as a more immediately relevant object for a "geoculturally" informed study of poetic influence, which I take, following Harold Bloom, to be an anxiety-ridden space of experience. Thus I argue that the disqualification of Ottoman literature through the efforts of both Western Orientalists and the modernizing Turkish cultural elite had the effect of relocating the sources and pathways of anxiety and so for a time acted as facilitator in successive outbursts of the New, with the "Second" New as the last and the most drastic one in a long line of such breakthroughs. That we are thus attempting to transfer the ideas of the author of *The Western Canon* to quite alien terrain, where they would seem to lose much of their relevance, and by way of a type of concern that has been branded as "the culture of envy" by the author of those ideas—is a move I hope will no longer sound so outlandish when we come to the end of this essay.

≡≡≡≡

Not in the very beginning but somewhere along the road, the Second New poets too had a taste of that "clean slate" feeling common to all poetic renewals. Again, Cemal Süreya was the first to formulate it, even while he tried to strike a balance between pure origination and causation. Thus the Second New was truly new only because the preceding generation had seen to it that everything smacking of tradition would sound ridiculous, improbable, at once weird and fake. Writing in 1967 on the fate of Orhan Veli and his *Garip* movement, Süreya claimed that Veli "had won the cause of Turkish poetry, and lost the cause of his own"; that is, in destroying what came before him, he also self-destructed, and so cleared the ground for "real innovation." True, but not specific enough, for this was what had been recurring for at least a century, with every new generation making a fresh start. At this point, some words on the defining moments of the history of modern Turkish poetry seem in order.

Toward the end of the nineteenth century, classical Ottoman poetry (*divan*) was deemed dead. More crucial than the accuracy of this judgment is the fact of its having been passed, and still more important is the identity of those who voiced it. These were Young Ottomans, a group of literati who had been shaped and employed by the new reformist, Westernizing bureaucracy, and who through their action and ideas would set the tone of much of the political and cultural transformation well into the Republican era.[6] Most of them had had some sort of classical education and some tried their hands at divan poetry; but on returning home after a stint in Paris as political refugees, they began to search for a different kind of writing, experimenting with genres like verse drama or the novel, both of which were hitherto unknown in Turkish literature. So what was the compelling motive behind their rejection of classical poetry? In turning to Western models, had they really felt the pull of Western literature? Namık Kemal (1844–1888), the most influential figure among the group, had come to know Hugo's and Musset's work while in Paris, but apparently did not notice Baudelaire. Victoria Holbrook has persuasively argued that the primary factor in the rejection of classical poetry was less literary than political: the Young Ottomans and some of their peers in the reformist bureaucracy regarded the divan style as the literary analogue of Ottoman decline, its rhetorical intricacies blocking the way to an effective representation and manipulation of social reality. Yet if the causes were political, the more immediate results were certainly literary, and catastrophically so: by discarding an entire tradition, Kemal's program was reducing the keepers of an age-old hieratic art to the rank of beginners, condemning any prospective poet to a state of infantile helplessness.[7]

Registering the full impact of this fall would take several decades. Many, at the time, may have experienced relief from a harrowing sense of belatedness in relation to past masters, a sense most poignantly expressed by the sixteenth-century poet Fuzuli: "What a perplexing circumstance: something said before cannot be said because it has already been said—and something not said before cannot be said because it has never been said. Past colleagues have so thoroughly pillaged the store of images and tropes that the space of poetry is now too narrow for us. Oh, this having someone come before us!"[8] With the annulment of the poetic past, this particular double-bind seemed to be suspended, and the ancient "blocking agents" finally laid to rest. But if one inhibitor was removed, and removed so easily, it was largely because another was already moving in to take its place: here, at first lightheartedly and then more apprehensively named, Western Literature—or rather, the idea of it—as the new model. But the action of the "external" model differed from that of the "internal" one in two important respects.

First, while the *divan* masters belonged to the past, the new model would always seem to be signaling from the future—its extraterritoriality, its arrival as part of that which compelled the Ottoman state to alter itself in the first place, adding a tantalizing aspect to its action. It would recurrently give fresh impetus to innovation, but like an ever-receding threshold would also frustrate the innovator. A wedge driven not only between the past and the future, but also between the future and the present, between what seems possible and what is attained, the New as the blocking agent would work to devalue what it itself called forth, thus making the history of modern Turkish poetry the history of its successive self-disqualifications.

There was also another, at first glance brighter, side to the picture. The exclusion of Turkish poetry from the "world" arena, from the scene of action of its new model, would provide something like a secluded space where the poet was free to act without feeling exposed to the gaze of the model. Most often escaping notice, this circumstance would prove to be a mixed blessing, imparting a somewhat facile, foreshortened aspect to both the triumphs and the downfalls. Moreover, its relieving effect depended on the external model remaining truly external and not becoming part of the psychical makeup of the Turkish poet. Both during the last decades of the Ottoman Empire and at the beginning of the republican era, there were deliberate attempts to keep the Western model at a distance; but even the formulation of such programs showed that some inner space had already been ceded to the foreign agent and a self-destructive momentum was at work.[9]

As might be expected, the first ones to fall victim to this self-destructive process were the initiators themselves. By the end of the century, a new generation of writers (the *Servet-i Fünun* group mentioned by Süreya) had looked at the output of their predecessors and found it wanting: they were comparing Kemal's works with his Western models. Ironically enough, this was Kemal's verdict too. "Comparing the progress made by our literature with the West's literary culture," he had written heedlessly toward the end of his life, "is like comparing the few words managed by an infant with the [expressive] powers of a man of learning"—the progress he was assessing was that of his own time. There was an aspect of unstoppability to the whole process: the futurity of the new source of influence, calling from an ever-changing locus, seemed to leave no time for consolidation. Halit Ziya Uşaklıgil (1866–1945), the greatest writer of the *Servet-i Fünun* group, in his novel *Mai ve Siyah* [The blue and the black] described the new poet in his slide toward the New:

> And so all the drafts were burnt . . . together with pieces written in the manner of Fuzuli, Baki, or Nedim [*divan* poets]. . . . At first, they were inclined to follow a chronological order . . . but attempting to read the Iliad and the Odyssey, they left the books unfinished. . . . They were in a hurry to come down to more recent times. . . . So they went forward until they reached Goethe, Schiller, Milton, Young, Byron, Hugo, Musset, Lamartine. . . . He knew that by following only his own impulses he would be confining his thinking inside too narrow a space . . . and that the poet had to stimulate his emotions with the marvels of poetry. Thus he emptied [his friend's] library, and carried to his tiny retreat works by those who came after Hugo and Musset; all the Parnassians, the Symbolists, the Decadents; that group of poets starting with Heredia and Théodore de Banville also; and then the Prudhommes, the Coppées. . . . As he read these, he marveled at the subtlety the art of poetry had gained in the half century leading to Verlaine.[10]

The emergence of the *Servet-i Fünun* group had made an impact on several important followers of Namık Kemal, to the point of forcing them to reconsider their premises, yet it would take only a decade for Uşaklıgil and his friends to be unseated in their turn. They were being disparaged precisely for having *remained* at the level of "a Coppée." Thus Yahya Kemal (1884–1958), variously regarded as the last of the divan poets or the first properly modern Turkish poet, commented on Tevfik Fikret (1867–1915), the leading poet of *Servet-i Fünun*: "Fikret understood nothing of the profounder aspects of the French poetry of his own time, from Baudelaire to the Symbolists. The poets he understood were Sully Prudhomme, Coppée, and the like."[11] Of course, there were also other, more directly political factors involved. The birth of Turkish nationalism during the Balkan Wars of 1912–13 had given rise to a National Literature movement, the members of which were now denouncing the *Servet-i Fünun* writers for having become "excessively Westernized" and failing to give expression to "the original Turkish spirit."[12] Nevertheless, it was Yahya Kemal's seemingly pure aesthetic judgment that finally did the Nationalists' political job for them: the "merely a Coppée" pronouncement, to be reiterated to this day, had finished Fikret as a poetic model.[13]

What gave weight to Yahya Kemal's position was the double-acting quality of his poetry, a poetry which at once deliberately assumed the Westward drift of Turkish literature (by now an irreducible datum), *and* held out the promise of arresting it. Simply put, his proposition was "Back to our Classics, through the Western Moderns," as described in his own account of his poetic itinerary:

> I had left behind the cruder sides of Hugo. I stayed for quite a while with the *Légende*, his true poem. After Hugo, I came to like Gautier and De Banville. I had just begun to appreciate the finer qualities of Romanticism, when I encountered Baudelaire's poetry, which left me enthralled. . . . After Baudelaire I began to see Verlaine in a different light. . . . On the other hand, those literary historians who would find a temporal progress in poetry are deceiving both themselves and their readers. I have tested this on myself. Though I understood Gautier and De Banville well, though I had a frenzied passion for Baudelaire and Verlaine, though the works of Maeterlinck and Verhaeren were not unknown to me, it was nevertheless on José Maria de Heredia's work that my tastes had finally come to rest, a poet regarded as quite backward in comparison with the others. Heredia was not a creator; he was a classical artist, if a very belated one. . . . Through him, I had a taste of classical Greek and Latin poetry too. And it was in this way that I realized I had come very close to the new Turkish that I had long sought: Our spoken Turkish was something like that *white language* found in classical Greek and Latin poetry. Thus I began to sense the wisdom and the rationale behind the beauty of our [divan] verses.[14]

After the catastrophe of disinheritance, the promise of a double patrimony, with each relieving the other from its burden of anxiety: if one looked to foreign models, it was only for the sake of recovering what is most oneself; and if the ancient masters were once again evoked, it was with the reassuring knowledge that they had already been rendered powerless, framed and sublimated into merely aesthetic phenomena, precisely by the gaze that had turned away.

This was an undeniable victory over both the "over-Westernizers" and the nationalists, but it was bought at the price of entanglement in their contradictory positions, in their desires, fears, repressions, and self-deceptions. Yahya Kemal thought he was reestablishing the poetic tradition, and the ease with which he seemed to do so was blinding him to the fact that what is called "tradition" precludes all facileness, that a tradition "re-established" can never regain the compelling force it once had.[15] But if "traditional tradition" had lost its grip, a still more compelling one, dubbed "the tradition of the New" by Harold Rosenberg, was in full force. Yahya Kemal had subdued the nationalists by *surpassing* their opponents: the Westward slide he would arrest was the condition of his victory—just as it would be the cause of his eventual dethronement. Though he had never used the term, many among his admirers called his move a "synthesis," thereby unwittingly pointing to its defensive nature but also glossing over the considerable self-curtailment involved: even as he seemed to break out of the new, West-related double-bind by energizing and manipulating its own terms, avowedly carried home by the outward drift itself, Yahya Kemal still had to station himself at a "backward" site out there—"Heredia" this time, in place of "Coppée." This deliberate retraction, aiming to curb the wasting of energies on necessarily insuperable tasks, like most defensive moves involved a substantial blockage of its own and marred the work in several important respects.

First, there was the short duration of actual production: the bulk of Yahya Kemal's poetry was already written by the time he was forty, with almost forty barren years still before him[16]—a fact which I think is indicative of something more fundamental than a premature dissipation of energy, something which precluded any kind of development in the first place. As significant as the absence of a late resurgence is the fact that this poetry seemed already fully formed when it first appeared.[17] Despite its effortlessly flowing rhythms (the result of the marriage of Ottoman *aruz* meter with Verlaine's mellifluous tones) there was a frozen quality at the core, as if the "synthesis" finally mastered had left no room for further experimentation, as if any move not already underwritten by the prior negotiation could readily trivialize the whole endeavor.[18] And what made this an ever-present danger was paradoxically the musicality of the work, its greatest achievement: everything was sedimented in the sounds, in the modulations, to such an extent that the poem, after some habituation, would begin to sound like a too easily achieved objectification of its idea—that is, a period piece.

This circumstance has not escaped the more perspicacious of his followers. Nurullah Ataç (1898–1957), a student of Yahya Kemal's at Istanbul University, having hailed the poet as "a God" in the 1930s, would later complain of the "théâtral" quality of the Master's poems, and point at its "somewhat facile beauty."[19] Ahmet Hamdi Tanpınar (1901–62), another student and perhaps the most loyal disciple, in scorning his own poems for a "musicism" that preempted any severe effort, was in fact condemning the whole Kemalian legacy: "These are things written at a time when a musicism stood for everything and a newly found Turkish rhyme was considered a triumph."[20]

And so it was that Yahya Kemal's true achievement, his rediscovery of spoken Turkish as an elevated poetic language, a feat believed to be unimaginable at the time, would come to be regarded as his major deficiency: a musicality that not only cannot stand sustained scrutiny (as during a translation), but is also powerless against new manifestations of the modern—against the onslaught of prose, of the prosaic. That Yahya Kemal's poetry (its audience and its ongoing reproduction) managed to survive the stormy arrival of Nazım Hikmet (1902–63) in the late 1920s and 1930s is a circumstance that has more to do with Hikmet's poetry—and politics—than with Kemal's resilience.

The first instance of dissonance set loose, Hikmet's work initially stood out as too strange to be assimilable. Coming after a period during which poetic energies were devoted to the domestication of alien forces, and coming from revolutionary Russia where Hikmet was exposed to Vladimir Mayakovsky's thundering performance, these strange-looking and strange-sounding poems threatened to start the whole process anew. When he later effected a retraction of his own, this time playing Yahya Kemal—and the familiar tone of Turkish songs—against Mayakovsky and the constructivists, it was too late: Hikmet was in jail, unable to exert much influence on—and be influenced by—the daily ups and downs of Turkish poetry.[21] It was too late in a more central sense too: Yahya Kemal and followers were already ousted, made to look not only old-fashioned but also bizarre and improbable—by a group of poets who would be collectively known as "the Strangers."

The same mechanism of selection by comparison, albeit having lost some of its immediacy in the secluded cultural life of Republican Turkey, was still at work: Max Jacob or Jules Supervielle now, instead of "Heredia" or even

Mallarmé. Oktay Rifat (1914–88), a member of the original Strange Trio, in an obituary for Orhan Veli (1914–50), the leader of the group, commented on the contemporaneity of his friend—contemporaneity with the West:

> When Orhan first began writing, people like Yahya Kemal and Ahmet Haşim [a symbolist, and a professed disciple of Remy de Gourmont] were looked up to as the Grand Old Men of our poetry. Those who came after Haşim have merely added certain nuances to this line of poetry. Our poetry at the time was busying itself with turning over and over the problems that had exercised French poets some seventy years ago. In saying this, I am not taking into account Nazım Hikmet. For he is an altogether separate starting point in our poetic tradition. Since the middle of the nineteenth century our poetry has been struggling to Westernize, all the while doing nothing more than following Western poetry sixty, seventy years behind: Orhan Veli has enabled our poetry to close the gap.[22]

The mechanism was still in effect, but its tenor had changed. For both Yahya Kemal and the nationalists the more immediate threat was Western literature, and their defenses were geared to checking its influence. For Orhan Veli's generation, on the other hand, the real barrier to imaginative independence was internal: something like a tradition of the moderately New had formed by the 1940s, with its attendant constraints and castrating figures.[23] Yahya Kemal, even through his followers, was a real enough presence (Orhan Veli's early poems sounded like second-rate imitations of Yahya Kemal). The Strange Trio's choice of French references had therefore to be disruptive in a special way: deliberately modern—even avant-garde—but preferably minor figures, with a sly, tongue-in-cheek plebianism if possible: Laforgue or even Charles Cros rather than Rimbaud; or Max Jacob more than Reverdy—needles to burst the balloon they called Yahya Kemal. Ruth Christie's superb translation of a programmatic piece by Orhan Veli should give an idea:

> His corn hurt him more
> than anything else in the world;
> it was even harder to bear
> than being born ugly.
> He didn't invoke God's name

except when in pain from his shoe;
you couldn't call him a sinner.
Poor Süleyman Efendi!

For him "To be or not to be"
wasn't such a big deal.
He went to sleep one night
and never woke up.
They came and took him away;
he was washed, prayed over and buried.
When his creditors hear he has died
they'll give up their claims, no doubt;
as for his credit—
the poor departed had none.[24]

Cemal Süreya of the Second New remarked that "all of Orhan Veli's poems were satirical parodies of old poetry . . . almost with a one-to-one correspondence." I would say there was a yet more destructive strain, not unrelated to that deep-seated sense of futility I have been trying to trace: a tendency that went against the very idea of poetry, even as it effected a defensive move of *askesis* toward the "old poetry."[25] More clearly than any single poem of the Strangers, this passage from the memoirs of Melih Cevdet describes and performs the telos of Strange poetry:

> It was during my first military service, for I have served twice, that I had a similar experience. . . . There was Saturday night party at the regiment hall, which the officers attended with their wives. . . . At this point, I must briefly dwell on the personality of our regiment commander. He was an engineer, educated in Germany. The colonel believed that our country would prosper through science and technology and viewed philosophy and literature as utter nonsense. When the dance halted, a lieutenant stood up, and after saluting our commander, said: "Sir! We have a poet in our midst. Please permit him to read a poem of his." So I went ahead with one of my short poems, so often mocked. Silence. As I was returning to my seat, the colonel called: "Lieutenant, come here." I went. "What is this that you have read?" "Poetry," I said. "But how can that be!" he said. Once again, the need for an explanation had arisen. "Sir! We three friends have expelled meter and rhyme from poetry, expelled simile and metaphor . . ." I didn't need to go on,

our commander was in raptures. "I've got it," he said, "bit by bit you're going to abolish poetry."[26]

Apparently, most readers and writers of poetry were not as astute as Anday's commander, and overlooking the abolition, would come to see only the poetry: a "strange" poetry dissipated enough to make no one "feel alienated, perplexed, ill at ease." If there was any *askesis* involved, it must have been of a weak kind: Orhan Veli became a good man long before he died, having been loved and easily imitated by most everyone. It is impossible not to be amazed at the sentimentality of some of his later poems, a sentimentality in every way more malleable than the one they were militantly against (the poem "I'm Listening to Istanbul," included in the modern Turkish poetry issue of *Agenda*, is an example). The tradition Orhan Veli had so effortlessly ridiculed out of existence had thus proved stronger in the end—stronger by default, by insufficient compulsion, allowing easy triumphs and just as easy defeats even through its flashes of negative grandeur.

The moment of Yahya Kemal had passed, together with the pressures weighed and negotiated in his poems. For more than a decade, poetry looked like a very diluted flow, it became poetry-as-usual. Then the Second New came with a feeling of renewed thickening, for a time doing away with all transparency. But the label was imprecise: it was not the second but arguably the fifth New, and if it was in any way second, it was with respect not to the "first New" of the Strangers, but to the first truly originary moment of modern poetry, that of Yahya Kemal. Like him, but more sovereignly than him, the Second New would turn the positional weaknesses of modern Turkish literature, its off-centeredness and its belated novitiate, into the formal law of great poetry.

———

It may still be too early, as Chou En Lai reportedly said of the French Revolution, to bring off a measured appraisal of the Second New. Pending that definitive evaluation, which the poetry itself has tended to put off (despite the frequent stock-taking essays of Cemal Süreya and the self-serving pronouncements of Ece Ayhan), one can still attempt, as I will shortly do, to describe its complexion or point out some of its salient features. But first, a recapitulation of the situational aspects of the work—the reason for this article.

Unlike other major poetries issuing from the ruins of Ottoman culture, the Second New had no authoritative *national* figure whom it was compelled to look back on. Ritsos had Constantine Cavafy, George Seferis, or even Kostas Karyotakis behind him, and Seferis must have truly agonized with Dionysios Solomos and Kostis Palamas. Modern Arabic poetry is perhaps a yet more useful point of comparison, as it was shocked into being roughly at the same time and by the same cataclysmic events.[27] The great modernists Adunis and Nizar Qabbani (the Second New's contemporaries) had the Romantics (Gibran) and the Neo-Classicists (Ahmad Shawqi) still standing behind them, just as Shawqi had to look back to Islamic and pre-Islamic Arab poets. "Do we have any classics of our own," M. C. Anday would rhetorically ask, back in the 1960s, and could hardly suppress his joy in saying "No, we have none." The successive dismissals of what was at hand, from the time of Namık Kemal, had made sure that the prospective Second New poet, after an abridged instruction, would find both interest and challenge, if any, only in his or her peers (a "regime of the brother," as J. F. McCannell has termed it). And the mediator—in the form of the latest French poet—which had been used repeatedly to disenfranchise the predecessor? It was still there, but its urgency had waned. Turkey's closing in upon itself—the government's effective cultural tariff wall in the 1930s and the dehistoricization or deactualization of "Western Culture" in the 1940s (see note 9 at the end of this essay)—had created a sort of sheltered cultural space relatively free from uncontrolled daily infusions of foreign influence. The earlier generations of poets all had firsthand knowledge of French—and often English—literature; some, like Yahya Kemal and Ahmet Haşim, had befriended figures like Jean Moréas and Jacques Lacan in Paris;[28] and even while disenfranchising their elders, they would themselves act as the self-appointed overseas franchises of the French. The poets of the Second New, by contrast, were all products of the state school system, coming—with one exception, Edip Cansever (1928–86)—from quite humble backgrounds; and two major figures in the group, Cansever and Turgut Uyar (1927–85), did not know any foreign language at all. Cemal Süreya, as the future director of the National Mint, commented on the "self-financing" capacities of Turkish poetry, in an essay (1969) that began with a consideration of Bulgarian poetry:

> It is true that Turkish poetry has been inordinately conditioned by Western poetry since the *Tanzimat*. . . . But simple imitation has gradually given way to a more vigorous engagement with Western poetry,

leading to an unexpected turn. . . . The number of translations of even second- and third-rate poets is probably greater in Turkish than in any language. These have created new linguistic undercurrents. A laboratory of world poetry has been established in Turkish . . . with the result that our poetry has acquired an additional means of "self-financing."[29]

Apparently, the poet felt secure enough to be able to admit the earlier insecurity *and* to reflect on its auspicious aftereffects. And yet, this late-won self-confidence was largely the work of earlier poets like Yahya Kemal or Orhan Veli, whom no Second New poet held in much regard. Was "the regime of the brother" all that mattered now? And that "unhappy, inwardly disrupted consciousness . . . where victory in one consciousness is really lost in its opposite" (Hegel, *Phenomenology of the Mind*)—had it truly been healed, and healed all by itself? But perhaps these are moot questions: all along, I have tried to describe the energetics of modern Turkish poetry through something like a lay Bloomian framework. So what I should really be asking, with the hope that the answer will have some bearing on those questions too, is this: Who was the precursor that had "chosen" the Second New poets as its "misreading" inheritors: what was it that "flooded" them, thereby turning them into Second New poets? All fresh imaginative space gained by a latecomer, according to the circular logic of this negative pragmatics, is territory forcibly regained: With the national tradition—even that of "the New"—already devalued, and the foreign model at a safe remove, where and how could the Second New poets find, before the "additional means of self-financing," the primary antithetical force that enabled them to at once beget themselves and seduce others?

That the precursor was not and could not have been any "French" poet must once again be emphasized: according to Bloom's revisionist Freudian framework, the force of the precursor acts through the *id*, whence it takes its daemonic power; in the Turkish case, by contrast, the psychical agency functioning as a receptacle for things "French" had always been the *ego ideal*, an agency that may put severe demands to the ego but has no sovereign force of its own. As H. Z. Uşaklıgil ably revealed in his novel *The Blue and the Black*, the modern Turkish poet first became *the* modern Turkish poet precisely by yielding his ideals to the action of "French" culture. The inner disruption was not between two undetermined "consciousnesses," but between a historically defined superego whose contents were given by State and Tradition (or better, the idea of national tradition as a mandate),

and an equally historical ego ideal formed through successive identifica-
tions with the "West."[30] The nationalist project was then a bid for a massive recapture of the yielded psychical space: Be your own ideal![31] What the
"French"-filled ego ideal, on the other hand, seemed to be whispering to the
poor ego was, "Be like me—as you know perfectly well that you can't." The
crippling joint effect of these two contrary offers must be obvious by now:
even Yahya Kemal had to suppress, Hikmet to move out, Orhan Veli to be
despairingly flippant, and by leaving himself fully exposed to the impact of
these opposite demands Tanpınar became the greatest Turkish critic and
a failed poet. So the demonic energy the Second New poet could muster
was not issuing from nor mobilized to the revision of any proper precursor,
whether foreign or Turkish. We thus seem to have reached a juncture where
even the laicized Bloom we have been using as a regulatory tool looses its
efficacy: if no precursor, then no *modern* poet, and the Second New becomes
a totally unaccountable phenomenon—which is exactly how Ece Ayhan, the
poet most given to the idea of a primal New, would have liked it to be, having
repeatedly described the movement's birth as a "mutation." And yet—

≡≡≡

Edip Cansever, the poet of an unabashed if broken sublime, in his perhaps
greatest medium-length poem, "A Firefly May Have Flickered," wrote:

> You will remember, there was a poem, a poem that would
>   end too late
> For everything for everything for everything
> Oh for everything ripening once at a time.[32]

In the long poem that is the Second New, more often toward the end, one
keeps on encountering scenes where the speaking subject seems to be
swerving with respect to the poem, or situating it outside himself (there
is no herself, strictly speaking), where it is either on the verge of its never-
culminating advent, or has already passed beyond, without ever having
become one with the subject's voice. This is all the more significant in a
poetry that has been noted for the directness of its mode of presentation—
"poetry as experience" or "experience as poetry."[33] Though it is true that
this inner disruption is more pronounced in later works, where it is often
conjoined with a sense of irreparable loss, one can find prefigurations in
quite early pieces, the jubilant records of their own birth, as in Ilhan Berk's

line: "My Soul, it's Ilhan Berk crossing the bridge, can you feel it?" The voice is addressing itself, urging itself not so much to behold as to hear the process of formation of that elated poem called Ilhan Berk.[34] In Ece Ayhan, the swerve takes on a harsher aspect, with much self-envy involved, in the end thrusting the poet out of poetry; in his voluminous interviews, which he said were an "extension" of his poems, Ayhan would insist that he was "coming not from poetry, but from music," and that "in any case" he was a moralist, or a historian, rather than a poet.[35] It is in Cemal Süreya, the poet who said he was wary of the overly self-referential character of recent poetry, that we find a more benign but still unmistakable mark of this swerve: a sense of poetry missed, and thereby reinstated even more securely—at a distance from the subject. In his late cycle, "Autumn-spent" (1988), the poems end with the refrain, "I wish I had loved you only for that [reason]." Three examples (quoting only the last stanzas): "You were faraway, right there, in the other continent, / I wish I had loved you only for that"; "We're walking in a failed silence[36] / I wish I had loved you only for that"; "I found a very short poem titled 'Divination' / I wish I had loved you only for that." Love, in Süreya as in Cansever and Uyar, is an analogue for the fulfillment of the poetic will, for its completion and therefore its death: by repeatedly dodging its fulfillment the will may be said to be giving itself a new lease on life.[37] On the other hand, the love (the poetic impulse) that is thus displaced back is made to seem forever other, as if never claimable in its entirety. It is at this point that Bloomian theory releases a sharp, incremental insight, an insight that has not been able to find adequate employment in the area Bloom covered, the "over-pre-determined" descent of post-Miltonian English poetry.

"When we say that the meaning of a poem can only be another poem, we may mean a range of poems: The precursor poem. . . . [Or a] rival poem, son or grandson of the same precursor. [Or a] *poem that never got written—that is—the poem that should have been written by the poet in question.*"[38] Here the argument seems to be on the verge of retreating from its boldest intent, which had a "realistic" enough basis: a real, because really other, because really prior precursor—whether a poet or a poem—who is also heavily present, acting in complicity with the later poet's id, thus compelling the later poet's ego to take some defensive action, the more or less successful effect of which would then be the later poem. But in the passage just quoted, the poetic act, and with it the precursor, was being re-internalized to be correlated with the poet's *own* unrealized possibilities—a turn that could reopen the door to the idealistic/solipsistic account of poetic birth, the principle target of Bloomian polemics. Rather than taking it as an escape clause or a momentary lapse in an otherwise relentless argumentation, I would see in the aporia an insufficiently realized potential of the theory itself.

Cansever wrote in another poem from the 1960s, "I'm the debt of a frenzied blue signet," which could also be translated as "I'm the promise of a red-hot blue signet," or again as "I'm the obligation—to perform—of a red-hot blue signet." To Cansever, the co-owner of an antique shop, signets and seals are part of a figural series that begins with the humblest unusable object (something like Paul Valéry's "found object") and extends to gems and to more talisman-like things; as for most poets, but perhaps more insistently than most, they also signify Poetry. Here, the emblematic object is made to perform and reveal the nature of its coming into being: It is a seal, the sign and guarantee of something sent by an other; it is a debt or a promise on the part of the receiver, the poetic subject; it is red-hot, frenziedly urging the subject to perform, to repay his debt; and its scorching action is in part self-inflicted, the result of the subject's partial identification with the object, an identification that at once activates the influencing object *and* sets it apart. And what of the "blue," the most invariable figuration? As several of the poems from the same cycle ("Sky-meaning") indicate, it is a name for that oceanic feeling, but with the ocean often appearing as a severe, uncaring parent who lets the child down.[39] And so it is that the poet, by definition always the later poet, has been driven to retroactively imagining his harsh family into existence, in the absence of a real one. The poem called "Divination," found as if accidentally by Süreya's subject, the precursor poem "that should have been written by the poet in question," would thus be the most preordained poem of all—precisely as the one that can *never* come off, the one that can only be represented by a poem of pure contingency.[40]

With time, this contingency would get to know itself as such and thus attain a sort of inner direction, imparting to the Second New's invented, ad-hoc forms an aspect of inevitability. And it was in the same period, too, that images of self-invention or self-begetting began to appear in their poems. As so often, the most emboldened one in this respect was Ece Ayhan, in whom perversity adjoined a total denial of father-as-cause: "A catamite was giving birth to himself, straight-eject." Inversion, both grammatical and semantic, was frequently the enabling instrument of that denial, and of the self-begetting toward immortality: "My dear! Beautiful horses are like beautiful poems / When dead they begin to race backward." Or: "The son of man is fatherless / 'In our next coming into the world, we shall be returning upstream.'" Images of self-sufficiency abound in the *Orthodoxies* (1968): sleep, sudden swoons; auto-eroticism; and a pointedly callous, blasé manner, not only reflected in the grammatical contraction but also taken up thematically: "A word he endlessly repeats: hermaphrodite. Makes love biting own lip. Plays the secondhand lute of terror. *I was reading The Jew of Malta. Inside a coffin where I dwell*" (emphasis original); "Was slipping into the sleep of cistern rain-water, a mortar pestle. With a diamond[-like] accustomedness"; "Adorned with gold dust leaves. Not only the ebbing of the sea, but even its revelation would not interest him"; "Yells would run on like arches, inside a cathedral. Couldn't confess, because of swaggering pride. / He was indifferent. The fingers of his cut-off right hand had made the sign required in his by-laws" (Nemet-Nejat's translations, but revised and made more literal). Ayhan was the most self-congratulatory poet; but even in Süreya, who with his long suppressed Kurdish origin devoted a considerable part of his energies to appeasing people (not least by writing many of the most beautiful poems in the language—a self-defeating move, always), even in him one can find a sense of rebirth, into love through poetry—and more often the other way around. His third volume, the most exultant one, was titled *Kiss Me, Then Give Me Birth*, as the closing lines of a poem had it: "My mother died too early / Kiss me, then give me birth."

But this second (poetic) birth, this self-begetting, was not, and perhaps can never be, a once-and-for-all attainment: the poet had to always re-experience it, had to repeatedly taste the terror of self-loss so as to be once more reborn. (More important than gaining a new lease on life was therefore the prospect of reaching life *through death*.) In Cansever the addictive nature of this cyclic experience emerges most clearly, as in the poem "After a Straying" (or "After a Swoon"):

> I've tested it often: when the carnation's stem touches the water
> Someone is shot inside me
> And there is a resurrection engraved in jade
> Every morning my doorbell rings
> I open it: it's me, the month of June
> Or the wish to live, to live indefinitely, maybe.

And "Dead Sirens," from roughly the same time (mid-1960s) ends thus:

> When the evening gave me back my eyes
> The city disappeared, as did the calm of the sea
> While a phoenix shuffled its ashes again
> And a grotto made itself used to emptiness
> I said: I was the sea, and I the one who dreamed it
> And at first light I will find myself
> Lying like a smile on top my depth.

If this is phoenix, it is a phoenix doing a very Turkish poetic act, assuming and imitating modern Turkish poetry's repetitions, its cycles of self-disenfranchisement and reenfranchisement. The opposition between conscious and unconscious does not apply at this level of hypostatization, that of the poetic act itself, just as the opposition between necessary and contingent is suspended. The Second New poet, now Second not even with respect to Yahya Kemal but Second as such, the incarnation of something like Freud's deferred action, a continuous afterwardness, sees himself, in this suspended moment, as willing his whole historical being into existence, himself creating the ruptured history that had produced him. And so the true manifesto of the Second New, which was not a "Movement" and did not publish any collective manifesto, would be Uyar's essay "Novitiate, Our Master," written in 1956:

> We have quite many poets who had written some pretty good love poems in their youth but later became silent. This was due, I think, to their inability to reinvent themselves. And I also think that one comes into this impasse only by aiming at mastery, at virtuosity. For that, you willy-nilly have to take a definite direction, allowing the reader to anticipate what is coming. . . . You will take a stone and carve it. A hammer each day. At the end, you will have produced an ornate, pretentious monument. Whereas novitiate. Our Master the Novice. You will take a stone and begin to carve. When it is just about to take shape you will throw it away. You will take another stone, and yet another. In the end, you will have left a host of imperfect, half-done forms. Maybe others will love and complete them. But each time you took a stone in your hand, your fear was new, was fresh. You had worked with the delight of the anxiety of not succeeding.[41]

The poet had been many times disinherited, deprived of a "direction," of a strong precursor with respect to whom he would swerve, or whom he would attempt to antithetically "complete": a severe dispossession leaving him with no choice but to work against the grain, to take the disinheritance itself as the precursor poem, and then throughout a lifetime to write it anew, so as to become the true author of his own descent.[42]

"I ascend to fall down from a height," Cansever had written, "I descend, I descend to a swan's uncertain adventure." In a narrowly stylistic sense, he would come through as the steadiest Second New poet, while the others agitated themselves into recurrent upheavals (between the 1950s and the early 1980s, each poet would expose his work to at least four drastic overhauls). All seemed to have a presentiment of the increasingly self-consuming character of such turbulences. "A tired poem is changing step," wrote Ayhan in *Poems for Second-Grade Dropouts* (1973), a volume that won him a wider readership, coming as a relief after the red-hot self-absorption of *Orthodoxies*. But it is in Uyar, the poet most given to self-curtailment, that we find the unerring figurations of the Second New's fate. Long before his late poems came to be described as "somewhat enervated," Uyar knew himself to be working toward that enervation: "Don't ever close, stay, O hole emptying me out," he implored in one of his first Second New poems (for there was a pre-Second period, in the 1940s). He knew himself, at the outset, to be given over to the labor of the negative, but one which foresees no positive outcome. He made the poem address itself as "O knife that by sharpening wears away." He made the audience, drawn as chorus into the poem, another one, to speak of "the now dead horse" of the poem (and of poetry) as "a willful dimunition." And in a later poem, "The Journal of Defeat," written in 1965, at the high point of a second ascent, we find the image of an extinguishment twice foretold:

> The puzzlement left over from an unachieved past
> the present nakedness. forming on a half-illumined wall
> an experience drawn out of a defeat. an agedness
> which worked to bleach the breath of a gold seam.

The absent precursor had foretold the futility of the latecomer's efforts. It was his only "severe poem": now the latecomer is writing back to make the precursor poem seem a pale imitation of the second catastrophe—a turning that would reappear as an irreparable yet exquisite time warp in M. C. Anday's post-Second poetry.

≡≡≡≡

"The literature of the outsider has become quite an inside thing, but I don't think we have heard anything like this voice." Thus wrote Chris King, the American reviewer of Murat Nemet-Nejat's translation of Ece Ayhan's *A Blind Cat Black and Orthodoxies*.[43] Certainly Anday had not heard anything like it either, at least not in Turkish. King notes the poetry's intoxicating effect, too: "This book has a way of lulling the reader into reverie, so that you complete the picture with your own colors, whistle the rest of the warped tune." And Nemet-Nejat, in his *Talisman* essay, "A Godless Sufism," described the *auditory* character of the intoxication, which was indeed a seduction:

> Turkish has no distinction between short and long syllables; that is to say, individual words in Turkish have almost no rhythmical value. Rhythm in Turkish is syntactical, in its cadences. . . . I believe two ideas underlie the Second New. The first is *Eda* . . . a term derived from folk poetry, which roughly means tone, sound, style. . . . [It] is a term also applied to women. A woman with Eda is one whose *totality* has allure. Eda as a poetic idea suggests an allure which is not concentrated on a single object, but is global, diffused in the body of the whole poem. The Second New can be seen as an extended, experimental exploration of the possibilities of Eda. . . . Even at its most elaborate or opaque, the physical and emotional impact of a poem, the cadences of its Eda, are always transparently clear. This global directness is at the heart of this poetry. . . . The simplest line in a satisfying Second New poem resonates with intimations beyond its actual sense. On the other hand, the most elaborate stylic riff has a relentless underlying clarity.[44]

No seduction without the seducer "preseduced": as Jean Laplanche most cogently argued, the "enigmatic signifier" coming from the others must have been enigmatic for them also—not completely worked out yet, demanding a further effort at "translation," and therefore relentless more in its constant pressure than in its clarity. Thus the auditory imagination of the Second New poet had to first seduce itself, precisely by bewitching his incoming auditory material. Something like an originary moment for this process is described by Ece Ayhan in an early interview:

> My grandmother concealed the war's outbreak from us. I would only hear the sirens, see the lights going out, but without understanding their meaning. I would only hear: the drawn out and undulating sound of the sirens, a suddenly deserted street, then the end of the sirens, the first stirrings in the street. . . . Nothing but these, and the war was a total mystery for me. I didn't know "the truth," and yet the contours of my poems were already being drawn there. The whole war consisted of mysterious signs for me.[45]

As Nemet-Nejat stressed, there is a distinctly auricular, "heard" quality in any satisfying Second New poem, as if the poet himself is still intently listening to his sentences, still hearing them sounding. Enis Batur, a perceptive poet-critic from the succeeding generation, commented on a related quality, the "bodily" character of Turgut Uyar's poems: "An orgasmic language: it has its special tempo, its contractions and quiverings, its flows and dammings. . . . No other poet represents this linguistic trauma: it is the work of two poets only, Uyar and Ayhan. . . . Uyar's poetry comes into being in an epileptic *eda*."[46] I would object only to the delimitation: even when lacking the flagellating effect of Ayhan's spurt-out sentences, the others' poems had their own vortexlike action, "so full of the threat of a sense of loss that the total effect is thrilling and disturbing," as Nemet-Nejat said of Süreya's poems.[47]

The facilitating musicism Tanpınar deplored in his own generation would thus seem to have resurfaced, as the *eda* that leaves no room for undue misunderstanding. That the Second New, like all major poetic overreachings, at once provoked and curbed its own misreadings is indisputable. But this second musicism differed in one important respect: it came from and was the instrument of a deliberately self-tantalizing, self-traumatizing intention: its felicitous reception entailed major disturbance on the part of the receiver.

It was Anday who lived the arrival of the Second New as a catastrophe. The other two poets who were able to seize on the forward thrust and use it to re-energize their own work, Oktay Rifat and Behçet Necatigil, had already hardened themselves to some extent: they seemed to be able to look at the Second New's development as the still uncertain unfolding of some of their own possibilities. Anday, by contrast, was caught unawares, and at one moment even his practical existence seemed to have come to a standstill: he had died one morning, when the landlady found him lying on the floor and called the doctor to restore him to life. This incident, thereafter making his life only a pretext for the poetry to come, would work to twist every fiber in the poetry too—even before it arrived. The poetry that issued out of a silence of eight years (1956–63) had a distinctly "inorganic" tincture about it. On the surface, it was a poetry of nature—not unlike Cansever's—but of a nature that had been irreparably sundered, split-off. At one polar extreme it would appear as sheer sensuousness, with no emotion attached, and at another as the object of something like pure intellection. Isolation, separation of affect from idea, and a neglectful, almost cruel speeding up of sensuous experience were the basic mechanisms. The poem "Always Afterward" from his penultimate volume, *In the Sun* (1990), may be a good example:

> The evening is about to end. Not evening.
> And then? I have seen coves
> Like unrecognized envoys. But it's the night
> I know. And then? Then the dreams,
> All dreams. I shot a small bird,
> It was left crippled in July. And then?
> Then it was morning, from the mountain I descended
> To the day's slope. I saw that it was not the one,
> Not the one that knew me while it was a bird.
> And then I saw the neighbors,
> As if they knew something, as if they could know,
> Were watching the evening and waiting for the night.

Night, for Anday, was not a moment in a cycle of deaths and rebirths; it meant irreversibility, marking what can only expire. The arrival of the Second New had warped his sense of orderly succession: he could regain at least a semblance of composure only by quickening time's passage even further. He had been benighted: he would pull the blinding agent itself into a yet denser darkness, into sleep, thereby also giving the most luminescent emblem of modern Turkish poetry's traumatized births: "A hastening world, this one. Everything is too early / And everything too late. The sun will go into eclipse while we are asleep."

Notes

1   Cemal Süreya, *Toplu Yazılar I* [Collected writings] (Istanbul: YKY, 2000), 425.
2   Melih Cevdet Anday (b. 1915) is the only surviving member of a trio labeled "Garip" (strange) in reference to the title of their first, joint volume of poems. The other two members were Orhan Veli Kanık (1914–1950) and Oktay Rifat (1914–1988); Rifat and Anday were two of the three early-comers who were able to make the late "leap," under the influence of the Second New. The third, Behçet Necatigil (1916–1979), had never been close to the original Garip movement, feeling a strong aversion to their ostentatiously anti-traditional, "antiromantic" stance, but later would not much object to his poetry's being associated with the "larger Second New movement."
3   I am of course not forgetting the brilliant translations by Talat Sait Halman, Murat Nemet-Nejat, Ruth Christie, Richard McCane, and Liam Blake, but I would nonetheless insist that the total output is still too fragmentary to provide an adequate picture. For some of the work by these translators, see the section "Contemporary Turkish Poetry" in *Talisman: A Journal of Contemporary Poetry and Poetics* 14 (1995): 32–59, in which all translations are by Nemet-Nejat, and *Agenda* 38: 3–4 (2001–2), which is devoted to modern Turkish poetry and offers work by different translators. Nemet-Nejat's introductory piece, "A Godless Sufism: Ideas on Twentieth-Century Turkish Poetry," in the same issue of *Talisman*, despite the inaccuracy of its main argument ("Sufism, even if godless"), is to my mind the best short account of the Second New that has so far appeared in English. Nemet-Nejat has also translated the entirety of two volumes of poetry by Ece Ayhan (1931–2002), arguably the most radically innovative poet of the Second New: *The Blind Cat Black* and *Orthodoxies* (Los Angeles: Sun and Moon, 1997). A risky undertaking by any standard, Nemet-Nejat's labor of love is also important in raising the question of the ultimate untranslatability of at least several of these poets.
4   There, Gibb offered a more generic explanation: "The great race to which the Ottomans belong, that race which includes not only the Turks both Western and Eastern, but all the so-called Tartars and Turkmans as well as the Mongols, has never produced any religion, philosophy or literature which bears the stamp of its individual genius. This is because the true genius of that race lies in action, not in speculation. The Turks and their kinsfolk are before all things soldiers." *A History of Ottoman Poetry*, 6 vols. (London: Luzac, 1900–1907), 1:6.
5   Walter G. Andrews, "Singing the Alienated 'I': Guattari, Deleuze, and Lyrical Decodings of *the Subject* in Ottoman *Divan* Poetry," *Yale Journal of Criticism* 6.2 (1993): 191–219. Andrews is the author of *Poetry's Voice, Society's Song: Ottoman Lyric Poetry* (Seattle: University of Washington Press, 1985), a superb introduction to the *gazel* form in Ottoman poetry. Victoria Rowe Holbrook, in her book on Ottoman *masnavi* poetry, is equally indignant: "A marvelous maze of absences is [the] point of departure for writing about Ottoman literature in the United States today. . . . The Middle East is widely perceived as an exclusively sociological area where humanities never happen (except, perhaps, in an ideal country called Persia). It has the strange reputation of being a place where only war occurs." *The Unreadable Shores of Love: Turkish Modernity and Mystic Romance* (Austin: University of Texas Press, 1994), 1. The constraint of discourse on an "absence," a "fade-

out," seems to have led both authors to introduce—and to the best effect—a distinctly poststructuralist sensibility to a discipline commonly characterized by extreme methodological conservatism.

6 Serif Mardin's *The Genesis of Young Ottoman Thought: A Study in The Modernization of Turkish Political Ideas* (Princeton, NJ: Princeton University Press, 1962) is still the best account of the movement.

7 "As to our poetry," he wrote in the preface to his verse drama *Celaleddin Harzemshah*, "with the exception of the majority of *munacat*s and *nat*s [the opening pieces in a divan, praising God and the Prophet, respectively], a few *masnavi*s and some isolated beautiful couplets, it has consisted of disconnected representations taken from an illusory realm altogether out of touch with the worlds of nature and reality." *Namık Kemal'in Türk Dili ve Edebiyati Üzerine Yazilari* [Namık Kemal's writings on Turkish language and literature], ed. Kazim Yetis (Istanbul: Alfa, 1996), 345.

8 The passage, taken from his preface to his Persian divan, deserves to be quoted in full: "As chance would have it, all the poets that came before me were men of immense wisdom. Every beautiful image, every subtle arrangement has been used by them, so much so that nothing is left for us now. One should have a full knowledge of everything they wrote, lest one admit already created meanings into one's own work. There have been times that, having labored all through the night, I was just able to find a trope and write it down—only to cross it out in the morning on finding that I had merely repeated other poets. There have been times, too, when I would immerse myself deep into the sea of reflection and bring up a virgin meaning; but on hearing others say that this trope was unintelligible, that it was not used and would not have been tolerated by the masters, I would at once lose all interest in it. What a perplexing circumstance: Something said before cannot be said because it has already been said—and something not said before cannot be said because it has never been said. Past colleagues have so thoroughly pillaged the store of images and tropes that the space of poetry is now too narrow for us. Oh, this having someone come before us!" Ali Nihat Tarlan, introduction to *Fuzuli Divani Şerhi* (Commentary on Fuzuli's divan) (Ankara: Akçag Yayınları, 1997), 10.

9 Ziya Gökalp (1876–1924), the leading theorist of early Turkish nationalism, gave the formula: into Western civilization with our national culture. Translated into aesthetic terms, this read as follows: "Civilization comprises the institutions common to all nations, its constituents being science, technique, and the arts. . . . Taking science and technique from Europe will greatly aid our progress. In addition, Europe will have positive effects on us in aesthetic and spiritual fields too. But these latter influences are helpful only to the extent that they combat and overthrow the Persian and Arabic influences. The moment they attempt to take the place of the influence they have overthrown, they begin to have harmful influences. . . . Let our poets read the whole of European poetry, beginning with Homer. . . . But let them be content with taking only the techniques, stopping short of adopting other nations' tastes also." Ziya Gökalp, *Hars ve Medeniyet* [Culture and civilization] (Istanbul: Toker Yayınları, 1995), 15, 17. An alternative, less consistent, but more effective policy, put into effect during the 1940s, was to counter the *current reality* of Western culture with the help of the *idea* of Western culture: the timeless classics and, to a

lesser extent, the nineteenth-century realists, for fear of the ever-new moderns. The State Publishing House's publication of the World Classics series in the 1940s was both an index and an instrument of this second tendency.

10 Halit Ziya Uşaklıgil, *Mai ve Siyah* (Istanbul: Hilmi Kitabevi, 1941), 43–44, 140. The novel was first published in 1897. The edition I have used is the one that was subsequently "purified" of much of its Arabic and Persian words by the author himself in response to the dictates of the Language Reform of the 1930s.

11 Yahya Kemal, *Siyasi ve Edebi Portreler* [Political and literary portraits] (Istanbul: Istanbul Fetih Cemiyeti Yayınları, 1986), 21. And further: "What stood out in [Fikret's] poems were the tastes of the French middle class, a bourgeois mindset. At a time when Paul Verlaine's poetry was exerting its most violent influence, this circumstance was on all counts an obvious backwardness." Yahya Kemal, *Edebiyata Dair* [Concerning literature] (Istanbul: Istanbul Fetih Cemiyeti Yayınları, 1984), 261.

12 Ziya Gökalp was the leading theorist of the National Literature movement. The progressive literary appropriation of the vernacular, gaining momentum through Gökalp's efforts well before the actual reform of the 1930s, would also work to diminish the *Servet-i Fünun* writers' readership. For the debate on "the original Turkish spirit," see Nurdan Gürbilek's essay in this issue.

13 Thus Nurullah Ataç, a student of Yahya Kemal and the leading critic of the 1940s and 1950s, wrote, "I thought I would find subtle emotions, great ideas and a rigorous sense of form in Fikret's poems. But for some time now, they have made me shudder. In fact, I cannot help noticing the pomposity and the inept diction. . . . He has taken from Europe what is perhaps its worst poetry, and tried to be like François Coppée." *Okuruma Mektuplar* [Letters to my reader] (Istanbul: Can Yayınları, [n.d.]), 20, 22. And Cemal Süreya wrote in the 1960s: "Despite the fact that Fikret had all the means to deepen his knowledge of Western culture, he remained ignorant of roughly contemporary figures like Mallarmé, Rimbaud, Lautréamont, Nietzsche, or Marx. . . . In the meantime, he had taken as his master a third-rate French poet, François Coppée." Ibid., 77–78.

14 Yahya Kemal, *Çocuklugum, Gençligim, Edebi ve Siyasi Hatıralarım* [My childhood, my youth, my literary and political reminiscences] (Istanbul: Istanbul Fetih Cemiyeti Yayınları, 1976), 106–8; emphasis original.

15 Harold Bloom, the theorist of poetic tradition, also seems to overlook this fact, even as he argues for the negative power of tradition: "I intend here . . . to assert for literary tradition its *currently* pragmatic as opposed to idealized function: it is *now* valuable precisely because it partly blocks, because it stifles the weak, because it represses even the strong. To study literary tradition *today* is to achieve a dangerous but enabling act of the mind that works against all ease in fresh 'creation.'" *A Map of Misreading* (Oxford: Oxford University Press, 1975), 29; emphasis added. But can we really summon the force of the long defunct? Adorno's observation, at the opening passage of *Aesthetic Theory*, that modern art has lost its newly found freedom *simultaneously* with the loss of its inner necessity or self-evidence, might be pointing at a more fruitful way of reflecting on the energetics of the "tradition of the New."

16 This drying up was a recurrent theme. In a famous poem ("Autumn") written well before

he was fifty, Yahya Kemal seemed to be foretelling his poetic fate: "Company is trouble, and solitude oppressive. / How should I spend the last five, ten years? / Mankind has been fathomed. And the world has no more secrets. / Had I a single golden arrow left in my quiver now / I wouldn't bother to shoot it for even the loveliest vision. / . . . / Let this futile autumn gracefully come to an end! / Dying is not the most terrible business of our lives; / That a person dies before dying is the real difficulty."

17   It had first appeared in oral form: "At the time of his return to his country in 1912, after nine years in Paris, not a single poem of his has yet been published. . . . But the poems he recites—with broad gestures and a modulating tone, somewhat under the influence of Parisian actors—fascinates the listeners at social gatherings. And so he becomes the first and the only poet in [modern] Turkish literature to rise to fame without having a single poem published." Sermet Sami Uysal, *Yahya Kemal Beyatlı: Siire Adanmıs bir Yasam* [Yahya Kemal: A life dedicated to poetry] (Istanbul: Yahya Kemal'i Sevenler Dernegi, 1998), 374. To this must be added the fact of his never bringing himself to collect his poems in a book. Some time in the 1930s, at a reception where he was present, a nervous young poet long among his watchers had dared to call out: "Yahya Kemal, a poet without poems." Kemal beckoned him to his side and whispered: "What you just said is your first real poem, let's hope it won't be the last." The fact that I cannot and need not cite any source for this bit of information, that hearsay suffices, this fact, taken together with the title of the above source and the name of the publisher (The Society of Those Who Love Yahya Kemal), if assimilable to a Pninian universe, is not unrelated to what made Kemal's triumph so easy: the absence of a compelling tradition.

18   The product of a double—and tormented—mediation, Yahya Kemal's poetry, even at its best, could still sound somewhat self-satisfied, as in these most famous lines: "Take a look at the pensive waters of the bay / You shall see, deep down, a night from the past lingering. / The moon, big roses, and your most beautiful likeness . . . / In short, the dream we've known is still in place."

19   Nurullah Ataç, *Letters to My Reader*, 90. Elsewhere, he wrote: "From the very first day, Yahya Kemal's poems have been admired and liked. They never made anyone feel alienated or perplexed. For he was bringing back a beauty we had lost but could not forget. . . . There were many who begrudged him, but none who did not understand his poetry. For there was no essential novelty in his poems, nothing to make you ill at ease. He said what other poets said, but said it better, more smoothly." Nurullah Ataç, *Söylesiler* [Conversations] (Istanbul: YKY, 2000), 224.

20   *Tanpınar'in Mektupları* [Tanpınar's letters], ed. Zeynep Kerman (Istanbul: Dergah Yayınları, 1992), 153. That Tanpınar was not exaggerating on the matter of "musicism" is attested by a strange, never fulfilled project of Yahya Kemal's. To those who would make a case of the absence of the novel genre in Ottoman literature, he would reply: "Our novels are inside our songs, in our music. One day I will have the chance to demonstrate this." A. Hamdi Tanpınar, *Yahya Kemal* (Istanbul: Dergah Yayınları, 1982), 26.

21   By ostracizing Nazim Hikmet, the only Turkish entry in a recent Routledge *Who's Who in Twentieth-Century World Poetry*, the Turkish cultural establishment ensured that there would be no authoritative, compelling canon of modern poetry to this day. We are left only

with preferences, group or personal, and every new anthology is a cause of major strife. On the other hand, Hikmet's easily achieved banishment (easy in literary terms) may be regarded as much a result as a cause of the difficulties in the way of canon-formation in modern Turkish literature: starting with Namık Kemal, it had pretty much been a matter of easy victories and easy exits.

22 Oktay Rifat, *Siir Konusmasi* [Poetic discourse] (Istanbul: Adam Yayınları, 1992), 78. He also wrote: "Orhan managed to pack into his very short life the poetic adventures of several generations of French poets. Thanks to him, our poetry has caught up with European poetry. Had he lived, he would have most certainly conquered the advanced poetry of twentieth century, too." Ibid., 77. (Rifat was a socialist, if a very evolutionary one. During the 1950s, the word "advanced" [*ileri*], instead of "progressive" [*ilerici*], was used as a euphemism for socialist.) Edward Said has made much the same point in his commentary on Mahfouz: "[His] work from the late thirties on compresses the history of the European novel into a relatively short span of time." Edward Said, *Reflections on Exile and Other Essays* (Cambridge: Harvard University Press, 2000), 318.

23 Tanpınar, the poet-critic who could not bring himself to evade difficult questions, bemoaned his persistent sense of futility in a letter written just before the Strangers made their debut: "I want your opinion of this latest version of the 'Nightingale' poem . . . I'm working—but like a mill turning in vain, grinding only time itself. What you see is the fruit of two months of labor, and how insipid it is, how elementary! . . . But here's some news for you. Yesterday evening I saw Yahya Kemal. He approached our table reciting the couplet: 'At the feast of pleasure cups of red wine come and go, to and fro / As with the ebb and flow of the tide the ocean surges to and fro.' We were quick with the compliment—'That is your coming, Sir!'—and flattered him no end. The master was drunk, and became effusive, cursing indiscriminately. Then for about a half hour he praised our prose and finally offered the fatherly advice: 'Quit writing poetry. Give it up, it has ended with me. Your humble servant has already done it, with your permission. You can no longer do it.' I was piqued at first, but thinking of 'Nightingale,' felt obliged to cede him a point. Poetry doesn't come to an end with Yahya Kemal, that much is certain, though it's true that I can't quite attain it." Tanpınar, *Tanpınar'in Mektuplari*, 35–37. In an open letter, written and published in 1951, the lament gains a wider resonance: "The first thing Yahya Kemal taught me was giving myself a respite. . . . I haven't contributed anything to Yahya Kemal's journal. I was used to suppressing the first thrust, always. I would find myself insufficiently prepared and would give up. . . . The most important events of my life consisted of my finding, one after the other, my own poets. Yes, because I was not able to find myself in due time, I was busy discovering others. . . . You see, my life is replete with delays." A. H. Tanpınar, *Yasadigim Gibi* [As I have lived] (Istanbul: Dergah Yayınları, 1996), 304–7.

24 Christie's translation can be found in *Agenda* 38 (2001–2).

25 The term is Bloom's, of course: "*Askesis*, or a movement of self-purgation which intends the attainment of a state of solitude. . . . The later poet . . . yields up a part of his human and imaginative endowment, so as to separate himself from others, including the precursor, and he does this in his poem by stationing it in regard to the parent-poem as to

make that poem undergo an *askesis* too; the precursor's endowment is also truncated." Harold Bloom, *Anxiety of Influence* (Oxford: Oxford University Press, 1997), 15.

26   Melih Cevdet Anday, *Akan Zaman, Duran Zaman* [Time flowing, time stopped] (Istanbul: Adam Yayınları, 1984), 35–36. The nihilistic strain was less prominent in the work of Oktay Rifat, who claimed that "the new poetry" (i.e., their poetry) was all about the senses, with little time for either reason or the emotions. Orhan Veli's lines are more in line with Anday's passage: "When dead we would be cleansed of our dirt, / When dead we would become good men too."

27   Thus the same self-disinheritance with respect to things Ottoman: "At the outset of the nineteenth century, Arabic poetry suffered from many weaknesses. These were caused by the onerous social, political, and cultural conditions inflicted on the Arab world by the oppressive domination of the Ottoman Empire . . . reflected most poignantly in our literature. Creative expression was checked and often stifled. Slowly, the Arabs were cut off from their brilliant intellectual and literary past, and, with time, the art of poetry began to inhabit a cultural vacuum . . . full of useless embellishments—nothing more than an exercise of wit and almost wholly devoid of substance." Salma Khadra Jayyusi, *Modern Arabic Poetry: An Anthology* (New York: Columbia University Press), 1. A similar view is expressed by M. M. Badawi in *A Short Introduction to Modern Arabic Literature* (Oxford: Clarendon Press, 1998).

28   The following passage is from Haşim's "Notes from a Journey," written in 1928: "We gathered at a small Russian restaurant in Montparnasse. The lady who had invited us, a young Austrian woman, and two French youths, both close watchers of artistic currents: Doktor Lakan and Vikont dö Santak [*sic*]. . . . I probed Doktor Lakan on the present state of French literature. He said: 'Cubism, futurism, dadaism, surrealism . . . Almost all of these professions mushrooming out of the putrefaction of symbolism are café-based movements, brought into our country by some foreigners. We are a hospitable nation. Our jails are full of foreign criminals, our hospitals with foreign patients, our schools with foreign students . . . Landovski, a Pole, is one of our greatest sculptors.'" Ahmet Haşim, *Bize Göre* [From our perspective] (Istanbul: Semih Lütfi Kitabevi, [n.d.]), 61–62.

29   Süreya, *Toplu Yazılar*, 81.

30   Freud had arrived at the notions of the ego-ideal and the superego through different routes, but finally conflated them in his second topography. Later authors like Lacan, Béla Grunberger, and Janine Chasseguet-Smirgel, though making a sharp distinction between the two terms and defining them as two separate substructures of the ego, did not specifically consider the possibility of an insistent and geoculturally determined conflict between the superego and the ego ideal—the two concepts in Freud's system that are best disposed to function as interfaces between individual depth psychology and the dynamics of the social life-world. A. H. Tanpınar, at various points in his critical writings—and especially in his monumental *A History of Nineteenth-Century Turkish Literature*—commented on the "ideal-less state" of the Ottoman intellectual before the advent of Namık Kemal and the Westernizers.

31   Ziya Gökalp called his cultural project "ideal-ism," the same term the mass ultraright movement that was born in the 1960s would adopt as its generic designation.

32 Edip Cansever, *Kirli Agustos* [Dirty August] (Istanbul: Adam, 1968). All translations of the Second New poets, with the exception of those of Ece Ayhan, are mine and have been made for this essay.

33 This immediacy, and the correlative overabundance of decontextualized imagery, are what later generations of poets would inherit from the Second New, with the inner disruption (the "askew positioning" of the subject) registered only by the three poets of the preceding generation that I mentioned (see n. 2 above), and most notably by M. C. Anday, for whom the coming of the Second New was a trauma.

34 The question clause, *duyuyor musun* in the original, can be translated alternatively as "can you hear it" or "can you sense it." Ilhan Berk (b. 1918) remains one the few still active poets associated with the movement. Though he first began publishing his poems in the 1940s, Berk would have no difficulty in moving ahead together with the younger poets of the Second New, whose coming he did not experience as a trauma, and at times Berk even stood out as the movement's most daring experimentalist.

35 This diremption in the poetic act, with the voice stepping back, as it were, or stepping aside from what it is saying, is most apparent in Beckett. "The Expelled" ends thus: "I don't know why I told this story. I could just as well have told another. Perhaps some other time I'll be able to tell another. Living souls, you will see how alike they are." And the ending of "The End": "The sea, the sky, the mountains and the islands closed in and crushed me in a mighty systole, than scattered to the uttermost confines of space. The memory came faint and cold of the story I might have told, a story in the likeness of my life, I mean without the courage to end or the strength to go on." As in Ece Ayhan, the poetic will wishes to be larger than any created poem, and precisely by being crushed to pieces it is propelled outward so as to encompass all.

36 The Turkish phrase could also mean "a silence that couldn't pass the exam" or "a silence condemned to incompleteness."

37 In an early poem Süreya had said, "He who has love, has nothing but." This sentence would be subsumed in another, from an essay against Strange's mock plebianism: "Not everything can become poetry, but poetry can become everything."

38 Bloom, *The Anxiety of Influence*, 95–96; emphasis added.

39 The child, let it be said, is an "alcoholic" one: liquid, just like the parent, even a more refined, sublimated liquid, but still a less worthy one: "O sea! even you can get wet / I'm an alcoholic child from your Infinity. // . . . / I ascend to fall down from a height / I descend, I descend to a swan's uncertain adventure / O sea, even you can get wet, so understand: / I'm an alcoholic child from your Infinity."

40 From an earlier poem of Cansever's: "Through a flock of trees / The sun falls like lemon slices / Into my vodka glass / I feel a joy that is not mine // . . . // Not in time, but somewhere / I grow old with something not mine / Consuming my earlier form I overtake / A slowly burning batch of bricks." Though less given to the typically Canseverian mixture of gloom and enchanted elation, Turgut Uyar also strongly embraced this sense of contingency: "What is a man, set against a sea, a moustached and baldheaded man, / what else than a bad habit . . ."

41 Turgut Uyar, *Sonsuz ve Öbürü* [The infinite and that other one], ed. Tomris Uyar (Istanbul:

Broy Yayınları, 1985), 156. Uyar never commented on the works of his confreres (except remarking once that "what Ilhan Berk touches, turns at once into poetry"), but I think he must have found the poems of Süreya and even Cansever, his closest friend, as just a bit too "monumental" for his taste. He was after what Adorno termed "the nonidentical," that which tends to elude its own concept and resist all repose, except the final one. M. C. Anday, at the receiving end of the forward thrust of this deadly pursuit, would succeed, after the event, in taking a side step and capturing the pursuit as the unerringly faltering pulse of his own poems.

42 Again, this daemonic vision finds its more arrogant version in Ece Ayhan, in the last stanza of "The Hunchback as His Own Tailor": "For every hunchback comes from a family of poets / That is, he can also become his own apprentice / In order to give life to dead words and children / So don't forget, whenever an anthem is played twice / It is for a hunchback at once master and apprentice."

43 Chris King, "Gay in Istanbul," *Nation*, July 7, 1997, 26–27. King continues: "God knows what the Turkish looks like (the translator assures us it has puzzled most readers); the English is a bizarre movement through invisible dogs, convulsed emotions, corpses, stolen kites, rats in sewers, blind black cats with dead babies . . . and the ghosts of jokes. Nothing obvious connects the riot of images and tide-turns of emotion."

44 Murat Nemet-Nejat, "A Godless Sufism: Ideas on Twentieth-Century Turkish Poetry," *Talisman: A Journal of Contemporary Poetry and Poetics* 14 (1995): 35.

45 Ece Ayhan, *Yort Savul* [Get out of the way!] (Istanbul: Agaoglu Yayinevi, 1977), 200. Bloom formulates the "pre-poeticization" of the extraliterary material thus: "Acts, persons, and places, if they are to be handled by poems at all, must themselves be treated first as though they were already poems, or parts of poems." Bloom, *A Map of Misreading*, 70.

46 Enis Batur, *Yazinin Ucu* [Writing's edge] (Istanbul: YKY, 1993), 87–88.

47 As in these lines by Süreya: "Today, this small Tuesday / Everything eludes Istanbul, except its hills / Only Galata / Galata / Like a mouth organ / Is slowly exuding to the sea / That inexhaustible passion for corrosion / Which the night feeds in its basements." Galata, once the central business district of Istanbul, is where the city most eminently slopes down to meet the sea, deigning to insinuate itself with the waters, as it were.

Nurdan Gürbilek

Dandies and Originals: Authenticity, Belatedness, and the Turkish Novel

Let's start with an impasse in our reading practices. Criticism in Turkey—not only social and cultural criticism but also literary criticism—is mostly the criticism of a lack, a critique devoted to demonstrating what Turkish society, culture, or literature lacks. Thus statements of lack ("We don't have a novel of our own" or similarly "We don't have a tragedy, a criticism, a philosophy, or an individual of our own") are typical of a critical stance that positions itself from the very start as a comparative one, presuming that it becomes convincing only when it talks about something the "other" has but "we" don't have, pointing out to the persistent lack, the irremovable deficiency, the unyielding inadequacy of its object: Turkish culture.

It would be unfair to say that this is merely a discursive fallacy. A whole set of social-economic-cultural reasons are at work here: a society that is "belatedly modernized,"[1] a system of thought that has come to accept its insufficiency before a modern one presuming to be superior, and a culture that has adopted an infantile role when confronted by foreign modern ideals. What the Greek scholar Gregory

The *South Atlantic Quarterly* 102:2/3, Spring/Summer 2003.
Copyright © 2003 by Duke University Press.

Jusdanis calls "belated modernity," what the Iranian scholar Daryush Shaye-gan describes as "a consciousness retarded to the idea,"[2] what the Turk-ish scholar Jale Parla explains by a sense of "fatherlessness"[3] and what the Turkish critic Orhan Koçak discusses within the framework of a "missed ideal"[4] are all related to the traumatic shifting of models generally discussed under the heading *Westernization*. This cultural context forced Turkish lit-erary criticism toward being an anxious effort of comparison programmed to discuss from the very start the deprivation, insufficiency, and shortage of its object: Turkish literature.

In fact not only the critic's but also the reader's critical response is rooted in a similar complaint of insufficiency that has become an almost automatic response, a reflex action throughout the years. Most theoretical works in Turkish give us the impression that they are translations from a Western lan-guage, crude adaptations of an alien theory, shallow imitations of an origi-nal model inevitably deformed when carried to a different cultural scene. It is as if the Western concepts have lost their viability or they have become somewhat decorative figures in an inert local theory that is belated and arti-ficial at the same time. There seems at least to be an irremovable tension between the foreign theory and the local reality, between the alien concepts and the native cultural scene.

Criticism of the novel gets its share from the tension. Most Turkish critics blame Turkish novelists for creating secondhand characters lacking spon-taneity and originality, characters who are prisoners of imitated desires, copied sensibilities, bookish aspirations, and belated torments. It is as if the critical attempt has eliminated itself because of a defect inherent in the object itself, the critic becoming a Western observer entrusted with the task of showing how "presence" is spared from the local object, someone in charge of declaring that the original version of everything local is elsewhere, making record of foreign debts, imitated books, stolen plots, and derived characters. Hence Turkish criticism is born into an arrogant detachment from its object presumed from the very start to be crude, primitive, and childlike.

The criticism of lack is in fact torn between two extremes. The first one assumes that what is original is elsewhere ("outside," namely in the West) while the second insists that we do have an authentic literature and a genuine native thought but in order to appreciate it we have to leave aside all those lifeless imitations and snobbish efforts related with the West.

The first one, accompanied by an unconditional admiration for the foreign model, devaluates its object by reducing it to an import, while the second takes sides with a true self that was almost crushed by the foreign ideal, waiting for the right moment when the oppressed tradition, the repressed past, or the autonomous inner world will speak with a language completely its own. Thus criticism in Turkey is torn between a detached observation reproaching its object for its inadequacy and an ardent search for an authentic localness, between snobbish arrogance and provincialist pride, between an unconditional admiration of the stranger and an unconditional hostility to it.

A fair evaluation will take notice of the desire for originality here: the desire for a novel that has a less traumatic life of its own, for a criticism equipped with concepts not alien to its object, for a critical theory that does not neglect the tensions of living in a cultural climate somewhat different from the others. This desire—before it was frozen into a reflex action—was neatly expressed by Ahmet Hamdi Tanpınar (1901–1962), poet, novelist, essayist, and literary critic, one of the most talented and enlightened figures in the wake of Turkish modernist literature. In the 1936 essay "Our Novel" ["Bizde Roman"] Tanpınar was trying to answer the question "Why don't we have a novel that is specifically ours?" and seeking ways to get rid of the inadequacy he called "the great lack." He explained this defect partly by the fact that Turkish culture does not have "an extensive and tense art life," partly by "the narrowness of individual experience" in Turkish society, sometimes by referring to the differences in class structure in Turkey, sometimes by "the lack of introspection," which he connected with the lack of religious confession in Islam, partly by the fact that visual arts are not that developed in Ottoman-Turkish culture, and mostly by the narrowness of the individual writer's imagination. He too was comparing the Turkish novel with the Western model, pointing out that there is a lack of originality in the Turkish scene. He was also the first critic who formulated the problem as a dilemma: the Turkish writer cannot escape the lack of vitality even when "he generously surrenders himself" to local daily life, but there is always an artificiality, a lack of genuineness when he sails into foreign horizons. Thus the writer is torn between a "funny and wretched" localness and a "crippled and incomplete" foreign model. He is either too much a Westerner or remains the "man of primitive taste." Both positions will bring forth "literary puppets" lacking real depth.[5]

The overwhelming presence of the dilemma had convinced Tanpınar of the necessity of creating a literature that is "totally our own." He believed that a literature which is neither "wretched" nor rootless, neither "funny" nor derivative, neither "primitive" nor imitative, which has both a "human warmth" and a "horizon" will be the result of an original synthesis of native characteristics and European ideals. Tanpınar's every suggestion toward this objective starts with the word *self*: We needed to "go back to ourselves," go back to our own past, go back to our own cultural wealth. In order to create a literature organically ours, we had to "be our own selves." But the dilemma appears once again in the very attempt to transcend it: Tanpınar is talking about creating a national literature rooted in an authentic national self, but the sentence itself is spoken under the very pressure of the foreign model, with the desire to rise to the level of the model, with the objective of winning the admiration of the admired model: "It is impossible for Europeans to admire us because of things that we have borrowed from them. The most they will say is a short 'Well done!' It is only when we introduce to them things that are specifically ours that they will like us, treating us as their equals in the path of beauty and self-realization."[6]

More than half a century later, Orhan Koçak analyzed the same dilemma within a psychoanalytic framework in the 1996 essay "Missed Ideal" on the late Ottoman modernist novelist Halit Ziya Uşaklıgil. The *Tanzimat* (the state-sponsored political reforms of the mid-nineteenth century) had introduced a rift in the Ottoman world by presenting Western culture as an ideal to be embraced, thereby reducing the "local ego" to "a state of infant-like helplessness before the foreign ideal." Later it was the republican state itself that first presented Western culture as an ideal to be embraced and then reprimanded those who embraced the ideal too wholeheartedly. This rift was experienced as a double-bind, resulting in a futility that defined the contours of much of modernist Turkish literature up to this very day. The Ottoman-Turkish writer is doomed to "a local self without an ideal" when he gets in touch with daily life, whereas he is under the command of "foreign desires, copied fancies, borrowed aspirations" when he steps into the world of ideals. There is a shallowness of vision and a sluggishness in the first case while there is a secondhandness and an affectation in the second one.[7]

Hence the double deformation: the local self will cause the foreign ideal to appear as a deformed one, while the foreign ideal has already deformed that local self. The localness ensures that the foreign ideal is artificial, incomplete, and snobbish, whereas the foreign ideal has already transformed that localness into an inert, clumsy, and worn-out provinciality. The ideal will always look like a caricature of itself, something *alafranga* in the local scene, but the local scene itself is already reduced to a caricature of itself, something *alaturka* before the foreign ideal.[8] Thus the double-bind that has defined the profile of the modern Turkish literary scene up to this day: the Turkish novelist is either a snob, a parvenu, a dandy, or an unrefined provincialist stuck in the narrow traditional world.

The question is, How can literature go beyond this double-bind? Is there an original area somewhere between Tanpınar's "funny and wretched" localness and "crippled and incomplete" foreign ideal, or between Koçak's "clumsy and narrow" daily life and the "borrowed" foreign ideal? The same rift is also valid for a literary criticism torn between the arrogant observer's gaze, where the literary work in question is presumed to be the product of an inadequate local self and a proud provincialism speaking on behalf of a local self made miserable by the foreign ideal. But the two divergent stances in fact share the same nationalistic paradigm. Let me remind you of the typical critical comment: the Turkish novel does not say anything to us about us and the characters are imitations of characters from Western works. This recurring complaint, generally accompanied by an accusation of theft, soon transforms the critic into a detective in search of imitated books, stolen plots, and derived characters, in charge of sorting out which is borrowed from which. A vicious circle indeed, but one that has influenced even some of the most talented critics in Turkey. Just to give an example: Tanpınar the critic says that there is "a lack of taste and warmth" due to "the lack of something substantial of our own" in Halit Ziya's novels and years later Tanpınar the novelist is faced with a similar accusation.[9] Suad, the evil-minded character of Tanpınar's 1949 novel *Peace of Mind* [*Huzur*] is said to be unconvincing, rather superficial, because he is a "translation" of Dostoyevsky's abject heroes, especially Stavrogin of *The Possessed*.[10]

But behind the obsession with originality there is the nationalistic reflex[11] which was overtly expressed by the republican literary scholar and historian Mehmed Fuat Köprülü (1890–1966): "Why hasn't the noble and *original Turkish spirit* that has gained 'national victory' and made the 'national reform,' that Turkish character, which is molded in a thousand years of emancipation and sovereignty, which longs for freedom but abhors being the prisoner of foreign cultures, why hasn't this spirit appeared in literature yet? When will we be able to celebrate the national 'masterpiece' which will tell us about the life and mystery of the Turkish people, which will make us conscious of our unconscious emotions?"[12]

In *The Rise of the Novel*, Ian Watt states that the English word *original* has taken its modern meaning by a semantic reversal in the eighteenth century, the period when the novel rose. The word that in the Middle Ages had meant "having existed from the first" came to mean "underived, independent, first-hand" and started being used as a term of praise meaning "novel or fresh in character or style."[13] The Turkish word *orijinal* also has the two meanings "not derived, borrowed or imitated; initial and pristine" and "brand-new, interesting or unique." But the two divergent meanings ("pristine" and "brand-new," "initial" and "inventive"), almost opposites, are united in a single meaning, *orijinal* taken as something interesting or unique since it is the very essence of something rather than its imitation, the product of an autonomous thought, an immediate experience, a spontaneous imagination—something open to the imitation of others rather than being an imitation itself. But the tension between the two meanings is still there. Moreover, the different usages of the word *orijinal*—itself of French origin—display the cultural rift in the Turkish scene. Köprülü's *orijinal Türk ruhu* [original Turkish spirit] refers to a nationalistic spirit imagined to be the spontaneous product of an autonomous national self, whereas the language of the capitalist market tells us that an *orijinal* perfume or an *orijinal* blue jean is an import, products of the domestic market mere imitations. The same ambiguity is also valid for the new Turkish word *özgün* (original) coined from the Turkic *öz* (essence). *Özgün* is both that which is translated into Turkish—or just the contrary, something which is genuinely ours, something related to an originary Turkish essence. But of course it is not only a matter of words. In the Turkish scene, where one constantly needs to translate terms of one culture to those of another (and of course dollars and euros to Turkish liras), meanings constantly shift. As a matter of fact, the Turkish "originality" itself is made up of that shift. The republican language reform, the attempt of producing an *öz Türkçe* (an essential, pure, and genuine Turkish vocabulary) by replacing terms of Arabic and Persian origin involves the enchantment with the West, since it involves the attempt to construct an originary Turkishness from a pre-Ottoman past through philological techniques learned from the West,[14] but it also represents the fear of losing one's identity in that of the Western outsider. Similarly the word *özgün* referring to the same *öz* (essence) as that of *öz Türkçe*, coined to replace the French *orijinal*, displays both the enchantment and the anger involved in Turkey's relationships with the Western world.

In this essay I discuss the specifically Turkish aspects of this desire for originality in the context of literary criticism and the novel. I argue that the overemphasis on originality and the obsessive attempt to create an authentically Turkish novel itself is part of the impasse of belatedness rather than a way out, that the obsession with authenticity itself is the outcome of the very divide that compulsorily made some of us snobs and the rest unrefined provincialists in each other's eyes. Is there or can there be a "Turkish novel that has a distinct identity"[15] working with an authentically Turkish material with a style specifically ours? In order to answer the question I go back to the prehistory of the Turkish novel, a prehistory not only of the Turkish novel but also of Turkish dandyism, focusing on a novel that owes not only its cultural context but also its subject matter to dandyism. This is *The Carriage Affair* [*Araba Sevdası*] by Recaizade Mahmut Ekrem (1847–1914), one of the second-generation *Tanzimat* writers.[16] Within the framework of this novel I try to see whether there are ways, at least in the domain of literature, of aesthetically transcending the dualities of the original and the imitation, the authentic and the derived, the self and the other.

It is accepted that realism—or a realistic romanesque that has moved away from romanticism—in the Turkish novel starts with a grotesque jest, with a novel made up of a "joke," as Tanpınar puts it. This is *The Carriage Affair*, about the spoiled son of an Ottoman aristocrat (Bihruz Bey) and his love for the lady (Periveş Hanım) he meets in Çamlıca, the excursion spot where noble ladies and gentlemen ride their elegant landaus. But Recaizade Ekrem's novel is a "carriage affair" also because it is the story of Bihruz Bey's infatuation with carriages. We soon understand that Bihruz the dandy is in love with the ornate landau that Periveş Hanım rides, with the modernized Çamlıca where he meets her, with Lamartine's poem "Le lac" [The pond] that the pond in Çamlıca reminds him of, with the *Belle Hélène* operetta that he listens to there, and finally, with the images of the French poets that he admires, rather than with the lady herself, whose face he does not properly see. Bihruz Bey's sorrow when he loses his love is no less an imitation: in the center of pain stands Lamartine's *Graziella*, the poem the French poet wrote after the death of the young girl he loved. Just like Bihruz's effort to tell love, his effort to tell pain paves the way for a series of translations (translations of French poems to Turkish), making *The Carriage Affair* a comic novel about misunderstood words.

Let me start with Ahmet Hamdi Tanpınar's interpretation of *The Carriage Affair*. Tanpınar describes the novel as "the work that prepares the Turkish romanesque," but he seems to be uneasy, rather anxious because of the "excessiveness," the "exaggerated mockery" and the "offensive realism" of the novel. According to Tanpınar, it is because of his poor imagination that Ekrem takes refuge in an exaggerated realism; he grasps the comical, but "since he wildly insists on it, beating the strings violently over and over again instead of just touching them, he breaks the instrument." Once again the double-bind: *The Carriage Affair* is a critique of snobbism, a novel about artificiality, rootlessness and excessiveness, a novel about a character made up of exaggerated gestures, but ironically the novel itself is just as excessive, exaggerated, and artificial as the thing it criticizes. *The Carriage Affair* is a "novel of rootless shadows" and the characters in the novel "live a shadowy life, a life exterior to themselves," says Tanpınar. And it is the main character of the novel that troubles him most. Bihruz Bey is a character "hardly present" and the novel lacks "the values that makes a human being a human being." Recaizade Ekrem is unable to tell us about "inwardly felt emotions" and a spontaneous experience.[17]

Let's not be unfair to Tanpınar. *The Carriage Affair* is indeed a grotesque comedy of errors starting and ending with a joke. Bihruz is indeed a character lacking an inner world, a hollow man made up of borrowed gestures. His infatuation with the lady is merely an infatuation with carriages. Thus *The Carriage Affair* is the story of a borrowed model rather than that of natural feelings, the story of romantic gestures rather than spontaneous passions, the story of a derived self rather than an autonomous inner world. But this is exactly what troubles Tanpınar. He says that the novel's main character is not a human being, but an object, the landau itself.

As I mentioned earlier, Tanpınar was one of the most enlightened figures in the wake of Turkish modernism. He was influenced by French poets and writers like Baudelaire, Valéry, and Proust, yet he did not have the aversion to the Ottoman most Westernized and republican intellectuals shared. He favored the idea of an unbroken continuum in cultural history and was occupied with problems of producing an authentic national literature, of creating an original synthesis of native characteristics and European ideals. He called for a "substantial return to our own realities" and to a "personal experience genuinely ours" and was in search of what he called the "inner man," an organically composed and genuine cultural self. Tanpınar's notion of culture was an organicist one, that of an inviolate culture having an integrity of its own. Hence he was for a cultural nationalism accompanied by the insistence to "go back to our own selves."

The conflicts and anxieties behind Tanpınar's stance are evident. The attempt to create a national literature without breaking the cultural continuum is a contradiction in itself, and the very obsession with authenticity represents the anxiety of losing one's self in the "superior" model. Tanpınar's critical responses to *The Carriage Affair* also betray this anxiety. It is unlikely for an organicist like Tanpınar to enjoy a novel about a character living "a life exterior to himself." But that is the whole idea behind Recaizade's novel. The characters in the novel are overshadowed by a landau riding full speed to and from Çamlıca; similarly, Bihruz's efforts to express his love are overshadowed by the texts of the French writers. Without Rousseau's *Nouvelle Heloise* or Lamartine's *Graziella*, without *Manon Lescaut, Paul et Virginie*, or *La Dame aux camélias*, Bihruz can neither fall in love nor shed a tear. He is a man without an interior, since the interior is already composed of the exterior—of borrowed gestures, romantic clichés, and quotations from French writers. For Tanpınar, Bihruz must have been the embodiment of futility, the adulterated "outer man" reminding us that the personal experience Tanpınar cherishes might not be *that* personal after all, or that futility itself is a component of what we call *personal experience* in the modern world. Tanpınar's interpretation of *The Carriage Affair* turns out to be a delimiting one, since he tries to fix a clear boundary between the genuine national self and *Tanzimat*'s snobbish one. He concludes that *The Carriage Affair* is significant since it is the critique of a certain period, the story of a certain generation, a satire on the psychology of an epoch full of Westernized dandies.

Now the question is, Is that so? Is *The Carriage Affair* significant merely because it is the story of a transient fancy, an *alafranga* ambition that has tormented the Abdülaziz period (1861–76) alone? Is it the critique of a rootless generation already left behind, parody of snobbism long surpassed? Is there an "interior," an inner man, and if there is, where shall we look for it?

═══════

Snobbism is defined as something excessive. The snob is not someone who imitates, but someone who imitates excessively, not someone who borrows, but someone who borrows beyond measure, not someone who desires the other's desire, but someone who exaggerates that desire. Thus the critique of snobbism is mostly the critique of excessiveness. There is always someone out there more excessive, more of a caricature than our own true self. The existence of the snob is the guarantee for our feeling genuine ourselves.

Bihruz of *The Carriage Affair* is a typical Westernized *züppe*.[18] He is estranged from traditional Ottoman values, has an unconditional admiration of Western culture and is easily carried away by the consumption regime accompanying modernization. He is intolerant of the "vulgar" folk culture and looks down on the "inadequate" Turkish language, having an inadequate knowledge of French himself. This figure, the Westernized dandy who previously appeared in Ahmet Mithat's novel *Felatun Bey and Rakım Efendi* [*Felatun Bey'le Rakım Efendi*], kept showing up again and again in later *Tanzimat* novels like *Quick to Fall* [*Şıpsevdi*] by Hüseyin Rahmi and *Efruz Bey* by Ömer Seyfettin.[19] In "Excessive Westernization after *Tanzimat*" ["Tanzimat'tan Sonra Aşırı Batılılaşma"], Şerif Mardin rightly says that there is a "Bihruz syndrome" that has affected most writers in the *Tanzimat* period. According to Mardin, the abundance of dandies (thus the strong opposition against them) in *Tanzimat* literature is a response to the shock Western civilization caused in the Ottoman Empire. It is the reaction of the man in the street to the ruling elite, the reaction of the Muslim neighborhood to the pretentious Çamlıca, the reaction of the traditional community to the sinful and carousing Beyoğlu (the Europeanized and cosmopolitan center of Istanbul that represented the new consumption regime, becoming the symbol of an adulterated culture for many Turkish writers, Tanpınar among them). In other words, the abundance of dandies in *Tanzimat* literature represented the discontent of the communitarian low classes who see the market economy and individual consumption as a threat to traditional society. The "Bihruz opposition" was a somewhat new version of folk man

Karagöz's mocking response to the verbose Hacivat, characters of the traditional shadow show. "Bihruz syndrome" represented both an admiration of the material features of Western culture and a communitarian conservatism against modernism, a conservatism that labels that admiration as something evil and sinful. Mockery of the dandy was an aspect of social control toward those not obeying communitarian norms, those deaf to people wearing *shalwars* and veils. It was a social control aiming to cast out the excessively Westernized elite in charge of modernization.[20]

Mockery of this rootless creature, this freak of nature, this pretentious extravagant called *züppe* also had a significant place in the political discourse of modern Turkey. The belittling Turkish terms *tatlı su frengi* (freshwater French) or *salon sosyalisti* (living-room socialist) are examples of a similar reaction. The *züppe*, who is both a snob, the slave of the fashionable, and a dandy who pays exaggerated attention to physical appearance "just like a woman," represented the opposite of both warlike manly values and those of the street and the community. Mardin rightly states that the opposition to the *züppe* was influential in Turkey up to the 1960s as an opposition to socialism. It is a response that left its traces in Turkish nationalism and anti-Western chauvinism. As a matter of fact, traces of the "Bihruz syndrome" are seen in Turkey even today in the opposition to intellectuals that was an important component of the cultural climate following the military coup in 1980. The *entel* figure (*entel* being the belittling abbreviation of the Turkish word *entellektüel* meaning "intellectual") was the main target of Turkish humor and especially of Turkish caricature in the 1980s and 1990s, and the word *entel* has a popular usage today designating people torn away from life and, of course, from manly virtues, people occupied with insignificant details, excessively sophisticated and rather effeminate. Hence *züppe* designates both the imitating snob and the effeminate dandy.

Now let's go back to *The Carriage Affair*, since there is a question about the novel we have not answered yet. Why does a Westernized writer like Recaizade Ekrem, famous for his literary refinement, make fun of the Westernized dandy? Previously Ahmet Mithat had done so, but he was a writer of artisan origins dedicated to enlightening the majority, expressing their sorrows, speaking for virtues such as laboriousness, thrift, and being content with what one has, an advocate of the "genuine Turks and blessed Muslims," a novelist who took "art for art's sake" to be an irrelevant fancy. What is rather complicated is Ekrem's case: How does a writer famous as a man of

Man with mannequin 1. Photo by Arif Aşçı.

Man with mannequin 2. Photo by Arif Aşçı.

alafranga comforts, an advocate of "art for art's sake," become hostile to the dandy? How is that possible?

Mardin's answer to the question is a sociological one. What makes Ekrem an opponent of the dandy is his closeness to the Young Ottomans, the elites that did not benefit from the blessings of the *Tanzimat* as much as they wanted, intellectuals discontent with the speed of social mobilization in the process of modernization, who stood for a populist critique making use of the discontent of the lower classes. Hence the Young Ottomans leaned on a "Bihruz opposition" in their political struggle against the upper bureaucracy, blaming the *Tanzimat* advocates for creating a new nobility and forgetting the man in the street. This opposition was instrumental rather than spontaneous and became an instrument in the hands of these intellectuals who themselves were advocates of modernization, an instrument of mobilizing the masses under their own limited and rather conservative modernization project. Thus the "Bihruz opposition" was a common denominator of the traditional upper- and lower-class cultures. It was the product of the estrangement of both the community and the communitarian Ottoman ruling elite from the new consumption regime.

Sociology explains why the dandy figure is so central in *Tanzimat* literature and why Ekrem made the effort to write a satire on dandyism. It also explains why the mockery of the dandy is so central even in today's Turkish political thought. But there are things that sociology does not explain. What makes *The Carriage Affair* unique among *Tanzimat* novels, what makes it something more than a document of the "Bihruz syndrome," is not its being a satire leaning on communitarian values, but rather its failure to be a satire. In satire there is an insurmountable wall, an unsurpassable boundary between the false other and the true self, and it is by mocking the false other that the writer ensures the true self. The satirical voice is a self-confident, determined, and clear voice. This is exactly what *The Carriage Affair* lacks. There is neither a firm narrator nor a resolute authorial voice in the novel to denounce the foppish Bihruz. It is rather a hesitant, faltering, and undecided voice that we find there, wavering between the third-person singular and the first-person plural, between the authorial voice of the narrator and the *alafranga* of Bihruz, a voice that does not differentiate itself from that of the mocked character. It is this faltering voice that makes *The Carriage Affair* a novel going out of order, a novel in which the writer loses its voice among voices and texts other than his own. Even if we presume that Ekrem shares the truth with his public (even if he is against the *züppe*, that *alafranga* malady threatening communitarian values) we soon understand that the possibility of telling the truth has already been lost. The writer is no longer the guardian of the true self, since language itself does not work.

The Carriage Affair is a patchwork of different styles. The *alafranga* of Bihruz, the high style of the first-generation *Tanzimat* writers, an artificial language borrowed from the French romantics, and Ekrem's own realistic voice exist side by side in the novel. But that is what this novel is all about. Bihruz spends all his time translating one language into another. He translates Rousseau into Turkish only to find that Turkish is not "adequate" enough. He translates a chansonnette from the *Divan* by Vâsıf (the Ottoman poet he calls "the Béranger of the Turks" and the only Turkish poet "worthy of his fame"), only to find that this language is "as strange to him as Chinese" and that he does not understand a word without the Ottoman dictionary prepared by the Englishman Redhouse. Thus *The Carriage Affair* turns out to be a work displaying "semantic dilemmas, communication impasses and strategies that negate its own text," a "symbol of the literary crises of the period," as Jale Parla has aptly shown in a detailed stylistic analysis.[21]

Rather than being a satire leaning on traditional communitarian values, *The Carriage Affair* is a text representing the unavoidable literary crises of the *Tanzimat* writer (who by definition proceeds by translating communitarian values into innovative ones), a text displaying the unavoidable accident that accompanies the act of translation itself, a black parody hinting at its own pretension—its own snobbism. As to snobbism itself, rather than being a ridiculous excessiveness, it points to the possibility of unveiling the characteristic feature of the weird creature called *Tanzimat novel*. It is the childlike desire of the snob that enables us to see that the carriage is "bought by debt," love is borrowed, emotions are bookish—and the novel imported.

Tanpınar criticizes Ekrem because it is the carriage rather than a human being that becomes the protagonist of *The Carriage Affair*. But rather than being a weakness, that is the main craft of Ekrem's novel. Both the carriage and the novel are symbols of the same foreign ideal, the same borrowed consumption regime, the same imported modern life. Hence the *Tanzimat* writer's infatuation with novels is as artificial as Bihruz's infatuation with carriages. Bihruz falls in love with the lady because he likes her landau; Ekrem has fallen in love with the novel since it is a Western import, something that will carry him away from that "clumsy bunch of words" called Turkish literature and closer to the admired world of Lamartine and Alfred de Musset. The car, which Henri Lefebvre calls the "king of objects" or the "king-object," the object that is the sign of consumption as well as a scene for the consumption of signs,[22] becomes in *The Carriage Affair* the symbol of not only changing places but also changing identities. (The "consumption of signs" has a vital importance for Bihruz; wherever he goes, "he aims not to see and be seen, but only to be seen.") It represents the promise of a second life, the effort of being someone other than one's inadequate self, the chance to imagine and show oneself as the other, the attempt to close the distance between traditional Süleymaniye and modern Çamlıca (or between the belatedly modern Çamlıca and Paris itself) and thus the worried exertion of closing the gap between the periphery and capital of desire—just like the novel itself. But let's not forget that the landau of *The Carriage Affair* is "bought by debt" and that it will be in an accident, its axle broken, its paint coming off—just like *The Carriage Affair* itself, which is a book of accidents and a novel going out of order. Thus the carriage turns out to be the very symbol of a modern technique that cannot be mastered, the symbol of the foreign toy called the novel borrowed at the same time from the very same place as the carriage itself. In the land of the "traffic monster"[23] and belated novels, it is as if the "king-object" is pointing to the unavoidable accident at the origin of the construct *Turkish novel.*

—————

Let's ask Şerif Mardin's question once again, this time trying to answer it while staying within the literary domain, by referring to the possibilities of literature itself rather than those of sociology. How come a Westernized writer like Recaizade Ekrem makes fun of the Westernized dandy?

Although close to Young Ottoman ideals, Ekrem was farther away from politics compared to the first-generation *Tanzimat* writers. At the time he was one of the few writers adhering to the principle of "art for art's sake," which was taken by his contemporaries as a self-indulgent, extravagant, and hence snobbish endeavor, since the supporters of "art for art's sake" were accused of not taking literature as a medium for social mobilization and of sacrificing meaning for art. Ekrem was the founder of *Servet-i Fünun* literature, accused by Ahmet Mithat and other contemporaries of being decadent, and was later accused by others of escapism, artificiality, and rootlessness. He was an advocate of the innovators opposing Muallim Naci, the chief spokesman for previous literature. He was not much interested in the Arabian or Persian literatures, influenced more by the French romantics who sublimate the autonomy of human emotions—just like Bihruz himself. He translated and dramatized the *Atala* of the romantic Chateaubriand, was influenced by Alfred de Musset and Lamartine, wrote the sentimental love story *Muhsin Bey* after reading Lamartine's *Graziella*, and entitled his volume of poems *Meditation* [*Tefekkür*]—just like Lamartine, the poet of *Méditations.* Tanpınar states that before he wrote *The Carriage Affair*, he composed sentimental poems displaying a "postcard sentimentality," liked things that were "sad and sentimental," was fond of "emotional and pathetic things" and insisted on a "weepy voice on the accidents of life." Even the poem he wrote for his dead son, *Nejad-Ekrem*, was a monument of romantic clichés. He probably wrote it after he read "La Mort de Julie," the poem Lamartine wrote for his daughter who died during the east journey.

Tanpınar's critical remarks on Recaizade Ekrem are significant. Ekrem was "a man wide open to all the influences around him," he was "under the influence of ideas spreading like malaria at the time," he wrote in "a language in utter confusion," he searched for a taste of language and tried to master the *aruz* verse, but "all in vain." He was "the victim of a crises of taste" and wrote "hollow verses under the influence of an excessive sensibility learned from French books" and composed "with a belated romanticism loose pieces of poetry of childish content, poems full of histrionic gestures displaying an uncontrolled taste and an empty sensibility."[24] It is as if Tanpınar is describing Bihruz, the man empty inside, the puerile dandy incapable of developing an inner world of his own. But it is not Tanpınar himself but his mentor, the poet Yahya Kemal, who openly accuses Ekrem (because of his *alafranga* behavior and dandyish attitudes) of being a Bihruz himself: "Ekrem Bey is just another Bihruz, that is all!"[25]

The state of belatedness concerns not only ideas and ideologies but also desires and aspirations, anxieties and fears, envies and resentments—the desire to be the other and the fear of losing one's self in the other. The writer is always already working in that space made up of aspirations and frustrations, prides and shames, the self and the other. Now the question is, Hasn't Recaizade Ekrem felt that he has his share of "bihruzness" himself? Hasn't he noticed that what he calls his *inner world* is also composed of romantic clichés, stolen similes, and verbosity? Can it be that he hasn't noted that his own love of novels is a love of changing identities? Let's ask ourselves: Could it be that reading *The Carriage Affair* merely as a satire of the foppish Bihruz—as we were taught by our teachers at school—involves the attempt to hide the inevitable snobbism at the origin of our own identities, the self we call the *original Turkish spirit*? Can it be that we haven't noticed that this national self established its very "originality" by hiding its own Westernized aspirations, constantly projecting snobbism to the excessive other, the dandyish *Tanzimat* self?

The mainstream critical opinion is that *Tanzimat* novelists filled their novels with clichés stolen from Western writers, with puppets complete strangers to us since they lacked introspection. Now it is time to move one step further. What if that is what they saw there? When they were looking inside themselves, what if someone else—a deformed and a distorted figure but someone else indeed—looked back at them? What if the place called *inside* consists of an outside? What if the inner world is made up of accidents and traumas rather than being a "natural treasure" that is always already there? What if it is "the ideas spreading like malaria" or the "unwanted guests"[26] themselves that make up the place we call the *interior*?

We surely do not know whether Ekrem was preoccupied by these questions. But we know that it is impossible to speak of a genuine self or an organic body in a culture in the big rush to translate French works, together with the classical works that have been models to the French themselves, where the self itself has become a noisy field of discourse, a procession of books, a battleground of models. Obviously Ekrem himself drifted in the same wind and probably felt thwarted by the same obstacles as the character Bihruz. Hence *The Carriage Affair* gives us the chance to think about the inevitable snobbism not only of the Ottoman dandy, but also of the Turkish writer, critic, and reader, since what is called Turkishness itself involves at the very origin the currently irremovable rift between a snobbish self and an authentic one, between an *alafranga* self and an *alaturka* one. This is what Mardin's sociological explanation of *The Carriage Affair* disregards. The attempt to read *The Carriage Affair* merely as a satire, as something less than what it is, places not only its writer but also its critic in an autonomous space uncontaminated by snobbism.

Tanpınar was well aware that the protagonist of *The Carriage Affair* was someone "almost absent," that the authorial voice itself was almost absent. Hence the anxiety: He described the prospective synthesis between the Western ideals and native characteristics with the metaphor of the body, the living organism whose parts functioned in perfect harmony, whereas Ekrem was talking about an utter oddity in which native characteristics and foreign ideals had irreparably deformed each other. Bihruz's inner world is a manufactured—or in his own *alafranga* Turkish—a *fabrike edilmiş* (fabricated) world. Moreover, not only the main character of the novel but the novel itself is a freak of nature, the product of the encounter of "two antagonistic epistemological systems."[27] Tanpınar was the man of possibilities: He longed for an inviolate culture and insisted on an aesthetics of harmony that can possibly reproduce the integrity and intactness lost in real life. As for Ekrem, his idea of the comical rested on impossibilities. He suggested that what we call *old culture* is reduced to a dictionary (the Ottoman dictionary prepared by an Englishman), that an East-West synthesis will necessarily be deformed and disfigured. Tanpınar was in search of what he called the inner man while Ekrem suggested that the inner man himself might be made up of foreign influences and external pressures. Tanpınar invited us to "go back to ourselves," while Ekrem implied that it may be too late to go back to an intact self.

In the Turkish cultural scene of the 1980s and 1990s, when there was an outburst of repressed "authentic selves," we noticed the impasse once more: We cannot go back to our selves, since what we call *self* always appears as something altered under the other's look, sometimes as a defense mechanism, sometimes as a nationalistic resentment, and mostly as a demand for power, at least as an element of decoration, since the true self can easily be reduced to a decorative Eastern effect—unless it is not problematized. Yes, it is always too late to go back to an original self, and in fact the invitation to go back to an original self is the expression of belatedness itself.

≡≡≡≡

I tried to problematize the specifically Turkish aspects of the obsession with originality, but we know that originality and authenticity are not problems of belatedly modernized cultures alone, that originality acquired a transcendent value also in nineteenth-century Western Europe—ironically when spontaneity itself was at stake. A comparison between Recaizade's Bihruz and Flaubert's Emma Bovary might enable us to observe the common features of the problem of borrowed personality in the novels of the periphery and the metropolis.[28] What makes the Ottoman dandy and the provincial French woman alike is that both lack spontaneity and are reduced to bookish passions.[29] Emma is provoked to love by the romantic novels "full of gloomy forests, romantic intrigue, vows, sobs, embraces and tears,"[30] as is Bihruz by the "desire-invoking novels" his French teacher Monsieur Piyer recommends. Emma craves for Paris once she breathes "the dust of cheap novels" she devours when only fifteen, and so does Bihruz, because he has read the French romantics at a young age. As a matter of fact, Bihruz and Emma are fond of the very same book. Emma reads Bernardin de Saint-Pierre's *Paul et Virginie*—the love story of unadulterated hearts in the midst of intact nature—in the monastery at a young age; Bihruz reads the same book just a few months before he falls in love with Periveş Hanım. *Paul et Virginie*'s influence is rather ironic in both cases. It is a book on intactness and naturalness, but it soon becomes the model to pretenders imitating the other's desire.

There is one more similarity between Emma and Bihruz worth mentioning. Both motherless Emma and fatherless Bihruz are provoked into conspicuous consumption. Emma, who gets to know the latest fashions of the capital from the press and who loves literature because it stirs her desires, is impelled to buy the latest goods so that she can make her bookish self real. Thus what is more significant in this first "tragedy of the consumer"[31] is the description of goods—silk curtains, silver candlesticks, champagne spilling out from slender glasses, feathery slippers of pink satin, and silver cigarette cases—rather than Emma's loving feelings. Similarly, readers of *The Carriage Affair* will recall the trademark of Bihruz's stylish overcoat, the label on his brightly polished ankle boots, the enameled watch he carries in the pocket of his white vest, and his silver stemmed walking cane rather than his feelings for Periveş Hanım. Furthermore, the central theme of *The Carriage Affair* is a secondary one in *Madame Bovary*: Emma has the secret desire of possessing a blue carriage pulled by English horses. The carriage is once again the symbol of changing places (from the peripheral Yonville to Paris) and thus of identities. The carriage will first whip desire and then carry the periphery closer to the capital of desire—just like the novels themselves. What René Girard describes as a "literary inculcation," what he calls the "seminal function of literature," is central to both Bihruz-ism and Bovarysm.[32] It is because of this literary inculcation that Emma deems Rudolphe a prince with the white horse and Bihruz takes the loose coquette for a noble lady.

Jules de Gaultier wrote his famous essays on Bovarysm at the turn of the century, defining Bovarysm as the lack of "an auto-suggestion from within," which made the Bovaryst character fated to obey the "suggestion of an external milieu."[33] Flaubert's characters were marked by "an essential lack of a fixed character and originality of their own," escaping from their insufficiencies by identifying with an image they took for their own, per-ceiving themselves as the other ("seeing themselves as they are not") since they were nothing of their own accord. Despite all their differences (Emma fails because nothing works out the way she pretends; Bihruz, on the other hand, standing somewhere between Gaultier's "Bovarysm triumphant" and "puerile Bovarysm," starts and ends as a childlike pretender never facing the tragic end) they shared the same lack of originality, the same lack of autosuggestion from within.

Girard's *Deceit, Desire, and the Novel* was written against the romantic thesis that mimetic desire is less powerful than spontaneous desire. Accord-ing to Girard, desire is not autonomous or spontaneous but mediated, involving the mediation of a model, the desire of the other—the desire to be another. Flaubert's Bovaryst characters, Stendhal's *vaniteux*, Proust's dandy, and Dostoyevsky's underground man revealed the dynamic relationship between individual and collective desire, the hostile dialogue between the self and the other, showing us that the "interior garden" so often praised by the romantic critics is never a "solitary garden." All great novels, to the extent they break the illusion of the autonomous self, show us that the snob's desire is not a stranger to us. Dostoyevsky's character descends to the underground to feel the pride and suffering of being unique but ends up with a principle of universal application: the moment he feels he has distanced himself from the others is the moment that he feels closest to them.

Girard's theory of "triangular" (or "metaphysical") desire provides an important framework for the discussion on snobbism. The snob is a caricature, and like all caricatures it exaggerates the lines, but while doing so it openly reveals the mimetic nature of all desire. Neither the desire of the child nor that of the lover is more spontaneous or original than that of the snob. Snobbism is significant here once again in relation to our reading strategies. There is an irony in the critic's sublimation of the originality of Don Quixote ("the imitation of imitations") or praising the underground man as the apostle of spontaneity. Such a reading represents the modern self's effort to differentiate from the other, being prone to forget the role the other plays in the genesis of one's own desire. In the destructive anger against snobbism—in the effort to carry Bihruzism outside the autonomous self—there is the troubled attempt to build an autonomy already lost. What Girard calls "romantic pride" is the tendency to see the natural child in our own self while seeing the artificial snob in the other. One will willingly reveal the role of the mediator in others, willingly mock snobbism as a "vice we ourselves have fortunately been spared," so that one can hide the role of mediation in one's own desire: "Ekrem Bey is just another Bihruz, that is all!" Yet at a closer look we should be able to notice that the snob enrages us because it is a "tasteless caricature" of our own desires. It is because of our own desire to be the other, because of the incompleteness of that desire, that the snob particularly arouses our disdain.

That Girard's theory of desire is a universal one hardly taking into account local, cultural, or national differences can be taken as a theoretical weakness. But the theory of mimetic desire takes its very universality from the fact that its object—desire itself—has already been universalized. It is not a mere coincidence that Girard bases his theory mostly on the novel of the nineteenth century, the epoch when spontaneity and originality both acquired a transcendent value and lost ground, when autonomous nature was both romanticized and overshadowed by a second nature made up of external suggestions, when not only capital and goods or ideas and ideologies but also desires and aspirations spread to virginal lands no matter what the race, the country, or continent is, when laws of desire themselves were universalized, all eyes turning from London ("the working house of the world") to Paris ("the capital of desire"), the concept "desire" becoming more important than that of "need."[34] Girard himself underlines that mimetic desire is the desire of an epoch of modern reconciliation rather than that of violence and arbitrariness, the desire of a society where individuals are "free and equal by law" in the sense that everyone imitates everyone else. Thus the new reader is a mimetic one, universal in the sense that he lives in the same universe of desire as the others, prone to make the other's desire his own. *Graziella* is the bedside book of both Flaubert and Ekrem and similarly *Paul et Virginie* is the bedside book of both Emma and Bihruz.[35]

But let's not disregard the disparity accompanying capitalist universalization. Not only the novels but also our own personal experiences tell us that the journey toward desire is always from the dull periphery toward the glimmering capital—even in reversed journeys where virgin wilderness, noble savage, exotic East, natural native, or innocent child become the object of longing. Desire always goes after capital from the periphery toward the homeland of capital, toward glittering goods and dazzling objects. In fact it is this very distance—distance to the capital of desire—that makes modern provinciality what it is. There is never an autonomous and self-sufficient province that can "go back to itself"; on the contrary, the province is always what is provincialized, seized, and seduced by the "superior" other. The novelistic characters who are slaves of external suggestions are imitative to the extent that they are seized by this seductive light. Emma has lost her originality because she has devoured books full of descriptions of wild desire, because the characters in these books "glimmer as comets in the dark sky of history," because this encounter with light has created an irreparable rift in her self. Hence numerous novels tell us how the glittering light has irrecoverably turned one's self to a dull district, a primitive and worn-out province. For Emma her husband is tasteless and unrefined because of his plain talk and ideas devoid of fantasy. Even nature gets its share from the conversion: The snowy mountains of Switzerland give Emma a sense of sublimation, whereas her own garden has turned into an uninspiring place blunting the soul. For Bihruz the Turkish language itself has become an uninspiring tongue incapable of expressing sublime feelings; thus the effort to speak of desire will always be hindered by the "inadequacy" of the Turkish language.

This provides us with a broader framework for discussing belatedness. In the modern world being belated is imagining oneself peripheral, provincial, underdeveloped, and inadequate, and it is precisely this inadequacy the snob hides. Thus the figures of the pretentious snob and the unrefined provincial, rather than being opposites, are the two faces of the same figure. Girard states that Don Quixote is merely a snob in the eyes of his peers, the petty squires. Similarly Emma must have been a snob in the eyes of the people of Yonville. And when we scrape off Bihruz's dandyism, we find underneath the orphaned Ottoman pushed to the periphery of the world, to a dull district culturally remote from the center called West. And it is no coincidence that the dual identity called Turkishness, that bipolar modern self involving both the state of drifting toward the foreign ideal and the effort to go back to an original self, that desire to be another and the fear of losing oneself in the other, is always preoccupied with exteriorizing the figures of the snob and the unrefined provincial in order to be autonomous and original itself. Therefore it is these tasteless caricatures themselves that precisely define this "original" self. That is why we prefer to read *The Carriage Affair* merely as a satire on snobbism, as a manifesto of the opposition to Bihruz.

‗‗‗‗‗

The effort to go back to a genuine self was linked with the invention of a belated national literature, but the problem of literary genuineness certainly involves more than that. I mentioned earlier that most Turkish critics accuse Turkish novelists of creating borrowed characters lacking a genuine voice of their own. The irony is that the history of the novel since *Don Quixote* is full of characters living in the world of borrowed ideals and bookish aspirations, characters who thereby fail in evaluating the real world. It is no coincidence that novelistic characters are condemned to an ordinary fate to the extent that they long for something exceptional: a genuine voice of their own. In *Crime and Punishment* Raskolnikov sheds blood because he wants to differentiate himself from the ordinary masses, taking great pains to be like Napoléon, just to see in the end that his bloody act is nothing but an ordinary judicial case, himself nothing but a "pale copy of characters from a foreign novel." The underground man curses the common laws just to see in the end that the curse itself is just as borrowed and bookish as the thing he curses. Krilov of *The Possessed* prefers death in order to challenge God with the "courage to desire nothingness," but his death itself will merely be an imitation of Christ's death. The Turkish scene is no different. In Tanpınar's *Peace of Mind*, Suad, the evil-minded dandy, commits suicide as a challenge to the intellectuals of mediocre ideas and moderate sensibilities, but his suicide (accompanied by a Beethoven concerto) is nothing but an imitation, a literary cliché borrowed from a Dostoyevsky book. In Oğuz Atay's 1971 novel *The Disconnected* [*Tutunamayanlar*], the bookworm Selim, coming from a small town, cannot grow up because he confuses what is bookish and what is real, perishing early in life because of the desire to be a Dostoyevsky, a Gorky, and an Oscar Wilde, all at the same time.[36] The case of Lado in Latife Tekin's 1984 narrative *The Berji Kristin: Tales from the Garbage Hills* [*Berci Kristin Çöp Masalları*] is no different. Lado, the hero of the shanties on the garbage hills adopting a new consumption regime — not with silver candlesticks and silk curtains as in *Madame Bovary*, nor with enameled watches and amber prayer beads as in *The Carriage Affair*, but with fruit powders and blue jeans — is also obsessed with books. He is secretly writing "the novel of his life" — but in vain.

The novel emerged with the claim to originality. It was to take its subject matter from individual experience rather than from mythology, legend, past history, or previous literature. It needed to be loyal only to individual experience rather than being loyal to previous models or canons. It was to benefit from all previous genres without the imperative to obey a rule. That is where the dilemma appears: in order to be original, the novel has to be loyal to an experience that is locally or individually unique, but in the epoch of contagious ideas and contaminative desires, local or individual experience is always faced with the problem of belatedness. Hence the history of the novel involves the claim to originality as much as the experience of losing that originality, an outburst of local color as much as the conquest of what we call *localness*, an eruption of individuality as much as the danger of losing that individuality. Likewise it involves an outburst of interiority as much as the awareness that the inner world is reduced to external suggestions, clichés, and affectations. In fact what we call *interiority* in the novel is mostly the awareness that interiority is endangered, nativity conquered, and naturalness lost forever.

These certainly do not explain the difference between Flaubert's objective seriousness and Recaizade's grotesque humor, or Flaubert's detached ironic attitude and Recaizade's black parody, or Flaubert's stylishness and Recaizade's "accidental" style, or the difference between the confessional tone of the French writer ("Madame Bovary, c'est moi!") and the accusative tone in the Turkish scene ("Ekrem Bey is just another Bihruz, that is all!"). In this essay I deliberately tried to underline the surprising similarities between the two scenes, the similar psychological ground nourishing different novels, so that we can draw outlines of a paradigm not disregarding cultural differences but free of discriminative culturalism.[37] Since it is these similarities that make novels something more than documents of nationalistic or local identity, calling our attention to the modern dilemma the Ottoman dandy shares with the French provincial, the French provincial with the hidalgo of La Mancha, the hidalgo of La Mancha with the Russian underground man, the Russian underground man with the "disconnected" Turkish intellectual.

Let's go back to *The Carriage Affair*. Though we have sparks of irony there, it is not a novel of an antagonistic self divided between longings and realities, suffering because of the failure to be genuine. As soon as he realizes that Periveş Hanım is in fact a loose coquette, that love is merely a provocation and pain a hackneyed gesture, the puerile dandy hops in the carriage and leaves the scene forever. The encounter with reality does not lead to a change, a conflict, a crisis, or a fragmentation in Bihruz's static character. But despite this novelistic weakness, *The Carriage Affair* is a significant work since it has drawn the irreversible line in the Turkish novel, pointing out that snobbism is the constitutive element of the "original Turkish spirit" itself, where not only gestures and appearances but the inner world itself is at stake. If there is a weakness in the modern Turkish novel, it is not because it has not returned to an original self, but because it has not faced the inevitable lack of originality, the fact that it is always too late to return to an original self.

There is a grotesque episode in the 1974 novel *Dangerous Games* [*Tehlikeli Oyunlar*] by Oğuz Atay, master of irony in the Turkish novel. In this dream episode, an encyclopedia of Hikmet (the main character of the novel, whose name means "wisdom" or "inner knowledge" associated with the East) is to be written by Hikmet himself and some others. But it turns out in the dream that those others are Englishmen and they have given up the project, saying, "The man of an underdeveloped country cannot have an inner world of his own." The strength of Atay's irony lies in the fact that the statement is true and of course false at the same time. Among other things, Atay told us about the pain and anger accompanying feelings of inadequacy, that feeling of "being duped," that of "being on the scene as a servant and a fool," but he handled that vast psychic material that is painful and comic at the same time both by dismantling the romantic discourse of victimization deemed proper to the Eastern people and by working through the literary problems of belatedness and affectation, problems not only of belatedly modernized literature but of all literature, itself always belated to what we call individual experience. It was this working through, this inner knowledge that the inner world becomes inner to the extent it faces its own inevitable dependency, which enabled Atay to create a genuine voice of his own in Turkish literature.

≡≡≡≡

Going back to the ideal of originality so pivotal in Turkish literary criticism, I will say that the two seemingly divergent approaches share the same reifying paradigm assuming a mechanical relationship between the self and the other. The first ("We don't have an original novel") takes originality as a standard applied merely to our "clumsy" reality, taking the Western model itself as a monument of originality, while the second (inviting us to "go back to our selves") disregards the fact that this self is already shaped by the other, that the effort to produce a national literature, an original novel, an autonomous aesthetic culture in a belatedly modernized culture itself is inevitably a belated strategy. This is the double-bind of Turkish criticism, treating its object either as a snobbish endeavor or as something primitive, childlike, and provincial. But this is also the source of critical authority. The critic thereby becomes either the guardian of an originality that is presumed to be elsewhere or that of a repressed true self unable to speak with a language its own.

Yet Turkish literary criticism—just like the Turkish novel itself—was born in the midst of ambivalent feelings of admiration and contempt, fascination and anxiety, felt before European culture. In other words, it was born as an anxious effort to explain the "great lack." This gives it the ability to be in empathy with the novel. But its effort to walk one step ahead, imposing a rigid standard of originality to the novelist, making an invoice of foreign debts, limits both itself and the novel. Rather than a simple-hearted call for originality, rather than constantly reproducing the discourse of lack and victimization, criticism should work with concepts that can appreciate the accidents and traumas that make up the space we call *self*, concepts that relate cultural belatedness to the belatedness of literature, of not only belatedly modernized literature but all modern literature, which is always belated to a genuine experience. I think that is the moment in criticism when both modern arrogance and romantic pride may fade out.

Notes

1 Gregory Jusdanis, *Belated Modernity and Aesthetic Culture: Inventing National Literature* (Minneapolis: University of Minnesota Press, 1991).

2 Daryush Shayegan, *Le Regard mutilé: Schizophrénie culturelle: Pays traditionnels face à la modernité* (Paris: Albin Michel, 1989), 83.

3 Jale Parla argues that the Turkish novel is born into a fatherlessness, not only because the first Turkish novels were about fatherless boys, but also because the first novelists had to assume the role of the father at an early age, being "authoritative children" themselves, to compensate for the lack of political and intellectual power in the society at large. Jale Parla, *Babalar ve Oğullar* (Istanbul: İletişim Yayınları, 1990).

4 Orhan Koçak, "Kaptırılmış İdeal: *Mai ve Siyah* Üzerine Psikanalitik Bir Deneme," *Toplum ve Bilim*, no. 70 (1996): 94–152.

5 For Tanpınar's remarks on the subject, see "Bizde Roman" (1 and 2), "Milli Bir Edebiyata Doğru," and "Türk Edebiyatında Cereyanlar," all in Ahmet Hamdi Tanpınar, *Edebiyat Üzerine Makaleler* (Istanbul: Dergâh Yayınları, 1992). Also see "Ahmet Hamdi Tanpınar'la Bir Konuşma," in *Yaşadığım Gibi* (Istanbul: Dergâh Yayınları, 2000).

6 Tanpınar, "Milli Bir Edebiyata Doğru," 91.

7 Koçak, "Kaptırılmış İdeal," 118, 147.

8 In Turkish, *alafranga* is the belittling term for "French style," "something or someone snobbish, imitating European ways" and *alaturka* is the belittling term for "Turkish style," "something or someone stuck in the narrow traditional world."

9 Halit Ziya Uşaklıgil was accused of escapism, decadence, and superficial Westernism not only by his Ottoman contemporaries but also by the literary guardians of the newly formed Turkish Republic. For Tanpınar's remarks, see Ahmet Hamdi Tanpınar, *Yahya Kemal* (Istanbul: Yapı Kredi Yayınları, 2001), 69.

10 Fethi Naci, "Huzur," in *Yüzyılın Yüz Romanı* (Istanbul: Adam Yayınları, 1999), 249; Mehmet Kaplan, "Bir Şairin Romanı: Huzur," *Türk Dili ve Edebiyatı Dergisi*, December 31, 1962, 37–38. See also Berna Moran, "Bir Huzursuzluğun Romanı," in *Türk Romanına Eleştirel Bir Bakış*, vol. 1 (Istanbul: İletişim Yayınları, 1987), 274–75. For a discussion of Suad's evil-minded dandyism, see Nurdan Gürbilek, "Kötü Çocuk Türk (1)," in *Kötü Çocuk Türk* (Istanbul: Metis Yayınları, 2001), 66–88.

11 Victoria Holbrook discusses how the search for an originary Turkishness was accompa-

nied by the undervaluation of traditional modes of expression as Ottoman, stating that "to be original was to be Turkish, not Ottoman." *The Unreadable Shores of Love: Turkish Modernity and Mystic Romance* (Austin: University of Texas Press, 1994), 23.

12 Mehmet Kaplan, Zeynep Kerman, and İnci Enginün, eds., *Atatürk Devri Fikir Hayatı II* (Ankara: Kültür Bakanlığı Yayınları, 1981), 131–33; emphasis added.

13 Ian Watt, *The Rise of the Novel* (London: Penguin, 1972), 15.

14 For a discussion of the relation between Turkish nationalistic ideals and Western philological techniques, see Holbrook, *Unreadable Shores*, 13–31.

15 Cemil Meriç, *Kırk Ambar*, vol. 1 of *Rümuz-ül Edeb* (Istanbul: İletişim Yayınları, 1988), 15.

16 Recaizade Mahmut Ekrem, *Araba Sevdası*, ed. Seyit Kemal Karaalioğlu (Istanbul: İnkilap Kitabevi, 1985). Ekrem's novel was first published in 1896.

17 Tanpınar, "Romana ve Romancıya Dair Notlar III," "Recâi Zâde Mahmud Ekrem," in *Edebiyat Üzerine Makaleler*, 67 and 248–53; "Recâi Zâde Mahmud Ekrem Bey," in Tanpınar, *19. Asır Türk Edebiyatı Tarihi*, vol. 1 (Istanbul: İstanbul Üniversitesi Edebiyat Fakültesi Yayınları, 1956), 467–96.

18 The Turkish term *züppe* is used for both the "dandy" and the "snob." Snobbism is generally defined as a blatant imitation and the state of openly seeking association with the "superior" other and rebuffing those regarded as inferior, whereas *dandyism* is distinguished by both an exaggerated attention to personal appearance and a cold indifference, a pretension to self-sufficiency and an "ascetism for the sake of desire," as René Girard puts it, the dandy "acting as a magnet for unattached desires." But in this essay I don't attribute a significant difference to the terms *dandyism* and *snobbism*. Bihruz is both a Westernized dandy and a snob, paying exaggerated attention to how he looks, openly imitating the "superior" other, rebuffing his own people, culture, and language as inferior. René Girard aptly discusses literary dandyism within the broader context of snobbism in *Deceit, Desire, and the Novel: Self and Other in Literary Structure*, trans. Yvonne Freccero (Baltimore: The John Hopkins University Press, 1988), 162–64.

19 Berna Moran, *Türk Romanına Eleştirel Bir Bakış*, vol. 1 (Istanbul: İletişim Yayınları, 1987), 73. For an essay on the transformation of the dandy figure in Turkish novel, see Moran's "Alafranga Züppeden Alafranga Haine" in the same volume.

20 Şerif Mardin, "Tanzimat'tan Sonra Aşırı Batılılaşma," in *Türk Modernleşmesi* (Istanbul: İletişim Yayınları, 2000), 21–79.

21 Parla, "Metinler Labirentinde Bir Sevda: *Araba Sevdası*," in *Babalar ve Oğullar*, 105–24. See also Jale Parla, "İstanbul'da İki Don Kişot: Meczup Okurdan Saf Okura," in *Berna Moran'a Armağan: Türk Edebiyatına Eleştirel Bir Bakış*, ed. Nazan Aksoy and Bülent Aksoy (Istanbul: İletişim Yayınları, 1997), 206–9.

22 Henri Lefebvre, *Modern Dünyada Gündelik Hayat*, trans. Işın Gürbüz (Istanbul: Metis Yayınları, 1996), 103.

23 Turkey is one of the leading countries in traffic accidents. The campaign to prevent traffic accidents has the slogan "Stop the Traffic Monster Inside You."

24 Tanpınar, *19. Asır*, 467–96.

25 Yahya Kemal, *Edebiyata Dair* (Istanbul: Yahya Kemal Enstitüsü Yayınları, 1997), 290.

26 Cemil Meriç's angry (but lucid) remarks reflect the awareness of the impossibility of a "fortunate" dialogue between the East and the West, that the "transition from *irfan* [East-

ern spiritual knowledge] to culture" inevitably involves both a loss of integrity and the impossibility of going back to an original self: "Getting to know ourselves . . . there are a crowd of guests living all by themselves in the cellars of our soul . . . knowing oneself, knowing that which is melting, dispersing, turning into smoke. You are the same with your pains, shames and degradations, but the other with your dreams, aspirations, and wishes." Cemil Meriç, *Bu Ülke* (Istanbul: İletişim Yayınları, 1985), 244.

27 Parla states that *The Carriage Affair* is the "textual negation" of the idea that "two antagonistic epistemological systems" can coexist. *Babalar ve Oğullar*, 103.

28 Berna Moran points out the similarity between Don Quixote and Bihruz, both characters living in the imaginary world of their own creation. Moran, *Türk Romanına Eleştirel Bir Bakış*, 69. Robert Finn states that Bihruz reminds one of Emma Bovary since he too is a character exemplifying "life's imitation of art." Robert Finn, *Türk Romanı*, trans. Tomris Uyar (Istanbul: Bilgi Yayınevi, 1984), 91. Süha Oğuzertem has also compared *The Carriage Affair* with *Don Quixote*, saying that both novels involve "a critique of the idealized discourse of love in the romances." Süha Oğuzertem, "Taklit Aşklardan Taklit Romanlara: Genel Kadın Yazarlığı," *Toplum ve Bilim*, no. 81 (1999): 68. Cemil Meriç underlines the literary kinship between Don Quixote and Emma Bovary, saying that "Emma Bovary is the sister of the hidalgo of La Mancha." Meriç, *Kırk Ambar*, 209.

29 We can't speak of a Flaubertian influence on Ekrem. The author of *Madame Bovary* entered the *Tanzimat* scene later. It was Ali Kemal, the author of *Edebiyyat-ı Hakikiyye Dersleri*, and Ahmet Şuayb, the author of *Hayat ve Kitaplar*, who introduced Flaubert to the *Tanzimat* reader. See Meriç, *Kırk Ambar*, 298, and Beşir Ayvazoğlu, *Geleneğin Direnişi* (Istanbul: Ötüken Neşriyat, 1997), 115–16.

30 Gustave Flaubert, *Madame Bovary* (Boston: Houghton Mifflin, 1969), 30.

31 Franco Moretti, *The Way of the World: The Bildungsroman in European Culture* (London: Verso, 2000), 173.

32 Girard, *Deceit*, 5.

33 Girard, *Deceit*, 5 and 63.

34 Moretti states that the "desiring subject," darling of the 1970s, "interpreted as a force hostile to the social order, de-legitimizing, even subversive," designates the "the new human type generated by the capitalist metropolis." Moretti, *The Way of the World*, 166.

35 For a detailed critique of Girard and its possible application to the Turkish novel, see Gürbilek, "Romanın Karanlık Yüzü," *Virgül*, no. 49 (2002): 8–13.

36 One of the writers who neatly articulated the provincial bases of being a "bookworm" (the desire and also the impossibility of changing places) is Cemil Meriç, who adored Balzac, Hugo, and Chateaubriand and became an intellectual mostly by reading novels. He says that he took refuge "in the peaceful seclusion of books from that noisy world he had drifted into because of provincial curiosity." "Books were my harbors. I lived in books. I loved the people in books more than those in the street. The book was my private garden . . . I was in exile. My homeland was the Spain of Don Quixote, the town of Emma Bovary. Then I met Balzac, I lived the whole century in him, sometimes becoming a Vautrin, sometimes a Rastignac, living four thousand lives in four thousand characters." Meriç, *Kırk Ambar*, 36.

37 The fact that Ekrem aesthetically transcends his own Bihruzism (his admiration of the

French romantics) by creating the effeminate Bihruz while Flaubert aesthetically transcends his own Bovarysm (his own craze for romantic novels) by creating a female character is thought provoking. Andreas Huyssen states that "woman (Madame Bovary) is
positioned as the reader of inferior literature—subjective, emotional and passive—while
man (Flaubert) emerges as the writer of genuine, authentic literature—objective, ironic,
and in control of his aesthetic means." Andreas Huyssen, "Mass Culture As Woman: Modernism's Other," in *Studies in Entertainment: Critical Approaches to Mass Culture*, ed. Tania
Modleski (Bloomington: Indiana University Press, 1986), 189–90.

Suna Ertuğrul

Belated Modernity and Modernity As
Belatedness in *Tutunamayanlar*

This essay explores the possibilities of a reading
of belated modernity in Oğuz Atay's *The Disconnected* [*Tutunamayanlar*].[1] Atay, an engineer
by training and a professor at Istanbul Technical
University, wrote his first novel, *The Disconnected*, in a relatively late period in his life. Before
his death, seven years after the publication of *The
Disconnected*, he finished another novel, *Tehlikeli
Oyunlar* [Dangerous games], a collection of short
stories, *Korkuyu Beklerken* [Waiting for fear], and
a play, *Oyunlarla Yaşayanlar* [Living with games].
In a very short time, as if pressed by death, Atay
broke the literary taboos of the 1970s cultural
milieu in Turkey, shattered the narrow frames
of discussion about the uses of art, and allowed
the Turkish language to find the possibilities of
expressing the distress of modern existence.

The Origin of Modernity and the
Question of Cultural Identity

Oğuz Atay's works are about the question of
cultural identity in the sense that Dostoyevsky
articulated at the end of the nineteenth century:
Who are the Russians? What is the essence of a

The *South Atlantic Quarterly* 102:2/3, Spring/Summer 2003.
Copyright © 2003 by Duke University Press.

Russian? At the turn of the century this question was also James Joyce's when he asked what it means to be Irish. Atay repeated the same gesture when he set out to write the great novel on "the spirit of the Turks." As in the works of Joyce and Dostoyevsky, the question of cultural identity and cultural difference is brought about and marked by a certain relation of belatedness vis-à-vis Western modernity and opens up the question of the limits of the modern project as such.

What happens in this experience of belatedness? What does it mean to be in a position of lack and imitation—that is, to be in a nonposition that prompts the question of identity in the first place? What happens to the self when it has lost the ground on which it interprets the world and is torn between two worlds without really belonging to either one? What happens when the traces of the old world still linger, while the new one violently takes over with its absolutely different configurations of the meaning of the human and the sacred? How does one respond to this suspension of the present, which does not offer a project of future?

However, this experience of the "loss of world" is not specifically belated modernity's problem, but belongs to the essence of modernity as such. What we call modern is essentially an experience of the loss of origin, the loss of the transcendental structure that guarantees the meaning of the human sojourn on earth.[2] The modern epoch is opened up simultaneously as the absence of origin and an attempt to ground it at the level of subjectivity.[3] In this sense modernity is always belated vis-à-vis itself.[4]

What in fact gets revealed in the experience of belatedness is the "unthought" origin of the modern project. The experience of belatedness is not being late to a historically determined essence; it is the recurrence of the essential lack of ground that defines the modern project. In its most radical expression, the experience of belatedness is the infinite "repetition" of this lack/loss without being able to turn it into a project of grounding. That is, to experience belatedness as an epochal destiny. I would claim that this radical experience of belatedness is at the same time an experience of the limits of the modern project.

The End of Modernity/The Closure of Metaphysics of Presence

When we formulate the question of modernity in terms of the crisis of ground that created an epochal turn in our relation to the world and things, we can safely assume that there is no outside to modernity in the sense of native and aboriginal traditions, or non-Western narratives that can open up the possibilities of an outside or alternative to Eurocentric modernity. Insofar as these discourses are provoked and generated by the loss of ground and by a desire for identity, they are modern through and through. In other words, the question of identity is a response given to the absolute loss of ground that opened up the modern epoch.

However, what I would like to argue in this article is that identity construction is just one way of responding to the crisis opened up by modernity. Another way of confronting this loss of world and marking something like a cultural difference is to take the modern crisis to its limits and to experience the impossibility of origin as the caesura of the future, as the end of history in which no "project of Being," no "common destiny" offers itself. This is an experience of the present that is suspended in its impossibility and through this suspension/halt opens up the possibility of thinking the world as an opening to the "origination" of sense, as an event of sense. This "event of sense" or "sense as an event" is the most radical way of thinking the other in its alterity. In other words, sense is the event of the coming of the other.[5]

Taking the crisis to its limits is possible insofar as the belated moderns think the question of belatedness not only as a question of cultural difference/identity but also as a world destiny in which the essence of modernity is at stake. In other words, the urgent task is to think belatedness from out of the closure of modernity in which the ground revealed itself as nothing, as always late vis-à-vis itself. But the closure at stake is not a chronological issue; that is, we have not finished off with modernity or with the postmodern times in which the ground finally exposed itself as nonground and allowed the space in which any and every identity formations have their relative values. The discourses of "alternative modernities" and the proliferation of identity politics already tell us that we are experiencing a spectral modernity, a modernity in which we can no longer experience the provenance of the distress, in which we no longer think the loss of the world and the ruination of language as such. In short, we do not heed the Nothing that is revealed in the absence of ground and we are trying to cover over this absence with an excess of determinations and positions.[6]

The crisis of the ground, this traumatic experience of loss of language and world, is a crisis of subjectivity, which, since Descartes, has determined the modern relation to the world and things. What is revealed in the works of Atay, as in the works of Dostoyevsky, Joyce, Beckett, and Kafka, is the impossibility of subjectivity as the ground of meaning. As opposed to the Enlightenment/modern project that grounds meaning in the unity of the subject and thereby secures the certainty of representations, the modern turn in literature questions this status of the subject and shows the limits of its supposed unity. Modern literature traces the traumatic breakdown of the subject and the world through which the self emerges as a response to that which overwhelms it.

As I stated at the outset of the essay, this double exposure—the loss of world as the withdrawal of the origin and the resulting manifestation of the limits of the modern project—is an experience of radical belatedness. In the next section I analyze *The Disconnected* under the light of this relation to the withdrawal of the origin, attempting to assess its implications vis-à-vis the question of cultural identity.

Hearing the Call

In *The Disconnected*, Atay stages the awakening of the subject through an experience of absolute loss incurred by the death of the other. The subject, by undergoing the unbearable pain of separation/absence, emerges as a response to a call to which it can never fully respond, in regard to which it is always late and always responsible. The birth of the subject, then, would be the breaking down of the economy of the everyday, and the opening up of an impossible responsibility to the other, which will lead to the question of the meaning of Being/world in its turn. In a certain sense, *The Disconnected* articulates something like a condition of the possibility of saying "cultural difference" in and as the emergence of singularity.

The Disconnected begins with the protagonist Turgut receiving the news of the suicide of his best friend, Selim, and thus with the shattering of the everyday order by the violence of death and loss. Turgut, absolutely devastated by the news of Selim's death, sits in his living room and reads Selim's suicide note. He feels that he is called "to do something" but does not know what it is. Turgut engages in an imaginary dialogue with Selim, as if trying to justify his own survival, his being left behind in the world of the living. This dialogue with Selim continues till the end of the novel, as if to mark the passage from the world of the living to the space of death and writing. What first begins as self-defense on Turgut's part to protect himself from this sliding away of the everyday turns into Turgut losing his hold on the world and joining the ranks of the "disconnected." The novel traces the transformation of the protagonist Turgut as he gradually approaches the unsettling experience of a limit from which he cannot return. The concepts of dispossession, failure, confusion, and dispersion are gradually developed in the novel, giving way to an experience of the other as denuded of all identity or position. And they mark the essentially negative character of the opening of the relation to the other as such. In a certain sense, the emergence of the ethical will go through the expropriation of the proper identity. We follow this movement of decentering and expropriation in Turgut's constant dialogue with dead Selim:

> He returned to the L-shaped living room, sat on his fake leather easy chair and pushed himself back. You got caught Turgut, you exposed yourself. Why Selim? Just as I am buying a new car for ten-thousand-now-fifteen-thousand-in-installments from the accountant of the firm, just as I am learning to drive, just as I am thinking of saving some money to buy an apartment . . . you can't fool me Selim, you can't meddle with my affairs. I know how to keep my cool . . . if this were ten years ago I would have thought more; I wouldn't have been scared of indeterminate dangers. (16)

The first part of the novel reveals Turgut's unwillingness, his panic in hearing the call of his friend. He tries to protect himself and his identity. Turgut in fact defends himself against Selim and against what he represents for Turgut: an impossible existence, an existence that, by going against every norm and order (and doing this without grounding itself in any other determinate order), perished in the end. Turgut tries to convince himself that what Selim was about, the way he experienced the world and relations, does not have any place in the world, in the economy of things. It leads one to absolute destruction:

> You too shattered the game with a horrifying truth, my dearest Selim. You just drifted alone in this huge world in which everybody busies himself or herself with something determinate. . . . Man stands against the realities, he lives and stays what he is, Selim. Moreover, you didn't send this letter to me, I am not appointed for this task. This is not my

job. I read your letter ten times. I couldn't reach any result. You could
have had another existence. You could have built a life, an order of your
own outside of the ones who rejected you. (16–17)

But Turgut, against his will, is appointed for this task, and there is no
"release from it." We might say that he has always already been appointed for
the task because he has always already heard the call of his friend by taking
it to heart. The difference that Selim made, both in his life and death, this
impossible holding oneself in the openness of sense, has already touched
Turgut and leads him to repeat this opening to sense in and as writing.

We can say that it is all about "hearing the call" as that which fissures
the illusionary unity of the "I" and leads one to undergo an experience of
absolute responsibility for the other. Turgut fails to accomplish a proper
mourning that enables one to separate life from death and to protect oneself from the contamination of the nothing. He fails to forget the call of his
friend, and he is drawn more and more to the void opened up by the absence
of Selim. The pain of loss turns into a desire to understand Selim in his
absence:

> He heard Burhan saying, "I don't know what to say." I don't know,
> either. You could have told me, Selim. Who wouldn't have listened to
> you in a situation like this? What did you do in the last months? Even
> if I didn't understand, I would have listened to you. The existence of
> another human being would have taken away the burden of your deadly
> thoughts. . . . How did we come here, Selim? . . . How can I fill this
> void between us? How can I learn you without you now? . . . Say some-
> thing, Selim, don't be silent. Speak, tell me: That I have to read a thou-
> sand books. That I have to stay awake at nights. That I have to exercise
> every day and at the end I will accomplish an epsilon of progress. . . .
> I am ready for everything. . . . Tell me that I have to go to the British
> Museum, that I have to work like Karl Marx . . . if you want I will even
> grow a beard. (72)

Now what happens in this dialogue with the dead? What is the significance of it? Right here, we see that Atay refuses to separate the realms of the
dead and living with clear-cut, unsurpassable boundaries. The dead enter
the realms of the living, or better, they do not leave them, as we assume
that a proper mourning would accomplish. There is a refusal of the closure

realized through mourning and a refusal to return to the economy of the living, in which memory, by interiorizing the rupture caused by death and loss, reconnects to itself, comes back to itself. This movement of the interiorizing memory (*Erinnerung*) is in fact what is at stake in the novel. The self-return, the self-discovery that goes through the dialectic of the same and the other and comes back to itself is destroyed in *The Disconnected* by Turgut's inability to stop the dialogue and come to a closure through proper mourning. Turgut hears the call of his friend against his will.

The first part of the novel articulates Turgut's resistance to the call of his dead friend. What is at stake here is the ego's panic in the face of something that disturbs the enjoyments of life, the fear of losing the sense of security one finds in the world and in the economy of meaning that sustains the daily. This would mean the loss of resistance against the unfamiliar and the uncanny that might overcome one if one leaves the realm of the home and everyday—in short, the realm of ideology. In other words, what is at stake in this resistance is nothing other than the loss of the world and ground as the referential frame in which we can more or less make sense of our lives. The danger, as Turgut senses, is absolute in hearing the call, since it leads to the shattering of the familiar and opens up the world no longer as the correlations of answers but as a realm of unanswered questions.

As Turgut lets himself be drawn into the world of Selim, as he reads the manuscripts Selim left behind and tracks down his friends in order to understand what happened, he slowly drifts away from the everyday. As he enters Selim's world, as he begins to see how Selim experienced the world, he begins to fall away from the security of everyday meanings. Things lose their solidity, and gradually a sense of solitude grows. Although this solitude is exciting in the sense of a newly found freedom, it also panics him insofar as he senses that this small crack in the edifice will bring an absolute isolation. Through the dissolution of the everyday and the disintegration of present meanings, a new sense of the world begins to emerge. As Turgut allows himself to feel how Selim felt, he begins to realize there is another "truth" behind the everyday, another way of seeing things, of being touched by the relations. This "other truth" is difficult to express in the hard and worn-out words of the everyday. He needs another syntax, another language to express it: "I feel a huge confusion and indeterminacy. All the meanings I gave to my experiences are running away. I can't give new meanings to the words" (379). At the end of the novel the task becomes for Turgut to tell the world the difference that Selim made in his existence. Selim had to die to say this difference; Turgut repeats it as writing.

> I wish you had left your eyes to me when you died. Now Being-Selim is left to the hard words spoken between two people. Even if we get a big funding how can we gather together all the Being-Selim? How can we gather your sweating over the Economy Notes in the heat of the summer to help your friend when everybody was at the seaside? Where can we collect your worries, your pain while you were working on them? How can the guide at the Museum of Selim express all these? How is he going to remember everything? And also, would his voice be as we want it? What if he skipped the most important moment? What if one of the visitors wants to look at the fly that flew through the window right at the most important moment? We can't afford such a danger. What would Being-Selim be in the hands of the ignorant museum guide when even we can't find the words to express it? Even if the highest-ranking staff, how can I say, the presidency, is assigned to this task, we can't find a fitting person for this job of keeping. I wish you had trained me before you went. I wish you had found for me a way to say the difference between your death and others. Now there is nothing but the pain of carrying you inside of me. The pain is growing as time goes. What will I say if someone stops me in the street and asks? Everybody will be relieved: they will say, after all there was nothing, since you can't tell, explain, express! They will return to their daily tasks with peace! I wish they all went blind by the excess of peace! Let the museum be closed also! Let no more Selims come to this world; let them live their scientific lives! Let a god-dammed peace of mind fill the whole world! (329)

The Disconnected articulates the shattering effect of the death of the other as the possibility of the opening of sense. The always inadequate and always belated response of the subject to the loss is the condition of the emergence of thought. In this sense, thought begins from the other, from the absence of the other. The decentered subject is the condition of the possibility of welcoming the other in thought.

The novel shows this opening of sense in thought (this transcendence, if you will) as an experience of difference between the significations of things and that which exceeds them; it is an experience of difference as an excess of "sense" over language, over representations. In other words, it is the experience of the "world" as the horizon of meaning in its excess of the determined meanings of things that take place in the world. In this sense, the emergence of the subject is the emergence of the world as sense.[7] The world and the other are disclosed with the same gesture. Likewise, this limit experience is an experience of the limits of language as representation. In the breakdown and ruination of the everyday, then, in the loss of the ground, what gets revealed is the world itself as that which is in excess of every determination of meaning and which no representational language can express. The amazing usage of irony and parody in Atay's texts and their unequaled humor are the signs of the failure of the representational usage of language to express this excess of sense over signification.

The lack of ground reveals itself, then, as the absolute necessity of making sense of the world. It is the engagement with the world in its historical dimensions. It is the return to the world and to everyday as resolutely naked—unveiled, unmasked, uncovered. It is the essential disclosedness of human subjectivity as making sense.

Inconsolably Late

But everything turns around Selim. Who is Selim and what is the meaning of his life and death that will lead Turgut to another experience of truth and eventually to writing? In *The Disconnected* Selim is the figure of pure disclosedness. The whole novel traces Selim's relation to an originary absence that cannot come to language as such, but opens up the imperceptible gap between words and things.

The themes of constant vigilance, fatigue, excess of feeling, and running ahead of oneself that characterize Selim in the novel are the articulations of this experience of the excess of sense over the givenness of everyday meanings of things. This excess is nothing, it is not in the register of the ontical, but neither is it a transcendental structure of meaning. It is the experience of hearing that which exceeds what is said in every communication and which we try to erase in our urge to reach a clear representation/signification of our everyday concerns. Even if we sense it, we pass over it by claiming that "it is nothing, really!" It is in fact nothing; it is the experience of the nullity/absence of the ground of meaning that relentlessly pushes the subject back to this originary withdrawal. Subject as the ground of meaning is absolutely late vis-à-vis this withdrawal of the origin. It is unable to ground itself in the presence of the origin. As Atay writes, "No one would be able to bear it if life were something that you had to begin anew everyday" (431).

Being drawn to the withdrawal of the origin is to experience the absolute groundless of (representational) meaning. This passion of/for the origin is the mark of the opening of alterity in thought. The thought is the index of finitude of truth, which, in the absence of the absolute ground, emerges as a response to the difference by offering a space of relation. In other words, the thought is the emergence of the relational space in which the world occurs as an event of history. The other appears in thought and as thought in its difference. This repetition of the nothing of the origin is the faithfulness to thought. Selim is the figure of faithfulness to thought as the opening up of the difference in which the other appears. The thought, then, is the ultimate relation to the other: "It was Selim who made me see that words were more important than the facts. He was faithful to his thoughts and he thought that everybody was the same. His sincerity and loyalty were different than the faithfulness of the people who make a career out of thinking. . . . When he had read Camus's statement that 'no one has ever died because of an ontological problem,' he had said someone had to. His faithfulness to the thought was something like a passion for life" (324).

Selim represents the ruination of the subject as the center/ground in its opening to the other as other. Turgut will be touched by Selim's relation to his own finitude and his awakening (to thought) will come about by repeating this relation to death/Nothing. Turgut finally accomplishes the mourning by repeating the expropriation that led Selim to thinking. He incorporates the absence of Selim, and he dies into writing: "Selim lived differently; that is, he could not live, he died. Maybe this task is given to you my Lord [Turgut begins to talk with an imaginary sidekick, Olric]. Selim was just giving us the light? Maybe, my Lord. I wished he taught me how to think before he died. I wish he did not hide. I don't think he was hiding, my Lord. I know, I learned a lot, Olric; but death, he is hiding the death. You will live, my Lord. I want to live with the knowledge of death, Olric" (314).

The Figure of the Other: Disconnectus Erectus

In his search for Selim after his suicide, Turgut comes across a manuscript that Selim wrote years ago, a fake autobiography, a parody of his own development and life. This is a song about the failure of identity and the resulting drift and dissemination of meaning: "The Song of the Disconnected." This hilarious parody of autobiography is made up of two parts; the first part is a poem written in different verse styles that tells the story of Selim's growing up, and the second part is the parody of the scientific/literary scholarship that gives an exegesis of the poem. In this parody of the myth of origin and the tradition of the bildungsroman, the question of identity is articulated in relation to the question of cultural identity. Being born to a culture torn between a failed modernity and an exhausted past, Selim describes his childhood as confused and disoriented. He tells of his aimless wanderings in the ugliness of the city, his lack of guidance, his growing up exposed to two radically different worlds existing side by side without forming any unity, creating only deformations and distortions. This duality/duplicity of culture and the resulting lack of originary unity prompts the question of identity: "Selim, as in all his endeavors, began to write these songs like a Turk, but despite his good will and effort, he could not finish them like an Englishman. He thought the best way to express the confusion in his mind would be to write in a free style. But the free style ended up looking like a deformation, a disorder of style, a lack of style" (134). The question of identity is provoked by cultural difference, then. Here cultural difference is articulated as that which refuses to be appropriated by the modern project without offering any ground in its turn. It is something like an outer limit, a certain outside that constantly dislocates modernity's attempts to appropriate the world in terms of a systematic organization of life. But the cultural difference exists as difference—that is, as a force of dislocation rather than a possible ground for an alternative world.

The question of identity eventually leads to the question of the meaning of history as an attempt to create a coherent narrative of identity. The "Song of the Disconnected" parodies official history in its desire to create an origin by appropriating the traditional elements into a narrative of modern progress that will guarantee an identity. According to this official version of history, modernity is not a sundering of the traditional but is embedded in tradition itself as a seed; thus, what is happening today is the dialectical progress of that which has been at the origin all along. Cultural schizophrenia is produced and kept in place by this effort to weave the traditional and the modern into a narrative fabric. What the "Song of the Disconnected" reveals by parodying these narratives is the failure of the project of modernity, its inability to build an identity on the exhausted forces of a defeated culture, and the confusion created by the legends of past victories and the reality of the sad and failed present. Thus, "The Song of the Disconnected" is also a legend of exhaustion, fatigue, and death at the cultural/historical level.

But beneath all these failures there is another defeat that does not even enter the history books. The song is dedicated to the hidden history of the "disconnected," of the dispossessed, the underdog, the defeated and crushed, the "abject," if you will. It is written in order to unearth the other history behind the official one. After parodying the myths of origin, the illegitimate and artificial institutions of the origin, and corrective historical writing, Selim talks about the "disconnected." In a parody of scientific definition he describes them:

> From the Encyclopedia of Bizarre Animals: The Disconnectus Erectus: They are clumsy and cowardly animals. . . . At first sight they even look like humans. But their claws are very weak. They can't climb hills. When they have to descend, they let themselves slide down (they fall frequently). They don't have much body hair. Although their eyes are big, their sight is not well developed, that is why they can't detect danger from afar. Their males cry in sad tones when they are left alone. They call for mating in the same sad tones. Usually they live in other animals' shelters as long as the hosts can bear the situation. Sometimes they live in deserted shelters. They don't have any family order. After birth, mother, father, and children go their separate ways. They don't know how to live in a community, and they can't organize against an attack. They don't have regular feeding habits. When they live with others, they eat what the others bring in. When they are left alone, they forget to eat. Since all their behavior depends on imitation, if they don't see the others eating, they don't understand they are hungry. It is forbidden to hunt them in these periods of weakness. Their instincts are not well developed. They don't know how to protect themselves. And again, because of their imitative nature, they constantly enter into fights because they see other animals doing it. No disconnectus erectus has ever been recorded to win a fight. Nevertheless, since their memories are weak, they keep forgetting the old defeats and keep fighting. Although religious books forbid eating these animals, they are illegally hunted. It is very easy to hunt them. If you look at them with

tenderness, they will approach you immediately. To kill them afterward is extremely easy. But since they carry some harmful bacteria,
the state health administration bans their slaughtering. Feelings such
as slight uneasiness, oppression, and a guilty conscience are thought
to be caused by the consumption of the disconnectus. Animal trainers
have worked hard to teach them some tricks and employ them in the
circus, but because of their clumsiness, they were unable to learn any
tricks. And some disconnectus that were brought to the stage made the
public sad rather than merry (people ran to the ticket office to get their
money back). It is generally believed that the disconnectus have the
strongest sense of religion after elephants. Some writers have claimed
that they go to heaven after they die. But this seems improbable since
they create chaos wherever they gather. (128)

Selim sings their song as the "coming kingdom" of the disconnected in a
carnivalesque moment in which the reign of reason will end, the wall of
impossibilities will be demolished, and pain and sorrow will be abolished:

Although scientists can't yet determine the exact date of its beginning,
the Brass Period will be the golden period of our people. According
to some theologians, this period will coincide with the second coming
of Christ. During the Brass Period the distinctions between people as
first-class versus second-class will cease to exist. . . . Drivers will not
torture people; they will always carry enough change. Peasants will no
longer squat in front of public offices under the sun with their thick
wool coats. The reign of the concierges in the buildings will end. The
dark-skinned man selling toys in the streets, the man selling belts who
looks twenty years older than he actually is, and the man who keeps
falling on the sidewalk because of his epilepsy, selling I don't know
what in small bottles, and the young man with glasses selling nuts in
bars, and Koco, who dances for the customers in taverns, and the senile
waiter Tanas, who brings wine when you order Ouzo . . . they will all
be saved from their miserable condition. Everybody will become what
they want to be. . . . No one will make fun of the mentally ill: kids will be
forbidden from running after the mad. . . . The condition of street dogs
will improve. . . . Cunning will be abolished. Strictest measures will be
taken in this regard. This heavy burden in our hearts, this pressure in
our heads will be lifted. Only then will the reign of the disconnected

begin, and it will last a thousand years. It will last a thousand more years, and a thousand more. (212)

The appearance of the disconnected is the failure of the modern project in its essence. The disconnected, the abject, is the remainder, the waste that the project of modernity creates in its desire to reorganize life content in terms of functionality. That which is created by modernity, and that which gives the modern project its life support, this abject remainder, is at the same time considered as outsider, as marginal by the same project. The disconnected are the improper of the system, of the systematic and coherent articulation of the identity/of the idea. They are those modernity has to repress and purge in order to ground its identity in an alleged purity and property. In this sense, the disconnected are the ones who are erased in the attempts to give a coherent narrative of origin. Everybody finds their place in the narrative of modernity, even the traditional, insofar as it is woven into the fabric of progress—everybody, that is, except the disconnected, the ones who cannot hold on to the world, the true products of the modern project. *Disconnected* is the final word of the novel, as the figure of the other to which the novel stages the opening in and through writing.

Conclusion

In my discussion of *The Disconnected* I focused on the question of the emergence of the subject as responsibility for the other through an experience of loss/absence, relating this opening of sense in terms of the emergence of thought in which the other appears.

Now, after tracing the emergence of subjectivity from out of an encounter with Nothing, with that which exceeds the order of the given, we need to ask, What is the importance of thinking the question of subjectivity in terms of this abyssal opening in relation to cultural identity and difference? As we know, the question of identity is strictly related to the metaphysics of subjectivity/presence. Any positing of cultural identity functions with the premises borrowed from a metaphysics of presence. But this does not mean that we should deny the question of cultural difference in a wholesale manner. How does *The Disconnected* write cultural difference?

The novel tells the impossibility of the present in terms of the suspension between a lost world and a failed modernity. What is manifested in this suspension of the present is the world itself as an event of sense. The question of cultural identity is articulated around this opening of/to sense. The text expresses the question of the cultural as an originary inscription, as a marking that needs to be repeated in writing in order to come forth. Cultural identity (if we can use the notion of "identity" at this level) does not give itself in any positive manner; the cultural "is" its own withdrawal. It is that which is closest, in the words of Friedrich Hölderlin, the most proper that is hardest to own or appropriate. In the repetition and writing of the withdrawal of the cultural, what comes forth, what appears, is not a cultural identity as such, but the way it marks or stamps the singular. In other words, what appears is the singular response to the marking of the cultural. If we push this line of thought further, there is no cultural identity as such, but always singular appropriations of it. In this sense, *The Disconnected* is the appearing of the singularity as the appropriation of the "alterity" of culture. It is the articulation of a singular response to that which one is born into, to that which marks one and through this marking expropriates one. In this sense, the cultural is said in/as the appropriation of this expropriation. As Derrida articulates it in *Writing and Difference*:

> Henceforth, what is called the speaking subject is no longer the person himself, or the person alone, who speaks. The speaking subject discovers his irreducible secondarity, his origin that is always already eluded; for the origin is always already eluded on the basis of an organized field of speech in which the speaking subject vainly seeks a place that is always missing. This organized field is not uniquely a field that could be described by certain theories of psyche or of linguistic fact. It is first — but without meaning anything else — the cultural field from which I must draw my words and my syntax, the historical field which I must read by writing on it.[8]

The singular articulation of this "historical field" in writing makes cultural identity manifest as difference. That is, not in terms of a representation of an essence, but as that which marks the speaking subject in its constant withdrawal, in its difference.

The Disconnected, as I said, is the articulation of something like a cultural difference/identity through the remarking of its withdrawal. If there is any positivity that comes out of this "writing" of difference, it is that by remarking the withdrawal of the "cultural," this writing shows the cultural as a certain outside that defeats the rational/systematic organization of factical life to which the modern project aspires. Eventually in *The Disconnected* the question of cultural identity and difference gives way to the question of the other and the outside as such. And the name of this outside is "Disconnectus," the ones who cannot hold on, no matter which culture they come from.

Notes

1　Oğuz Atay, *Tutunamayanlar* (Istanbul: İletişim Yayınları, [1971] 1984). *Tutunamayanlar* literally means "those who cannot hold on." But Atay turns the word *tutunamayan* into a term that unearths other possible meanings, such as "disconnected," "dispossessed," "underdog," "marginalized," "outsider," "loser."

2　At this point we need to refer to Heidegger's reading of Friedrich Hölderlin's poetry as the most radical experience of modernity, in terms of the withdrawal of gods. The withdrawal in question is the manifestation of the finitude of Being as the absence of ground. Heidegger will place this ruination of ground and the resultant manifestation of the structure of signification as a shift in our understanding of Being. He interprets this shift as an epochal turn in which the destiny of humankind is at stake. See Martin Heidegger, *Holderlins Hymnen "Germanien" und "Der Rhein"*, vol. 39 of *Gesamtausgabe* (Frankfurt am Main: Klostermann, 1980) and *Holzwege* (Frankfurt am Main: Klostermann, 1972).

3　For a detailed discussion of the relation between the question of subjectivity and the metaphysics of presence, see Martin Heidegger, *Being and Time*, trans. John Macquarrie and Edward Robinson (New York: Harper and Row, 1962), *Basic Problems of Phenomenology*, trans. Albert Hofstadter (Bloomington: Indiana University Press, 1982), *Nietzsche*, trans. David Farrel Krell (San Francisco: Harper San Francisco, 1991), and also Jacques Derrida, *Margins of Philosophy*, trans. Alan Bass (Chicago: University of Chicago Press, 1982), *Of Grammatology*, trans. Gayatri Chakravorty Spivak (Baltimore: The Johns Hopkins University Press, 1976).

4　Modernity, in its self-grounding gesture as a metaphysical project and its failure in terms of the originary delay, is analyzed in Jacques Derrida, *La voix et le phenomene: Introduction au probleme du signe dans la phenomenologie de Husserl* (Paris: PUF, 1990).

5　See Derrida's work on the "coming/advenant," especially Jacques Derrida, *Parages* (Paris: Galilee, 1986) and *Spectres de Marx* (Paris: Galilee, 1993).

6　"Contemporary thought has approached a limit beyond which a new epochal-religious unveiling of the word no longer seems possible. The primordial character of the word is now completely revealed, and no new figure of the divine, no new historical destiny can lift itself out of language. . . . For the first time, what preceding generations called God, Being, spirit, unconscious appear to us as what they are: names for language. . . . Nihilism experiences this very abandonment of the word by God. But it interprets the extreme revelation of language in the sense that there is nothing to reveal, that the truth of language is that it unveils the Nothing of all things. The absence of a metalanguage thus appears as the negative form of the presupposition, and the Nothing as the final veil, the final name of language." G. Agamben, *Potentialities*, ed. and trans. Daniel Heller-Roazen (Stanford: Stanford University Press, 1999), 45.

7   The manifestation of the world as the horizon of meaning and the coming of the other must be thought together. In *Being and Time* Heidegger bases his analyses of the structure of the disclosure of *Dasein* on the equiprimordiality of Being-in-the-world and Being-with.

8   Jacques Derrida, *Writing and Difference*, trans. Alan Bass (Chicago: University of Chicago Press, 1978), 178.

Erdağ Göknar

Ottoman Past and Turkish Future: Ambivalence
in A. H. Tanpınar's *Those outside the Scene*

> We're the children of a crisis of mind and iden-
> tity; we're living the question "To be or not to be"
> more poignantly than Hamlet. As we embrace this
> dilemma, we will more fully take control of our lives
> and our work.
> —A. H. Tanpınar, "Istanbul" from *Five Cities*

Reductive perceptions of Turkey as a nation
caught between East and West, or moving gradually from the former toward the latter, give way
to more meaningful insights when approached
through the works of culturally astute writers
like A. H. Tanpınar (1901–63), whose value in
understanding the Turkey of tomorrow rests
in his understanding of the late-Ottoman past.
Tanpınar's attention to the psychological effects
of the Kemalist cultural revolution of the 1920s
and 1930s, his recognition of the persistence
of an Ottoman Islamic cultural legacy, and his
depiction of the individual alienated and divided
by modernization make his work indispensable for anyone interested in modern Turkish
society. His novels, articles, and critical essays
provide insights into the contradictory aspects
of a society that has been actualizing a "civili-

The *South Atlantic Quarterly* 102:2/3, Spring/Summer 2003.
Copyright © 2003 by Duke University Press.

zational shift" since at least the 1839 *Tanzimat*. Tanpınar's work has taken on even more significance as Turkey enters the twenty-first century, attempts to realize membership in the EU, and positions itself as the model of a "secular Muslim country."

The tone of Tanpınar's novels might be characterized as part lament for the loss of a late-Ottoman cultural past and part anxiety about the future of Turkish national society. *Those outside the Scene*, Tanpınar's third novel, set in Istanbul during the post–World War I period of European colonial threat, captures the psychological dilemma of a people whose identity has been transformed as a result of rapid sociocultural change. Faced with a decision between "East" and "West," modernity and tradition, and Ottoman past and Turkish national future, Tanpınar's characters cannot, or perhaps refuse to, decide. Indecision is their form of bourgeois protest. Indeed, Tanpınar's worldview is Janus-faced, implying that these choices are false, or even absurd. Rather than seeing the "two worlds" as alternatives, he sees them as synchronic, two cultural springs feeding his identity and his art. His cultural ideal thereby involves a lived synthesis of apparently contradictory identities (Eastern and Western, traditional and modern, Istanbulite and Anatolian, Islamic and secular) manifested by the people of Turkey.

Our approach to Tanpınar will be clearer if we set him against the generation of writers and thinkers that preceded him.[1] Broadly, that group of nationalist writers witnessed an Ottoman state whose desperate "*Tanzimat*-style" Westernization led it into semicolonial status. In response, they helped establish a new sociocultural narrative that imagined what might emerge out of the collapse of the Ottoman Empire: an independent Turkish nation-state. This involved not only a shift away from Ottoman-Islamic historiography, but also the creation of a new identity based on Enlightenment ideals. In order to reinforce this secular identity, the golden age of the new "Westernizing" Turkish Republic would be "pre-Islamic" and situated in Turkic Central Asia.

Thus, the generation that established the Turkish Republic in 1923 also articulated a didactic metanarrative that helped guide and imagine the transition from empire to republic, that is, from Ottoman Muslim to secular Turk. This narrative, which I've elsewhere termed the Turkish national core narrative (NCN) has four major plot points: (1) colonial encounter (foreign military occupation); (2) the Anatolian turn (a movement toward the people); (3) national consciousness (nation over self); and (4) cultural revolution (a new history and identity).[2] Though this historically based narrative is a subtext in *Those outside the Scene*, Tanpınar leaves his characters in a Hamlet-like indecision regarding the break in history, culture, and identity that it necessitates.

Those outside the Scene: Those outside the NCN

Those outside the Scene is woven out of the protagonist Dr. Cemal Bey's recollections and the sociohistorical events of the occupation of Istanbul (1918– 23) by the Allied powers after World War I.[3] In a doubled narrative movement, the novel unfolds on both psychological and historical levels. This is a period of intense sociopolitical change and increasing national consciousness as the War of Independence progresses in Anatolia. The novel is structured in the form of Cemal Bey's memoirs and opens with his return on September 20, 1920, to the city of his youth, now occupied by Allied armies, in order to begin medical school. Two strong emotional magnets for Cemal in the city are İhsan, his mentor and former teacher, and Sabiha, the object of his unrequited love since childhood. The novel develops through a tension between Cemal's personal interests (represented by Sabiha) and his pressing duty to the nation (represented by İhsan). This tension echoes one of the didactic functions of the NCN: fostering a change in consciousness from one that is individually delimited to one that encompasses the nation. Thus, İhsan draws an ambivalent Cemal into underground work for the Istanbul resistance; specifically, he assigns him to help an aging Ottoman statesman, Nâsır Pasha, who is undecided about whether to join the nationalists or to work with the comprador Ottoman Istanbul government, write his memoirs (in a way that will serve the nationalists). The climax of the novel focuses on the pasha's murder, in which İhsan is implicated. All the while, Cemal's thoughts are preoccupied with a now-married Sabiha. He is caught between Sabiha and İhsan, between self and nation, between Istanbul and Anatolia, and between a cosmopolitan late-Ottoman cultural past and the nationalistic Turkish future.[4] Tanpınar's portrayal of Cemal's debilitating state of ambivalence provides a psychological corollary to the historical crises represented by the occupation of the Ottoman capital. The novel ends without any resolution in Cemal's personal or social situation. In turn, the implied unanimity-of-purpose of the national project is questioned and subverted. The novel ends with the line, "Come on, let's go!" but as we might expect from Tanpınar, the destination and intent of the command are anything but certain.

Continuity and Synthesis: The First Person ("I") and the National Collectivity ("We")

Continuity and *synthesis* are important psychosocial concepts in Tanpınar's approach to Ottoman/Turkish culture and history. In a short article entitled "People and Society," Tanpınar conflates *continuity* and *society* (and by extension the *nation*), ascribing to the individual a diminished and weakened state of being:

> When the idea of society is introduced, the tragedy of fate diminishes, because unlike for the individual, there is no death for society. Continuity exists there. The chain continues for all eternity. . . . As individuals—that is, as people diverge from the consciousness of society— they are nothing but an aggregate of weaknesses. As they enter into and adopt the life of society, they overcome these weaknesses. . . . Only society, and its historical manifestation, the nation, can withstand fate and time.[5]

Why, then, in Tanpınar's fictional world, and specifically in Cemal's character, do we witness a reluctance to relinquish individuality and introspective thought for the sake of the national collective? One cause is the dilemma of cultural rupture. The call to national resistance also inherently implies a "rupture" in Ottoman history and identity because the Ottoman state itself is one of the declared targets of the national revolution. The rupture, codified by the national core narrative, contradicts Tanpınar's vital notion of continuity and gives rise to intense anxiety about cultural loss. Cemal states, "As individuals everyone was personally willing to give his life for the sake of national honor, but as a social body we were overcome with anxiety about the future."[6] Thus, a predicament arises: an individual willing to sacrifice himself for the nation (NCN point 3), realizing the uncertain future of that social body—which is the object of his self-sacrifice—can no longer act. This psychosocial "double-bind" infuses *Those outside the Scene*, alluding to doubts about the entire nationalist, and later Kemalist, project. Indeed, one of Tanpınar's literary achievements is his narrative aestheticization of the anxiety of a society on the verge of permanent yet uncertain change. Unable to rely on a disintegrating past or on a forseeable future, the Istanbul society under occupation in *Those outside the Scene* can seek deliverance only at the greatest cost: either by forsaking the past for the "new" (in the form of the national) or by accepting the compromise of Western rule in the form of occupation, mandate, or colonial authority.

For Tanpınar, this situation results in the destruction of social and historical "synthesis," which he sees as vital to culture and identity. Tanpınar writes, "The national life is a synthesis of yesterday and today. At present, we're manifesting this synthesis through our individual effort. . . . In short, when our life becomes stable and ordered, perhaps this task that falls to the individual will diminish some. But the synthesis will always persist. That is the gift presented to us by geography and history."[7] Even the structure of *Those outside the Scene* reflects the author's conception of synthesis: the novel is presented as Cemal's memoir, a retrospective look at his youth and the past, which he incorporates into the "present time" of republican Turkey. Cemal's story resurrects the late-Ottoman past, folds history into the "present," and attempts to achieve continuity by synthesizing "old" and "new" and "Eastern" and "Western" cultural elements. Even so, instead of describing social synthesis, *Those outside the Scene* highlights the ambiguities of nationalism by offering descriptions of psychological torment in the face of the new life represented by cultural revolution (NCN point 4). Rather than articulating a didactic plan for actualizing "nation over self," Tanpınar exhibits individual consciousness as reticent to meld into the national collective. Juxtapositions between the "I" of the first person and the "We" of the nation set the rhythm that drives *Those outside the Scene*.[8] Though Tanpınar hints at the narrative development from individual to nation demonstrated by the NCN, we are continually drawn back to Cemal's subjective first-person point of view in a way that counters any greater national-social momentum. Ultimately, we are left with an ambivalent chronicle of the effects of national consciousness on the individual, rather than the wholehearted assimilation of a national ideal. *Those outside the Scene* recasts this period as one of confusion, indecision, and hopelessness experienced by a people dispossessed of political and social cohesion. In other words, from Tanpınar's perspective, "occupation" isn't the *first* act or genesis of the national story, as it is presented in the core narrative, but one link in a sociohistorical chain linking the late-Ottoman and the republican eras.

Furthermore, by conveying the anxiety of the individual suspended in the quiet interstices between empire and republic, Tanpınar invites us to reconsider what has been presented and received as a Kemalist project of progress, nationalism, and secular Turkish identity created as if out of nothing. Throughout *Those outside the Scene*, the dramatic tension arises out of the struggle of characters who must acknowledge and accept the determining cultural force of social nationalism. In the final analysis, is it Cemal's personal obsession with Sabiha that colors the novel or Cemal's increasing awareness of the implications of the national struggle in Anatolia (represented by İhsan)?[9] Social, national, and historical plot elements appear intermittently and then give over to pages and pages of character description. These interludes, glimpses of the national core narrative as subtext, emphasize how the fate of the individual in Istanbul, however "outside the scene" he or she might seem, is inextricably bound to the fate of the collectivity in Anatolia.

Colonial Encounter: Between "Ottoman" and "Turk"

In the novel's opening paragraph, we learn that the ship that brings Cemal to Istanbul is delayed for nine hours due to two intense Allied searches by occupying military forces (NCN point 1). The date is September 20, 1920, Cemal's first time in the city in six years, and a little more than a month after the Ottoman government has signed the Treaty of Sèvres, which, though never ratified, divided up Ottoman territory, leaving only north central Anatolia to the Ottomans. The foreign battleships anchored in the Bosphorus and the harsh treatment of passengers during the inspections make Cemal long for the quiet of the small Aegean town he has come from, though thoughts of his childhood love, Sabiha, and the true reason for his decision to return to Istanbul (completing his education in medicine) prevent him from doing so. (Note that the national resistance is not a motivating factor for Cemal.) Tanpınar, from the very first pages of the novel, sets up an equivalence between occupied Istanbul—an Istanbul whose very future, history, and culture are under question—and Cemal's own psychological ambivalence.

The Ideal Synthesis: İhsan and Sabiha

The morning after his arrival in Istanbul, Cemal goes to visit his old neighborhood (*mahalle*), where he meets with İhsan, who is actively working for the national resistance. At times assuming a detached "voice of history," Cemal proceeds to describe and reflect upon the neighborhood of his youth, where his grandfather had settled after the Crimean War (1853–56). Personal recollection and Ottoman history intertwine, and the symbolic references to Islam and folk religion are noteworthy because there is little room for them in the articulation of the national core narrative. Cemal's neighborhood is grouped around a seventeenth-century mosque, the center of its social life. Within the neighborhood are four saints' tombs (*türbes*), a wooden small mosque (*mescit*), and two *medresses* (one dating to the Tulip period, one a little older). Cemal comments on the role of everyday lived religion in the neighborhood society of the past: "Whether one felt faith within, everybody sought cover in faith when out and about. Faith wasn't only what bound us to God, it was the sole source of interpersonal relations, of unified dress, expression, etiquette, in short, of what we called politeness and formality in social life."[10] Cemal associates the fabric of society itself with a tradition of faith. Though religion makes no direct appearance in the novel, it constitutes a subtext through the manner of social interaction, the *mahalle*, and the cultural symbols of Ottoman architecture. Furthermore, as Cemal discusses his neighborhood, the "secure" nature of the local *mahalle* emerges: there are no occupying soldiers here.

The theme of continuity is highlighted by Cemal's historical comments on the neighborhood and its inhabitants, from nineteenth-century Ottoman historical figures like Şirvanizade Rüştü Paşa and Mithat Paşa, to immigrant communities of Cretans and Moreans, to refugees from war-torn Balkan provinces, all the way to Cemal's childhood friends, İhsan and Sabiha. Indeed, we learn that the neighborhood has developed through four late-Ottoman historical phases: the early-nineteenth-century era of Sultan Mahmut II (when İhsan's forebears settled here); the midcentury Crimean War and the era of Sultan Abdülaziz (when Cemal's grandfather arrived); the Russo-Ottoman War (1877) and the first half of the era of Sultan Abdülhamid (Cemal's father's generation); and the 1908 Second Constitutional period and the subsequent Balkan Wars (when Sabiha moved in and the neighborhood took its present shape) (21–24). The "social geology" Cemal describes not only situates the neighborhood into the larger narrative of late-Ottoman history, it unites this history with Cemal's personal life, inscribing a movement from the "we" of history and society to the "I" of individual memory. In short, through the narrative horizon of the neighborhood, Tanpınar enacts an identification between Cemal and a century of Ottoman history.

The conflict that divides and debilitates Cemal is best represented by the poles of İhsan and Sabiha, the former symbolizing the future and self-sacrifice in the face of national-social obligation, and the latter representing connection to the past and emotional wholeness. He cannot decide between them, and on a certain level he wants both; indeed, when Cemal first arrives in Istanbul he happily fantasizes that İhsan and Sabiha have married: "Suddenly hope overcame me. Sabiha might be married to İhsan. . . . My god, if this were the case, how easy everything would become!" (148). If such were the case, Cemal would be freed from making any decision at all, as the "synthesis" between İhsan and Sabiha would have resolved his dilemmas between self, past, and future. This imagined union of past (represented by Sabiha) and the prospect of a new future (represented by İhsan) might be read as the personification of Tanpınar's ideals of continuity and synthesis.

Cemal ends up at İhsan's house, where İhsan is having a discussion with Arif Bey and İbrahim Bey, who have come in an attempt to persuade İhsan to join the antinational Istanbul government. İhsan refuses in no uncertain terms, telling them to inform the Grand Vizier that "İhsan Bey doesn't believe in the legitimacy of your government. . . . as long as there is a struggle in Anatolia, he doesn't want to cooperate with those who are involved in city affairs, with a government that has taken a stance against the National Struggle" (152). He continues, "There's a struggle there [in Anatolia], a war. Our fate will be determined there! The actual scene is there. Here, unfortunately, we are only spectators. We're outside the scene" (152).

It is through this scene that İhsan immediately pulls Cemal into working for the nationalists. A conflicted Cemal, however, seems noncomittal and confused, unable to think of much besides Sabiha and the past. Regarding İhsan and his cause, Cemal muses, "But was this İhsan, the İhsan whom I knew so well?" (157).

The Persistence of the Past: Cemal and Nâsır Pasha

On only his second day in Istanbul, Cemal expresses his doubts about the national resistance:

> Were they really doing anything? Or had a few people come together to play a game of "secret society." . . . I decided to cut my ties with these people who had no consideration whatsoever for my own freedom. . . . Let me say this as well, this anger and the sensation of not believing in the seriousness of those around me would last until the end. But if I

said this was only the fault of those in my immediate circle I'd be doing an injustice. In truth, I was stuck in a strange lethargy. I sought only solitude, quiet, and daydream. (195)

Though Cemal resolves to distance himself from İhsan and his circle, as we have come to expect, the dutiful social side of his character takes hold (switching from "I" to "we"). He immediately thinks differently when he sees the terrible condition of the people waiting at a ferry dock. Seeing the suffering and the destitution of the mass of Istanbulites affects Cemal in such a way that by the time he meets with İhsan again he has changed his mind and is able to tell himself, "What İhsan wanted would happen" (197). Though İhsan seems to have won out, Cemal's wavering indecision persists throughout the novel.

The two go to a restaurant in Tepebaşı opened by White Russian refugees recently arrived in Istanbul. İhsan informs Cemal that he is to help Nâsır Pasha, a former ambassador and minister in the Ottoman government, write his memoirs. Cemal is to work with the pasha three times a week, gain his trust, and obtain documents that will allow Cemal and the resistance to put the desired political slant onto the memoir with the goal of weakening the comprador Istanbul government. In short, it is İhsan's intention to use this memoir as a means to destroy political figures who oppose the nationalists.

Ironically, Nâsır Pasha echoes Cemal's own ambivalence. Caught between Istanbul and Anatolia (NCN point 2), the pasha's position is described as follows:

> The Pasha insisted on the need for cooperation between Istanbul and Anatolia, though he offered no positive suggestions. He enumerated what were in his opinion the justified points in the opinions and claims on both sides, and then declared that only by the skill of "an experienced individual who was possessed of political wisdom, yet who hadn't been rattled by the onus of recent and persisting failures, an individual who was not unfamiliar with progressive schools of thought, yet who was also bound to the sublime caliphate" could the differences between them be overcome. (210)

But, like Cemal, the pasha is also unable to "overcome differences" in any meaningful way. In desperation, he considers fleeing the country. Meanwhile, Cemal's recurring urges to flee Istanbul, his spiritual alienation, and his unrequited obsession with Sabiha intensify into a climax wherein he considers suicide:

> I was able to sleep only for a couple hours toward morning. . . . When I opened my eyes, I saw the dilapidated window through which filtered a murky light. At that very moment I was overcome with an intense desire to kill myself. I wanted to hurl myself into this ashen void. . . . I was disgusted with people, with nature, and objects . . . I was disgusted by the various faces of existence. . . . Everything seemed comic, foolish, and grotesque. (268)

The image of the window, and its invitation to death, haunt him as he roams the streets of Istanbul. On his way to Nâsır Pasha's home that very night, he is overcome by thoughts of the changed or ruined lives of the people of his youth and his own loneliness and displacement in the occupied city.

That evening Cemal is a guest of Nâsır Pasha, whom he describes as "looking at a past that will die with him" (290). The two, an old Ottoman pasha of the civil service and a young potential Turkish nationalist, retire to the pasha's study after eating. Rather than representing two opposing poles, however, Nâsır Pasha and Cemal share great empathy and respect for each other. Snubbed by the Ottoman palace, the pasha agrees by default to help the resistance. Preparing to leave Istanbul for Italy, he gives personal papers to Cemal, saying that İhsan is free to use them in any way he sees fit (later we learn that the pasha has duped Cemal and İhsan by giving them the wrong documents and by withholding his memoir).

Next, the pasha instructs Cemal that they are to burn all the letters, documents, and photographs in his study. This "ritual sacrifice/burning" scene is perhaps one of the most important in the novel, as it is an allegory for the all-important cultural and historical break between "old/Ottoman" and "new/Turk" that occurs in the transition from empire to republic as represented in the NCN. Cemal, witness to this sad ritual of the pasha's, cannot conceal his reluctance to participate. When the pasha is on the verge of tossing a photograph of his own son, who perished at the battle of Sarıkamış (1915), into the flames, Cemal objects, "But Nâsır Pasha wasn't listening. And he didn't want to forgive anyone. He was going to burn his past. He was going to burn all of it, everything. Seeing that everything was transitory, realizing the uselessness of all dreams of success, considering that he had witnessed the collapse of institutions that ought to have defied the life span of generations, he was going to destroy everything" (300). Soon afterward, Cemal gets caught up in the ritual himself: "The desire to burn had passed onto me as well. I, too, wanted to surrender whatever surrounded me, all of it, to this fire, to its insatiable mouth, to the rising and falling rhythm of the dance. . . . We burned whatever we could lay our hands on" (301–2). As the burning ritual continues, Cemal has an epiphany about the cultural nature of the past, in keeping with Tanpınar's own views: "We were persistently burning that peculiar entity we called the past! But burning was useless. Everything we burned oddly stuck in our minds, the names were calling to one another, lives were separating, and memories were joining together. The mouth of the void had opened, and it was spitting back upon us seemingly three or four times what it had just consumed" (302).

Cemal's realization that the past is a sociocultural force also challenges the foundations of the NCN, which is predicated on a historical break with the late-Ottoman past. Again, it bears emphasis that Tanpınar's novel is in the form of a *memoir*, a retrospective personal account and reckoning with the past. Cemal's epiphany about the persistence of the past through memory carries allegorical significance: a past that persists in memory cannot be elided. In an article titled "The Essential Source," Tanpınar writes, "We are possessed of a past whose voice it is impossible to ignore when it speaks through us in its genuine essence."[11] Cemal echoes this belief in the force of the past when he comments, "In truth, the trick was being played on us. Outside, everything persisted as per usual. . . . At the very least I had rid myself of a fable. Fire does not abolish anything. It doesn't purify anything. It only destroys matter."[12]

In short, the sacrifice of "burning" has no lasting effect. As Tanpınar writes in "Identity and the Exchange of Civilizations," "What's for certain, if anything, is that the 'past' stands right beside us, sometimes like a victim, sometimes as a lost paradise—it's a treasure that ensures our wholeness of spirit; and at the slightest uncertainty the past opens before us with the glimmer of an oasis; it calls to us, and when it doesn't, it makes us doubt our lives, [causing] hesitation and a kind of guilty conscience."[13] The past is an integral component of Tanpınar's ideals of synthesis and continuity, a notion contrary to the national core narrative and the Kemalist cultural revolution. The next morning, when Cemal asks the pasha why he doesn't go to Ankara, the pasha replies ironically, "They need New Men there. I'm too old and far more experienced than necessary!"[14]

In the last chapter of the novel, with the pasha's decision to leave Istan-bul, Cemal has practically forgotten the resistance and the nationalist cause. Sabiha has invaded his thoughts, and he hopes that she will keep her word and visit him at the boarding house. When she does, Cemal states, "At that moment, as always, I could've happily died for Sabiha" (330). Though he feels the call to national duty in a vague and unspecified Anatolia, he is immobilized: "I knew that somewhere, somewhere unknown to me, there was something that I absolutely had to do. . . . But I couldn't save myself from the weight that had smothered me, I couldn't manage to find myself" (333). In a moment of transformation near the end of the novel, Cemal states, "However it happened, an hour later, I was another kind of man. The social man had reawakened and saved me from thoughts and anxieties about myself" (337). This is hardly convincing, however, for in the closing pages of the novel, at a point when İhsan is in danger of being accused in the murder of Nâsır Pasha, Cemal is more preoccupied with Sabiha, who is set to begin a life in theater "as the first Turkish stage actress" (340). As was the case in the opening pages of the novel, Cemal is still divided hopelessly between "İhsan" and "Sabiha."[15]

Divided Selves: Memoir and the Story of the Nation

In *Those outside the Scene*, Tanpınar alludes to both the historic and the psychic effects of the Allied occupation and the collapse of the Ottoman Empire. Of course, his perspective is that of a writer/intellectual who has lived through the republican cultural revolution (NCN point 4) and wit-nessed the establishment of a new Turkish nation. (*Those outside the Scene* first appeared serially in 1950, almost thirty years after Allied troops left Istanbul and the Republic of Turkey was declared.) Why then does he revisit the period of the occupation in a manner that emphasizes ambivalence and problematizes the transition from empire to republic? For Tanpınar, undoubtedly, this historical transition period is so complex that it neces-sitates great delicacy. From his perspective, the ambivalence between East and West, tradition and modernity, and Ottoman and Turk is not resolved during the period of occupation, the national struggle, or even after the republic is established. It persists. In "Identity and the Exchange of Civili-zations," Tanpınar describes a pervasive duality extant in Ottoman/Turkish culture since the *Tanzimat*: "The reason for this crisis [of mind] is the duality brought about by moving from one civilization to another. . . . This duality first began in public life, then it split our society in two in terms of mentality, and in the end, deepening and changing its progress, it settled within us as individuals."[16] Thus, Tanpınar might conclude, the duality of modern Turkish society should not be read as a problem needing a solution, but rather, as the foundation(s) of modern Turkish cultural identity.

Furthermore, Tanpınar teaches us that the rupture represented historically by the period of occupation and socioculturally by the Kemalist cultural revolution must not be conceived of as an actual "break," but must be understood as a bridge to the past. The national story, as articulated through the national core narrative, disrupts continuity and synthesis and diminishes the cultural wealth of the nation. Tanpınar asks us to contemplate this paradox: How shall I live in an environment that doesn't acknowledge my own (its own) past? And, in many ways, this paradox defines his crisis as an intellectual.

Tanpınar's understanding of the "national life" is bound to his ideals of synthesis and continuity, which he believes will transcend the pervasive crisis of the "divided self." He explains: "National life is continuity. National life means persevering by changing and changing by persevering—because the first condition of being able to create is continuity. Real breaks and ruptures only produce freaks of nature and half-formed creatures."[17] In an attempt to overcome the monsters created by historical and cultural "rupture," Tanpınar advocates tapping a "third source," a synthesis between binaries like tradition and modernity in order to manifest the "reality of the nation":

> We can consider the East or the West only as two separate sources. Both exist for us, and quite extensively; that is to say, they are part of our reality. However, their presence alone can't be of any value, and remaining [separate] that way, they are an invitation to create a vast and comprehensive synthesis, a life meant for us and particular to us. For the encounter and fusion to be fruitful, it must give birth to this life, to this synthesis. And this is possible by attaining the vital third source, which is the reality of the nation.[18]

Tanpınar's "third source" is a call for a more inclusive "re-writing" of the national core narrative so that it reflects the realities of everyday life and the influences of the recent Ottoman past, of its society, its religious traditions,

and its culture. The goal would seem to be to ease the persistent and unre-
solved tension between the individual story (memoir/"I") and the national
story (history/"We") that is so evident in *Those outside the Scene.*

Notes

All translations in this essay are mine.

1   These predecessors include Ziya Gökalp, H. E. Adıvar, Peyami Safa, Y. K. Karaosmanoğlu,
    Ahmet Ağaoğlu, Fuat Köprülü, and Yusuf Akçura.

2   This emplotment can be traced in much of the literature of the period and forms the basis
    of Turkish Republican historiography and Turkish national identity.

3   *Those outside the Scene (Sahnenin Dışındakiler)* is Tanpınar's third novel. Published seri-
    ally in 1950, its characters and themes are interrelated with his first two novels, *Song in
    the Mahur Mode [Mahur Beste]* and *Peace of Mind [Huzur].* In *40 Novels in 40 Years [40 Yılda
    40 Roman]* (Istanbul: Oğlak, 1994)], Fethi Naci puts forth convincing evidence that *Those
    outside the Scene* is an unfinished novel. Based on the plot development of *Between Two
    Fires [İki Ateş Arasında]* (Istanbul: İyi Şeyler, 1998)], the screenplay based on the novel,
    this claim would seem to be reasonable.

4   Cemal's ambivalence echoes that of Mümtaz, the protagonist of Tanpınar's preceding and
    related novel *Peace of Mind.* Mümtaz, like Cemal, wavers between his personal happiness
    and his responsibility to society.

5   Ahmet Hamdi Tanpınar, *Yaşadığım Gibi* (Istanbul: Dergâh, 1996), 22–23.

6   Ahmet Hamdi Tanpınar, *Sahnenin Dışındakiler* (Istanbul: Dergâh, 1973), 253.

7   Canan Yücel Eronat, ed., *Tanpınar'dan Hasan-Ali Yücel'e Mektuplar* (Istanbul: Yapı Kredi,
    1997), 42–43.

8   In his article "Ahmet Hamdi Tanpınar and Turkish Modernism" (*Defter* 8.23 [1995]: 41),
    Orhan Pamuk makes the following comment on Tanpınar's unorthodox use of the pro-
    noun "we" in *Peace of Mind* (a novel otherwise written in the third person): "Who is this
    'we'? Evidently the Turks, the Ottomans, those living in Istanbul, a nation that this text
    desires to produce, a culture, an environment. . . . As we hear this voice of plurality, 'we'
    begin to exist—by Tanpınar's creation." Tanpınar makes the same narrative gesture in
    Those outside the Scene; however, since this novel is written in the first person, the use of
    the "we" isn't as jarring.

9   Pamuk, again in the article cited above, identifies in *Peace of Mind* what he terms one
    of Tanpınar's greatest narrative "tricks": "This is a typical Ahmed Hamdi Tanpınar sub-
    stitution. Two people are in love, then 'love' alternates with 'culture.' . . . Love, thereby,
    is mixed up with the mystery and the bewilderment of a substitution of culture. Thus,
    the tension between characters assumes a new dimension" (Pamuk, "Tanpınar ve Türk
    Modernizmi," 37–38). The love Cemal feels for Sabiha in *Those outside the Scene*, in simi-
    lar fashion, alternates, not with "culture," but with the "nation." Mehmet Baydur, in his
    preface to Tanpınar's *Between Two Fires*, puts it this way: "It's as if Tanpınar is making
    variations on [the themes of] Love, Affection, and Passion. In the end, he masterfully
    adds in patriotism and love of country" (Tanpınar, *Between Two Fires*, 9).

10   Tanpınar, *Sahnenin Dışındakiler*, 28.

11   Tanpınar, *Yaşadığım Gibi*, 40.

12   Tanpınar, *Sahnenin Dışındakiler*, 302, 304. For Cemal, the "fire" is an illusion. Cemal states, "It seems we both believed that the fire would abolish everything, that it would purify life and renew it!" (303). Note how Tanpınar's use of this metaphor differs from Halide Edib Adıvar's. For Tanpınar everything cannot begin anew, whereas Adıvar's *The Turkish Ordeal* [*Türkün Ateşle İmtihanı*] and "Shirt of Flame" ["Ateşten Gömlek"] represent a very real life-or-death struggle that defines and determines the future of a "New Turkey," which is separate and distinct from the old. In short, even their uses of the metaphor of "fire" reflects how these writers approach Ottoman-Turkish history and historiography differently, the one advocating continuity and the other rupture.

13   Tanpınar, *Yaşadığım Gibi*, 39.

14   Tanpınar, *Sahnenin Dışındakiler*, 305.

15   Mümtaz, the protagonist of Tanpınar's related novel *Huzur* [Peace of mind], occupies a position similar to Cemal's. Berna Moran writes of Mümtaz: "*Peace of Mind* articulates a petit bourgeois intellectual's vacillation between the personal happiness he finds in aestheticism and his responsibility to society. Tanpınar doesn't take the easy way out by turning Mümtaz into a positive protagonist who undertakes social and political burdens. Uneasiness is Mümtaz's fate, because he knows he will not be able to escape the dilemma he is in." Berna Moran, *Türk Romanına Eleştirel Bir Bakış: Ahmet Mithat'tan Ahmet Hamdi Tanpınar'a* [A critical analysis of the Turkish novel: From Ahemt Mithat to Ahmet Hamdi Tanpınar] (Istanbul: İletişim, 1983), 222–23.

16   Tanpınar, *Yaşadığım Gibi*, 34.

17   Ümit Meriç Yazan and Selma Ümit Karısman, *Edebiyatın Huzurunda: Ahmet Hamdi Tanpınar* (Istanbul: Ufuk, 2000), 252.

18   Tanpınar, *Yaşadığım Gibi*, 42–43.

Notes on Contributors

HÜLYA ADAK is an assistant professor of comparative literature in the Program of Cultural Studies at Sabancı University. Her teaching experience and research interests include theories of autobiography, nation-building myths and the novel, culture and literature of the Middle East and Turkey, postcolonial theory and literature, and theories of self and subjectivity.

MELTEM AHISKA is an assistant professor of sociology in Boğaziçi University, Istanbul. She completed her Ph.D. at Goldsmiths College, University of London, in 2000. She is currently working on a book based on her dissertation, "An Occidentalist Fantasy: Early Turkish Radio and National Identity." Her articles have appeared in various journals, including *Defter*, *Toplum ve Bilim*, and *New Perspectives on Turkey*, and she was a member of the editorial board of *Defter*, a journal of cultural criticism published in Turkey from 1987–2002.

BEHİÇ AK is a cartoonist, architect, film director, and writer. His play *The Building* received a special award from the Turkish Ministry of Culture in 1993. His film on the history of censorship in Turkish cinema was named best documentary at the Ankara film festival in 1994. He has also written and illustrated several children's books. His cartoon albums have been published in Turkey and Germany, and his cartoons have appeared in the daily *Cumhuriyet* since 1982.

TANIL BORA, a political scientist and journalist, is the editor of the nonfiction series *İletişim Yayınları* and the chief editor of the quarterly social science journal *Toplum ve bilim*. He is also editing a book series on political thought in modern Turkey, *Modern Türkiye'de siyasi düşünce*. He is published regularly in the monthly socialist culture journal *Birikim*. His publications on political thought in Turkey, especially rightist ideologies and nationalism, include *Devlet Ocak Dergah—1980'lerde Ülkücü Hareket* (with Kemal Can), *Milliyetçiliğin Kara baharı* (1995), and *Türk Sağının uç Hali* (1998).

AYŞE BUĞRA is a professor of political economy at Boğazici University, Istanbul. Her publications include *İktisatçılar ve İnsanlar* (1989), *State and Business in Modern Turkey: A Comparative Study* (1994), *State, Market, and Organizational Form* (coedited with Behlül Üsdiken, 1997), and *Islam in Economic Organizations* (1999). She has also published articles in such journals as *Economics and Philosophy*, *International Journal of Middle Eastern*

Studies, Middle Eastern Studies, International Journal of Urban and Regional Research, Technological Change, and Social Forecasting, Current Anthropology, Review of Radical Political Economy, and *Revue du Mouvement Anti-Utilitariste dans les Sciences Sociales (MAUSS).*

ÜMIT CIZRE is an associate professor at Bilkent University, Ankara. She is a former Fulbright Research Scholar (Princeton University) and Jean Monnet Research Fellow (RSC, European University Institute, Florence). Most recently she has published "The Military and Politics: A Turkish Dilemma," in *Middle Eastern Armies: Politics and Strategy,* ed. Barry Rubin and Thomas Keaney (2002); "Turkey's Kurdish Problem: A Critical Analysis of Boundaries, Identity and Hegemony," in *Rightsizing the State,* ed. Ian Lustick (2002); and "The Truth and Fiction about Turkey's Human Rights Politics," *Human Rights Review,* no. 3 (October–December 2001).

MENDERES ÇINAR is an assistant professor of political science in the Department of Political Science and International Relations, Başkent University, Ankara. His main research interests are political Islam and the republican political tradition. He has most recently published a theoretical discussion of Islamism as a "political" question in *Totalitarian Movements and Public Religions* (2002). His forthcoming book, *Kemalist Republicanism and Islamist Kemalism: Reproductions of Anti-Politics in Turkey,* will be published in Turkish.

ANDREW DAVISON is a member of the political science department at Vassar College. His publications include *Secularism and Revivalism in Turkey: A Hermeneutic Reconsideration* (1998) and *The Philosophic Roots of Modern Ideology: Liberalism, Communism, Fascism, and Islamism,* 3d ed. (coauthored with David Ingersoll and Richard Matthews, 2001).

SUNA ERTUĞRUL is an assistant professor in the Western languages and literatures department of Boğazici University. She works between literature and philosophy, having specialized on Heidegger and contemporary French philosophy. She is currently working on a book-length project on the question of modernity and belatedness.

KATHERINE PRATT EWING is an associate professor of cultural anthropology and religion at Duke University. She is currently investigating diasporic Islamic practice in Europe. In her book *Arguing Sainthood* (1997), she examines how the Sufi mystical tradition has been a focus of religious and political controversy in Pakistan. Recent publications include "Legislating Religious Freedom: Muslim Challenges to the Relationship between Church and State in Germany and France," *Daedalus* (2000).

ERDAĞ GÖKNAR is visiting assistant professor of Turkish language and culture at Duke University. He is also the translator of Orhan Pamuk's novel *My Name Is Red* (2001).

HALDUN GÜLALP is professor of sociology at Boğazici University, Istanbul, and currently a fellow at the Woodrow Wilson International Center for Scholars, Washington, D.C. He is the author of *Kimlikler Siyaseti* (2003).

NURDAN GÜRBILEK is the author of *Vitrinde Yaşamak* (1992), an analysis of the cultural dynamics of the 1980s in Turkey. Her other publications include *Yer Değiştiren Gölge* (1995) and *Ev Ödevi* (1999), both collections of essays on Turkish writers Ahmet Hamdi Tanpınar, Oğuz Atay, Yusuf Atılgan, Bilge Karasu, Tezer Özlü, and Latife Tekin. She is also the author of *Kötü Çocuk Türk* (2001), an analysis of some of the significant images and archetypes in modern Turkish literature and popular culture.

GÜVEN GÜZELDERE is an assistant professor of philosophy at Duke University. He is the editor of *A Brief History of Consciousness* (forthcoming) and the coeditor of *The Nature of Consciousness: Philosophical Debates* (1997), and *Constructions of the Mind*, a special issue of *Stanford Humanities Review* (1995). He has published numerous articles in edited collections and such journals as *Behavioral and Brain Sciences* and *Journal of Consciousness Studies*.

AHMET INSEL teaches development economics, nonmarket economics, social change and politics, and philosophy of economics in Galatasaray University and Paris 1 Pantheon Sorbonne University. He is on the editorial board of *Revue du Mouvement Anti-Utilitariste dans les Sciences Sociales (MAUSS)* and *Birikim*. He is the author of *Türkiye Toplumunun Bunalımı* (1991) and *Düzen ve Kalkınma Kıskacında Türkiye* (1996). Among his recent publications are "On Unachieved Democracy" in *The Living Legacy of Marx, Durkheim and Weber* (1998), "Quelle autre mondialisation" with Alain Caille in *Quelle autre Mondialisation* (2002), and "Free Movement of Labour Versus Labour Market Harmonization," *Industria* (forthcoming).

SIBEL IRZIK teaches English and comparative literature in Boğaziçi University. She is the author of *Deconstruction and the Politics of Criticism* (1990). She has edited a collection of selected writings by Mikhail Bakhtin, *Karnavaldan Romana* (2001), and published articles on modern British, American, and Turkish authors in various journals and edited collections in Turkey. Her most recent publication is *"The Black Book*: How to Be a Novelist of Istanbul," forthcoming in *Il romanzo*, a history of the world novel edited by Franco Moretti.

ORHAN KOÇAK, a literary critic and the editor of *Virgül*, a book review monthly, has published widely on modern Turkish poets and novelists.

BRUCE K. KUNIHOLM is a professor of public policy and history at Duke University, where he has also been director of the Sanford Institute for Public Policy and vice provost for academic and international affairs. His four books include *The Origins of the Cold War in the Near East: Great Power Conflict and Diplomacy in Iran, Turkey, and Greece*, which won the Bernath Prize. Most recently, he has published several articles, including one on Turkey's accession to the EU, in *Diplomatic History, Middle East Journal, Turkish Studies*, and *Journal of American History*.

JALE PARLA taught English literature at Boğaziçi University from 1975 to 2000. She is now teaching in the comparative literature department of Bilgi University. Among her publications are *Efendilik, Kölelik, Şarkiyatçılık* (1985), *Babalar ve Oğullar: Türk Romanının Epistemolojik Temelleri* (1990), and *Don Kişot'tan Bugüne Roman* (2000).

LEVENT SOYSAL is currently visiting assistant professor of anthropology at the European College of Liberal Arts, Berlin. He has coedited *Youth and Identity: Transition, Culture, and Relations* (a special issue of *Europæa: Journal of the Europeanists*, 2001). His recent publications include "Beyond 'Second Generation': Rethinking the Place of Migrant Youth Culture in Berlin," in *Challenging Ethnic Citizenship: German and Israeli Perspectives on Immigration* (2002) and "Diversity of Experience, Experience of Diversity: Turkish Migrant Youth Culture in Berlin," in *Cultural Dynamics* (2001).

NECMI ZEKA is a poet, translator, and painter. In 2002, he published his collected poems *Yavru Aslan'dan Konu Komşu'ya* (1981–2001) and opened his second solo exhibition of paintings *Surprise Witness* at the Dirimart Gallery in Istanbul.

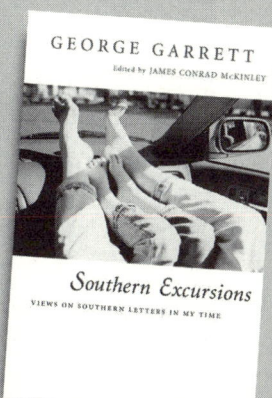

Southern Excursions

Views on Southern Letters in My Time

GEORGE GARRETT

Edited by James Conrad McKinley

This book contains more than fifty of the best essays, reviews, and other short pieces of Garrett's career, covering topics that include southern publishing houses and literary quarterlies, the alliance between writers and academia, the state of criticism and theory, and, most eloquently, the persistence of place, memory, and the Civil War as themes in southern letters.

"Garrett may well be a critic of genius. This book will be a great pleasure to every serious reader."—James Whitehead

$34.95

Orphans' Home

The Voice and Vision of Horton Foote

LAURIN PORTER

Porter's in-depth examination of Pulitzer Prize–winning playwright and Oscar-winning screenwriter Foote's masterpiece, *The Orphans' Home Cycle*, demonstrates why it is a unique accomplishment in the canon of American drama. Porter shines much-needed light on this talent who proves to be a vital American voice.

"There is no better place to learn why these plays were made, the best way to read them, and what they will mean for future generations."
—Gerald C. Wood, author of *Horton Foote and the Theater of Intimacy*

$49.95 cloth, $22.95 paper

Southern Literary Studies
Fred Hobson, *Editor*

LOUISIANA STATE UNIVERSITY PRESS
Baton Rouge 70808 • (800) 861-3477 • www.lsu.edu/lsupress

RADICAL HISTORY *Review*

Looking for something radically different?

For more than a quarter of a century, *Radical History Review* has stood at the point where rigorous historical scholarship and active political engagement converge. The journal is edited by a collective of talented historians—men and women with diverse backgrounds, research interests, and professional perspectives. Positioning itself unabashedly to the left of center, it carries its political legacy as a sacred trust.

Recent and forthcoming special issues include "Health Politics/Health Workers," "Radicalism in Transition," "The Uses of the Folk," and "Terror and History."

SUBSCRIPTION INFORMATION

Three issues annually
Institutions: $90
Individuals: $35
Students: $22

Please include $12 postage for subscriptions outside the U.S.
Canadian subscribers must include 7% GST.
To place your order using a credit card, please call 888-651-0122
(toll-free within the U.S. and Canada) or 919-687-3602.
www.dukeupress.edu.   RADICAL

boundary 2

Benjamin Now:
Critical Encounters with The Arcades Project

Volume 30, Issue 1 March 2003
Philip Rosen and Kevin McLaughlin, special issue editors

The Arcades Project is the unfinished, final work of the
influential cultural theorist, critic, and historian Walter
Benjamin. Until 1999, this huge, unruly manuscript, which
provides a more complete picture of the diversity of
Benjamin's work than formerly available, had not been fully
translated into English. "Benjamin Now" is the first collection
of essays in English to focus on that text.

While this essential text's title refers to its ostensible
subject—the nineteenth century shopping arcades of Paris—
The Arcades Project is a mass of cultural, political, and
social material presented in the form of a vast montage.
"Benjamin Now" reconsiders the significance of Benjamin's
theories and writings in light of this final project.

*Contributors: T. J. Clark, Howard Eiland, Peter Fenves,
Tom Gunning, Michael Jennings, Claudia Brodsky Lacour,
Kevin McLaughlin, Philip Rosen, Henry Sussman,
Lindsay Waters, Samuel Weber, Peter Wollen*

U.S. $14 for single issues
U.S. $32 for individual subscriptions
U.S. $133 for institutional subscriptions

Outside the U.S. add $16 for postage

Available from Duke University Press
1-888-651-0122 (toll-free in the U.S. and Canada)
or 1-919-687-3602
www.dukeupress.edu

Good news!
SAQ back issues are available.

For only $12 each (plus shipping), selections include

Diaspora and Immigration
V. Y. Mudimbe and Sabine Engel, special issue editors
98:1/2, Winter/Spring 1999
ISBN: 0-8223-6464-6

Domestic/Tragedy
Julie A. Carlson, special issue editor
98:3, Summer 1999
ISBN: 0-8223-6470-0

After the Garden?
Michael Crozier, special issue editor
98:4, Fall 1999
ISBN: 0-8223-6465-4

Harbin and Manchuria: Place, Space, and Identity
Thomas Lahusen, special issue editor
99:1, Winter 2000
ISBN: 0-8223-6475-1

Mysterious Actions: New American Drama
Jody McAuliffe, special issue editor
99:2/3, Spring/Summer 2000
ISBN: 0-8223-6502-2

Millennial Japan:
Rethinking the Nation in the Age of Recession
Tomiko Yoda and Harry Harootunian,
special issue editors
99:4, Fall 2000
ISBN: 0-8223-6527-8

Atlantic Genealogies
Ian Baucom, special issue editor
100:1, Winter 2001
ISBN: 0-8223-6533-2

Michel de Certeau—in the Plural
Ian Buchanan, special issue editor
100:2, Spring 2001
ISBN: 0-8223-6473-5

The South
Atlantic
Quarterly

Anglophone Literatures and Global Culture
Susie O'Brien and Imre Szeman, special issue editors
100:3, Summer 2001
ISBN: 0-8223-6523-5

Culture and the Law
Gaurav Desai, special issue editor
100:4, Fall 2001
ISBN: 0-8223-6530-8

Vicissitudes of Theory
Kenneth Surin, special issue editor
101:1, Winter 2002
ISBN: 0-8223-6537-5

Dissent from the Homeland: Essays after September 11
Stanley Hauerwas and Frank Lentricchia,
special issue editors
101:2, Spring 2002
ISBN: 0-8223-6540-5

Medium Cool
Andrew McNamara and Peter Krapp, special issue editors
101:3, Summer 2002
ISBN: 0-8223-6542-1

Enduring Enchantments
Saurabh Dube, special issue editor
101:4, Fall 2002
ISBN: 0-8223-6544-8

For a complete listing of all available back issues, visit
www.dukeupress.edu/saq.

To order, contact customer service at
1-888-387-5765 (in the U.S. and Canada) or **919-687-3602**.

African American Studies

American Studies

Anthropology

Art

Asian Studies

Film & Television Studies

Gay & Lesbian Studies

History

Latin American Studies

Law

Literary & Cultural Studies

Political Science

Sociology

Women's Studies

DUKE

Are you getting *e*buzz ?

Sign up today for Duke
University Press's quarterly email
notification listserv and receive
news about our latest books,
journal special issues, award-
winning publications, and other
news from the Press.

www.dukeupress.edu/ebuzz